THE SACRAM

# Confirmation

A COMPLETE PREPARATION COURSE
and Activities with Parents & Sponsors

[DID-uh-kay]

The *Didache* is the first known Christian catechesis. Written in the first century, the *Didache* is the earliest known Christian writing outside of Scripture. The name of the work, "*Didache*," is indeed appropriate for such a catechesis because it comes from the Greek word for "teaching" and indicates that this writing contains the teaching of the Apostles.

The *Didache* is a catechetical summary of Christian Sacraments, practices, and morality. Though written in the first century, its teaching is timeless. The *Didache* was probably written by the disciples of the Twelve Apostles, and it presents the Apostolic faith as taught by those closest to Jesus Christ. This series of books takes the name of this early catechesis because it shares in the Church's mission of passing on that same faith, in its rich entirety, to new generations.

Below is an excerpt from the *Didache* in which we see a clear example of its lasting message, a message that speaks to Christians of today as much as it did to the first generations of the Church. The world is different, but the struggle for holiness is the same. In the *Didache* we are instructed to embrace virtue, to avoid sin, and to live the Beatitudes of Our Lord.

> My child, flee from every evil thing, and from every likeness of it. Be not prone to anger, for anger leads the way to murder; neither jealous, nor quarrelsome, nor of hot temper; for out of all these murders are engendered.
>
> My child, be not a lustful one; for lust leads the way to fornication; neither a filthy talker, nor of lofty eye; for out of all these adulteries are engendered.
>
> My child, be not an observer of omens, since it leads the way to idolatry; neither an enchanter, nor an astrologer, nor a purifier, nor be willing to look at these things; for out of all these idolatry is engendered.
>
> My child, be not a liar, since a lie leads the way to theft; neither money-loving, nor vainglorious, for out of all these thefts are engendered.
>
> My child, be not a murmurer, since it leads the way to blasphemy; neither self-willed nor evil-minded, for out of all these blasphemies are engendered.
>
> But be meek, since the meek shall inherit the earth.
>
> Be long-suffering and pitiful and guileless and gentle and good and always trembling at the words which you have heard.[1]

The *Didache* is the teaching of the Apostles and, as such, it is the teaching of the Church. Accordingly, this book series makes extensive use of the most recent comprehensive catechesis provided to us, the *Catechism of the Catholic Church*. The *Didache Series* also relies heavily on Sacred Scripture, the lives of the saints, the Fathers of the Church, and the teaching of Vatican II as witnessed by the postconciliar Popes.

1. "The Didache," *Ante-Nicene Fathers*, vol.7. tr. M.B. Riddle. ed. Alexander Roberts, James Donaldson, and A. Cleveland Coxe (Buffalo, NY: Christian Literature Publishing Co., 1886).

# The Sacrament of Confirmation

## A Complete Preparation Course
### and Activities with Parents & Sponsors

Author: Rev. James Socias
Editor: Eric Sammons

MIDWEST THEOLOGICAL FORUM
Downers Grove, Illinois

Published in the United States of America by

**Midwest Theological Forum**
4340 Cross Street, Suite 1
Downers Grove, IL 60515

Tel: 630-541-8519
Fax: 331-777-5819
mail@mwtf.org
www.theologicalforum.org


Revised First Edition
ISBN 978-1-939231-73-4

*Nihil Obstat*
Reverend John Balluff, S.T.D.
Censor Deputatus
April 5, 2017

*Permission to Publish*
Most Reverend Joseph M. Siegel, D.D., S.T.L.
Vicar General
Diocese of Joliet
April 6, 2017

The *Nihil Obstat* and *Permission to Publish* are official declarations that a text is free of doctrinal and moral error. No implication is contained therein that those who have granted the *Nihil Obstat* and *Permission to Publish* agree with the content, opinions, or statements expressed. Nor do they assume any legal responsibility associated with publication.

---

**Author:** Rev. James Socias

**Editor:** Eric Sammons

**Editorial Board:** Rev. James Socias, Rev. Peter V. Armenio, Randal Powers

**Other Contributors:** Stephen J. Chojnicki, Beth Mortensen

**Design and Production:** Marlene Burrell, Jane Heineman of April Graphics, Highland Park, Illinois

## Acknowledgements

Excerpts from the English translation of the *Catechism of the Catholic Church* for the United States of America, copyright ©1994, United States Catholic Conference, Inc.—Libreria Editrice Vaticana. Used with permission.

Excerpts from the English translation of the *Catechism of the Catholic Church: Modifications from the Editio Typica*, copyright ©1997, United States Catholic Conference, Inc.—Libreria Editrice Vaticana. Used with permission.

Scripture quotations are from the Catholic Edition of the *Revised Standard Version of the Bible*, copyright ©1965, 1966, National Council of the Churches of Christ in the United States of America. Used by permission. All rights reserved.

Excerpts from the *Code of Canon Law, Latin/English Edition*, are used with permission, copyright ©1983 Canon Law Society of America, Washington, DC.

Citations of official Church documents from Neuner, Josef, SJ and Dupuis, Jacques, SJ, eds., *The Christian Faith: Doctrinal Documents of the Catholic Church*, 5th ed. (New York: Alba House, 1992). Used with permission.

Excerpts from *Vatican II: The Conciliar and Post Conciliar Documents, New Revised Edition* edited by Austin Flannery, OP, copyright ©1992, Costello Publishing Company, Inc., Northport, NY, are used with permission of the publisher, all rights reserved. No part of these excerpts may be reproduced, stored in a retrieval system, or transmitted in any form or by any means—electronic, mechanical, photocopying, recording or otherwise, without express written permission of Costello Publishing Company.

*Disclaimer: The editor of this book has attempted to give proper credit to all sources used in the text and illustrations. Any miscredit or lack of credit is unintended and will be corrected in the next edition.*

The Subcommittee on the Catechism, United States Conference of Catholic Bishops, has found this text, copyright 2018, to be in conformity with the *Catechism of the Catholic Church.*



Printed in Canada

# TABLE OF CONTENTS

# TABLE OF CONTENTS

# TABLE OF CONTENTS

# TABLE OF CONTENTS

# TABLE OF CONTENTS

"Let the children come to me, do not hinder them; for to such belongs the kingdom of God. Truly, I say to you, whoever does not receive the kingdom of God like a child shall not enter it." And he took them in his arms and blessed them, laying his hands upon them. (Mk 10:15-16)

## ABBREVIATIONS USED FOR THE BOOKS OF THE BIBLE

### OLD TESTAMENT

| | | | | | |
|---|---|---|---|---|---|
| Genesis | Gn | Tobit | Tb | Ezekiel | Ez |
| Exodus | Ex | Judith | Jdt | Daniel | Dn |
| Leviticus | Lv | Esther | Est | Hosea | Hos |
| Numbers | Nm | 1 Maccabees | 1 Mc | Joel | Jl |
| Deuteronomy | Dt | 2 Maccabees | 2 Mc | Amos | Am |
| Joshua | Jos | Job | Jb | Obadiah | Ob |
| Judges | Jgs | Psalms | Ps | Jonah | Jon |
| Ruth | Ru | Proverbs | Prv | Micah | Mi |
| 1 Samuel | 1 Sm | Ecclesiastes | Eccl | Nahum | Na |
| 2 Samuel | 2 Sm | Song of Songs | Sg | Habakkuk | Hb |
| 1 Kings | 1 Kgs | Wisdom | Wis | Zephaniah | Zep |
| 2 Kings | 2 Kgs | Sirach | Sir | Haggai | Hg |
| 1 Chronicles | 1 Chr | Isaiah | Is | Zechariah | Zec |
| 2 Chronicles | 2 Chr | Jeremiah | Jer | Malachi | Mal |
| Ezra | Ezr | Lamentations | Lam | | |
| Nehemiah | Neh | Baruch | Bar | | |

### NEW TESTAMENT

| | | | | | |
|---|---|---|---|---|---|
| Matthew | Mt | Ephesians | Eph | Hebrews | Heb |
| Mark | Mk | Philippians | Phil | James | Jas |
| Luke | Lk | Colossians | Col | 1 Peter | 1 Pt |
| John | Jn | 1 Thessalonians | 1 Thes | 2 Peter | 2 Pt |
| Acts of the Apostles | Acts | 2 Thessalonians | 2 Thes | 1 John | 1 Jn |
| Romans | Rom | 1 Timothy | 1 Tm | 2 John | 2 Jn |
| 1 Corinthians | 1 Cor | 2 Timothy | 2 Tm | 3 John | 3 Jn |
| 2 Corinthians | 2 Cor | Titus | Ti | Jude | Jude |
| Galatians | Gal | Philemon | Phlm | Revelation | Rev |

## GENERAL ABBREVIATIONS

*AG* — *Ad Gentes Divinitus* (Decree on the Church's Missionary Activity)

*CA* — *Centesimus Annus* (On the Hundredth Anniversary)

CCC — *Catechism of the Catholic Church*

CDF — Congregation for the Doctrine of the Faith

CIC — *Code of Canon Law* (*Codex Iuris Canonici*)

*CPG* — *Solemn Profession of Faith*: Credo of the People of God

*CT* — *Catechesi Tradendæ* (On Catechesis in our Time)

*DCE* — *Deus Caritas Est* (God is Love)

*DD* — *Dies Domini* (The Lord's Day)

*DH* — *Dignitatis Humanæ* (Declaration on Religious Freedom)

*DoV* — *Donum Vitæ* (Respect for Human Life)

*DV* — *Dei Verbum* (Dogmatic Constitution on Divine Revelation)

DS — Denzinger-Schonmetzer, *Enchiridion Symbolorum, definitionum et declarationum de rebus fidei et morum* (1985)

*EV* — *Evangelium Vitæ* (The Gospel of Life)

*FC* — *Familiaris Consortio* (On the Family)

*GS* — *Gaudium et Spes* (Pastoral Constitution on the Church in the Modern World)

*HV* — *Humanæ Vitæ* (On Human Life)

IOE — *Iura et Bona* (Declaration on Euthanasia)

*LE* — *Laborem Exercens* (On Human Work)

*LG* — *Lumen Gentium* (Dogmatic Constitution on the Church)

*MF* — *Mysterium Fidei* (The Mystery of Faith)

*PH* — *Persona Humana* (Declaration on Sexual Ethics)

PL — J.P. Migne, ed., *Patrologia Latina* (Paris: 1841-1855)

*PT* — *Pacem in Terris* (On Establishing Universal Peace)

*QA* — *Quadragesimo Anno* (The Fortieth Year)

*RP* — *Reconciliatio et Pænitentia* (On Reconciliation and Penance)

*RH* — *Redemptor Hominis* (The Redeemer of Man)

*SC* — *Sacrosanctum Concilium* (The Constitution on the Sacred Liturgy)

*SRS* — *Sollicitudo Rei Socialis* (On Social Concerns)

*SS* — *Spe Salvi* (In Hope We Are Saved)

USCCB — United States Conference of Catholic Bishops

*VS* — *Veritatis Splendor* (Splendor of the Truth)

# Preface

**Midwest Theological Forum** is proud to offer *The Sacrament of Confirmation*, which is our first book in the *Didache Sacramental Preparation Series*.

This series stands alongside the *Didache Complete Course Series*, the *Didache Semester Series*, the *Didache Parish Series*, and the *Didache Bible*. It was prepared for the catechetical needs of dioceses across the country and in accordance with guidelines from the Committee on Evangelization and Catechesis of the U.S. Conference of Catholic Bishops.

This book was designed with preteen and early teenage students in mind, but it may be used profitably by Catholics of all ages. My prayer is that it brings you toward a closer union with Christ and a deeper intimacy with the Holy Spirit, "in order to be more capable of assuming the apostolic responsibilities of Christian life" (CCC 1309).

I encourage you to read the material at the end of each chapter. These special sections will teach you how to pray and discern God's will for you (*Sealed in the Spirit*). They will also strengthen your relationship with your parents, who are your first teachers in the faith (*You and Your Parents*), and help you grow in spiritual friendship with your sponsor (*You and Your Sponsor*).

Most especially, since the Holy Spirit's "actions, his gifts, and his biddings" (CCC 1309) can be seen most clearly in the lives of the saints, each chapter highlights a particular holy person who has powerfully manifested the fruits of the Holy Spirit. As you read the stories of these heroic Christians, I invite you to pray for their intercession and open your heart to a closer friendship with each of them.

I hope you enjoy this book as you prepare—with the loving help of your sponsor, parents, catechist, parish priest, bishop, guardian angel, and patron saint—to receive the Sacrament of Confirmation.

**Rev. James Socias**
Pentecost Sunday
June 4, 2017

"Thou dost show me the path of life;
in thy presence there is fulness of joy."
Ps 16:11

THE SACRAMENT OF

# Confirmation

Introduction

# WHY DO WE NEED CONFIRMATION?

*Pentecost* by Bentele.
God is working to transform your life and get you ready for the next life with him in the happiness of heaven.

## INTRODUCTION

**Confirmation deepens our baptismal life that calls us to be missionary witnesses of Jesus Christ in our families, neighborhoods, society, and the world. Through Confirmation, our personal relationship with Christ is strengthened.***

If you are reading this book, then you are probably preparing to receive the Sacrament of Confirmation. You might feel that you know what Confirmation is, or you might not be sure. You might be excited, or you might just be doing this because everyone else your age is. No matter how much you already know, or why you are preparing for Confirmation, God has been waiting for you to be confirmed. Before you were even born, God knew in his love for you where he wanted you to go: heaven. And Confirmation is a gift given to you by God to help you get there. Furthermore, Confirmation can change your life here on earth. As you read this book and prepare for Confirmation, be aware of all the ways God is working to transform your life and get you ready for the next life with him in the happiness of heaven.

After reading this chapter, you will be able to answer these questions:

- What is each person's final destination?
- What is the Sacrament of Confirmation?
- What are the gifts and the fruits of the Holy Spirit?
- What are the four elements of being a disciple of Christ?

* United States Catholic Catechism for Adults (Washington, DC: United States Conference of Catholic Bishops, 2006), 207.

# OUR JOURNEY TO HEAVEN

***Confirmation is an important step along the way to your eternal destination.***

**We are but travelers on a journey without as yet a fixed abode; we are on our way, not yet in our native land; we are in a state of longing, but not yet of enjoyment. But let us continue on our way, and continue without sloth or respite, so that we may ultimately arrive at our destination. (St. Augustine, *Sermon on Martha and Mary*)**

You probably have heard it said that "life is a journey." The Bible likens our earthly life to a journey, urging us to keep our eyes fixed on heaven as our final goal. Every journey has a beginning, a direction, and a destination. When you plan a vacation with your family, you choose what the destination will be, the best way for you to travel there, when you want to arrive, and what you want to do while you are there. The life of a Christian is also a journey. It begins at **Baptism**, which starts us on the right path by cleansing us of sin and making us God's adopted children—members of his family. The Christian journey also has a direction. God invites us to choose to follow the example of his Son, Jesus Christ, by turning away from sin and living the Christian life. And the Christian journey has a destination: heaven, where we can be with God forever.

Christ calls you, personally and directly, to follow him and become his **disciple**. It is not always easy to live as his disciple. Life is often hard, so Christ promises you the help and guidance of the Holy Spirit to keep you on the right track. The Holy Spirit will help you steer away from sin, to focus on God's will, and to search for and travel the path that God has planned for you.

You first received the Holy Spirit when you were baptized. The Holy Spirit purified you, cleansed you of all sin, and made you holy. Through the Holy Spirit you became an adopted child of God and were made ready for eternal life in heaven. That is God's ultimate plan for you: happiness forever, far greater than the human mind can imagine, far greater than anything we could possibly experience during our earthly lives.

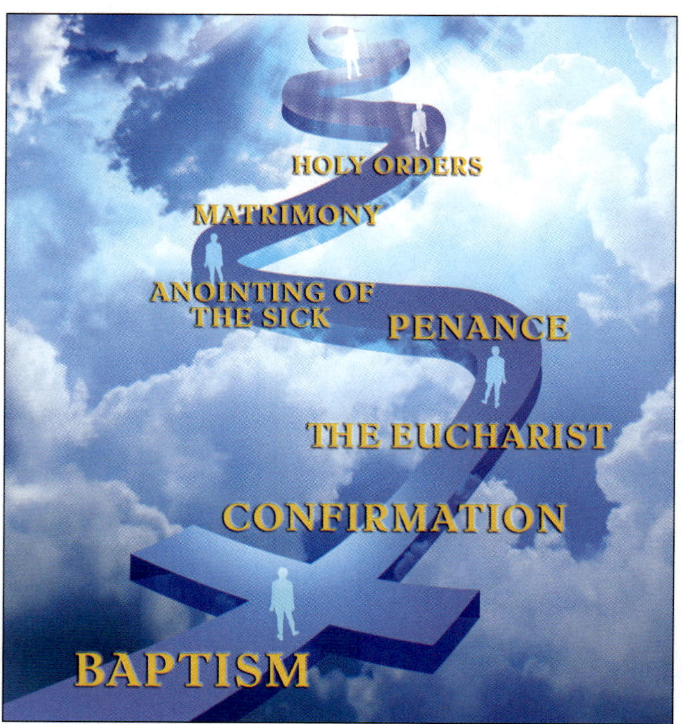

Confirmation is the next stop on your journey to heaven.

Throughout life, the Holy Spirit helps us live as true disciples of Christ. The divine help that he gives us is called **grace**. Grace makes us holy and pleasing to God and guides us along the way. But the challenges and temptations of this world can lead us away from that pure and holy state that we enjoyed after Baptism. Sometimes we make bad choices. When life is difficult we might find ourselves feeling weak or frustrated; we might give in to sin and lose our way. We might decide that following Christ is too hard. We can forget that we are sons and daughters of God, destined for eternal happiness. We need help to be strong on our journey to our eternal destination.

That is where the Sacrament of Confirmation comes in. At your Confirmation you will be sealed with the gift of the Holy Spirit and receive an outpouring of grace that strengthens you to live as a faithful Christian. The Holy Spirit, which you received already in Baptism, will work in you more powerfully through the sacramental grace of Confirmation.

Confirmation is the next stop on your journey to heaven. Just as you have to be prepared and ready to take a family vacation, so too must you be prepared for this important step along the way to happiness with God in eternity. This book will help you in your preparation for the Sacrament of Confirmation.

## WHAT IS GRACE?

Grace is the divine assistance, the help from God, that we receive in order to live as faithful followers of Christ. We can further describe grace as a share in his divine life or the presence of God dwelling within us. This inner presence of God helps us to "stay on track," to have a good attitude so that we can think and act as God wants us to think and act. Grace also helps us figure out the path that God wants us to take in our lives.

The more we allow God's grace to work in us, the more intimately we are united with the Blessed Trinity: the Father, Son, and Holy Spirit. Grace can bring us so close to God that we actually share in his divine life. This expression means that God draws us into his own life, making us more and more like him.

### Grace.

**Our justification comes from the grace of God. Grace is favor, the free and undeserved help that God gives us to respond to his call to become children of God, adoptive sons, partakers of the divine nature and of eternal life.**

**Grace is a participation in the life of God. It introduces us into the intimacy of Trinitarian life: by Baptism the Christian participates in the grace of Christ, the Head of his Body. As an "adopted son" he can henceforth call God "Father," in union with the only Son. He receives the life of the Spirit who breathes charity into him and who forms the Church.**

**This vocation to eternal life is supernatural. It depends entirely on God's gratuitous initiative, for he alone can reveal and give himself. It surpasses the power of human intellect and will, as that of every other creature.**

**The grace of Christ is the gratuitous gift that God makes to us of his own life, infused by the Holy Spirit into our soul to heal it of sin and to sanctify it. It is the sanctifying or deifying grace received in Baptism. It is in us the source of the work of sanctification:**

**Therefore if any one is in Christ, he is a new creation; the old has passed away, behold, the new has come. All this is from God, who through Christ reconciled us to himself.**

**Sanctifying grace is an habitual gift, a stable and supernatural disposition that perfects the soul itself to enable it to live with God, to act by his love. Habitual grace, the permanent disposition to live and act in keeping with God's call, is distinguished from actual graces which refer to God's interventions, whether at the beginning of conversion or in the course of the work of sanctification. (CCC 1996-2000)**

Grace helps us figure out the path that God wants us to take in our lives.

# THE SACRAMENT OF CONFIRMATION

### *Understanding Confirmation will help us prepare to receive it.*

What is the Sacrament of Confirmation? How can you prepare yourself to receive so great a gift? These two questions should be on your mind as you move toward your Confirmation.

Confirmation is one of the Seven Sacraments of the Catholic Church. A **Sacrament** is an efficacious sign, instituted by Christ and entrusted to the Church, that gives grace to the person who receives it. What does "efficacious" mean? It means something that can bring about the result (or effect) it signifies. Christ meets us today in the Sacraments. We are not able to walk with Jesus and speak with him as those who lived in his time could, but in the Sacraments, we can encounter him in a real, tangible way. The Seven Sacraments—Baptism, Confirmation, the Eucharist, Penance (also called Reconciliation or Confession), the Anointing of the Sick, Matrimony, and Holy Orders—are the primary ways that we meet Jesus. Through them, he gives us his grace by the power of the Holy Spirit.

Baptism, the Eucharist, and Confirmation are called the Sacraments of Christian Initiation because they are the foundation for the Christian life and have always been celebrated as part of the process of welcoming new believers into the Church.

> **Confirmation perfects Baptismal grace; it is the sacrament which gives the Holy Spirit in order to root us more deeply in the divine filiation, incorporate us more firmly into Christ, strengthen our bond with the Church, associate us more closely with her mission, and help us bear witness to the Christian faith in words accompanied by deeds. (CCC 1316)**

Confirmation will perfect the grace that you received at Baptism. In Confirmation the Holy Spirit will bind you more deeply as an adopted child of God and bring you more closely into the Body of Christ, which is his Church. Confirmation will help you to have life in the Holy Spirit, a life of prayer, holiness, witness, and service to the will of God.

If you welcome this outpouring of the Holy Spirit and cooperate with the grace that it gives you, your life will change, and you will be strengthened to touch the lives of many people in a positive way. As St. Paul wrote, "We are ambassadors for Christ, God making his appeal through us" (2 Cor 5:20).

The Sacrament of Confirmation *will* change you if you allow God's grace to work within you.

> **This Sacrament brings a growth of Baptismal grace: it unites us more firmly to Christ; it brings to fulfillment our bond with the Church; it gives us the special strength of the Holy Spirit to spread and defend the faith, to confess the name of Christ and never to be ashamed of His cross. (Pope Francis, *On the Sacrament of Confirmation*, General Audience, January 29, 2014)**

To get the most benefit out of the grace that is given in a Sacrament, we should be properly prepared to receive it. This means not only understanding what the Sacrament is and does but also having a *good interior disposition*. To have a good interior disposition means that we desire the Sacrament and commit ourselves to making use of the grace that it offers us. We set our sights clearly in the direction of Confirmation, and do all we can to let it change us. The Holy Spirit gives us grace through the visible sacramental sign, but the good that this grace can accomplish depends on our good interior disposition toward it. The goal of this book and this period of preparation is not only that you learn all about Confirmation, but also that you learn how to have a good interior disposition to receive the Sacrament.

## THE SEVEN SACRAMENTS

| SACRAMENT | EFFICACIOUS SIGN | SOURCE |
|---|---|---|
| **Baptism** | We die to our sins, including Original Sin, and rise to new life in Christ, becoming adopted children of God and receiving sanctifying grace so as to share in the divine life of the Blessed Trinity; we become members of the Church, the Sacrament of Salvation, and incorporated into the Body of Christ. | Mt 28:19-20 |
| **Confirmation** | It confirms our baptismal commitment and increases in us the gifts of the Holy Spirit, which we first received in Baptism, so as to grow in virtue and have the courage to evangelize. The Holy Spirit "[seals us] for the day of redemption." | Acts 19:6<br>Lk 24:49<br>Acts 2:1-4<br>Eph 4:30 |
| **Eucharist** | We receive the Body and Blood of Christ, the bread of life, the source of eternal life. When we do so, we "proclaim your death, O Lord, and profess your Resurrection until you come again." | Mt 26:26-28<br>Mk 14:22-25<br>Lk 22:19-20<br>Jn 6:22-23 |
| **Penance and Reconciliation** | With a spirit of conversion and repentance, we are redeemed from our actual sins, returned to the state of sanctifying grace, and restored to full communion with Christ and his Church. | Jn 20:22-23<br>Mt 16:19, 18:18 |
| **Anointing of the Sick** | Our sins are indirectly forgiven in preparation for the journey to eternal life. We are strengthened so that our suffering may have redemptive value, and it can even help our body to get well. | Jas 5:14-15<br>Mk 6:13 |
| **Holy Orders** | Men are ordained to the service of the Church through her liturgy and Sacraments, so as to confer the grace of the redemption to the faithful. | Lk 22:19<br>Acts 6:6 |
| **Matrimony** | A man and a woman become cooperators with God in creation and redemption. The love, sacrifice, chastity, and gift of self required in marriage reflect the love in the Blessed Trinity. | Mk 10:7-9<br>Jn 2:1-11 |

## THE GIFTS AND FRUITS OF THE HOLY SPIRIT

***Confirmation brings about an outpouring of the Holy Spirit.***

**The moral life of Christians is sustained by the gifts of the Holy Spirit. These are permanent dispositions which make man docile in following the promptings of the Holy Spirit. (CCC 1830)**

**The seven gifts of the Holy Spirit are wisdom, understanding, counsel, fortitude, knowledge, piety, and fear of the Lord. They belong in their fullness to Christ...They complete and perfect the virtues of those who receive them. They make the faithful docile in readily obeying divine inspirations. (CCC 1831)**

At your Confirmation—as with all of the Seven Sacraments—God will fill you with abundant graces. You might not *feel* anything different after you are confirmed, you might not have an emotional experience, and you probably will not go out into the streets preaching like the first **Apostles** did at Pentecost. Yet the Sacrament of Confirmation *will* change you if you allow God's grace to work within you.

First and foremost, through the Sacrament of Confirmation, we are given the seven **gifts of the Holy Spirit**. Here is a brief summary of them:

- **Wisdom** gives us God's perspective of the world.
- **Understanding** allows us to comprehend God's Revelation.
- **Counsel** helps us to recognize the voice of the Holy Spirit in making moral decisions.
- **Fortitude** enables us to profess the faith despite difficulties, disappointments, suffering, and lack of understanding from others.
- **Knowledge** is an understanding of God's creation and the plan God has established for his creatures.
- **Piety** is the love that we have for God as reflected in reverence.
- **Fear of the Lord** is our recognition of the majesty, awe, and wonder of God and our dependence on him.

The gifts of the Holy Spirit help us to live and grow as sons and daughters of God. They are not magical powers that change us. Rather, they are inner strengths that we must choose to embrace by our own free will. They come from God the Father, by God the Son, and through the Holy Spirit in this Sacrament. We will learn more about these gifts in Chapter 8.

Confirmation has a further effect on those who receive it, called the **fruits of the Holy Spirit**. Think about an orange tree—when it is healthy and growing, it bears fruit. This fruit is the result of the orange tree growing to its full potential. Likewise, when we accept the gifts of the Holy Spirit in our lives, they will bear fruit, and bring perfection to our daily lives:

**The fruit of the Spirit is love, joy, peace, patience, kindness, generosity, faithfulness, gentleness, and self-control. (Gal 5:22-23)**

After receiving Confirmation, a person is given the grace to live differently. Instead of being motivated and guided by fear, anger, hatred, jealousy, or greed, the person who receives Confirmation receives joy and peace, patience and love in their lives. These fruits of the Holy Spirit will be discussed in more detail in Chapter 8.

**The fruits of the Spirit are perfections that the Holy Spirit forms in us as the first fruits of eternal glory. The tradition of the Church lists twelve of them: "charity, joy, peace, patience, kindness, goodness, generosity, gentleness, faithfulness, modesty, self-control, chastity." (CCC 1832)**

## WHAT GOD ASKS OF YOU

***God has a mission for you: he wants you to be his disciple in the world.***

God wants us to be happy with him forever in heaven, and in response, we are called to be his *disciples*. A disciple doesn't just say that he believes in God; he follows him in all his words, thoughts, and actions.

**Faith by itself, if it has no works, is dead. (Jas 2:17)**

A disciple follows the Holy Spirit. However, there is another "spirit" that is not from God: the "spirit of

## WHAT CONFIRMATION IS

**The Sacrament of Confirmation** has the power to transform the lives of those who receive it. But many people have misconceptions regarding this Sacrament, so let's make clear what Confirmation really is:

**Confirmation gives us the capacity to become true Christians.**
Although it is a common practice for Catholics to prepare for Confirmation at a certain age or during a certain grade in school, Confirmation is not a "rite of passage" toward adulthood like graduating or getting a driver's license. Confirmation gives graces that will help you handle all the complex challenges that you are likely to face both as a young adult and for the rest of your adult life.

**Confirmation is one stage in our Christian vocation.**
Receiving Confirmation does not mean that we are finished learning about the Catholic faith. Even if you do not take formal classes like this Confirmation preparation course in the future, as a disciple of Christ, you will always have more to learn. Even the greatest mind can't fully understand God.

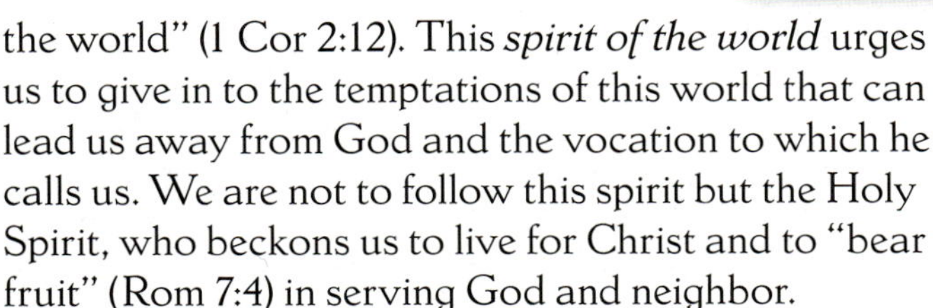

**Confirmation continues our Christian formation that will continue throughout our lives.**
It is not like a "carrot on a stick" that is dangled in front of you in order to keep you coming back to learn more about the faith. Confirmation is one of many milestones on your journey of life, a journey that began with Baptism and leads to heaven.

**Confirmation supplies us with the necessary strength to live out our Christian vocation.**
When you were baptized, you were adopted by God as his child. Confirmation strengthens your union in the Family of God and helps you cooperate with God's grace. Even if a person chooses not to be confirmed, he or she cannot "opt out" of the graces that were given in Baptism. Confirmation unites us more closely to Christ and his Church and increases the gifts of the Holy Spirit within us so that we can love and serve God and our neighbor more fully.

the world" (1 Cor 2:12). This *spirit of the world* urges us to give in to the temptations of this world that can lead us away from God and the vocation to which he calls us. We are not to follow this spirit but the Holy Spirit, who beckons us to live for Christ and to "bear fruit" (Rom 7:4) in serving God and neighbor.

What it means to be a disciple can be summarized in four main elements: (1) a disciple prays; (2) a disciple obeys the laws of God; (3) a disciple witnesses to others; and (4) a disciple serves others.

**Prayer.** Being a disciple requires a special relationship with God: we must be in communion with him in a personal way. This occurs primarily through prayer. Think about being part of a sports team, but never talking to the coach and never listening to him. You wouldn't be a very good team member, would you? Likewise, to be on God's "team"—to be his disciple—we have to talk to God and listen when he talks to us. This is the life of prayer, which will be discussed in more depth in Chapter 9.

**Holiness.** Holiness means living in conformity with Christ's way of life.

> **Becoming a disciple of Jesus means accepting the invitation to belong to *God's family*, to live in conformity with His way of life: "For whoever does the will of my Father in heaven is my brother, and sister, and mother." (CCC 2233)**

Of course, none of us will live *exactly* like Jesus did: we might be fathers or mothers, or work as artists or zookeepers. Part of living a life of holiness can include living a specific **vocation**, such as the vocation to marriage, Holy Orders, or the consecrated life. A life of holiness, including discovering your vocation, will be discussed more in Chapter 10.

> **Holiness, therefore, has its deepest root in the grace of baptism, in being grafted on to the Paschal Mystery of Christ, by which his Spirit is communicated to us, his very life as the Risen One. (Benedict XVI, General Audience, St. Peter's Square, April 13, 2011)**

**Witness.** As disciples we are called to be witnesses for Christ:

> **The disciple of Christ must not only keep the faith and live on it, but also profess it, confidently bear witness to it, and spread it. (CCC 1816)**

What does the word "witness" mean? It means to see something happening, but it also means to testify to something. To be a witness for Christ in the world, then, includes testifying to the truths that God has revealed. These truths are kept safe and made known by the Catholic Church. We will learn about being a witness in Chapter 11.

**Service.** Finally, being a disciple means that we live a selfless life. A selfless life is one that reaches out in service to others, just as Jesus lived. He gave his entire life for the salvation of the world. Our service to others is based upon our imitation of Christ himself.

> **"The Son of man came not to be served but to serve, and to give his life as a ransom for many." (Mt 20:28)**

Becoming a disciple might sound difficult, even impossible. But God gives us his Spirit to help us live as he calls us to live. Through the Sacrament of Confirmation, we are sealed with the gift of the Holy Spirit, which gives us the strength to be God's faithful disciples. Chapter 12 will cover the topic of service.

## CONCLUSION

### *Preparation is important for receiving the graces of Confirmation*

Every person is called by God to live for him and eventually to be with him in love and complete happiness forever in heaven. In order to help us reach this destination, God gives us help, especially through the Sacraments. In the Sacrament of Confirmation, God will pour out his grace upon you so that your life can be guided by the Holy Spirit.

Confirmation can change your life. It will help you to be a more faithful disciple of Christ, giving you the necessary strength to live out your Christian life. It is not the "end of the road" of being a Christian. It is a grace-filled stage in our journey towards God.

To get the most out of Confirmation you need to prepare well for it. This book and your Confirmation preparation course are designed to help you live the Christian life. The gifts that you will receive in Confirmation will give you the strength to cooperate with the grace that God freely gives. To receive them, you should be open to the Holy Spirit and cultivate your relationship with God. If you do this, you will be transformed into a disciple of Jesus Christ.

## POINTS TO REMEMBER

1. Your destination in life is heaven. You began your journey to this destination at Baptism, and God continues to help you in your journey through the Sacraments.
2. The Sacraments of Baptism, Confirmation, and the Eucharist are the Sacraments of Initiation. Confirmation brings an increase and deepening of baptismal graces and equips you to live out your vocation more fully so that you can serve as Christ's disciple in the world.
3. The Sacrament of Confirmation brings about an outpouring of the Holy Spirit in your life. Specifically, you receive the seven gifts of the Holy Spirit—wisdom, understanding, counsel, fortitude, knowledge, piety, and fear of the Lord.
4. In Confirmation, you are responsible for being a disciple of Christ. You will be a true Christian: live a life of prayer, strive for holiness, be a witness to the world, and help and serve those around you.

# WITNESS OF CHRIST

## ST. DOMINIC SAVIO

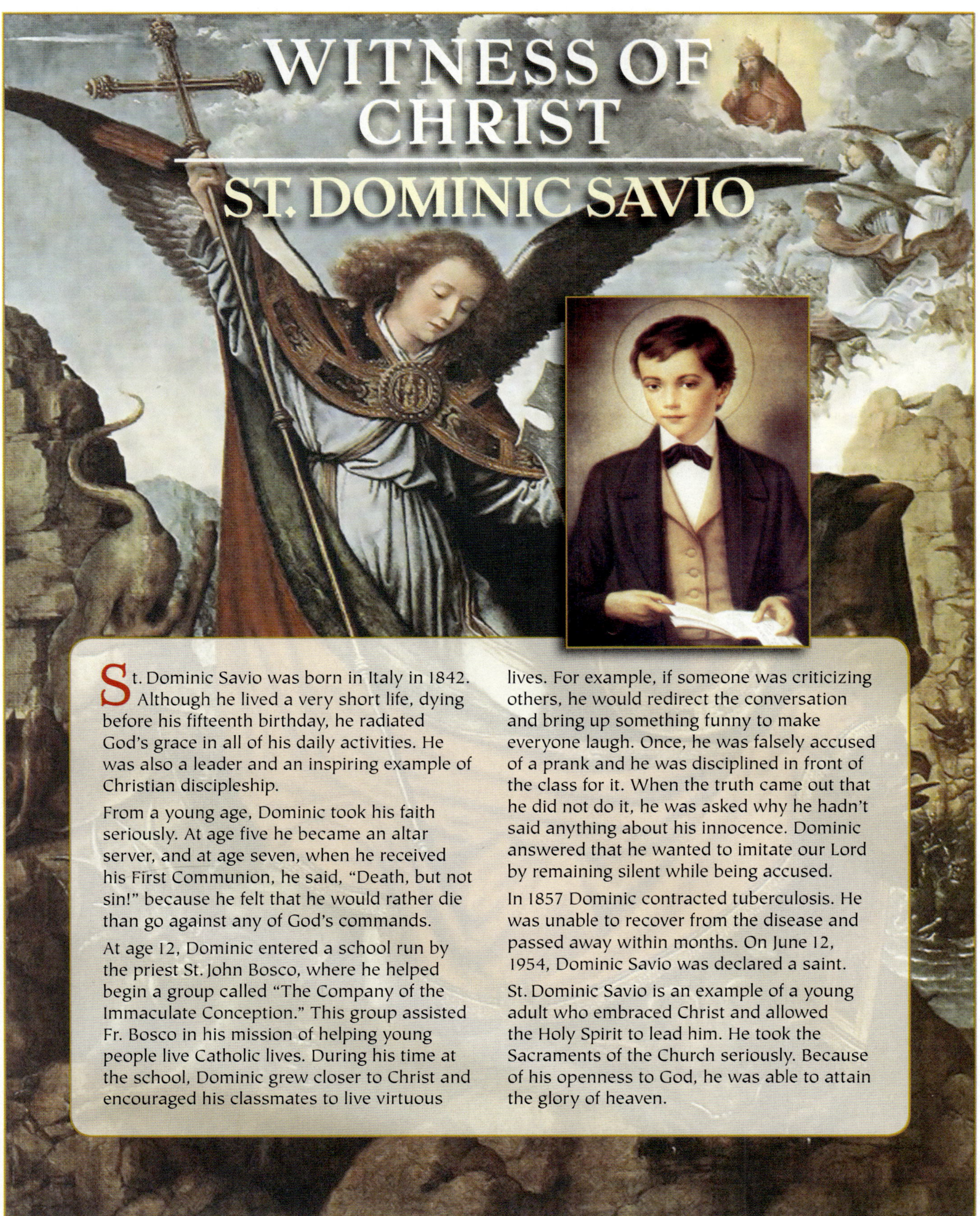

St. Dominic Savio was born in Italy in 1842. Although he lived a very short life, dying before his fifteenth birthday, he radiated God's grace in all of his daily activities. He was also a leader and an inspiring example of Christian discipleship.

From a young age, Dominic took his faith seriously. At age five he became an altar server, and at age seven, when he received his First Communion, he said, "Death, but not sin!" because he felt that he would rather die than go against any of God's commands.

At age 12, Dominic entered a school run by the priest St. John Bosco, where he helped begin a group called "The Company of the Immaculate Conception." This group assisted Fr. Bosco in his mission of helping young people live Catholic lives. During his time at the school, Dominic grew closer to Christ and encouraged his classmates to live virtuous lives. For example, if someone was criticizing others, he would redirect the conversation and bring up something funny to make everyone laugh. Once, he was falsely accused of a prank and he was disciplined in front of the class for it. When the truth came out that he did not do it, he was asked why he hadn't said anything about his innocence. Dominic answered that he wanted to imitate our Lord by remaining silent while being accused.

In 1857 Dominic contracted tuberculosis. He was unable to recover from the disease and passed away within months. On June 12, 1954, Dominic Savio was declared a saint.

St. Dominic Savio is an example of a young adult who embraced Christ and allowed the Holy Spirit to lead him. He took the Sacraments of the Church seriously. Because of his openness to God, he was able to attain the glory of heaven.

# VOCABULARY

### APOSTLE

From the Greek *apostolos* ("one sent forth"), it refers to the Twelve chosen by Jesus during the course of his public ministry to be his closest followers. The term also extends to a few other early followers of Christ: Sts. Matthias, Paul of Tarsus, and Barnabas. The Apostles were the first bishops of the Church.

### BAPTISM

The first of the Seven Sacraments that gives access to the other Sacraments. It is the first and chief Sacrament of Forgiveness of Sins, because it forgives both personal and Original Sin. It incorporates the baptized person into the Church, the Body of Christ, and makes us children of God.

### DISCIPLE

From the Latin verb *discere*, "to learn." One who accepted Jesus' message to follow him, especially one of the Twelve; this term can also refer to a Christian of any time period because he is a follower of Christ.

### FRUITS OF THE HOLY SPIRIT

According to Scripture and Tradition, twelve virtues that a person is enabled to live when exercising the gifts of the Holy Spirit. They include charity, joy, peace, patience, kindness, goodness, generosity, gentleness, faithfulness, modesty, self-control, and chastity.

### GIFTS OF THE HOLY SPIRIT

Seven special graces of the Holy Spirit that help us attain the fullness of Christian life: wisdom, understanding, counsel, fortitude, knowledge, piety, and fear of the Lord. They complete and perfect the virtues of those who receive them. They make the faithful docile in readily accepting divine inspirations. These gifts are given to Christians to assist them in following Christ and are conferred in a special way in Confirmation.

### GRACE

The favor of God given, first of all, through the Sacraments. Grace is a share in the divine life infused into the soul by the Holy Spirit to heal from sin, overcome sin and error, and lead one towards perfect knowledge of God. It is free and unmerited—we do nothing to earn it; God gives it as a gift.

### SACRAMENT

An efficacious sign of grace, instituted by Christ and entrusted to the Church, by which divine life is dispensed through the work of the Holy Spirit. Sacraments are effective in that they produce what they intend. There are Seven Sacraments. In Eastern Christianity, a Sacrament is often called a "mystery."

### VOCATION

The universal call to holiness, which is given in Baptism, is a call to love and serve God. Further, a vocation is also the particular plan or calling that God has for each individual in this life and hereafter. It could be a vocation to marriage, Holy Orders, or consecrated life. Some also live out their universal call to holiness in the single life.

*St. Philip Baptizing the Ethiopian* by Rembrandt. Baptism is the first of the Seven Sacraments that gives access to the other Sacraments.

## STUDY QUESTIONS

1. What is our ultimate destination in life?
2. When does a person first receive the Holy Spirit?
3. What is grace?
4. What is a Sacrament? Name the Seven Sacraments.
5. What is the Sacrament of Confirmation, and why do we need it?
6. Why is it important to prepare properly to receive a Sacrament?
7. What is a "gift of the Holy Spirit"? Name the seven gifts of the Holy Spirit.
8. Comment on this statement, explaining why it is right or wrong: *Confirmation is like your graduation from religious education, when you decide for yourself to be a Catholic.*
9. What are the four elements of living as a disciple of Christ?
10. What is a vocation?

## PRACTICAL EXERCISES

1. Set aside some time on two different days, about fifteen minutes each, to think about ways that you might prepare yourself spiritually to receive Confirmation. Begin and end each session with a short prayer to God to ask for his help. (The prayer can be in your own words or from Scripture, for example: "O LORD, make haste to help me" [Ps 70:1], or, "Give thanks to the LORD, for he is good" [Ps 106:1].) At the end of your time the second day, write down four of the ideas you have. Be sure these are things that you can do and that you might be willing to do with the help of God's grace. Save the paper to look back at it throughout your preparation. To help you with ideas, you might want to ask yourself these questions:

- What do I want to improve in my Christian life?
- What do I want to add to my life to make it more meaningful?
- What do I hope to gain through the reception of the Sacrament of Confirmation?
- How will Confirmation help me deepen my personal relationship with God?

2. The basic call of all Christians is to love and serve both God and neighbor. Start thinking about how you might put this into practice. Research and make a list of local volunteer opportunities or service projects that you might be willing to pursue as part of your preparation for Confirmation. Why do each of these options appeal to you?

"Give thanks to the LORD, for he is good." (Ps 106:1)

# SEALED IN THE SPIRIT

***How will you reflect in your daily Christian life that you have received the gifts of the Holy Spirit?***

This chapter emphasizes the importance of the Sacrament of Confirmation and the need to prepare well to receive it. What are some practical ways that you can prepare? How will your daily life reflect the fact that you have received the gifts of the Holy Spirit? It is important to understand what the Sacrament of Confirmation is and how it benefits you. So make a sincere effort to learn what you can from this course and book.

There is more to your Confirmation preparation than just learning facts about your Catholic faith, as important as that is. Preparation involves not only the mind but also the heart and soul. You read about how your reception of the Sacraments is affected by your interior disposition.

- *Why do you earnestly desire to receive this Sacrament?*
- *Why do you truly want to receive the grace that it offers so that you can be a disciple of Christ?*
- *How do you know that you are committed to allowing this grace to work within you?*

To have a good interior disposition, to set your sights properly, you must build the habits of a good spiritual life. The spiritual life is sometimes called the "interior life" because it forms your interior disposition. Here are a few essential ways to practice a good interior life as you prepare for Confirmation:

**Learn how to pray, and pray well.** Prayer is your personal conversation with God. There are many ways to pray, as we will discuss in a later chapter. Prayer does not always come easily; even the greatest saints sometimes struggled with prayer. The important thing is that you make a habit of daily prayer, because only in conversation with God—both speaking and listening—can we deepen our friendship with him.

**Go to Mass on Sundays and Holy Days of Obligation.** Do this not only because the Church requires it of you but also because you need to pray with the Catholic community. Most of all, the Mass provides you with the greatest opportunity and privilege of all: to receive the Body and Blood of Christ in the Sacrament of the Holy Eucharist. The Eucharist is our spiritual "food for the journey" as we face the challenges of life, and we ought to receive Christ in this way as often as possible. If you can, arrive a few minutes early and stay a few minutes late to be alone in God's presence. You can use this time to talk with him about your joys and struggles as well as thank him for the gifts that you have.

**Read the Bible and meditate on it.** In the Holy Scriptures, especially in the Gospels, we read of God's wonderful plan of salvation for the whole world. If we want to understand how God will work in our lives, we need to discover how he has worked in the lives of others before us.

**Go to Confession regularly.** The Sacrament of Penance is a great gift of healing. When we confess our sins to a priest with true repentance and a firm resolution never to sin again, we receive the forgiveness of Christ and the grace to become stronger against temptation. Everyone sins, so everyone needs this Sacrament. Confessing your sins on a regular basis—monthly would be a good practice—will help you stay on the right path.

**Marian Devotions.** Marian devotions are those prayers and acts undertaken to honor Mary, with the intent of seeking her intercession with her Son, Jesus, and his Father. The *Hail Mary*; the *Memorare*; the *Rosary*; the *Angelus*; the *Little Office of the Blessed Virgin Mary*; the *Litany of Loreto*; and the *Consecration to Jesus Through Mary* are some of the more popular Marian devotions.

**Seek out your parents and sponsor for guidance.** Your parents and sponsor have a vital role to play in your preparation for Confirmation. It is good to be able to speak with them freely about matters of the Catholic faith and ask their advice about things that concern you. At the end of each chapter there will be practical suggestions of ways to involve your parents and sponsor in this process.

**Seek out a Spiritual Director.** It is never too early in life to ask a priest (preferably), a religious, or a trusted family member or friend who practices the faith, to guide you in your spiritual journey. This spiritual coach can assess your spiritual strengths and weaknesses, and point the way for you to achieve the salvation of your soul.

# You and Your Parents

***Encourage your parents to be involved in your Confirmation preparation.***

At the end of every chapter, this section will suggest something to talk about or do with your parents. God gave you parents to be your primary teachers in the faith, and this section will help them prepare you for Confirmation.

Of course not everyone lives at home with a mother and a father. One or both of your parents might have passed away, or live outside your home because of separation or divorce. Perhaps you are blessed to have grandparents or an aunt and uncle who have stepped in to play a major role in your upbringing. Or perhaps you are living with foster parents. When this book asks you to talk about or do something with your *parents*, you can understand that to be the adults who are responsible for your care and for supporting you in your Confirmation preparation.

Your parents play a profound role in your life. They provide for your needs and help you mature from infancy and childhood into your teenage years and adulthood. Most importantly, they form you in the Catholic faith. The very fact that you are preparing for Confirmation indicates that one or both of your parents places a value on the Catholic faith and wants you to deepen and practice your faith as well.

This book will encourage you to talk about some aspects of your life of faith with your parents. You might be someone who has open communications with your parents and can "talk about anything," so these conversations may come easier for you. Use this section to go deeper than you have in the past. Or, you might find it is awkward to discuss faith and religion within the family. Even if it is difficult at first, please try to start these conversations. Your parents have wisdom and experience that might assist you in growing in faith and preparing for this great Sacrament. A simple request—"Would you help me prepare for Confirmation for a few minutes?"—might be all it takes to get started.

Find a few minutes when you can talk with your parents—perhaps after dinner, on a Sunday afternoon, or while going to school one morning—sharing your thoughts about your Confirmation preparation with them. Ask them these questions:

1. What is the best thing I can do to prepare for Confirmation?
2. What did you find most helpful when you were preparing for Confirmation?
3. Where were you confirmed, and what patron saint did you pick for your Confirmation name?
4. Who was your sponsor, and why did you choose that person?
5. What do you remember about the Confirmation Mass and how it felt to be confirmed?

Be prepared to report back to the class on your talk with your parents.

*Continued*

Find a few minutes when you can talk with your parents about your Confirmation preparation—perhaps after dinner, on a Sunday afternoon, or while going to school one morning.

# YOU AND YOUR PARENTS Continued

## FOR PARENTS: WHAT IS YOUR ROLE?

**Since parents have given children their life, they are bound by the most serious obligation to educate their offspring and therefore must be recognized as the primary and principal educators. (St. Paul VI, *Declaration of Christian Education*, October 28, 1965, no. 3)**

The Church has always taught that parents are the primary educators of their children. As such, parents are the primary guides for their children as they prepare for Confirmation. What are some things parents can do to help prepare a child for Confirmation?

1. **Praying with your child.** Encourage a life of prayer in your child. Pray with him or her regularly, and pray that the Holy Spirit will help your child be prepared for Confirmation.

2. **Helping your child prepare.** Be sure that your child is doing her assignments and reading along with the class. Encourage him to ask for help if he doesn't understand something or falls behind.

3. **Going to Mass and Confession regularly.** Confirmation is just one of the Seven Sacraments. It is important that your child (and you!) go to Mass each Sunday, and also that you all receive Confession on a regular basis (perhaps monthly). This will allow your child to be spiritually prepared to receive Confirmation, and will build habits that can last a lifetime.

4. **Learning more about Confirmation.** This will give you a chance to learn more about your faith together with your child.

## FOR CONFIRMANDS: WHAT IS YOUR ROLE?

You are going to be confirmed soon. What does that mean? How should you prepare? That is what this book is all about—helping you to understand Confirmation and how to prepare for it. Here are some things you can do to get ready to receive this wonderful Sacrament:

1. **Praying.** A regular prayer life is essential to being a follower of Christ. You will learn more about prayer in Chapter 9, but that should not stop you from praying now. Take time every day to ask for God's help.

2. **Keeping up with your assignments.** Your parents, your teachers, and this book will all help you prepare for Confirmation. Be sure to keep up with the reading and assignments you are given so that you can better understand the gifts—and responsibilities—you receive at Confirmation.

3. **Going to Mass and Confession regularly.** Being prepared for Confirmation is not simply a school activity. It is primarily a ***spiritual*** activity. To prepare your soul to receive this great gift, continue to receive the Sacraments regularly. This means going to Mass at least every Sunday and going to Confession regularly (perhaps monthly).

4. **Learning about Confirmation.** This is a great chance to learn more about the Catholic faith and to share your own faith with your parents.

For Parents:
Go with your child to Mass and Confession regularly.

For Confirmands:
A regular prayer life is essential to being a follower of Christ.

# You and Your Sponsor

***Serving as a Confirmation sponsor is both an honor and a responsibility.***

At the end of each chapter you will find this section which includes some suggestions for conversations and activities to engage in with your sponsor.

Along with your parents, your sponsor will play an important role in your preparation for Confirmation. Choosing a sponsor is not something to take lightly; it is something that you should do with careful thought and prayer.

You may choose one of your godparents from your Baptism to be your Confirmation sponsor. In fact, this practice is encouraged as a sign of the link between Baptism and Confirmation (CCC 1311).

Your sponsor may be male or female. He or she should be strong in the practice of the Catholic faith —attending Mass faithfully, going to Confession regularly, living a good moral life, and having a good prayer life. Your sponsor should know you and should be knowledgeable about the faith, too. He or she should be willing to take on the serious responsibilities of serving as your sponsor.

The Church lays out five minimum requirements for Confirmation sponsors (cf. CIC 874):

1. A sponsor must be suitable for the role of a sponsor and intend to fulfill it.
2. A sponsor must be at least 16 years old (unless your bishop or parish priest determines that there is an important reason to allow someone younger).
3. A sponsor must be a Catholic who has received the Sacraments of Initiation—Baptism, Confirmation, and the Eucharist—and who lives a life in harmony with the faith.
4. A sponsor, if he or she is married, must be in a marriage recognized by the Church. (A Catholic whose marriage has not been blessed by the Church or is living together with a romantic partner outside of marriage cannot be a sponsor.)
5. A sponsor must not be your father or mother.

Many people are tempted to select a sponsor mainly as a way of honoring that person—a favorite aunt or uncle, for example—and it is very good to want to honor our relatives and friends. Indeed, it is a great compliment to be a Confirmation sponsor! But that should not be the main reason for your choice. A sponsor is someone who will share part of his or her life of faith with you and help you as you prepare for Confirmation. Your sponsor should be a kind of advisor and role model, someone who will help guide you as you continue to grow in the Catholic faith after Confirmation.

## How to Choose Your Sponsor

So pray and think carefully about your choice of sponsor. Here are some suggestions to help you in your choice:

1. Pray to the Holy Spirit and ask him for guidance in choosing a sponsor.
2. Write down some of the qualities that you think a good sponsor would possess. Then brainstorm a list of people in your life who have those qualities. Check this list against the Church's requirements, above.
3. Your parents and your parish priest must ultimately approve of your choice of a sponsor. Ask them what qualities they think a good sponsor should have in order to assist you in your journey of faith.
4. Do two or three people stand out as possibilities? Write a letter to each of your possible sponsors, asking him or her to be your sponsor; explain the role of the sponsor and why you think that he or she would make a good sponsor for you. (Do not send these letters; it is just an exercise to help you when you make your choice.)

*Continued*

# YOU AND YOUR SPONSOR Continued

## FOR SPONSORS: WHAT IS YOUR ROLE?

**Insofar as possible, there is to be a sponsor for the person to be confirmed; the sponsor is to take care that the confirmed person behaves as a true witness of Christ and faithfully fulfills the obligations inherent in this sacrament. (CIC 892)**

Sponsors fill an important role in the life of the confirmand. He or she are to witness to the candidate how to be a faithful disciple of Christ. This obligation extends throughout the life of the sponsor and the confirmand. Once he or she has met the requirements on the previous page, what are some things a sponsor can do now as the candidate prepares for Confirmation?

**1. Praying for the candidate.** As the sponsor, your primary responsibility is the spiritual welfare of the confirmand. You should begin praying for him or her now, and continue this habit for the rest of your life.

**2. Being a model for the candidate.** The confirmand looks to his or her sponsor as a model for how to live the Catholic faith. This is a great responsibility! Strive to live each day as Christ would want you to live, so as to be an example of a Christian disciple. This should include making a rough plan to mentor the candidate, both before and after Confirmation.

**3. Expressing your faith to the candidate.** At an appropriate time during the preparation for Confirmation, tell the confirmand why you are Catholic. What has God done for you? It is important that the confirmand begins to see how God has worked in the lives of those he or she loves and admires. You should meet on a regular basis with the candidate to address any questions or concerns.

**4. Learning more about Confirmation.** This will give you a chance to learn more about your faith together with the candidate.

For Sponsors:
The confirmand looks to his or her sponsor as a model for how to live the Catholic faith.

## INTRODUCTION

***We naturally want to be happy; true and lasting happiness is found only in God.***

**The desire for God is written in the human heart, because man is created by God and for God; and God never ceases to draw man to himself. Only in God will he find the truth and happiness he never stops searching for. (CCC 27)**

Deep down, we all desire to know God; we were created for this. Whether we realize it or not, we want to know who God is and what he is like. We also wonder about the meaning or purpose of our lives. We are created with a desire to know the truth about who we are and why we are alive.

All of us search for the answers to these mysteries. Some of us look to various religions and philosophies, trying to discover the key to the meaning of existence. Others come up with their own conclusions based on their life experiences apart from religion.

Do you ever want something, get it, and then still feel unsatisfied? This happens to all of us, because we cannot find complete, full happiness here on earth.

So we are restless beings. The desire to be happy is a natural desire, and it comes from God himself. Our desire for perfect happiness is a desire for God, and God alone can satisfy us. *God alone can satisfy you.* As St. Augustine famously wrote, "You have made us for yourself, O Lord, and our heart is restless until it finds its rest in you."

It may amaze you to learn that just as you have an innate desire for God, God deeply desires you, too. He wants to enter into a personal relationship with you. He is always actively seeking you out, even when you hide from him or ignore him. But God will not force himself upon you. Instead he will invite you to freely choose a friendship with him, a friendship which will lead to perfect happiness with him forever in heaven.

After reading this chapter, you will be able to answer these questions:

- What is natural revelation?
- What is supernatural Revelation?
- What is the Deposit of Faith?
- What is the Magisterium?

Our desire for perfect happiness is a desire for God.

## ST. AUGUSTINE, Convert and Teacher

St. Augustine is one of the greatest philosophers and theologians of the Church. However, before he was a bishop, priest, or even a Christian, he was a brilliant, highly educated man who refused to seek God. Instead, he tried to fulfill his desire for happiness with many worldly things.

Augustine was born in 354, and his mother, St. Monica, prayed continuously for her son. Eventually, when Augustine was in his 30's, he experienced a religious conversion and embraced Christianity. Before long, he was appointed Bishop of Hippo, a diocese in North Africa. His writings and influence helped to develop our understanding of Original Sin, the Sacraments, the nature of the Church, and many other teachings of the faith.

St. Augustine is well known for his book *Confessions*, which is his spiritual autobiography and describes his search for God, his attraction to sin, and his pursuit of true happiness in God. It is still considered one of the greatest spiritual classics of all time. In this book, St. Augustine famously writes, "You have made us for yourself, O Lord, and our hearts are restless until they rest in you," meaning that God made us to be fulfilled only by loving him, and if we try to find fulfillment anywhere else, we will not be satisfied.

*The Conversion of St. Augustine* by Fra Angelico. Augustine's mother, St. Monica, prayed continuously for her son who had refused to seek God.

# GOD RESPONDS TO OUR SEARCH FOR HIM

***God wants us to find him, so he reveals himself to us in both natural and supernatural ways.***

God wants us to know that he exists and that he loves each of us. So, since the creation of the world, he has been giving us ways to find out about him. This is called "Revelation"—God revealing himself to us. Revelation comes to us in two different ways: through creation (natural revelation) and through his direct action in the world (supernatural Revelation).

**Natural revelation** refers to what we can know about God through human **reason** by looking at the world around us. In his letter to the Romans, St. Paul goes as far as to say that the law of God is "written on their hearts" (Rom 2:15). This is true even of those unaware of having ever encountered God.

> **From the greatness and beauty of**
> **created things**
> **comes a corresponding perception of their**
> **Creator. (Wis 13:5)**

Scripture tells us that every person, no matter his or her background, is capable of coming to know God. Why? Because God reveals his presence even in nature. In his Epistle to the Romans, St. Paul writes of nonbelievers:

> **What can be known about God is plain to them, because God has shown it to them. Ever since the creation of the world his invisible nature, namely his eternal power and deity, has been clearly perceived in the things that have been made. (Rom 1:19-20)**

St. Paul explains here that we can come to know God through the use of reason simply by observing his creation. The entire created universe reveals that there is a God. After all, where there is creation, there must be a Creator. Creation also reveals something about the nature of God, particularly his infinite power and goodness.

> **When he listens to the message of creation and to the voice of conscience, man can arrive at certainty about the existence of God, the cause... of everything. (CCC 46)**

Scripture tells us that we are made in the "image and likeness of God" (Gn 1:26-17). This means that, like God, we have both a free will to make choices, and an intellect to think. The intellect gives us the power to use reason to discover truth. Through reason, simply by observing and contemplating the world around us, we can come to know that there is indeed a God. The First Vatican Council stated:

> **God, the source…of all things, can be known with certainty from the consideration of created things, by the natural power of human reason: ever since the creation of the world, his invisible nature has been clearly perceived in the things that have been made. (Vatican I)**

The Council was simply echoing St. Paul when he wrote in the passage cited above that God can be "clearly perceived in the things that have been made."

But there is an obstacle: we all have a sinful nature, which makes us vulnerable to sin. This vulnerability is called **concupiscence** (any desire to satisfy our senses, in a manner contrary to what is good for us).

It clouds our reason and intellect, which makes it more difficult for us to know God. So God reveals himself to us through direct means as well. This is called **supernatural (or Divine) Revelation.** This type of revelation refers to certain truths that can only be known when God reveals them to us directly. Supernatural Revelation, which began at the time of Adam and Eve, unfolded gradually for centuries and was made perfect and complete in the person of Jesus Christ.

## A Dialogue
## GOD'S EXISTENCE

**Eddie:** I don't believe God exists.

**You:** Why not?

**Eddie:** Because science has shown that there is no God.

**You:** Well, science does help us to understand the world and how it works, but it doesn't really tell us *why* it exists.

**Eddie:** What do you mean?

**You:** Remember that big car accident last week? Where that guy ran into the back of a truck and then the truck ended up running into another car, until there were like 20 cars involved?

**Eddie:** Yeah, that was pretty wild. But what's that got to do with God?

**You:** Did anything cause that accident to happen? Or did it just happen on its own?

**Eddie:** Well, I guess the first guy who ran into the truck caused it. If he had just stopped in time, it never would have happened.

**You:** Exactly. The same is true of the universe. Science can tell us how it works and how it runs, but how did it start? Who caused it? Someone had to be the first cause that got it all started, just like someone had to start that car accident. The someone who created the universe is God.

**Eddie:** I guess that makes some sense. I'll think about it.

## GOD IS REVEALED IN NATURE

St. Paul taught in the New Testament that even those who have never heard of God can come to know him in nature. Even many centuries before Christ came to earth, in the Old Testament people recognized this truth. In poetic form in the Psalms, we read:

> **The heavens are telling the glory of God;**
> **and the firmament proclaims his handiwork.**
> **Day to day pours forth speech,**
> **and night to night declares knowledge.**
> **There is no speech, nor are there words;**
> **their voice is not heard;**
> **yet their voice goes out through all the earth,**
> **and their words to the end of the world.**
> **(Ps 19:1-4)**

## ST. THOMAS AQUINAS, the Angelic Doctor

St. Thomas Aquinas was a Dominican friar who lived in the thirteenth century. He is considered one of the greatest theological minds that the Church has ever known, and his insights into theology are still studied today.

However, when Thomas was in school, his classmates would have been shocked to know what he would become. They nicknamed him "dumb ox," not only because of his large build, but because he was usually silent. They didn't realize that he was quiet because his mind was always working!

During his life Thomas wrote many theological and philosophical works that help us to understand both God and the human race better. But Thomas was not just an intellectual; he was a great saint. He loved God deeply, and near the end of his life had a heavenly vision, after which he cried out, "All that I have written appears to be as so much straw after the things that have been revealed to me!" This was not meant to denigrate his writings, but to show that even the best knowledge of God pales in comparison to the awesome reality that is God.

St. Thomas Aquinas is called the "Angelic Doctor" and his feast day is January 28.

## WE CAN KNOW BY REASON SOME ATTRIBUTES OF GOD

We see that natural reason informs us that God exists. Natural reason can also tell us things about God beyond the fact that he exists—that he is perfect: eternal, all-powerful, all-knowing, present everywhere, unchanging, and that there is only one God. Let's look at a few of those attributes.

We say that God is the first cause of all things, which means that God was not created, but that he was the one who did the creating. But if he was not created and yet he exists, then he must always have existed—and always will exist. Therefore, God is *eternal*. Further, if God is ultimate perfection, that means he can do anything. So God is *all-powerful, all-knowing,* and *present everywhere*.

If God is perfect and eternal, then he need not change—he can't learn more information, or become stronger or go somewhere he is not. So we say that God is *unchanging*. Finally, there can only be one perfect being. If two or more beings were the source of all perfection, they would be the exact same being. If one was "more perfect" than the other, then the one who was less than perfect could not be God. So there is only one God.

These attributes of God can be known through reason, but even this understanding remains limited. It still doesn't tell us why God created us, whether he loves us, or what his plans for us are. These questions can only be answered through the direct action of God—his supernatural Revelation.

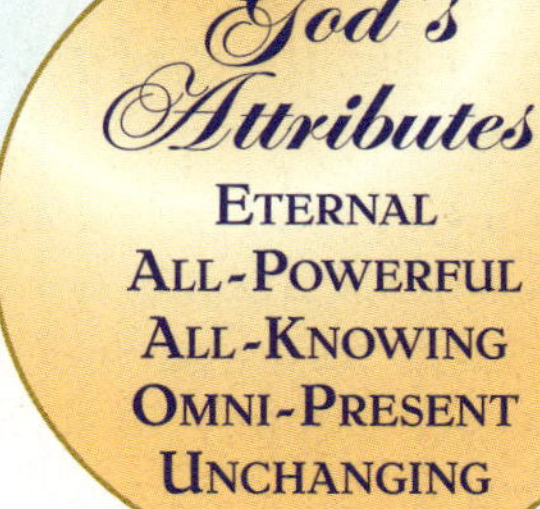


## SUPERNATURAL REVELATION

***God reveals himself throughout human history in order to reconcile sinful man to himself.***

As we read, through our use of reason we can know things *about* God. We can know he exists and we can know some of his attributes. But God does not want us to simply know facts about him, he wants us to know him in a deeply personal and intimate way.

Think of the first time you met your best friend. You immediately knew things *about* her, such as her hair color, how tall she is, what she likes to wear, etc. But over time you began to know her and have a relationship with her. God wants to have a relationship with us. That's why he has revealed himself to the world in supernatural ways—so that we can come to know him intimately.

God created the world for us. Out of perfect love, he made us uniquely in his "image and likeness." He gave us an immortal soul, free will, and an intellect. These gifts allow us to choose to love him and be united with him for all eternity. But when our first parents, Adam and Eve, misused their free will and chose sin, they broke their friendship with God and infected all of humanity with the stain of **Original Sin**.

Adam and Eve chose sin over obedience when they freely ate of the fruit God had forbidden them to eat. These are five results of that act:

- Our human nature is disordered, meaning we often desire what is not good for us.
- Our original state of being holy and just has been lost.
- We are now subject to death.
- Sin is now present everywhere in the world.
- Every person is born into this condition.

Like a genetic disease, Adam and Eve passed Original Sin on to every human being throughout time. We are all born with it and affected by it. Yet God did not give up on the human race. Instead, he sought to gather us back into his friendship.

But immediately after the first sin broke the friendship between God and man, God began reaching out to man. He didn't leave things as they were, broken. He promised that one day he would send someone, born of a woman, who would crush the head of Satan (Gn 3:15). Since that time, God has continued to repair this broken relationship through a series of covenants, which we will discuss in the next chapter.

The Old Testament shows us how the Revelation of God was a gradual process. Humanity was so affected by sin that God had to reveal himself slowly. He taught his people and guided them until they were ready to receive the promised **Redeemer**.

> **God communicates himself to man gradually. He prepares him to welcome by stages the supernatural Revelation that is to culminate in the person and mission of the incarnate Word, Jesus Christ. (CCC 53)**

St. Paul writes that the Son of God was born at the proper time ("when the time had fully come") to free us from our slavery to sin:

> **When the time had fully come, God sent forth his Son, born of woman, born under the law, to redeem those who were under the law, so that we might receive adoption as sons. (Gal 4:4-5)**

Christ is the fullness of Divine Revelation. Everything that God wants to reveal to the world can be found in who Christ is, what he said, and what he did. Everything that God promised to his people as described in the Old Testament comes to fulfillment in his Son.

To come to a deeper knowledge of God and his will for us, we need to look to the word and example of Jesus Christ. As Christ said to his Apostle Philip, "He who has seen me has seen the Father" (Jn 14:9). The author of the Letter to the Hebrews spoke of Christ as the fullness of the Revelation of God:

> **In many and various ways God spoke of old to our fathers by the prophets, but in these last days he has spoken to us by a Son. (Heb 1:1-2)**

Christ is the fullness of God's Revelation. He showed us what perfect happiness is. He revealed completely the Father's love and mercy. He showed compassion for all in healing the sick, casting out demons, raising the dead, and forgiving sinners. He proclaimed the Kingdom of God, and invited everyone to enter it by

*The Transfiguration* by Bellini.
Christ is the fullness of Divine Revelation. "He who has seen me has seen the Father" (Jn 14:9).

*The Holy Trinity* by Balen.
Christ revealed that God is a Trinity of three divine Persons: the Father, the Son, and the Holy Spirit

turning away from sin and believing in the Gospel. He taught the truth with love, even when he met with opposition and threats of violence. He also revealed that God is a Trinity of three divine Persons: the Father, the Son, and the Holy Spirit, something that is impossible to know by human reason alone.

> **Christ, the Son of God made man, is the Father's one, perfect and unsurpassable Word. In him he has said everything; there will be no other word than this one. (CCC 65)**

Ever since the Fall of Adam, God has been revealing himself to the world. The culmination of that Revelation—that which all Revelation points to and is fulfilled in—is Jesus Christ. Through him we come to know God and have a relationship with him. As Jesus himself proclaimed, "no one comes to the Father, but by me" (Jn 14:6).

## *A Dialogue*

## WHO IS JESUS CHRIST?

**Peter:** "Hey, Dad, my teacher said today that Jesus is the most important thing—more important than the Bible, even. Do you think that's true?"

**Dad:** "Oh, yes. Your teacher's right. Do you know why?"

**Peter:** "Well, he taught us how to live. Like 'Love your neighbor' and all that stuff."

**Dad:** "True. And who's your neighbor?"

**Peter:** "Everyone?"

**Dad:** "Right. Now why else is Jesus important? If he only taught us how to live, there are a lot of other people who did that, too."

**Peter:** "Um...he started the Church."

**Dad:** "That's right, and without the Church we wouldn't really know how to follow him. How could we go to Mass or be baptized or learn his teachings without the Church? And can you think of any other reasons Jesus is important?"

**Peter:** "No..."

**Dad:** "So far we've talked about living on earth. Is that all there is?"

**Peter:** "Oh! He made it so we can go to heaven."

**Dad:** "Yes! Without Jesus dying and rising for us we wouldn't be able to live for eternity with God in heaven. Life would just end. That's pretty important!"

**Peter:** "Yeah. But did Jesus have to be the one to do that? Because he never sinned?"

**Dad:** "Well, in a way it was because he never sinned...But it was much more than that. Mary never sinned but she couldn't have died for all of mankind. What was unique about Jesus?"

**Peter:** "You mean that he is God?"

**Dad:** "Exactly. Unlike any other religious leader in history he didn't just tell us about God, he was God. He let us see God and know him."

**Peter:** "Ok, I guess Jesus really is that important!"

# THE DEPOSIT OF FAITH: SCRIPTURE AND TRADITION

***Divine Revelation is handed on through Scripture and Tradition.***

Although Divine Revelation has been completed in Christ, it is not always entirely clear to us. During Christ's life even the Apostles sometimes failed to understand what he was trying to teach them. After Christ rose from the dead and ascended into heaven, the Apostles still wrestled with who Christ was and what he expected of them.

**That very day two of [Jesus' disciples] were going to a village named Emmaus, about seven miles from Jerusalem, and talking with each other about all these things that had happened. While they were talking and discussing together, Jesus himself drew near and went with them. But their eyes were kept from recognizing him. And he said to them, "What is this conversation which you are holding with each other as you walk?" And they stood still, looking sad. Then one of them, named Cleopas, answered him, "Are you the only visitor to Jerusalem who does not know the things that have happened there in these days?" And he said to them, "What things?" And they said to him, "Concerning Jesus of Nazareth, who was a prophet mighty in deed and word before God and all the people, and how our chief priests and rulers delivered him up to be condemned to death, and crucified him. But we had hoped that he was the one to redeem Israel. Yes, and besides all this, it is now the third day since this happened. Moreover, some women of our company amazed us. They were at the tomb early in the morning and did not find his body; and they came back saying that they had even seen a vision of angels, who said that he was alive. Some of those who were with us went to the tomb, and found it just as the women had said; but him they did not see." And he said to them, "O foolish men, and slow of heart to believe all that the prophets have spoken! Was it not necessary that the Christ should suffer these things and enter into his glory?" And beginning with Moses and all the prophets, he interpreted to them in all the scriptures the things concerning himself.**

*Supper at Emmaus* by Velasquez.
"And their eyes were opened and they recognized him."

**So they drew near to the village to which they were going. He appeared to be going further, but they constrained him, saying, "Stay with us, for it is toward evening and the day is now far spent." So he went in to stay with them. When he was at table with them, he took the bread and blessed, and broke it, and gave it to them. And their eyes were opened and they recognized him; and he vanished out of their sight. They said to each other, "Did not our hearts burn within us while he talked to us on the road, while he opened to us the scriptures?" (Lk 24:13-32)**

We can see from this Scripture passage that during the life of Christ, and even immediately following his Resurrection, his followers did not understand what the Lord was accomplishing. They were timid and afraid. Then came the Descent of the Holy Spirit at Pentecost, as recounted in the second chapter of Acts. After this, the Apostles went about preaching the Gospel boldly, relying on the Holy Spirit instead of their own human strength and knowledge. Scripture describes how the Apostles and other Church leaders would debate how to interpret and apply what they had been taught (see, for example, Acts 15).

Christ entrusted to his Church the authority and mission to make him known throughout the world and to teach in his name.

> **Jesus came and said to [the disciples], "All authority in heaven and on earth has been given to me. Go therefore and make disciples of all nations, baptizing them in the name of the Father and of the Son and of the Holy Spirit, teaching them to observe all that I have commanded you; and lo, I am with you always, to the close of the age." (Mt 28:18-20)**

When the Apostles went forth preaching and teaching the Gospel as Christ had commanded them, they did not have written notes and instructions from Christ. They had only their own testimony of what they had heard Christ say and what they had seen him do.

Think of it: the Gospels had not yet been written, nor had the letters of St. Paul and the other books that make up what we know as the New Testament. The "Word of God" was contained in the preaching of the Apostles as they handed on what Christ had taught them. This preaching was the beginning of **Sacred Tradition**.

Sacred Tradition refers to how the Church has taught, interpreted, preached, and practiced since apostolic times what God has revealed.

> **"[Sacred Tradition] transmits in its entirety the Word of God which has been entrusted to the apostles by Christ the Lord and the Holy Spirit." (CCC 81)**

*St. Paul Preaching in Athens* by Raphael.
The "Word of God" was contained in the preaching of the Apostles.

## WHERE DID THE BIBLE COME FROM?

Although the Bible is sometimes referred to as "the good book," it is actually a collection of "books" of varying lengths. In its canon of 73 books, Sacred Scripture tells the story of salvation history, God's unfolding Revelation of himself.

The 46 books of the Old Testament reveal how God formed and prepared his people for the coming of Christ, who would redeem them from sin. The Old Testament canon follows the *Septuagint*, the Greek translation of Scripture that was used by the early Church. The Church later declared this canon to be the inspired Word of God.

The 27 books of the New Testament present the life and redemptive mission of Christ, the foundation of the Church, and the life of the early Church as the Apostles began to make the Gospel known throughout the world. These books were written between about 50-100 AD. They were widely read in Christian communities and used in prayer and at Mass. There were many other books circulating in the early Church that told stories about Christ, and there were other letters said to be written by the Apostles or other early Christian figures. Some of these other writings were even held in high esteem by some Christians. Yet many of these writings are not included in the Bible. It was the duty of the Church to determine which books would comprise the New Testament by deciding which of these books were truly inspired by God.

The Bible used by Protestant Christian communities has fewer books than the Catholic Bible. When the first Protestant reformers broke away from the Catholic Church in the sixteenth century, they rejected several books and sections of the Old Testament that were not written originally in Hebrew. That is why most of the Protestant Bibles have only thirty-nine books in its Old Testament. (Some Protestant Bibles contain the books and sections that were deleted by the reformers, including them in a separate section, but noting the widespread Protestant belief that they are not inspired).

*St. Matthew and the Angel* by Reni.
Sacred Scripture is the Word of God recorded by human writers under the inspiration of the Holy Spirit.

As the early Church grew and developed, the Apostles and others began to record their teachings and their recollections of the life of Christ in writing. Among these writings are those books and letters of the Church that have been handed down to us as the New Testament. Together with the books of the Old Testament, they make up **Sacred Scripture**, the written Word of God, commonly called the Bible.

Sacred Scripture is the Word of God recorded by human writers under the inspiration of the Holy Spirit. God, then, is the author of Scripture. God did not dictate the books of the Bible word for word, the way an executive might dictate a letter to an assistant. Instead, God allowed the human authors to express his truth in their own words and writing style. Yet through this process God ensured that the writings express what he wants them to communicate. This is called "inspiration."

> **God is the author of Sacred Scripture. "The divinely revealed realities, which are contained and presented in the text of Sacred Scripture, have been written down under the inspiration of the Holy Spirit." (CCC 105)**

> **God inspired the human authors of the sacred books. "To compose the sacred books, God chose certain men who, all the while he employed them in this task, made full use of their own faculties and powers so that, though he acted in them and by them, it was as true authors that they consigned to writing whatever he wanted written, and no more." (CCC 106)**

Further, because God is all truth and does not contain error, so too Scripture does not teach any error. This does not mean that when men and women interpret the Bible they cannot err. In fact you will find many contradictory interpretations, which proves that they often do make errors! However, when the Bible is interpreted officially by the Church, under the guidance of the same Holy Spirit that inspired the Sacred Writings, we can know that the interpretation is true.

> **There exists a close connection and communication between sacred tradition and Sacred Scripture. For both of them, flowing from the same divine wellspring, in a certain way merge into a unity and tend toward the same end. (*DV* 9)**

Sacred Scripture and Sacred Tradition together make up the single sacred contents of the Word of God, which we call the **Deposit of Faith**. Together they provide the foundation for the teachings of the Church.

## WHAT IS THE *CATECHISM*?

A catechism is a book that compiles all the teachings of a church usually using a question-and-answer format. In the history of the Catholic Church, there have been many catechisms, some created for specific countries or regions of the world, and some intended for use by the whole Church. The most recent catechism is called the *Catechism of the Catholic Church*, and it is a universal catechism authorized by St. John Paul II as an official summary of Church teaching. The first English translation was published in 1994. In 1997, the authoritative edition was approved and published for use in the Universal Church.

This book quotes the *Catechism of the Catholic Church* frequently to show that the doctrines and explanations in the *Didache Sacramental Preparation Series* are presenting the authentic teachings of the Catholic Church.

## MAGISTERIUM: INTERPRETER OF SCRIPTURE AND TRADITION

***Revelation is communicated to us today through the teaching authority of the Church.***

Christ handed on to the Apostles his authority and commanded them to teach the Gospel to the whole world. With their disciples, the Apostles carried out this mission both orally and in writing —in preaching and, later, in the inspired works of the New Testament. Furthermore, the Apostles ordained bishops as their successors so that the teachings of Christ would be communicated faithfully to future generations.

Interpreting Sacred Scripture and Sacred Tradition is the role of the teaching office of the Church, called the **Magisterium**. The Magisterium is exercised by the Pope and the bishops in union with him. Since the time of the Apostles, the Magisterium has preserved the truths of the Deposit of Faith with the assistance of the Holy Spirit. Christ promised this assistance when he told the Apostles: "But the Counselor, the Holy Spirit, whom the Father will send in my name, he will teach you all things, and bring to your remembrance all that I have said to you" (Jn 14:26).

The Magisterium has been at work communicating the faith for almost 2,000 years. Over this time, as the Church has continued to reflect on the content of the Deposit of Faith, she has arrived at a deeper and more complete understanding of the nature of God and the person and teachings of Christ. This unending reflection has, for example, led to a deeper understanding of the mystery of the Trinity, the Holy Eucharist, and other articles of the faith over the centuries.

> **This sacred tradition, therefore, and Sacred Scripture of both the Old and New Testaments are like a mirror in which the pilgrim Church on earth looks at God, from whom she has received everything, until she is brought finally to see Him as He is, face to face. (*DV* 7)**

In every age, the teaching authority of the Catholic Church applies the teachings of Christ to new challenges and situations in our world.

> **It is [the] Magisterium's task to preserve God's people from deviations and defections and to guarantee them the objective possibility of professing the true faith without error. (CCC 890)**

## THE CALL TO FAITH

***God seeks us, but we must respond to his love in order to remain in his friendship.***

Revelation is God's way of seeking us, of calling us to seek him in return. God is constantly initiating a relationship with us. It is up to us to respond.

One of God's great gifts to mankind is free will—the ability to choose for ourselves. God will not impose himself upon us; instead, we must use our free will to accept his call and choose to follow him. We all know that you cannot make someone become your friend. God does not make us follow him. Christ tells

### TO TRUST AS MARY DID

Mary, the mother of Christ, is a model for us of perfect faith.

Mary was a young unmarried woman when the Angel Gabriel appeared to her to announce that God had chosen her to bear his Son. Although she did not understand how, as a virgin, she could conceive a child, she trusted in God's plan and submitted herself to his will:

> **"Behold, I am the handmaid of the Lord; let it be to me according to your word." (Lk 1:38)**

With her consent, Mary became the mother of our Savior, Jesus Christ, because she trusted in God's Revelation.

us, "Behold, I stand at the door and knock; if any one hears my voice and opens the door, I will come in to him and eat with him, and he with me" (Rev 3:20). He approaches us with urgency, but we must choose to open the door and let him into our lives.

Faith is a gift from God. This means that in order to believe, we need supernatural help. We need the assistance of the Holy Spirit so that our hearts can make those first steps toward a closer union with God. Faith is never the result solely of our own efforts; rather, faith is the result of God's promptings and inspirations and our response to his invitation. In the Sacrament of Confirmation you will receive the Holy Spirit in a new way, which will help strengthen your own faith.

## CONCLUSION

***God's Revelation requires a response from us so that we fulfill our destiny: eternal life.***

Some people speak as if it is impossible to know anything about God. "Nobody knows if God exists." "Nobody knows what really happens after death." These statements highlight an ignorance of God's Revelation, both natural and supernatural. We can know that God exists through the use of our human reason. And, we can know he loves us and wants a relationship with us through Divine Revelation, especially through his Son Jesus Christ. We need God's Revelation in order to gain eternal life. God wants to prepare us to spend eternity with him, and to be happy while here on earth.

Christ is the fullness of Revelation. His teachings, which comprise the Deposit of Faith, were entrusted to his Church. It is through his Church that each new generation has access to the truth. God does not want us to remain in ignorance and confusion but rather to come into an intimate and personal relationship with him through Christ. We must freely cooperate with God's gift of faith and accept that Revelation. In Christ alone can we obtain eternal life with the Father.

> **"Eternal life" is not—as the modern reader might immediately assume—life after death, in contrast to this present life, which is transient and not eternal. "Eternal life" is life itself, real life, which can also be lived in the present age and is no longer challenged by physical death. This is the point: to seize "life" here and now, real life that can no longer be destroyed by anything or anyone.**
>
> **This meaning of "eternal life" appears very clearly in the account of the raising of Lazarus: "He who believes in me, though he die, yet shall he live, and whoever lives and believes in me shall never die" (Jn 11:25-26).**
>
> **(Pope Benedict XVI, *Jesus of Nazareth*, "Holy Week")**

## POINTS TO REMEMBER

1. Every human person has a natural desire for God. We cannot find perfect and lasting happiness apart from God. As St. Augustine wrote, "You have made us for yourself, O Lord, and our heart is restless until it rests in you."
2. We can know about God through natural reason, although our reason is limited. We can also know God's inner life and his plans for mankind through Divine Revelation. Through what we can see for ourselves of the created world we can come to know of God's existence and some of his attributes. God's supernatural Revelation occurred slowly over time until it was fulfilled in Jesus Christ, the Son of God and Word of the Father, who is the promised Redeemer sent by the Father.
3. Sacred Scripture and Sacred Tradition comprise the one Deposit of Faith, and both are the Word of God. The Church's teaching authority, or Magisterium, continues to fulfill its role as the authentic interpreter and teacher of what God has revealed.
4. God reveals himself to us personally and provides for us the gift of faith. By living our faith, we make God present in our lives. We believe in God himself, not merely the things that God has revealed to us. We in turn must respond by cooperating with that gift, putting it to work and so transforming our lives to be united with Christ in a personal relationship based on prayer and knowledge.

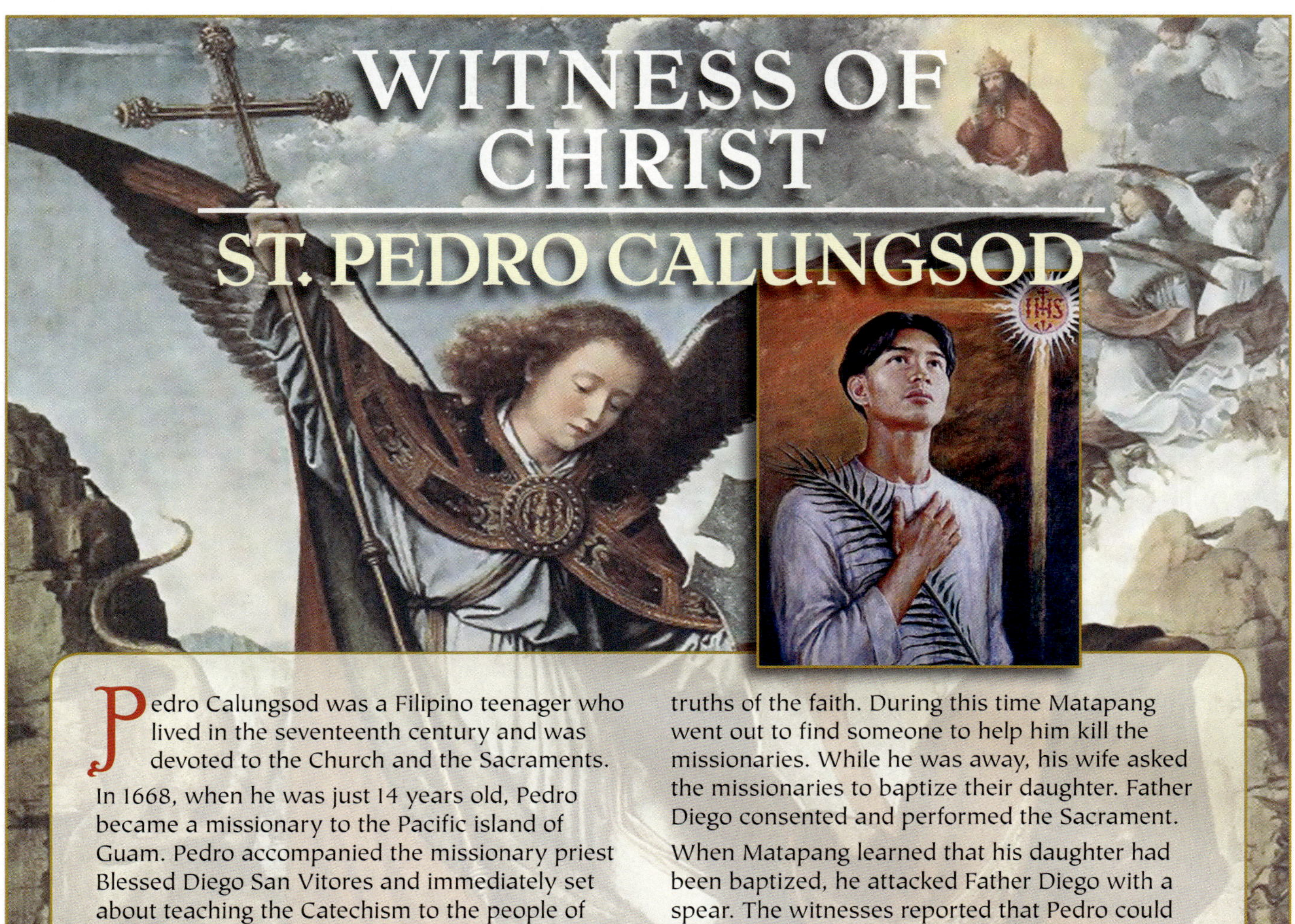

# WITNESS OF CHRIST

## ST. PEDRO CALUNGSOD

Pedro Calungsod was a Filipino teenager who lived in the seventeenth century and was devoted to the Church and the Sacraments. In 1668, when he was just 14 years old, Pedro became a missionary to the Pacific island of Guam. Pedro accompanied the missionary priest Blessed Diego San Vitores and immediately set about teaching the Catechism to the people of Guam.

The mission was soon blessed with many converts to the Catholic faith; however, the missionaries did face opposition. The local medicine men disliked the missionaries and began to circulate rumors that the priests were poisoning babies through the Sacrament of Baptism. A few of the babies who had been baptized had died, and so the medicine men were able to convince a number of the islanders to turn against the missionaries.

One morning Father Diego and Pedro traveled to one of the villages. They had received news that one of the women had just given birth to a baby girl, and Father Diego and Pedro wished to baptize the baby. However, when they arrived, the child's father, Matapang, refused to allow his daughter to be baptized.

Father Diego and Pedro gathered some of the other villagers together and began to teach the truths of the faith. During this time Matapang went out to find someone to help him kill the missionaries. While he was away, his wife asked the missionaries to baptize their daughter. Father Diego consented and performed the Sacrament.

When Matapang learned that his daughter had been baptized, he attacked Father Diego with a spear. The witnesses reported that Pedro could have gotten away, but he stayed and tried to protect Father Diego. As a result, Pedro was struck in the chest with the spear. One of the other men with Matapang charged at Pedro and hit him in the head with a machete, killing him immediately. Father Diego was then killed. Rocks were tied to their feet and their bodies were thrown into the sea, never to be found.

It has been said that "the blood of the martyrs is the seed of the Church," meaning that their witness inspires more and more people to become Catholic. Pedro Calungsod's passion for Christ and his eventual martyrdom became one of the seeds that helped to make the Catholic faith grow and spread to subsequent generations.

In March 2000, St. John Paul II beatified Pedro Calungsod, and, in 2012, Pope Benedict XVI canonized him. St. Pedro Calungsod is the patron saint of altar servers, Filipino youth, and the island of Guam.

# VOCABULARY

### CANON (OF SCRIPTURE)
The definitive list of the books of the Bible, by virtue of having been declared by the Church as inspired by the Holy Spirit.

### CONCUPISCENCE
The disordered state of human appetites or desires due to the temporal consequences of Original Sin. This situation remains even after Baptism, and results in inclination to sin.

### DEPOSIT OF FAITH
All of the Divine Revelation granted to the Church by Jesus Christ, contained in Sacred Scripture and Sacred Tradition, and expressed by the Magisterium. The Magisterium draws from the Deposit of Faith all that it proposes for belief as being divinely revealed.

### MAGISTERIUM
The universal teaching authority of the Church, entrusted to the Pope and the bishops in communion with him. The magisterium guides the members of the Church without error in matters of faith and morals, through the interpretation of Sacred Scripture and Tradition.

### NATURAL REVELATION
What God communicates to us about himself through the existence of creation. When God creates us, he writes knowledge of himself on our hearts, and through that mark we can learn something about God.

### ORIGINAL SIN
Adam and Eve's abuse of their human freedom in disobeying God's command. As a consequence, they lost the grace of original holiness and justice, and became subject to the law of death; sin became universally present in the world, with every person being born into this condition. This sin separated mankind from God, darkened the human intellect, weakened the human will, and introduced into human nature an inclination toward sin. The term is also used to describe the fallen condition that affects all human beings as a result of that transgression.

### REASON
Broadly, this is the guiding principle of the human mind in the process of thinking; more specifically, it is the intellectual power or faculty that is ordinarily employed by man in adapting thought or action to some purpose.

### REDEEMER
The expected Messiah (Jesus Christ), the one whom God promised would come and save his people from their sins.

### SACRED SCRIPTURE
The Bible; the canonical writings validated by the Church as inerrant and inspired by the Holy Spirit. The Bible contains the 46 books of the Old Testament and the 27 books of the New Testament. Together with Sacred Tradition, it makes up a single deposit of the Word of God—the *Deposit of Faith*—a single gift of God to the Church.

### SACRED TRADITION
From the Latin *traditio*, meaning "handing down," *Sacred Tradition*—often simply called *Tradition*—is part of the Deposit of Faith. It is the Word of God entrusted by Christ to the Apostles and their successors and communicated by preaching and teaching to every generation of Christians under the guidance of the Holy Spirit, who keeps it free from error. Sacred Tradition preceded Sacred Scripture, which grew out of Sacred Tradition with the inspiration of the Holy Spirit. *Human traditions* or *traditions of men* are man-made acts and rituals that did not originate with Christ. See also *Oral Tradition*.

### SUPERNATURAL REVELATION
Also known as Divine Revelation, and often simply called Revelation, God's communication of himself through the prophets and eventually in his Son, Jesus Christ, by which he makes known the mystery of his divine plan. The fullness of Divine Revelation was the sending of his Only-Begotten Son, Jesus Christ. The truths of Divine Revelation are transmitted through Scripture and Tradition.

## STUDY QUESTIONS

1. Why do we say that every human person searches for God?
2. What is natural revelation?
3. What is supernatural, or Divine, Revelation? How is it different from natural revelation?
4. What does it mean when we say that Christ is the fullness of Revelation?
5. What are Sacred Scripture and Sacred Tradition?
6. Did God dictate the Bible? What does it mean that God is the primary Author of Scripture?
7. What is the Deposit of Faith?
8. What is the "canon" of Scripture?
9. What is the purpose of the Magisterium?
10. What does the Church mean when it states that 'faith is a gift?'

## PRACTICAL EXERCISES

1. Suppose that you encountered someone who told you that he was an atheist. How could you explain to him, using only reason, that it is illogical not to believe in God?

2. The Magisterium is made up of the Pope and all the bishops united to him. Do some research, and find out who the previous three Popes have been, as well as the previous three bishops of your diocese. Find out when they became Pope/bishop.

*Pentecost* by Restout.
After Pentecost, the Apostles went about preaching the Gospel boldly, relying on the Holy Spirit instead of their own human strength and knowledge.

# Sealed in the Spirit

***Your Confirmation name is significant, so choose it thoughtfully and prayerfully.***

Congratulations! By beginning your preparation and taking this class, you can officially be considered a confirmand, or in other words a candidate for the Sacrament of Confirmation. (If you are not yet baptized and are preparing to receive the Sacrament of Baptism as well, then you are a catechumen.) You are a candidate because by wanting to be confirmed, you are seeking full initiation into the Catholic Church.

This section contains a quick history lesson. It should give you an appreciation for the history of the practice of Confirmation and help you understand why it is celebrated differently in some dioceses.

In the early Christian communities, what we now call the Sacraments of Baptism, Confirmation, and Holy Communion were all given in the same liturgical celebration, even to infants. A person who was ready to be initiated into the Church was baptized by the local priest, deacon, or by the bishop himself; received the Eucharist in Holy Communion from the local priest or the bishop; and then was anointed with oil by the bishop to "confirm" his or her initiation into the Church.

As the Church grew in membership and spread to more remote areas, it became impractical for the bishop to attend all the initiations of new Christians. So, as the practice developed in Western Europe and most of North Africa, the local priests continued to administer Baptism and the Eucharist, but the bishop would confirm the new Christians at a later date. It would often be several years before the bishop could visit and "catch up" on Confirmations. Yet the Church felt it was important to maintain the sense of union with the whole Church that comes from receiving the bishop's anointing. So even today in the Western Church, Confirmation is ordinarily given at a separate time, so that the bishop may administer it.

The faithful in the Eastern Churches, in locations such as Eastern Europe, the Middle East, and India, however, arrived at a different practice. The local priest, not the bishop, would administer the three Sacraments of Initiation in a single liturgical celebration. The sense of union with the whole Church came from the priest using the holy oils that were blessed by the bishop.

Both practices reflect the centuries-old traditions of the Church and faithfully express the teaching of the Church. The Magisterium of the Church does not teach that either practice is better than the other.

The practice today in the Western Church, which includes the United States, is to offer Confirmation to baptized Christians who at least have acquired the use of reason. This is usually considered to be the age of seven. However, Confirmation should be administered to any baptized Christian who wants or would have wanted to receive it when there is a danger of death, regardless of his or her age.

The bishops of the United States have determined that the Sacrament be celebrated between the ages of seven and about sixteen. Each local bishop may decide when Confirmation should be received in his own diocese.

You are in this preparation program because your bishop and parish priest believe that you are ready for it. And so do you, or else you wouldn't be reading this. As we continue through this book, make an earnest effort to get all you can out of your preparation so that you may be fully prepared when the big day comes and the bishop anoints your head, calls you by your chosen patron saint's name, and says, "Be sealed with the Gift of the Holy Spirit."

"Be sealed with the Gift of the Holy Spirit."

# You and Your Parents

***The importance of attending Mass, praying, and participating in discussions.***

In the introductory chapter we explained that your parents will play a vital role in your preparation for Confirmation. There's a very good reason for that: your parents love you, and they are responsible for your upbringing. They serve as your primary role models, and they are your first teachers, especially in the Catholic faith. Your parents ought to be very active in your religious education and sacramental preparation. As the *Catechism* teaches,

> **Parents have the first responsibility for the education of their children. They bear witness to this responsibility first by *creating a home* where tenderness, forgiveness, respect, fidelity, and disinterested service are the rule. (CCC 2223)**

Because of this grave responsibility, your parents should expect to attend Sunday Mass with you and your siblings as a family, pray with you and for you, and discuss with you the things you are learning in this book as you prepare for Confirmation.

In addition to making sure that you attend every preparation class and activity yourself, they should seek to participate in the required retreats, service work, meetings, information classes, or other events that your Confirmation preparation may require.

Sometimes parents feel too busy or overwhelmed with work, taking care of a sick relative, household responsibilities, or other duties. As much as they might want to, they may not believe that they have the time to discuss what you are learning in your Confirmation preparation. Try to find a way to get them involved in discussions anyway. Perhaps you can talk about it while preparing dinner, sitting down to eat, or washing the dishes together afterwards; while driving to practice or rehearsal; while working out together in the morning; while fixing the car together; or while getting ready for Mass on Sunday. By taking the initiative you can make it easier for them. You and your parents will probably find that you have a lot of ideas and experiences to share with one another that can enrich you all. Besides, when they see that preparing for Confirmation is important to you, they might find more time and energy to get more involved themselves.

Here are some ideas for questions that might help you open a discussion with your parents:

1. When did you first start teaching me about God?
2. When did you learn the meaning of being a true Christian?
3. Do you remember the first time that you took me to Mass?
4. When did I begin to become curious about the Catholic faith?
5. Have you ever struggled with having faith in God? (Do not be surprised if they have struggled with faith and doubt. Most people have.)
6. What did you do to overcome your struggle with faith?
7. Why do you go to Mass?

Talk to your parents about your Confirmation preparation during dinner or while helping with the dishes. By taking the initiative you can make it easier for them in their busy day.

# You and Your Sponsor

***A sponsor can help you choose your Confirmation name.***

Your Confirmation sponsor is intended to be your mentor in the Catholic faith. He or she is a source of encouragement and support as you prepare to approach the Sacrament and also should serve as a good role model as you continue to live in the world as a faithful Catholic. That mentoring role does not end the day you will be confirmed! That is why it is important to have a sponsor who seriously practices the faith as their most important quality. He or she will assume the responsibility to be your mentor in matters concerning your faith if your parents cannot do this.

The practice of having a Confirmation sponsor is rooted in the early Church. In the first centuries of Christianity, as we read earlier, the Sacraments of Christian Initiation—Baptism, Confirmation, and the Eucharist—were administered together to the new convert. Each convert had to have a sponsor in order to be received into the Church. The sponsor served as a guide and friend as the catechumen went through the preparation process, called the **catechumenate**. The sponsor would also vouch for the sincerity of the catechumen and would present him or her to the community for acceptance.

The sponsor of the catechumen, in effect, filled what today is often regarded as two roles in the Western Church: *godparent* at Baptism and *sponsor* at Confirmation. His or her word as to the sincerity and readiness of the catechumen was especially important in the early centuries of Christianity because the Church frequently experienced violent persecution, so the Mass and the Sacraments were often celebrated in secret. The sponsor's word assured everyone that the catechumen was not a spy or infiltrator helping the persecuting authorities who wished to arrest the ministers and the faithful, convert them by force, or even kill them.

Thankfully in most of the world today, Christians are not actively persecuted in that manner. The sponsor's role, however, is not merely symbolic, but still very practical. As you will be doing with your parents throughout this course, you should engage in prayer and discussions with your sponsor. If you can, have your sponsor join your family for Sunday Mass. Discuss what you are learning and other matters of faith with him or her. Try to discuss as much as you can in person, but if your sponsor lives far away, be sure to communicate with them frequently by phone, or email and text messages. Establish this communication early in your preparation process.

Here are some ideas for questions that might help you open a discussion with your sponsor:

1. Do you read the Bible often? If so, when? What is your favorite book or story of the Bible, and why? Share about your own favorite book or story and your own reasons.
2. How do you prepare for Sunday Mass?
3. How do you use the Bible to assist your personal prayer? Share how you have incorporated or would like to incorporate Scripture into your own prayer.
4. Can you teach me how to use the Bible in my prayer?

It is important to have a sponsor who seriously practices the faith as their most important quality.

The Sacrament of

# Confirmation

## Chapter 2

# The History of Salvation

## INTRODUCTION

### *God reaches out to us.*

In the last chapter we discussed how God has revealed himself to the human race, through both natural and supernatural Revelation. The *Catechism* provides a summary of this truth:

> **By natural reason man can know God with certainty, on the basis of his works. But there is another order of knowledge, which man cannot possibly arrive at by his own powers: the order of divine Revelation...God has revealed himself and given himself to man. (CCC 50)**

From the very beginning, God has been at work in the world. Since the Fall of humankind, he has been preparing the world for its eventual redemption in Jesus Christ. This preparation is called "salvation history." We can look to salvation history to better understand how God works in the world, and how we can participate in God's great plan for us.

Studying salvation history does not mean simply pondering events of the past. Rather, we are invited by Christ to live out *our* role in God's plan to redeem the world. Every Christian, including you, has a part in God's story of salvation. God is calling *you* to serve him in this way, to be his disciple in how you live your life. The Holy Spirit is at work to include *you* in salvation history. The grace that you receive in the Sacraments will help you to carry out this mission. In particular, the Sacrament of Confirmation will give you the spiritual gifts you need to be Christ's disciple.

*Christ Carrying the Cross* by Lotto.
The Sacrament of Confirmation will give you the spiritual gifts you need to be Christ's disciple.

After reading this chapter, you will be able to answer these questions:

- What does it mean to say that you are made in God's image and likeness?
- What is Original Sin, and how does it affect your ability to seek holiness?
- How has God revealed himself throughout history?
- Who is Jesus Christ, and what was his mission?
- What is meant by the "Paschal Mystery"?
- What are the Last Things?

## CREATOR AND FATHER

***Made in God's own image and likeness, we have the ability to become his children.***

God is the source of all creation. Everything that exists, has existed, or ever will exist owes its origin to God. Further, God created everything out of *nothing*. When human beings "create" something—for example, a work of art, a piece of furniture, a relaxing environment, a piece of music—we use, modify, and rearrange materials that already exist. This was not the case with God.

Out of all God's creation, human beings are special and unique, the "summit of the Creator's work" (CCC 343). In the physical world, only we were created in God's own "image and likeness." Both male and female are made in this divine image. This does not mean that we "look" like God. Rather, we are given certain gifts that are otherwise unique to God. Let us review them here:

- Every human being has an immortal soul so that he or she can live forever.
- Every human being has a rational intellect so that he or she can use reason to interpret and evaluate ideas and experiences. We can come to know ourselves, and we can use reason to control our feelings and instincts.
- Every human being has a free will that allows him or her to choose how to think and act, and even to choose between doing good and doing evil.

Because we are created in God's image, we possess a dignity that can never be taken away from us. It does not depend upon race, creed, nationality, sex, education level, age, health, social standing, or any other factor. We have this dignity simply due to our existence.

Many religions refer to God as "Father" because he is the source of all creation, the "father" of the world. But Christ revealed that God is more than just the source of our existence. We become God's adopted children through the Sacrament of Baptism. As St. John wrote in his Gospel, "...to all who received him [Christ], who believed in his name, he gave power to become children of God" (Jn 1:12).

With God as our father, we are called to a family relationship with God. "We adore the Father because he has caused us to be reborn to his life by adopting us as his children in his only Son" (CCC 2782). In the Gospels Jesus often referred to God as the Father, and he taught his disciples the prayer we all know that begins "Our Father." St. Paul told the Christian faithful to call God "*Abba*," an affectionate term used by children for their father:

> **Because you are sons, God has sent the Spirit of his Son into our hearts, crying, "Abba! Father!" (Gal 4:6)**

The Christian faith is not about worshiping some remote deity. It is about a personal relationship with God, our Father, who loves us to perfection and is always present among us.

### THE OUR FATHER

The "Our Father"—often called the Lord's Prayer because of who taught it to us—is the prayer that Christ taught his disciples when they asked him how to pray. It has been called the "perfect prayer."

> Our Father who art in heaven,
> Hallowed be thy name.
> Thy kingdom come,
> Thy will be done,
> On earth as it is in heaven.
> Give us this day our daily bread;
> And forgive us our debts,
> As we also have forgiven our debtors;
> And lead us not into temptation,
> but deliver us from evil. (Mt 6:9-13)

## THE BLESSED TRINITY AND CREATION

Although the work of Creation is often attributed solely to God the Father, it is actually the work of the Blessed Trinity as a whole. The Blessed Trinity is a profound mystery, and is a central and essential belief of the Christian faith.

What is the Blessed Trinity? The Trinity is the three Divine Persons—Father, Son, and Holy Spirit. As Christians, we worship the one and only God; however, God is made up of three distinct, yet inseparable, Persons. The Father, the Son, and the Holy Spirit are not parts of God as if God were a committee. The three divine Persons are not modes of God as if each has a particular function. In some mysterious fashion we cannot completely understand, there is only one God, but three Persons: the Father, Son and Holy Spirit are each divine.

Since the three Persons are one God, all three Persons are eternal, and all were active in the work of Creation. The Book of Genesis tells us that God accomplished his creation by his spoken Word (he commanded, "Let there be light"), and St. John's Gospel equates this with Christ, who is the Word of God:

> **In the beginning was the Word, and the Word was with God, and the Word was God. He was in the beginning with God; all things were made through him, and without him was not anything made that was made. (Jn 1:1-3)**

St. John further tells us that this Word of God was with God the Father in the beginning, and that it was through the Word of God that all of creation came to exist. This Word of God is the Second Person of the Blessed Trinity, Jesus Christ. Through him we are made a "new creation" by his act of redemption that reconciled us with the Father: We are restored to the friendship with God that our first parents had at creation but lost through sin. As St. Paul wrote:

> **If any one is in Christ, he is a new creation; the old has passed away, behold, the new has come. All this is from God, who through Christ reconciled us to himself. (2 Cor 5:17-18)**

The Holy Spirit, too, was active at creation. The very beginning of the Bible states that "the Spirit of God was moving over the face of the waters" (Gn 1:2). Later God breathed life into the nostrils of the first man; this "breath" of God is his Spirit. This same breath of God, the Holy Spirit, gives life to creation; this same Holy Spirit communicates the "new life" of grace that we receive in the Sacraments, particularly in Baptism and Confirmation. The Holy Spirit works closely with Christ and reveals Christ to us.

> **The Old Testament suggests and the New Covenant reveals the creative action of the Son and the Spirit, inseparably one with that of the Father...Creation is the common work of the Holy Trinity. (CCC 292)**

*The Rebuke of Adam and Eve* by Domenichino.
The damage done by the selfish act of Adam is restored by the selfless act of Jesus Christ.

## ORIGINAL SIN AND THE PROMISE OF REDEMPTION

***The sin of our first parents wounded human nature, placing us in need of redemption.***

**God said, "Let us make man in our image, after our likeness; and let them have dominion over the fish of the sea, and over the birds of the air, and over the cattle, and over all the earth, and over every creeping thing that creeps upon the earth." So God created man in his own image, in the image of God he created him; male and female he created them. And God blessed them, and God said to them, "Be fruitful and multiply, and fill the earth and subdue it; and have dominion over the fish of the sea and over the birds of the air and over every living thing that moves upon the earth." And God said, "Behold, I have given you every plant yielding seed which is upon the face of all the earth, and every tree with seed in its fruit; you shall have them for food. And to every beast of the earth, and to every bird of the air, and to everything that creeps on the earth, everything that has the breath of life, I have given every green plant for food." And it was so. And God saw everything that he had made, and behold, it was very good. And there was evening and there was morning, a sixth day. (Gn 1:26-31)**

In the beginning, our first parents Adam and Eve lived in a state of original holiness and original justice, in friendship with God, sharing in his divine life. They were in harmony with God, with the created world, and with each other.

God expressed this special relationship by making human beings his stewards to manage all of creation, giving Adam and Eve dominion and control over all other earthly creatures. God wanted them to take care of the created world, to use its resources to fill their needs. He also told them to "be fruitful and multiply" (Gn 1:22, 28)—to conceive and bear children and raise them as a family. The human race was created to be cooperators with God in his act of creation by caring for the earth and producing new life.

But Adam and Eve gave in to the temptations of Satan and misused their free will to disobey God. By choosing to do so, they rejected his love and friendship. This descent of the human race into sin is called the **Fall**.

The Fall affected not only our first parents. It affected all of their descendants: the entire human race for all of history. Every human person born since Adam and Eve, with the exception of the Blessed Virgin Mary, has been afflicted with Original Sin. (Jesus Christ, of course, was not afflicted with Original Sin, but he is a divine Person). Human beings became vulnerable to actual sin as well. Our intellect and use of reason became clouded, and our will to do what is good and pleasing to God became weakened. We no longer lived in harmony with creation, and we became subject to sickness and physical death. This is why we need God. Without him, we cannot be saved—we cannot have eternal happiness. Original Sin closed the door to God, and only he can reopen it.

In response to Original Sin, God did not condemn or destroy his creation. Instead he immediately promised to save us from sin. To the serpent that tempted Adam and Eve, he said:

> **"I will put enmity between you and the woman, and between your seed and her seed; he shall bruise your head, and you shall bruise his heel." (Gn 3:15)**

This passage from Genesis is God's first promise of a Redeemer. The "woman" mentioned here is the Blessed Virgin Mary. Mary's obedience to the will of God reversed the harm done by Eve's disobedience. Mary's "seed" is her Son, Jesus Christ, who came to redeem the world from sin, which had enslaved all of Eve's children. Christ will "bruise" the head of the serpent, Satan, meaning he will deliver a fatal blow. But all the serpent can do is "bruise" the heel of Christ, which is a reference to the wounds of his Crucifixion and Death.

St. Paul compares and contrasts Adam and Christ:

> **As by a man came death, by a man has come also the resurrection of the dead. For as in Adam all die, so also in Christ shall all be made alive. (1 Cor 15:21-22)**

In other words, the damage done by the selfish act of Adam is restored by the selfless act of Jesus Christ. Although the human race continued to disobey God by sinning, now there was hope that salvation was possible.

## APOLOGETICS 101:

### INCLINATION TO SIN

(Adapted from the *Didache Bible*)

***Why are we inclined to sin?***

> **The desires of the flesh are against the Spirit, and the desires of the Spirit are against the flesh; for these are opposed to each other, to prevent you from doing what you would. (Gal 5:17)**

Because of Original Sin we suffer from weakness in our will, intellect, and passions and are inclined to sin—an inclination called *concupiscence*. In order to avoid sin, we must rely on the grace of God and actively seek to choose good and to grow in holiness and virtue.

The sin of our first parents, called Original Sin, is "transmitted by propagation to all mankind" (CCC 404). As a result, every person is conceived in a fallen state that includes concupiscence, or the tendency to sin, which is now part of the human condition. Although Baptism washes away Original Sin, i.e., fills us with sanctifying grace by which we can triumph over temptation, the Sacrament does not remove concupiscence.

With our conscience, will, and intellect weakened, we must actively remain faithful and struggle to overcome our disordered passions—primarily our passions of the flesh, for material possessions, and for self-indulgence in pride. To master sin we must rely on God's grace and strive to master ourselves. The struggle must go on for a lifetime. We are comprised of body and soul—flesh and spirit—and "the flesh" possesses passions that "the spirit" must control (see Galatians 5:17 above). The great gift of Christ's forgiveness—the grace given especially in the Sacrament of Penance as well as the practices of prayer and self-denial for self-mastery—is an invaluable help in our continuing battle against sin.

Many Protestants believe that concupiscence in itself is sinful, and that even Baptism cannot wash away this sinfulness. This contradicts the Church's teaching and Christian tradition, which has always held that concupiscence is real but that, with grace, we can resist the inclination to evil and do truly good acts.

## THE PRESENCE OF EVIL IN THE WORLD

**As sin came into the world through one man and death through sin, and so death spread to all men because all men sinned... As by one man's disobedience many were made sinners, so by one man's obedience many will be made righteous. (Rom 5:12, 19)**

The question is often raised, particularly in the face of human tragedy or natural disaster: Why would an all-loving and all-powerful God permit so much evil and suffering in the world? If he is all-loving, he would want only what is best for us, and if he is all-powerful, he has the ability to alleviate suffering and death.

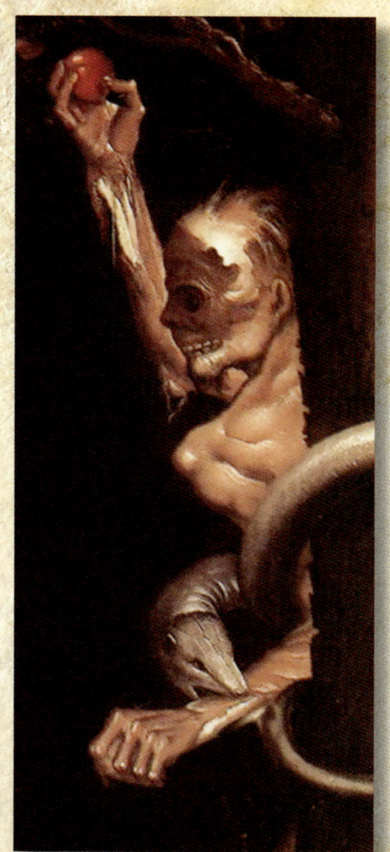

The answer to this question is difficult to understand. We know that God loves us and that he is all-good, but we also know from experience that God allows suffering in the world. Even "good" people suffer the effects of evil, sometimes even more so than "bad" people.

To begin, we need to recognize God did not create evil. Evil is experienced wherever there is an absence of good, which comes from God. What we call "evil" is really the result of the failure of created beings to act as they ought—in accordance with their nature—and to live up to the purpose of their existence. Evil is the "vacuum" created whenever humans do not strive to reach the true purpose and fulfillment of their lives: holiness, perfection, and unity with God. In the words of the *Catechism*:

> **Why did God not create a world so perfect that no evil could exist in it? With infinite power God could always create something better. But with infinite wisdom and goodness God freely willed to create a world "in a state of journeying" towards its ultimate perfection. (CCC 310)**

God gave us free will. This means that we are truly free to choose—for good and evil. God doesn't force us to choose the good. If he did, it wouldn't really be "free will." Exercising our free will, we can choose to follow God's will or reject it. When we consider the evils of this world, such as murder, drug abuse, or war, we can easily see their connection with choices people freely make to reject God's will. All evil and suffering result directly from a lack of respect for human life, a lack of love for neighbor, greed, envy, lust, and other vices. God allows these evils because they result from our free choice, which is his gift to us. Sadly, the sins of some also affect many who are not guilty of those particular sins, so the innocent suffer along with the guilty.

All suffering is rooted in Original Sin. Even suffering that results from natural disasters—tidal waves, hurricanes, or earthquakes—can be traced to the disharmony in nature that resulted from Original Sin. We wish that God would take away all the evil and pain of the world. But if he did he would be taking away our free will. Instead, God respects our freedom, even our freedom to choose evil over good. One day, however, all things will be restored in Christ and all evil will be overcome. Scripture calls that restoration a "new Jerusalem:"

> **I saw the holy city, new Jerusalem, coming down out of heaven from God, prepared as a bride adorned for her husband; and I heard a great voice from the throne saying, "Behold, the dwelling of God is with men. He will dwell with them, and they shall be his people, and God himself will be with them; he will wipe away every tear from their eyes, and death shall be no more, neither shall there be mourning nor crying nor pain any more, for the former things have passed away." And he who sat upon the throne said, "Behold, I make all things new." Also he said, "Write this, for these words are trustworthy and true." (Rev 21:2-5)**

## GOD'S COVENANTS

***God interacts with his people through sacred promises, or covenants.***

After the Fall, God began to reestablish his relationship with mankind. He did this through a series of **covenants**. Covenants are solemn agreements between God and his people that involve both sides making commitments to each other. Covenants in general bind people together into family-like relationships, and God's covenants bind him to his people as a father to his children. God entered into his covenants with specific persons, who represented all of God's people. These include Adam, Noah, Abraham, Moses, and David. Each covenant prepared the way for the final covenant God would make through his Son, Jesus Christ. Each was another step toward reopening the door to salvation.

To ***Adam***, God promised to send a Redeemer, as we discussed in the previous section. Even though his words were directed to the serpent, the message was a promise to Adam, Eve, and all of their descendants. The Redeemer would reconcile God and mankind, restoring the friendship they had lost through sin. In Christian tradition, this is called the *Protoevangelium*, which is a word that means "First Gospel," or "First Good News." It was the first promise by God to save the human race after the Fall.

> **After his fall, man was not abandoned by God. On the contrary, God calls him and in a mysterious way heralds the coming victory over evil and his restoration from his fall. This passage in Genesis is called the *Protoevangelium* ("first gospel"): the first announcement of the Messiah and Redeemer, of a battle between the serpent and the Woman, and of the final victory of a descendant of hers. (CCC 410)**

Many generations later, ***Noah*** and his family were saved when God decided to wipe out all the corrupt people on earth. In the familiar Bible story, God instructed Noah to build the Ark so that he and his family, who had remained faithful, would be saved while the earth was cleansed by the Flood. After the floodwaters had receded and the Ark had come to rest on dry land, God made a covenant with Noah. He promised that he would never again destroy the world in a flood.

After human beings had been scattered and divided into nations, God called Abram out of the land of Ur. Abram showed great faith and obeyed God, who eventually changed his name from Abram ("exalted father") to ***Abraham*** ("father of a multitude"). God promised that this "multitude" of Abraham's descendants would become his chosen people.

> **The people descended from Abraham would be the trustee of the promise made to the patriarchs, the chosen people, called to prepare for that day when God would gather all his children into the unity of the Church. (CCC 59-60)**

God later entered into a covenant with his people through ***Moses***. God gave the Israelites the Law through Moses on Mt. Sinai, beginning with the Ten Commandments, as their moral guide. The Law was a source of unity and guidance against the temptations brought by the idolatrous practices and immoral lives of the various pagan nations. Most importantly, the Law helped prepare Israel for the coming of the Messiah.

> **You have seen what I did to the Egyptians, and how I bore you on eagles' wings and brought you to myself. Now therefore, if you will obey my voice and keep my covenant, you shall be my own possession among all peoples; for all the earth is mine, and you shall be to me a kingdom of priests and a holy nation. (Ex 19:4-6)**

After a time of being ruled by men and women called judges, the Israelites asked God to grant them a king like other nations of the world. The Twelve Tribes

*Noah Releases the Dove, Stories of Noah Mosaic.*
God made a covenant with Noah. He promised that he would never again destroy the world in a flood.

had become divided among themselves. The people believed a king who was appointed by God would unite all of Israel.

Saul, the first king, turned out to be unfaithful, so God called a young shepherd boy named ***David*** whom he directed the prophet Samuel to anoint as king:

> **The LORD said, "Arise, anoint him; for this is he." Then Samuel took the horn of oil, and anointed him in the midst of his brothers; and the Spirit of the LORD came mightily upon David from that day forward. (1 Sm 16:12-13)**

David became "a man after God's own heart" (1 Sm 13:14). As a mighty warrior-king, he led Israel to victory over its enemies. As a great leader, he established Jerusalem as an influential city and made it the spiritual center of God's people. He called for a Temple to be built there where God would dwell among his people and where the whole nation could worship him. God promised him that David's kingdom would last forever. Although the kingly line of David eventually crumbled, we will see how God still fulfilled this promise.

## THE OLD TESTAMENT COVENANTS FORESHADOW OUR REDEMPTION

Many people and events in the Old Testament point to someone or something that appears in the New Testament. These "types" illustrate how, in the words of St. Augustine, "The New Testament lies hidden in the Old and the Old Testament is unveiled in the New." Each of the Old Testament covenants are types which point to the covenant with Jesus.

| COVENANT MEDIATOR | OLD TESTAMENT COVENANT EVENTS | COVENANTS FULFILLED IN CHRIST |
|---|---|---|
| ADAM | First Man of Creation | First Man of New Creation |
| | Disobeyed God—leads to Fall | Perfectly Obedient—leads to eternal life |
| NOAH | Forty days and forty nights of rain prepare for the new creation | Forty days and forty nights of fasting and penance to prepare for the new creation |
| | Flood waters cleansed sinfulness of world | Water of Baptism cleanses man of his sins |
| ABRAHAM | Circumcision was sign of covenant | Baptism is sign of New Covenant |
| | Faith is means to enter covenant | Faith is means to enter covenant |
| MOSES | Led chosen people from slavery to freedom in Exodus | Christ leads us from slavery of sin to freedom |
| | Sacrificial lamb spares firstborn of the Israelites | Christ is the sacrificial lamb who offers redemption to all |
| | Passage through waters of Red Sea brings people to freedom | Passage through waters of Baptism brings people to freedom from sin |
| DAVID | Promised an everlasting kingdom | Receives a truly everlasting kingdom |
| | God declares to David, "I will be his father, and he shall be my son" (2 Sm 7:14) | The true Son of God |

# CHRIST FULFILLS THE COVENANTS

***Everything God did in the Old Testament was to prepare the world for his Son.***

In each of God's covenants with the Israelites, God used a mediator—someone to represent the people to God, like Adam, Abraham, or David. In his final covenant that would bring redemption to the world, God willed that his Son would be that human mediator. This meant that his Son would need to be born of a woman, like any other man. He would need to actually be a man, not just pretending to be one.

> **The Father of mercies willed that the Incarnation should be preceded by assent on the part of the predestined mother, so that just as a woman had a share in the coming of death, so also should a woman contribute to the coming of life. (CCC 488)**

The reality that God became man is called the **Incarnation**, literally, "going into flesh." The Holy Spirit came upon Mary and she conceived the baby Jesus. As the Angel Gabriel told her:

> **"The Holy Spirit will come upon you,**
> **and the power of the Most High will**
> **overshadow you;**
> **therefore the child to be born will be called holy,**
> **the Son of God." (Lk 1:34)**

The Son of God, without losing his divinity, took on our humanity, body and soul. His divine nature and his human nature were united in his one divine Person. He experienced everything that human beings experience—joy, pain, emotion, fatigue, hunger, thirst, and even temptation. "He shared our human nature/in all things but sin," as we pray in the Mass (*Roman Missal*, Eucharistic Prayer IV, no. 117). Scripture also speaks of Christ in this way, saying he is "one who in every respect has been tempted as we are, yet without sin" (Heb 4:15).

St. John summed up the Incarnation in his Gospel:

> **The Word became flesh and dwelt among us, full of grace and truth; we have beheld his glory, glory as of the only Son from the Father. (Jn 1:14)**

Why did the Son of God become man? The man Adam disobeyed God and broke the covenant with him, placing humankind in an infinite debt to God. Just as Adam represented all of humanity, it would likewise need to be a man to represent his race in restoring us to God's friendship. Only an infinitely perfect man, however, could truly make up for the sin committed against an infinitely good God. Thus it was Jesus, true God and true man, who was the perfect Redeemer, reconciling God and all human beings through his Death and Resurrection. He made it possible for us to rise to new life.

*The Transfiguration* by Carracci.
Christ gave meaning and understanding to the figures, events, and symbols of the Old Testament.

The covenants, promises, and prophecies of the Old Testament were all designed to prepare God's people for the coming of the promised Redeemer. St. Paul wrote:

> **In many and various ways God spoke of old to our fathers by the prophets; but in these last days he has spoken to us by a Son, whom he appointed the heir of all things, through whom also he created the world. He reflects the glory of God and bears the very stamp of his nature, upholding the universe by his word of power. (Heb 1:1-3)**

Christ fulfilled all that the Old Covenant promised. He gave meaning and understanding to the figures, events, and symbols of the Old Testament. He fully revealed the plan and will of the Father.

# WHO IS JESUS CHRIST?

***With the help of the Holy Spirit, the Church came to understand Christ's identity.***

Who is Jesus? We have all heard of him, and we could all tell the basic story of his life, but who truly is he? Over the years, the Church, guided by the Holy Spirit, has found ways to speak about the identity of Jesus Christ.

**Jesus is the Messiah, the Christ.** "Christ" and "Messiah" mean "Anointed One." Anointing was used in Old Testament times to consecrate priests, prophets, and kings. Jesus was anointed by God as all three: priest, prophet, and king. He is the Eternal High Priest who intercedes and makes sacrifice for his people, he is the prophet who proclaimed the Good News of salvation, and he established the Kingdom of God on earth. We'll read in Chapter 7 how at your Confirmation you, too, will be anointed priest, prophet, and king.

**Jesus Christ is the Son of God.** Scripture teaches this plainly. The first verse of St. Mark's Gospel identifies it as "the gospel of Jesus Christ, the Son of God" (Mk 1:1). St. John ends his Gospel by explaining why he wrote it: "that you may believe that Jesus is the Christ, the Son of God" (Jn 20:31). The preaching of the Apostles in the rest of the New Testament also affirms this truth.

**Jesus Christ is the Second Person of the Blessed Trinity.** Christ identified himself as one with the Father: "He who has seen me has seen the Father... Believe me that I am in the Father and the Father is in me" (Jn 14:9,11). His place in the Trinity is expressed in his mandate to make disciples by baptizing them "in the name of the Father and of the Son and of the Holy Spirit" (Mt 28:19).

**Jesus Christ is fully God and fully man.** Christ is fully and eternally God, but he humbled himself by becoming man:

> **Though he was in the form of God, [Christ] did not count equality with God a thing to be grasped, but emptied himself, taking the form of a servant, being born in the likeness of men. And being found in human form he humbled himself and became obedient unto death, even death on a cross. (Phil 2:6-8)**

Christ is fully divine, and he is fully human. In fact, he is the perfect human being, a model for how we ought to live our own humanity, one like us in all things but sin.

> **The Word became flesh to be our model of holiness. (CCC 459)**

By his life, Christ gave his followers a model of the perfect way to live. He continually:

- ***prayed*** to his Father in heaven;
- fulfilled God's command to "be ***holy*** as I am holy" (Lv 20:26);
- ***witnessed*** to the Father's love in all his words and deeds;
- and ***served*** those around him, even to the point of giving his life for them.

## PROPHECIES FULFILLED IN CHRIST

Many Old Testament prophecies were not fully understood except in light of the life of Christ. Here are some examples:

- He was born of a virgin (Is 7:14).
- He was born in Bethlehem (Mi 5:2).
- He was born in the ancestral line of David (Ps 132:11, Jer 23:5).
- He was filled with and anointed by the Spirit of God (Is 11:2, 61:1-2).
- He healed the sick and cured those who were deaf, blind, or unable to speak (Is 32:3-4, 34:5-6).
- He was rejected by his people (Is 53:3; Ps 118:22; Is 8:14).

To be a faithful disciple of Christ, we must model our lives after him and do the same. Later in this book we will be exploring how we can go about living as Jesus did through the grace of the Sacrament of Confirmation.

## THE PASCHAL MYSTERY

### *Christ's whole mission led up to his Passion, Death, Resurrection, and Ascension.*

Christ is not merely a model of how to live, however; he is also our Savior. Christ was born in order to die, and it is through his Death that he made salvation possible for all people. This is what we mean by "redemption." More precisely, Christ redeemed us through his Passion, Death, Resurrection, and Ascension. The Church refers to these events as the **Paschal Mystery**.

From the time of the Last Supper until he died on the Cross, Christ suffered greatly. We call this his *Passion* (from the Greek word that means "to suffer"). Being fully man, Christ truly endured all the pain and suffering of his arrest, torture and Crucifixion—he was not just acting as if he were suffering.

Then, Christ truly experienced *death* and was laid in a tomb. As true man, Christ really died. He did not just appear to die, but actually died in the flesh. Through his Sacrifice Christ was able to reconcile mankind to God.

On the third day some women disciples of Christ visited the tomb to anoint his Body. They found the tomb empty, and they rushed to tell the Apostles. Soon they all understood Christ's own words that he would die and rise again to life:

> **"The Son of man must suffer many things, and be rejected by the elders and chief priests and scribes, and be killed, and on the third day be raised." (Lk 9:22)**

The *Resurrection* of Christ from the dead "is the crowning truth of our faith in Christ" (CCC 638). His Resurrection affirms his teachings and his life; St. Paul explained that "if Christ has not been raised, then our preaching is in vain and your faith is in vain" (1 Cor 15:14). Our faith is centered on the belief that Christ really and truly rose from the dead. Many people saw him in his glorified Body after his Resurrection. They spoke with him, ate with him, and touched him.

*The Resurrection* by Rosa.
Our faith is centered on the belief that Christ really and truly rose from the dead.

Forty days after his Resurrection, Christ *ascended* into heaven. Before he was lifted up, he gave the Apostles their final instructions. He asked them to wait in Jerusalem until the Holy Spirit comes, and then proclaim the Gospel and make disciples of all nations through Baptism. Scripture says that after his Ascension, Christ was seated at the right hand of the Father, signifying that he had fulfilled his Father's mission.

We call Christ's act of redemption a *mystery* because human reason is not capable of fully comprehending it. We call it *paschal* because it relates to the Passover (in Hebrew, *pesach*; in Greek, *pascha*).

## EVERLASTING LIFE

### *Death and judgment face us all, with heaven or hell our final destination.*

Ten days after Christ's Ascension, there was the great outpouring of the Holy Spirit at Pentecost, which we will explore more fully in the next chapter. Pentecost originated the Church's public ministry and inaugurated the final phase in salvation history, or what Scripture calls the "last days."

**Since that day, the Kingdom announced by Christ has been open to those who believe in him…By his coming, which never ceases, the Holy Spirit causes the world to enter into the "last days," the time of the Church, the Kingdom already inherited though not yet consummated. (CCC 732)**

The "last days" does not simply refer to the end of the world. It includes the whole time from Pentecost until Christ's **second coming** which will occur at the end of time. During these "last days" we experience Christ's kingdom, though imperfectly, through the Church. Scripture warns us that the Church and her faithful must undergo much suffering and many trials before the end of time. Yet it is through these trials that Christ will return and triumph over evil. Those who are faithful to him will enjoy the eternal happiness that God so desires for us.

So as Christians we live in the hope that we will be raised again to eternal life. Man's final events as an individual and as a race are called the **last things**: death, judgment, heaven, and hell.

- **Death** is a consequence of Original Sin, and is thus inevitable for every human person. Every person inflicted with Original Sin either has

## THE NEW PASSOVER OF THE EUCHARIST

Christ instituted the Eucharist at the Last Supper, which was a Passover meal. In doing so he made this great Sacrament the "new Passover." The Passover meal was an annual remembrance of when God delivered the Israelites from slavery in Egypt.

At the first Passover, Israelite families sacrificed an unblemished lamb and splashed its blood on their doorposts in order to be saved from the final plague. The lamb was then eaten in a shared meal. In the new Passover, Christ himself is the sacrificial Lamb whose Blood is shed in order to deliver all people from slavery to sin. His real Body and Blood are consumed in the Sacrament of the Eucharist. The Passover in Egypt is a foreshadowing of the Sacrifice of Christ.

**By celebrating the Last Supper with his apostles in the course of the Passover meal, Jesus gave the Jewish Passover its definitive meaning. Jesus' passing over to his father by his death and Resurrection, the new Passover, is anticipated in the Supper and celebrated in the Eucharist, which fulfills the Jewish Passover and anticipates the final Passover of the Church in the glory of the kingdom. (CCC 1340)**

There is yet another connection between Christ and the Israelites. During his earthly ministry, Christ likened himself to the food of the Israelites, calling himself the "Bread of Life." As St. John recorded in his Gospel:

**"I am the bread of life. Your fathers ate the manna in the wilderness, and they died. This is the bread which comes down from heaven, that a man may eat of it and not die. I am the living bread which came down from heaven; if any one eats of this bread, he will live for ever; and the bread which I shall give for the life of the world is my flesh." (Jn 6:48-51)**

The "manna in the wilderness" refers to the breadlike food that God provided to the Israelites during their forty-year journey in the desert from Egypt to the Promised Land. The manna was their daily food. It gave them life and was a sign of God's providence and loving presence among his people.

Similarly, Christ offered himself, his own Body, as the "bread of life" for the People of God. This bread is greater than the manna in the desert. The "bread of life," which is the Real Presence of God among his people, gives us eternal life.

The sacrifice of the lamb at the first Passover is a prefigurement of the Sacrifice of Christ, the Lamb of God. Everyone who finds salvation is redeemed through the Passion, Death, Resurrection, and Ascension of Christ, just as all those saved during the final plague in Egypt were saved by the blood of the Passover lamb.

died or will die. This death is only physical, however; our souls live on to face our judgment.

- **Judgment** occurs in two stages. Immediately upon his or her death, every person will have the *Particular Judgment,* where that person will be judged individually according to the state of his or her soul. Each person then goes to heaven, hell, or purgatory. At the end of the world comes the *General Judgment*—sometimes called the Last Judgment or the Final Judgment. Our bodies will rise from the dead and be reunited with our souls. The General Judgment will confirm the Particular Judgment and make it known to all the universe. Further, at the General Judgment all the souls remaining in purgatory will enter into heaven.
- **Hell** is eternal separation from God. Those who reject God's love and his offer of redemption will be in hell because of the choices they made. True human freedom—including the choice of evil over good—requires that persons are able to choose to be separated from God forever. While God is always ready to forgive us, we still have the freedom to reject him forever by our attachment to mortal sin.
- **Heaven** is eternal happiness and communion with God. Those who love God and remain faithful until death will be invited into his heavenly kingdom forever. They will attain the perfect happiness that is the deepest desire of every human heart.

Aside from the Four Last Things, there is a temporary state after death for many people. *Purgatory* is a time of purification for those who die in God's friendship but who were not completely purified in this life. In purgatory they undergo a final cleansing to enable them to enter heaven. Purgatory is temporary. The suffering souls in purgatory exist in a state of grace and are assured of eternal life in heaven, but they must endure the inability to see God completely for a time, in order to be freed from their sins and earthly attachments.

**All who die in God's grace and friendship, but still imperfectly purified, are indeed assured of their eternal salvation; but after death they undergo purification, so as to achieve the holiness necessary to enter the joy of heaven.**

*The Last Judgment* by Memling.
Man's final events as an individual and as a race are called the last things: death, judgment, heaven, and hell.

**The Church gives the name Purgatory to this final purification of the elect, which is entirely different from the punishment of the damned. The Church formulated her doctrine of faith on Purgatory especially at the Councils of Florence and Trent. The tradition of the Church, by reference to certain texts of Scripture, speaks of a cleansing fire:**

**As for certain lesser faults, we must believe that, before the Final Judgment, there is a purifying fire. He who is truth says that whoever utters blasphemy against the Holy Spirit will be pardoned neither in this age nor in the age to come. From this sentence we understand that certain offenses can be forgiven in this age, but certain others in the age to come.**

**This teaching is also based on the practice of prayer for the dead, already mentioned in Sacred Scripture: "Therefore [Judas Maccabeus] made atonement for the dead, that they might be delivered from their sin." From the beginning the Church has honored the memory of the dead and**

> **offered prayers in suffrage for them, above all the Eucharistic sacrifice, so that, thus purified, they may attain the beatific vision of God. The Church also commends almsgiving, indulgences, and works of penance undertaken on behalf of the dead:**
>
> **Let us help and commemorate them. If Job's sons were purified by their father's sacrifice, why would we doubt that our offerings for the dead bring them some consolation? Let us not hesitate to help those who have died and to offer our prayers for them. (CCC 1030-1032)**

When Christ comes again in his second coming, the Kingdom of God will be established completely:

> **At the end of time, the Kingdom of God will come in its fullness. After the universal judgment, the righteous will reign for ever with Christ, glorified in body and soul. The universe itself will be renewed. (CCC 1042)**

No one can be sure that he or she will live to an old age or have time to prepare for the moment of death or the second coming of Christ. Several of Christ's parables warn of the need to be prepared for the end at all times. With the help of the Holy Spirit and the grace received through the Sacraments, we can maintain our friendship with God in hopes of attaining our life's very purpose: eternal happiness in heaven.

## CONCLUSION

***God's plan of salvation began with Adam, and includes you.***

Since the time of Adam and Eve, God had a plan to redeem the human race. His plan began to unfold immediately after the Fall, and continued unveiling itself through covenants with Noah, Abraham, Moses, and David. Then God fulfilled his plan completely in his Son, Jesus Christ.

It is through the Paschal Mystery—the Passion, Death, Resurrection, and Ascension of Christ—that every person can be saved, becoming a part of God's great plan of salvation for the whole world.

> **"The wonderful works of God among the people of the Old Testament were but a prelude to the work of Christ the Lord in redeeming mankind and giving perfect glory to God. He accomplished this work principally by the Paschal mystery of his blessed Passion, Resurrection from the dead, and glorious Ascension, whereby 'dying he destroyed our death, rising he restored our life.' For it was from the side of Christ as he slept the sleep of death upon the cross that there came forth 'the wondrous sacrament of the whole Church.'"**
>
> **For this reason, the Church celebrates in the liturgy above all the Paschal mystery by which Christ accomplished the work of our salvation. (CCC 1067)**

In order to enter into this plan, we must become part of Christ's Body, the Church. Through the Church we can receive the Sacraments—such as the Sacrament of Confirmation—which allow us to be a part of the story that God began with his first promise of salvation to Adam and Eve, and that will not be completed until Christ's second coming at the end of time.

## POINTS TO REMEMBER

1. Human beings are unique because we are created in the image and likeness of God. Every person has an immortal soul, a rational intellect, and free will.
2. Original Sin is transmitted from our first parents to the human race. It makes us vulnerable to sin because it distorts our view of God and clouds our intellect and use of reason. Immediately after the Fall of Adam and Eve, God promised to send a Redeemer. God continued to reveal himself as he gathered his people and prepared them to receive the Messiah.
3. God formed a relationship with his people through his promises and covenants with people in the Old Testament. All the covenants, promises, and prophecies of the Old Testament are fulfilled in Jesus Christ.
4. Christ is perfect God and perfect man. He retained his full divinity and took on human nature in his Incarnation, becoming "a man like us in all things but sin." Through the Paschal Mystery Christ made salvation possible for every member of the human race.

# WITNESS OF CHRIST

## BL. CHIARA BADANO

Blessed Chiara Badano was born in Italy in 1971. Her parents had hoped to conceive a child for more than ten years, until finally God granted their desire. This child did things that few people have accomplished at such a young age.

Chiara exemplified devotion to the Catholic faith from the time that she was a little child. At the age of four, Chiara went through her toys to give some of them to poorer children. She did not give away just any toys; she gave away the toys that she liked most. As a young girl Chiara invited the poor to her home to spend holidays, and she spent time visiting the elderly in a senior center.

Aside from being a devout Catholic, Chiara was a typical girl. She loved to play tennis, go mountain climbing, and swim. Like most girls her age, Chiara liked to "hang out" and she especially took pride in her beautiful hair. However, her life changed when she was diagnosed with bone cancer at age seventeen.

Despite her diagnosis, Chiara's faith remained strong. Instead of feeling sorry for herself, she dedicated herself to loving those around her. She refused to take pain medication so that she could be alert. While in the hospital, Chiara spoke with a girl who was addicted to drugs; Chiara took walks with her, in spite of the fact that she was in extreme pain. Even when she began to lose her beloved hair, she offered the hardship up as a prayer to Jesus. Eventually, her cancer worsened and she became paralyzed. Despite her immobility, her heart still radiated love. One of the doctors said, "Through her smile, through her eyes full of light, she showed us that death doesn't exist; only life exists."

Bl. Chiara died in October 1990, but her impact was just beginning. After her death, the parents of a boy in Italy who was dying of meningitis asked Chiara to intercede for him. He recovered completely. The doctors were baffled and had no explanation for the healing. As a result of this miracle, in 2010 she was declared "blessed."

Before she died, Chiara said, "Now I feel enfolded in a marvelous plan of God, which is slowly being unveiled in me."

# VOCABULARY

### COVENANT
A solemn agreement between people or between God and man involving mutual commitments and guarantees. A covenant is more than a contract; whereas a contract establishes a temporary relationship beneficial to both parties, a covenant is intended to bind both parties in kinship forever.

### FALL
The commission of the Original Sin by Adam and Eve, which resulted in their loss of original holiness and justice as well as concupiscence, suffering, death, and loss of friendship with God.

### INCARNATION
From the Latin for "to make flesh." The mystery of the hypostatic union of the divine and human natures in the one divine Person, the Word, Jesus Christ. To bring about man's salvation, the Son of God was made flesh and became truly man.

### LAST THINGS
The elements that directly pertain to eternity, specifically death, judgment, heaven, and hell. A longer list would include purgatory, the resurrection of the body, and the end of time.

### PASCHAL MYSTERY
Christ's work of redemption accomplished principally by his Passion, Death, Resurrection, and Ascension, whereby, "dying he destroyed our death, rising he restored our life" (CCC 1067). The Paschal Mystery is celebrated and made present in the liturgy of the Church, and its saving effects are communicated through the Sacraments (CCC 1076), especially the Eucharist, which renews the Paschal Sacrifice of Christ as the sacrifice offered by the Church (CCC 571, 1362-1372).

### SECOND COMING
The coming of Jesus Christ at the end of time. At his second coming, Christ will come as Judge and will inaugurate his eternal kingdom.

*The Incarnation* by Piero. The reality that God became man is called the Incarnation, literally, "going into flesh."

## STUDY QUESTIONS

1. What does it mean to be made in the "image and likeness" of God?
2. Why do we call God "Father"? Describe two ways in which God is truly our Father.
3. How were all three Persons of the Blessed Trinity involved in our creation?
4. When did God first promise the redemption of the human race?
5. What is the Incarnation, and why did Jesus become incarnate?
6. How is Christ our model of discipleship?
7. What are the events that make up the "Paschal Mystery"?
8. What did Christ's Passion and Death accomplish?
9. How does the Eucharist relate to the Passover?
10. Why is the entirety of the Catholic faith centered on Christ's Resurrection?

## PRACTICAL EXERCISES

1. As a Catholic, you are part of a family history that goes back to Adam and Eve. Do some research on your immediate family history. Find out on what day and where you were baptized. Also try to find out where and when your parents were baptized.

2. Read Chapters 1 and 2 of the Gospel of Matthew. Find at least four different places that Matthew says Jesus fulfilled a prophecy. List them.

As a Catholic, you are part of a family history that goes back to Adam and Eve.

# Sealed in the Spirit

***Confirmation has a long history as a Sacrament of Initiation in the Catholic Church.***

At Confirmation, we recommit to participate in the Church's work and mission.

Sealing with the gift of the Spirit at Confirmation strengthens us for ongoing service in the Body of Christ in the Church and in the world. It prepares us to be active participants in the Church's mission and to

> **bear witness to the Christian faith in words accompanied by deeds. (CCC 1316)**

Finally, the Spirit sends us as workers in the vineyard and instruments of the Holy Spirit in renewing the earth and promoting God's Kingdom of justice and peace. Thus, Confirmation is not only an *anointing*, but also a *commissioning* to live out our faith *in the world.* We are already called to mission by virtue of our Baptism, but at Confirmation we are endowed with gifts of the Spirit (like the Apostles in Acts 2) to be

> **ever greater witness[es] to the Gospel in the world. (Pope Benedict XVI, *Sacramentum Caritatis* [*Sacrament of Charity*], no. 17)**

As disciples and witnesses to Christ in both Church and world (cf. CCC 1319), we are sent out to act on behalf of the poor and vulnerable, promoting the life and dignity of every human person.

In some dioceses, when you are confirmed, the bishop (or the priest, in some cases) will call you by your Confirmation name as he applies the Sacred Chrism (the holy oil), making the Sign of the Cross on your forehead. For example, if a young woman has chosen St. Gianna as her Confirmation name, he will say: "Gianna, be sealed with the Gift of the Holy Spirit."

This name is something you must choose for yourself. It ought to be a thoughtful and prayerful choice.

Choosing a name for Confirmation is not like naming a pet or coming up with a nickname. Confirmation is a Sacrament; it is something sacred. You should not select a name because, for example, it is the name of your favorite musician or athlete or because it happens to sound good.

It cannot be just any name, either. Your Confirmation name must be the name of a saint of the Church. That should not be a problem, however, since there are many, many saints with many, many different names.

Your Confirmation saint should be important in your Christian life—someone to whom you feel drawn and have a devotion. You should learn about the saint's life on earth and why he or she is a holy example. It is a good idea to include the saint in your personal prayers, asking him or her to pray for you. After all, the saints are in heaven, so they know how to help make you perfectly happy! The saint you pick for your Confirmation name will become your personal patron saint.

In Scripture we see that God sometimes changed the names of people when he was calling them to a particular mission; for example, Abram/Abraham, Jacob/Israel, and Simon/Peter. This is also true at Confirmation: you are receiving a mission to be a disciple of Christ in the world. Your new Confirmation name reflects that mission.

So pray and think carefully about your choice of a Confirmation name. It might help to discover a few saints who interest you and learn something about the life of each one. If you want to use your baptismal name, find out about the different saints who have that same name. Discuss this choice with your parents and sponsor. Think about which saints might be good models of holiness for you. When you do choose, learn everything you can about your patron saint and, whenever you pray, ask him or her to pray for you.

Finally, some confirmands may question whether they may use their baptismal name as their Confirmation name—the answer is 'yes.'

*(Excerpted from "Confirmation: Strengthened by the Spirit, Called to Action" handout, Copyright ©2013, United States Conference of Catholic Bishops, Washington, DC. All rights reserved.)*

# You and Your Parents

***The Church requires our attendance at Mass on Sundays and Holy Days of Obligation.***

A creed is a statement of basic beliefs. It is sometimes called a symbol of faith or a profession of faith. At Sunday Mass we recite either the Nicene Creed or the Apostles' Creed. Each of these creeds lists the fundamental beliefs of the Catholic faith.

The Nicene Creed and the Apostles' Creed developed in the early centuries of the Church. During those years there were sometimes disagreements over the humanity and divinity of Jesus Christ, whether he truly suffered and died, and similar questions. These Creeds help Christians know what exactly it is they believed about Christ.

The Nicene Creed is the central declaration of the Catholic faith. With your parents, read the Nicene Creed together (below), and then discuss answers to these questions:

1. What does this creed teach about God the Father?
2. What does this creed teach about God the Son?
3. What does this creed teach about God the Holy Spirit?
4. How do these truths relate to what you have read and learned in this book?

This papyrus fragment is believed to be the oldest copy of the Nicene Creed dated to the 6th century, Egypt.

## The Nicene Creed

I believe in one God,
the Father almighty,
maker of heaven and earth,
of all things visible and invisible.

I believe in one Lord Jesus Christ,
the Only Begotten Son of God,
born of the Father before all ages.
God from God, Light from Light,
true God from true God,
begotten, not made, consubstantial with
the Father;
through him all things were made.
For us men and for our salvation
he came down from heaven,
and by the Holy Spirit was incarnate
of the Virgin Mary,
and became man.

For our sake he was crucified under
Pontius Pilate,
he suffered death and was buried,
and rose again on the third day
in accordance with the Scriptures.
He ascended into heaven
and is seated at the right hand of the Father.
He will come again in glory
to judge the living and the dead
and his kingdom will have no end.

I believe in the Holy Spirit, the Lord,
the giver of life,
who proceeds from the Father and the Son,
who with the Father and the Son is adored
and glorified,
who has spoken through the prophets.
I believe in one, holy, catholic and apostolic
Church.
I confess one Baptism for the forgiveness
of sins
and I look forward to the resurrection
of the dead
and the life of the world to come. Amen.

(*Roman Missal*, The Order of Mass, no. 18)

# YOU AND YOUR SPONSOR

***Your sponsor has a serious obligation to help prepare you for Confirmation.***

Your parents will help choose a Confirmation name. However, you can also ask your sponsor for help in deciding on a name. These points should help you talk with your sponsor about your name.

- Once you have narrowed down your options to two or three saints, discuss them with your sponsor. Explain why you are drawn to each of these saints, and tell your sponsor some details about their lives. For each saint discuss the personality traits or talents you admire.
- Ask your sponsor to share his or her thoughts about the saints on your list. He or she may know something about you that may help you make a decision, maybe even suggesting you expand your search to a saint that you had not considered before.
- Ask your sponsor about his or her own Confirmation name: what name he or she chose and why. How does your sponsor see that saint as an example to follow in the Christian life? How often does your sponsor ask that saint to pray for him or her?
- When you decide on a Confirmation name, offer to pray for your sponsor to his or her patron saint, and ask him or her to pray for you to your patron saint. Find prayers to your patron saint and your sponsor's patron saint, and pray them regularly.

St. Catherine of Alexandria is the patron saint of librarians, students, philosophers, secretaries, and nurses.

St. Christopher is the patron saint of travelers, bookbinders, gardeners, mariners, drivers, surfers, athletes, and pilots.

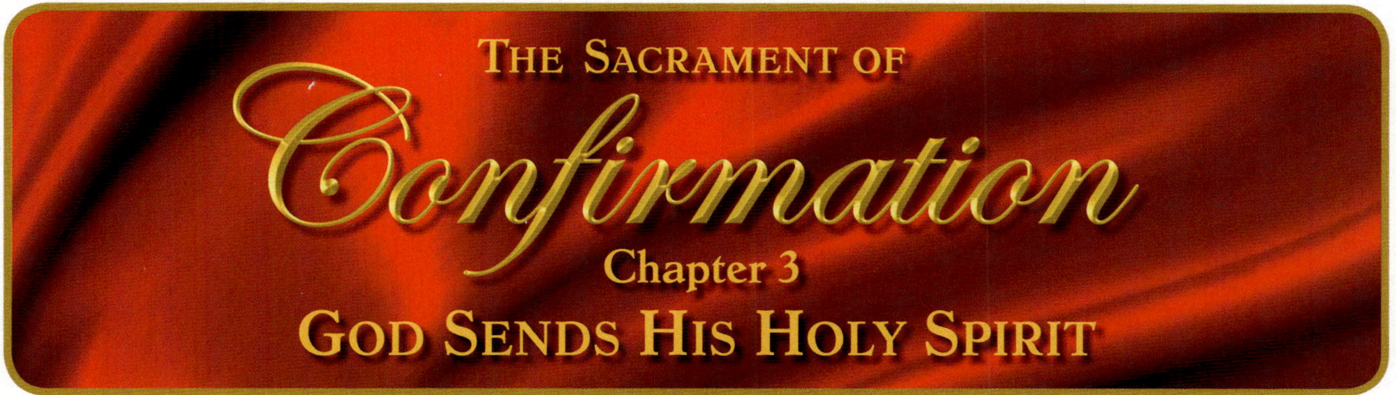


## INTRODUCTION

***Get to know the Holy Spirit and all that he can do for you and through you.***

After Christ ascended into heaven, he did not leave his followers forsaken. Ten days after the Ascension, the Holy Spirit descended upon the Apostles at the Feast of Pentecost. The Holy Spirit came to enliven the Church and guide all its members to become disciples of Christ.

> **I will not leave you desolate; I will come to you. (Jn 14:18)**

You are preparing to receive the Sacrament of Confirmation, when you will receive the gift of the Holy Spirit in a special way. It is important, therefore, that you understand who the Holy Spirit is, and how he works in your life and in the world.

Since you believe in Christ, the Holy Spirit has already touched you in some way. In Baptism, when you first received the Holy Spirit, you were given the grace to encounter Christ. Now in Confirmation you will be empowered by the Holy Spirit to have a closer encounter with Christ and to serve and follow him more faithfully.

After reading this chapter, you will be able to answer these questions:

- Who is the Holy Spirit?
- How has the Holy Spirit worked throughout salvation history?
- What are some of the other names and titles of the Holy Spirit?
- What are some of the symbols of the Holy Spirit?

*The Trinity in Glory* by Titian.
It is not easy to picture God the Holy Spirit.
After all, what does a "spirit" look like?

## GOD THE HOLY SPIRIT

***The Third Person of the Blessed Trinity gives us the graces we need to live as Christians.***

> **I believe in the Holy Spirit, the Lord, the giver of life, who proceeds from the Father and the Son. With the Father and the Son he is worshiped and glorified. He has spoken through the Prophets. (Nicene Creed)**

God is a Trinity of three Divine Persons: Father, Son, and Holy Spirit. While it is easy for us to picture God the Father and God the Son, Jesus Christ, it is not as easy to picture God the Holy Spirit. After all, what does a "spirit" look like?

*The Holy Trinity* by El Greco.
The Holy Spirit is the result of the relationship between the Father and the Son: he is the *love* between them. Their love is so real that it is a divine Person.

> **"Holy Spirit" is the proper name of the one whom we adore and glorify with the Father and the Son. The Church has received this name from the Lord and professes it in the Baptism of her new children. (CCC 691)**

In the Old Testament we see the Father revealed clearly in Creation and in his care for his people, Israel. The Old Testament also looked forward to Christ, foretelling the coming of the Messiah who would save God's people. It was not until the New Testament, however, that the Holy Spirit was fully revealed, by Christ, who promised that the Father would send him to the Apostles after the Ascension.

> **These things I have spoken to you, while I am still with you. But the Counselor, the Holy Spirit, whom the Father will send in my name, he will teach you all things, and bring to your remembrance all that I have said to you. (Jn 14:25-26)**

God the Holy Spirit is the Third Person of the Blessed Trinity. He is a divine Person, distinct from God the Father and God the Son yet **consubstantial** (completely united as one substance) with them. The Holy Spirit is equal to the Father and the Son and, like them, is adored and worshiped. It is important to understand that the Holy Spirit is a "who," not a "what," just like the Father and the Son.

It can be difficult to picture the relationship of the Holy Spirit to the other two divine Persons of the Trinity. The relationship between the Father and the Son is straightforward. The Father *generates* the Son, meaning that the Father is the source of the Son's life. (We have to remember that this does not mean there was a time the Son did not exist—this generation is eternal and has always existed.) The human generation of a son from a father is like this generation, although in God's case it is not physical and in a fixed point in time, but instead spiritual and eternal.

But what about the Holy Spirit? The Creed states that he "*proceeds* from the Father and the Son," but what does that mean, "proceeds"? Do we have anything in our experience that would help us to explain it in another way? Let us think about our own nature. Human beings are made in the image and likeness of God. The human family reflects the Trinitarian love of God, who is Father, Son, and Holy Spirit. Both a mother and a father participate in God's creative work when the result of their union is a child.

These comparisons between family relationships and the relationships within God are not perfect, but they do help us at least a little to understand the Blessed Trinity.

The Holy Spirit plays an important role in salvation history, in the Church, and in your life. This role becomes even more prominent through the Sacrament of Confirmation, when you will be anointed with the gift of the Holy Spirit.

> **The Holy Spirit is at work with the Father and the Son from the beginning to the completion of the plan for our salvation. But in these "end times," ushered in by the Son's redeeming Incarnation, the Spirit is revealed and given, recognized and welcomed as a person. (CCC 685)**

## The Lord

The Nicene Creed states "I believe in one Lord Jesus Christ," but then later proclaims "I believe in the Holy Spirit, *the Lord*..." If we believe in "one Lord Jesus Christ," how is it that the Holy Spirit is also "the Lord"? As we mentioned above, the Holy Spirit is "consubstantial" with the Father and the Son. This means that although the three Persons of the Trinity are distinct, they are one God. So we look to the Holy Spirit as our Lord—someone we serve and obey.

## The Giver of Life

In Chapter 2, we noted that all three Persons of the Trinity were involved in creation. As the sacred author of Genesis wrote, "the Spirit of God was moving over the face of the waters" (Gn 1:2). But the Holy Spirit is not just involved in physical creation—he also gives us spiritual life. We receive the Holy Spirit at Baptism, which fills us with God's life. At Confirmation, this gift of the Holy Spirit is strengthened in us, making us disciples of Jesus Christ. Through the Sacraments, the Holy Spirit gives us life.

## He Is Worshiped and Glorified

To "worship" means to show reverence and adoration for someone. God alone is deserving of worship. As God, the Holy Spirit is worshiped equally with the Father and the Son. We also glorify him, meaning that we try to live each moment of our lives for him, in a way that brings him glory.

The Holy Spirit is worshiped equally with the Father and the Son.

## APOLOGETICS 101:

### THE BLESSED TRINITY

(Adapted from the *Didache Bible*)

***How can we understand the mystery of the Blessed Trinity as "three Persons in one God"?***

> **Jesus came and said to [the eleven disciples], "Go therefore and make disciples of all nations, baptizing them in the name of the Father and of the Son and of the Holy Spirit." (Mt 28:19)**
>
> **The grace of the Lord Jesus Christ and the love of God and the fellowship of the Holy Spirit be with you all. (2 Cor 13:14)**

Because it is a mystery, the Blessed Trinity is impossible to understand by reason alone. By faith we can affirm the truths about the Blessed Trinity that have been divinely revealed to us and handed down to us through Sacred Scripture and Sacred Tradition.

The Blessed Trinity is the central mystery of the Christian faith, the very source and light of all other mysteries of faith. As such, it is the most fundamental and indispensable truth of Christianity, one that has been revealed to the Church and articulated by her through her reflection upon Sacred Scripture and Sacred Tradition.

The Most Holy Trinity is one God in three divine Persons. The Father is God, the Son is God, and the Holy Spirit is God, and each is of the same divine "substance," "essence," or "nature." They are differentiated as three Persons only in their relationship to one another: "It is the Father who generates, the Son who is begotten, and the Holy Spirit who proceeds" (Lateran Council IV). Yet we ought not attempt to distinguish the three Persons of the Blessed Trinity by their perceived "functions," as though it is the Father alone who creates, the Son alone who redeems, and the Spirit alone who sanctifies. All three are united in will and share in all divine works.

The Church celebrates the Solemnity of the Most Holy Trinity on the first Sunday after Pentecost.

## He Has Spoken Through the Prophets

We will read in the next section how the Holy Spirit worked during Old Testament times. Through the prophets, the Holy Spirit delivered God's Word to his people. He also speaks by inspiring the writers of the Scriptures to reveal God's plan of salvation. He continues to speak to us through those around us—our parents, priests, and holy people.

*Anointing of David* by Barrias.
In the days when kings ruled Israel, the Spirit of God came upon a king after a prophet anointed him with oil.

# THE HOLY SPIRIT IN THE OLD TESTAMENT

***The Holy Spirit is present in the Old Testament in a veiled way.***

You read in Chapter 2 that the Holy Spirit was active in the creation of the world. In Genesis we read that "the Spirit of God was moving over the face of the waters" (Gn 1:2). Later, God "formed man of dust from the ground, and breathed into his nostrils the breath of life; and man became a living being" (Gn 2:7). This "breath" is a translation of the Hebrew *ruah*, which also means "wind" or "spirit." So God gave the first human being his Spirit, which gave the man life.

The Holy Spirit continued to be active in the world during the entirety of Old Testament times, however, but his activity was hidden. God had not yet revealed the mystery of the Trinity to the world. Yet we can still detect the work of the Holy Spirit in the Old Testament, particularly in his impact on certain individuals. When God needed someone to accomplish a specific task, or a prophet to call the people back to himself, or a king to lead them, God's Spirit came down upon these individuals in a special way.

In the language of the Old Testament, the Spirit of God often *comes upon*, *falls upon*, *rests upon*, or *takes possession of* a prophet, judge, or another divinely appointed leader of Israel. This gives the sense that the Spirit of God guided these individuals and gave them special gifts to help them carry out their sacred tasks. In this way, the presence of the Spirit of God prefigures the Sacrament of Confirmation.

For example, when the Ark of the Covenant was to be built, God chose Bezalel to build it, saying this:

> **"I have filled him with the Spirit of God, with ability and intelligence, with knowledge and all craftsmanship, to devise artistic designs, to work in gold, silver, and bronze, in cutting stones for setting, and in carving wood, for work in every craft." (Ex 31:3-5)**

### HOLY GHOST OR HOLY SPIRIT?

The word "spirit" is sometimes translated as "ghost." In some prayers, hymns, and Bible translations, we refer to the "Holy Ghost"; for example the Catholic hymn, "Come, Holy Ghost." The word "ghost" comes from the German *Geist* and the Anglo-Saxon *Gast*, while "spirit" comes from the Latin *spiritus*. The two words have the same meaning.

When God was leading his people to the Promised Land, he chose 70 elders to help Moses govern the Israelites. God "took some of the spirit that was upon [Moses] and put it upon the seventy elders" (Nm 11:25), and they began to prophesy.

Although often the Spirit of God came upon a person without any human intervention, he also would come upon someone through the **laying on of hands**. Joshua, who succeeded Moses as leader of the Israelites, "was full of the spirit of wisdom, for Moses had laid his hands upon him" (Dt 34:9). Scripture often uses the laying on of hands as a sign of handing on the Holy Spirit.

The **anointing** with oil was another way the Spirit of God would come upon someone. In the days when kings ruled Israel, the Spirit of God came upon a king after a prophet anointed him with oil. A person who had this spirit might be called an *anointed one* or the *anointed of God*. Anointing is therefore also a sign of the Spirit of God.

As the prophets began to reveal the expectation of a Redeemer who was to come, he would be spoken of as the *Anointed One*. In Hebrew, he was called the "*Messiah*"; in Greek, "*Christ*." This promised one would be anointed in a special way by the Holy Spirit:

> **The Spirit of the Lord shall rest upon him,**
> **the spirit of wisdom and understanding,**
> **the spirit of counsel and might,**
> **the spirit of knowledge and the fear of the Lord.**
> **(Is 11:2)**

We will see in Chapter 7 how laying on of hands and anointing are still used in the Sacrament of Confirmation to signify the coming of the Holy Spirit.

The prophets also proclaimed that, in the time of the Messiah, a *new spirit* would come upon the People of God, offering them hope in the midst of their centuries of division, oppression, and exile:

## THE DIFFERENCE BETWEEN PERSON AND NATURE

The Trinity is a great mystery—the greatest mystery there is, in fact. We will never completely understand it. But we can make attempts to at least understand it as best we can. Over the centuries the Church created a certain "language" for referring to the Trinity to help us. The main two terms are "person" and "nature." But what do they mean?

Imagine you have a friend named Sarah Jones. *What* is she? She is a girl. That is her *nature*. *Who* is she? She is Sarah Jones. That is her *person*. There is more than one person with the nature of a human being (all humans, in fact), but only one of this specific person, who is named "Sarah Jones." (Note, other people might have the same name, but they are not the same *person*).

Now let's use those terms when referring to God. *What* is he? He is God. That is his nature. *Who* is he? He is Father, Son, and Holy Spirit. Those are his Persons. Notice the difference: God isn't just one *person*, like Sarah Jones, he is three *Persons*. But he is still only one God.

Don't worry if you still don't really understand the Trinity. Just remember that there is only one God, but he is Father, Son, and Holy Spirit.

*The Trinity* by Previtali.
The Trinity is the greatest mystery of all.
We will never completely understand it.

**I will pour out my spirit on all flesh;**
**your sons and your daughters shall prophesy,**
**your old men shall dream dreams,**
**and your young men shall see visions.**
**Even upon the menservants and maidservants**
**in those days, I will pour out my spirit.**
**(Jl 2:28-29)**

These prophecies regarding the Spirit of God—those that spoke of the coming Spirit-filled Messiah, as well as those that foretold a new Spirit that would fall upon God's people—found their fulfillment in Jesus Christ.

## CHRIST AND THE HOLY SPIRIT REVEAL EACH OTHER

***The Holy Spirit shares in Christ's redeeming mission.***

With the coming of Jesus Christ, the time promised by the prophets—the time of a Spirit-filled Messiah and God's Spirit being poured out onto his people—had arrived. In the New Testament, we see the work of Christ the Redeemer, but also the revelation and work of the Holy Spirit.

The Holy Spirit is involved in every aspect of Christ's mission, beginning with his conception in the womb of the Blessed Virgin Mary. When the Archangel Gabriel visits Mary to tell her that she will be the mother of the Messiah, he says:

**"The Holy Spirit will come upon you, and the power of the Most High will overshadow you; therefore the child to be born will be called holy, the Son of God." (Lk 1:35)**

As the Gospel of Matthew puts it simply,

**When his mother Mary had been betrothed to Joseph, before they came together she was found to be with child of the Holy Spirit. (Mt 1:18)**

Just as the Holy Spirit worked during Old Testament times to prepare people for the coming of the Messiah, he continued to do so in the New Testament. Speaking of John the Baptist, the Archangel Gabriel also said: "He will be filled with the Holy Spirit, even from his mother's womb" (Lk 1:15). John the Baptist was filled with the Holy Spirit because of his unique role in the plan of salvation. He would bear witness to Christ and prepare the world for Christ's mission.

*Madonna of the Forest* by Lippi.
The Holy Spirit is involved in every aspect of Christ's mission.

When the time came for the public ministry of Jesus to begin, the Holy Spirit was finally revealed to the world in an overt way. At Christ's baptism, the Holy Spirit descended upon him in the form of a dove:

**When Jesus was baptized, he went up immediately from the water, and behold, the heavens were opened and he saw the Spirit of God descending like a dove, and alighting on him; and lo, a voice from heaven, saying, "This is my beloved Son, with whom I am well pleased." (Mt 3:16-17)**

In this moment we see the Blessed Trinity revealed, through the presence of all three Divine Persons: the Father declaring that Jesus is his Son, the Son (Jesus Christ) being baptized, and the Holy Spirit descending like a dove.

**The descent of the Holy Spirit on Jesus at his baptism by John was the sign that this was he who was to come, the Messiah, the Son of God. He was conceived of the Holy Spirit; his whole life and his whole mission are carried out in**

**total communion with the Holy Spirit whom the Father gives him "without measure." (CCC 1286)**

Immediately after his baptism, Christ was "led by the Spirit" into the wilderness to fast and pray (Lk 4:1). He "returned in the power of the Spirit" to Galilee (Lk 4:14) and began preaching in the synagogues. There he announced that he is the fulfillment of the prophecies regarding the Messiah:

> **He stood up to read; and there was given to him the book of the prophet Isaiah. He opened the book and found the place where it was written,**
>
> **"The Spirit of the Lord is upon me,**
> **because he has anointed me to preach good news to the poor.**
> **He has sent me to proclaim release to the captives**
> **and recovering of sight to the blind,**
> **to set at liberty those who are oppressed,**
> **to proclaim the acceptable year of the Lord."**
>
> **And he closed the book, and gave it back to the attendant, and sat down; and the eyes of all in the synagogue were fixed on him. And he began to say to them, "Today this scripture has been fulfilled in your hearing." (Lk 4:16-21)**

Jesus Christ is the Spirit-filled Messiah promised in the Old Testament.

The second aspect of the Old Testament prophecies regarding God's Spirit—that it would come upon his people—was also fulfilled in Christ's time. During his public ministry, Christ taught that a person must be "born of water and the Spirit" in order to enter the Church (Jn 3:5). This refers to the Sacrament of Baptism, during which the baptized person receives the Holy Spirit. Also, Christ gave his Apostles the Holy Spirit when he instituted the Sacrament of Penance:

> **He breathed on them, and said to them, "Receive the Holy Spirit. If you forgive the sins of any, they are forgiven; if you retain the sins of any, they are retained." (Jn 20:22-23)**

Before he ascended into heaven, Christ also promised the power of the Holy Spirit to every Christian:

> **I will pray the Father, and he will give you another Counselor, to be with you for ever, even the Spirit of truth, whom the world cannot receive, because it neither sees him nor knows him; you know him, for he dwells with you, and will be in you. (Jn 14:16-17)**

This promise was fulfilled at Pentecost when the Holy Spirit descended upon the Apostles in the Upper Room, as we will read in the next section.

At Christ's baptism, the Holy Spirit descended upon him in the form of a dove.

## WHAT DOES IT MEAN THAT THE HOLY SPIRIT IS THE PARACLETE—A "COUNSELOR"?

What did Christ mean when he called the Holy Spirit "Counselor"? What is a counselor?

A counselor does a number of things:

- He guides a person to make wise decisions.
- He helps a person in need.
- He defends (or advocates) for a person in trouble.

All these things the Holy Spirit does for Christ's disciples. He imparts the gift of Wisdom (which we will read about in Chapter 7); he is always ready to help those who call upon him in times of need; and he fights for us in our battle against Satan and his demons.

*Pentecost* by Maino.

## PENTECOST

***The Holy Spirit came upon the Apostles and gave them power and courage.***

After the Ascension, Christ's disciples must have been both confused and frightened. The Resurrection had filled them with many hopes and dreams of the establishment of the Kingdom of God on earth, but then Christ ascended into heaven. Had he left them alone? No, Christ had promised to send the Holy Spirit, which he called a "Counselor," to guide and help them:

> **I will pray the Father, and he will give you another Counselor, to be with you for ever, even the Spirit of truth, whom the world cannot receive, because it neither sees him nor knows him; you know him, for he dwells with you, and will be in you. (Jn 14:16-17)**

This promise was to be fulfilled shortly after Christ's Ascension.

> **On the day of Pentecost when the seven weeks of Easter had come to an end, Christ's Passover is fulfilled in the outpouring of the Holy Spirit, manifested, given, and communicated as a divine person: of his fullness, Christ, the Lord, pours out the Spirit in abundance. (CCC 731)**

Ten days after the Ascension, the Jewish People were commemorating the Feast of Pentecost. This festival celebrated the giving of the Law to Moses, fifty days after Passover. During this time, the Apostles were gathered together in Jerusalem when they heard "a sound…like the rush of a mighty wind."

> **When the day of Pentecost had come, they were all together in one place. And suddenly a sound came from heaven like the rush of a mighty wind, and it filled all the house where they were sitting. And there appeared to them tongues as of fire, distributed and resting on each one of them. And they were all filled with the Holy Spirit and began to speak in other tongues, as the Spirit gave them utterance. (Acts 2:2-4)**

Miraculously, people in Jerusalem from various places who spoke many languages all understood what the Apostles were saying. In a real way, this was a reversal of the Tower of Babel, which divided humanity by confusing human speech into many languages.

Peter, the leader of the Apostles, then began to preach to the crowds regarding Jesus and his Resurrection (see sidebar "Peter's Sermon on Pentecost"). Many responded to his call to conversion, and the book of Acts tells us that "about 3,000 souls" were baptized that day! The Holy Spirit not only gave Peter the words to preach, but also opened the hearts of the people to receive his message of salvation.

After Pentecost, the Apostles were transformed. During Christ's public ministry, they often didn't understand his message and argued with each other about petty matters. Most sadly, at the time of Christ's greatest need—when he was arrested, tortured, and killed—all but John fled in fear. Yet after Pentecost, these same men became powerful and courageous preachers of the Gospel. In fact, other than St. John, all were eventually martyred for their faith. They preferred to be killed rather than abandon Christ again.

What made the difference in the Apostles' lives? The Holy Spirit. He gave them courage, knowledge, and many other gifts that they then used throughout their lives. This same Holy Spirit will come upon you in a new and special way at your Confirmation, which could be considered your own Pentecost!

## PETER'S SERMON ON PENTECOST
**(Acts 2:14-36)**

Peter, standing with the eleven, lifted up his voice and addressed [the crowd], "Men of Judea and all who dwell in Jerusalem, let this be known to you, and give ear to my words. For these men are not drunk, as you suppose, since it is only the third hour of the day; but this is what was spoken by the prophet Joel:

'And in the last days it shall be, God declares,
that I will pour out my Spirit upon all flesh,
and your sons and your daughters shall prophesy,
and your young men shall see visions,
and your old men shall dream dreams;
yea, and on my menservants and my maidservants
in those days
I will pour out my Spirit; and they shall prophesy.
And I will show wonders in the heaven above
and signs on the earth beneath,
blood, and fire, and vapor of smoke;
the sun shall be turned into darkness
and the moon into blood,
before the day of the Lord comes,
the great and manifest day.
And it shall be that whoever calls on the name of the Lord shall be saved.'

"Men of Israel, hear these words: Jesus of Nazareth, a man attested to you by God with mighty works and wonders and signs which God did through him in your midst, as you yourselves know— this Jesus, delivered up according to the definite plan and foreknowledge of God, you crucified and killed by the hands of lawless men. But God raised him up, having loosed the pangs of death, because it was not possible for him to be held by it. For David says concerning him,

'I saw the Lord always before me,
for he is at my right hand that I may not be shaken;
therefore my heart was glad, and my tongue rejoiced;
moreover my flesh will dwell in hope.
For thou wilt not abandon my soul to Hades,
nor let thy Holy One see corruption.
Thou hast made known to me the ways of life;
thou wilt make me full of gladness with thy presence.'

"Brethren, I may say to you confidently of the patriarch David that he both died and was buried, and his tomb is with us to this day. Being therefore a prophet, and knowing that God had sworn with an oath to him that he would set one of his descendants upon his throne, he foresaw and spoke of the resurrection of the Christ, that he was not abandoned to Hades, nor did his flesh see corruption. This Jesus God raised up, and of that we all are witnesses. Being therefore exalted at the right hand of God, and having received from the Father the promise of the Holy Spirit, he has poured out this which you see and hear. For David did not ascend into the heavens; but he himself says,

'The Lord said to my Lord, Sit at my right hand,
till I make thy enemies a stool for thy feet.'
Let all the house of Israel therefore know assuredly that God has made him both Lord and Christ, this Jesus whom you crucified."

## LITANY OF THE HOLY SPIRIT

Lord, have mercy on us.

Christ, have mercy on us.

Lord, have mercy on us.

Father all-powerful, have mercy on us. Jesus, Eternal Son of the Father, Redeemer of the world, save us. Spirit of the Father and the Son, boundless life of both, sanctify us. Holy Trinity, hear us.

Holy Spirit, Who proceeds from the Father and the Son, enter our hearts. Holy Spirit, Who art equal to the Father and the Son, enter our hearts.

Promise of God the Father, have mercy on us.

Ray of heavenly light, have mercy on us.

Author of all good, have mercy on us.

Source of heavenly water, have mercy on us.

Consuming fire, have mercy on us.

Ardent charity, have mercy on us.

Spiritual unction, have mercy on us.

Spirit of love and truth, have mercy on us.

Spirit of wisdom and understanding, have mercy on us.

Spirit of counsel and fortitude, have mercy on us.

Spirit of knowledge and piety, have mercy on us.

Spirit of the fear of the Lord, have mercy on us.

Spirit of grace and prayer, have mercy on us.

Spirit of peace and meekness, have mercy on us.

Spirit of modesty and innocence, have mercy on us.

Holy Spirit, the Comforter, have mercy on us.

Holy Spirit, the Sanctifier, have mercy on us.

Holy Spirit, Who governs the Church, have mercy on us.

Gift of God, the Most High, have mercy on us.

Spirit Who fills the universe, have mercy on us.

Spirit of the adoption of the children of God, have mercy on us.

Holy Spirit, inspire us with horror of sin.

Holy Spirit, come and renew the face of the earth.

Holy Spirit, shed Thy light in our souls.

Holy Spirit, engrave Thy law in our hearts.

Holy Spirit, inflame us with the flame of Thy love.

Holy Spirit, open to us the treasures of Thy graces.

Holy Spirit, teach us to pray well.

Holy Spirit, enlighten us with Thy heavenly inspirations.

Holy Spirit, lead us in the way of salvation.

Holy Spirit, grant us the only necessary knowledge.

Holy Spirit, inspire in us the practice of good.

Holy Spirit, grant us the merits of all virtues.

Holy Spirit, make us persevere in justice.

Holy Spirit, be Thou our everlasting reward.

Lamb of God, Who takes away the sins of the world,

Send us Thy Holy Spirit.

Lamb of God, Who takes away the sins of the world,

Pour down into our souls the gifts of the Holy Spirit.

Lamb of God, Who takes away the sins of the world,

Grant us the Spirit of wisdom and piety.

V. Come, Holy Spirit! Fill the hearts of Thy faithful,

R. And enkindle in them the fire of Thy love.

Let us pray. Grant, O merciful Father, that Thy Divine Spirit may enlighten, inflame and purify us, that He may penetrate us with His heavenly dew and make us fruitful in good works, through Our Lord Jesus Christ, Thy Son, Who with Thee, in the unity of the same Spirit, lives and reigns, God, forever and ever.

R. Amen.

## THE HOLY SPIRIT— THE SOUL OF THE CHURCH

***The Holy Spirit is the lifeblood of the Catholic Church.***

**The mission of Christ and the Holy Spirit is brought to completion in the Church, which is the Body of Christ and the Temple of the Holy Spirit. This joint mission henceforth brings Christ's faithful to share in his communion with the Father in the Holy Spirit. (CCC 737)**

The Acts of the Apostles in the Bible is the story of the early Church, and it is really about how the Holy Spirit led the Church. In fact, Acts is sometimes called the "Gospel of the Holy Spirit." In Acts the power of the Holy Spirit is shown in miraculous healings and the understanding of foreign languages. But the most important action of the Holy Spirit is shown in the conversion of people to Christianity. At the beginning of the book we find only a handful of disciples, but at its end Christianity has spread throughout the Roman Empire. It has reached the center of the world at that time, Rome. The Church is founded on the Holy Spirit, and all she does—then and now—is through the Holy Spirit's power.

The Holy Spirit gives life to the Church in three particular ways:

***Teaching.*** Christ told his disciples, "When the Spirit of truth comes, he will guide you into all the truth" (Jn 16:13). The Holy Spirit protects the Church from teaching error in her official pronouncements. This is important, for if a disciple of Christ could not be sure that the Church teaches truth, he or she would not know the path to follow to eternal life.

***Sanctifying.*** The goal of the Christian is to become holy—to become like Christ. This process is called "sanctification," and it is the work of the Holy Spirit. St. Peter wrote that followers of Christ are "chosen and destined by God the Father and sanctified by the Spirit for obedience to Jesus Christ" (1 Pt 1:1-2). The Holy Spirit's work of sanctification is primarily done through the Sacraments, which give us the grace to be more and more like Christ.

***Governing.*** The Church is a worldwide institution. Like any institution, it needs rules and laws in order

### NAMES OF THE HOLY SPIRIT

The authors of Sacred Scripture used many various names and titles to refer to God the Holy Spirit. These names and titles reveal to us different features of the mysterious nature of the Third Person of the Blessed Trinity. Here are some of them:

***Paraclete, Counselor, Comforter,*** or ***Advocate*** (Jn 14:16, 26; 15:26; 16:7). When explaining the power and mission of the Holy Spirit to his Apostles at the Last Supper, Christ referred to him as the *Paraclete*. In some Bibles this is translated as *Counselor, Comforter,* or *Advocate*.

All these names are appropriate. A *counselor* offers someone direction or advice, and the Holy Spirit counsels us in the truth in order to lead us on the path to God. A *comforter* provides care and assistance to those who suffer, and the Holy Spirit is our guarantee that God will never abandon us. An *advocate* looks out for our best interests and supports us in times of trial. The Holy Spirit is always there to support us when we face temptation.

***Spirit of truth*** (Jn 14:17; 15:26; 16:13; 1 Jn 4:6). Christ disclosed this title to his disciples. It demonstrates the Holy Spirit's inseparable link to our Lord. Christ declared, "I am the way, and the truth, and the life" (Jn 14:6). The *Spirit of truth* helped the Apostles and their successors to preserve the authentic teachings of Christ and safeguard them for all generations.

***Spirit of Christ*** (Rom 8:9), ***Spirit of the Lord*** (2 Cor 3:17), or ***Spirit of God*** (Rom 8:9; 15:19; 1 Cor 6:11; 7:40). These titles are revealed in the New Testament and reflect the close relationship between the three Persons of the Trinity.

***Spirit of the promise*** (Gal 3:14; Eph 1:13), ***Spirit of adoption*** (Rom 8:15; Gal 4:6), or ***Spirit of glory*** (1 Pt 4:14). The Holy Spirit is the *Spirit of promise* because he fulfilled the promises made by the prophets in the Old Testament. The Holy Spirit is the *Spirit of adoption* because he makes us children of God through Baptism and restores us to God's likeness by cleansing us of sin. We affirm in the Nicene Creed that the Holy Spirit is "the Lord, the giver of life"; he is the *Spirit of glory* because his grace makes us holy and leads us to the glory of heaven.

## THE HOLY SPIRIT IN THE NEW TESTAMENT LETTERS

Nearly every letter of the New Testament makes generous reference to the Holy Spirit, his gifts, his guidance, and his power in the Church. This is a short list of what the sacred authors teach about him:

- God's love is poured into our hearts through the Holy Spirit (Rom 5:5);
- The Holy Spirit guides our conscience (Rom 9:1);
- The Holy Spirit gives us hope, makes us holy, and produces signs and wonders (Rom 15:13-19);
- Our bodies are temples of the Holy Spirit (1 Cor 6:19)
- We are sealed for redemption by the Holy Spirit (Eph 1:13, 4:30);
- The Holy Spirit brings us joy (1 Thes 1:6);
- The Holy Spirit entrusts us with truth and dwells within us (2 Tm 1:14);
- The Holy Spirit distributes his gifts as he pleases (1 Cor 12:1-13; Heb 2:4).

to accomplish its mission. The Holy Spirit guides the Pope and bishops to properly govern the faithful.

Often the Holy Spirit is called the "soul of the Church." This reflects the role he has in giving life to the Church. As the Church is the Body of Christ, so the Holy Spirit is the soul that animates it and moves it to do God's will in this world. Individually, we cannot live the Christian life without the work of the Holy Spirit. Collectively, the Church cannot be faithful to Christ's command without the power of the Holy Spirit within her.

## CONCLUSION

The Holy Spirit, the Third Person of the Blessed Trinity, has been active in salvation history since the creation of the world. During the time of the Old Testament, his actions were veiled. But when Christ came, he revealed the Holy Spirit fully. Christ also promised that he would send the Holy Spirit after his Ascension. This occurred at Pentecost, ten days after Christ ascended into heaven.

When the Spirit descended upon the Apostles at Pentecost, they went out immediately to proclaim the Gospel with courage. The Holy Spirit calls all the baptized to pray and act, to seek deeper communion with God, and to help others find that communion as well. The gifts of the Holy Spirit in Confirmation will help you to do all this and more.

The Holy Spirit not only guides each individual follower of Christ, but he also guides the Church. He helps her teach the truth, sanctify her members, and govern wisely those entrusted to her care. The Church is the Body of Christ, and the Holy Spirit may be thought of as the "soul" of that Body, giving it life.

## POINTS TO REMEMBER

1. God is a Trinity of Persons: Father, Son, and Holy Spirit. The Holy Spirit is the Third Person of the Trinity who has been active throughout salvation history.
2. Christ revealed the Holy Spirit to the world during his life and mission, and promised the Holy Spirit would come after his Ascension. At Pentecost this was fulfilled when the Holy Spirit descended on the disciples.
3. The Holy Spirit is the soul of the Church, giving her life so that she may teach, sanctify, and govern the faithful.

## PRAYER TO THE HOLY SPIRIT

**Come Holy Spirit, fill the hearts of your faithful and kindle in them the fire of your love. Send forth your Spirit and they shall be created. And You shall renew the face of the earth.**

**O, God, who by the light of the Holy Spirit, did instruct the hearts of the faithful, grant that by the same Holy Spirit we may be truly wise and ever enjoy His consolations, Through Christ Our Lord, Amen.**

## SYMBOLS OF THE HOLY SPIRIT

We see in Scripture that the Holy Spirit uses everyday things such as fire, wind, water, and oil to show God's presence among his people.

***Cloud*** and ***light.*** In the Old Testament, the Spirit of God was present in the light-filled pillar of cloud that led and protected the Israelites on their journey to the Promised Land. The cloud also filled the tabernacle, a portable tent that represented the dwelling place of God. In a similar way in the New Testament, a bright, luminous cloud appeared during the Transfiguration of Christ. Both events portray the presence of the Holy Spirit.

***Wind.*** The presence of wind can be refreshing and pleasant. At other times it can be powerful and destructive. Christ referred to this unpredictable quality of wind:

> **The wind blows where it wills, and you hear the sound of it, but you do not know where it comes from or where it goes; so it is with every one who is born of the Spirit. (Jn 3:8)**

Wind is an especially appropriate symbol of the Holy Spirit because of what happened on the day of Pentecost. The Holy Spirit came upon the Apostles as "the rush of a mighty wind" that "filled all the house where they were sitting" (Acts 2:2).

***Fire.*** The transforming power of the Holy Spirit can be compared to a fire. Fire can destroy, but it can also refine and purify. Its power transforms whatever it touches. Likewise, when a person encounters the Holy Spirit, he or she is transformed. This aspect of the Holy Spirit was notable especially on the day of Pentecost:

> **There appeared to them tongues as of fire, distributed and resting on each one of them. And they were filled with the Holy Spirit and began to speak in other tongues, as the Spirit gave them utterance. (Acts 2:3-4)**

***Breath.*** Without breath, we cannot have life—it is essential to our existence. In this image we see the Holy Spirit as "the giver of life" (Nicene Creed). In Genesis we read that God created the first man and "breathed into his nostrils the breath of life" (Gn 2:7). This is the Holy Spirit. Christ breathed on his Apostles in order to give them the Holy Spirit and the power to forgive sins (Jn 20:22-23).

In the Old Testament, the Spirit of God was present in the light-filled pillar of cloud that led and protected the Israelites on their journey to the Promised Land.

***Water.*** Water is essential for life; without it life perishes. It refreshes and makes pure. In Baptism, where we first receive the Holy Spirit, water thus represents cleansing and new life. As St. Paul wrote,

> **By one Spirit we were all baptized into one body—Jews or Greeks, slaves or free—and all were made to drink of one Spirit. (1 Cor 12:13)**

***Anointing.*** The action of applying blessed oil is used at both Baptism and Confirmation as well as in Holy Orders and in the Anointing of the Sick. It is a symbol of strength and healing.

A ***hand.*** The laying on of hands, which is used in Confirmation and Holy Orders, invokes the Holy Spirit. When the priest extends his hands over the bread and wine at Mass, he asks the Holy Spirit to descend upon the gifts so that they may become the Body and Blood of Christ.

A ***dove.*** This image of peace and purity of heart refers to the appearance of the Holy Spirit in the form of a dove at the Baptism of the Lord in the Jordan River.

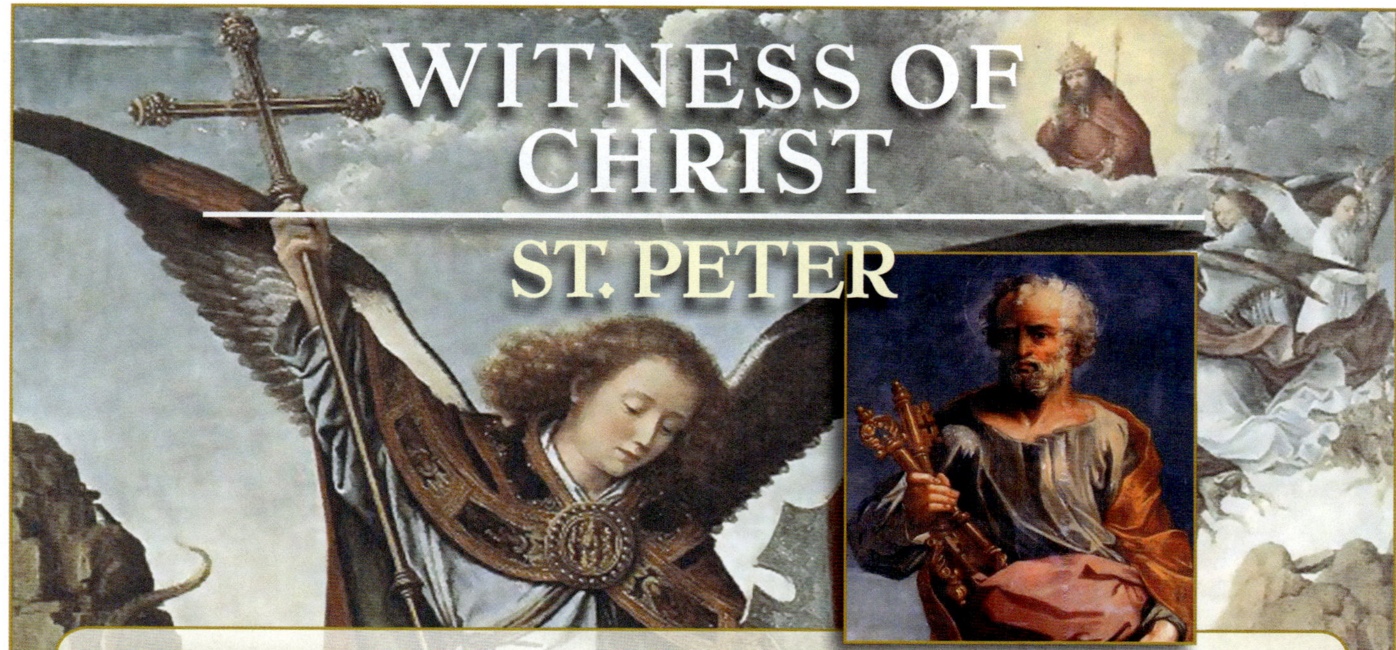

# WITNESS OF CHRIST

## ST. PETER

St. Peter is one of the most famous and influential Christians in history. It is unlikely anyone would have suspected his eventual fame and influence when he was growing up. However, the Holy Spirit entered his life and changed the direction of it forever.

St. Peter, born Simon, was the son of Jonah in Galilee and a fisherman. He probably had little formal schooling, because people in his level of society could not afford (and did not need) much education. From what we know about him, he must have been an outgoing, impulsive person from an early age. He was the type that was always the center of attention in any gathering.

One day Simon's brother Andrew introduced him to Jesus of Nazareth. Simon quickly decided to follow him (he decided everything quickly!), giving up his work as a fisherman to become one of Christ's Twelve Apostles. He came to love Jesus very much, and wanted nothing more than to serve him. One day, Jesus asked his Apostles who they thought he was. Some of the Apostles told him what other people thought about him. But then Simon spoke up and said, "You are the Christ, the Son of the living God." This was the first time someone declared that Jesus was the long-promised Messiah, and that he was the Son of God. In response, Jesus gave Simon a new name, "Peter," which means "rock," telling him, "on this rock I will build my church, and the powers of death shall not prevail against it" (Mt 16:18). Thus Christ made Peter the leader of the Apostles, and the first Pope.

Even as a leader, Peter was still confused at times regarding Christ's mission. When Christ was arrested, Peter denied three times that he even knew Jesus, something he deeply regretted later. After his Resurrection, Christ forgave Peter and entrusted him with the flock of his followers.

At Pentecost, Peter, like the other Apostles, received the Holy Spirit. In response, Peter preached a powerful sermon that attracted over 3,000 people to the Church. He then travelled the Roman Empire tirelessly telling people about Jesus Christ and urging them to repent and be baptized. Eventually, he ended up at Rome, becoming the head of the church there—the first Bishop of Rome. During a fierce persecution by the Roman authorities, he was arrested and sentenced to crucifixion. Not believing he was worthy to die as his Master had, he had the fortitude (courage) to ask to be crucified upside-down. His request was granted.

After Peter's death, the Church in Rome appointed a successor, who became the next Bishop of Rome and second Pope.

Peter's life shows clearly the effect the Holy Spirit can have on someone. From being a simple fisherman to the first Pope of the Universal Church, Peter allowed the Holy Spirit to guide him throughout his life.

## VOCABULARY

### ANOINTING

The application of oil to the body. This is a symbol of the Holy Spirit, whose anointing of Jesus as Christ fulfilled the Old Testament. Christ (in Hebrew, *Messiah*) means "Anointed One." This is the "matter" of Confirmation and the Anointing of the Sick, and it is one of the accompanying rites in Baptism and Holy Orders.

### CONSUBSTANTIAL

A Latin translation of the Greek *homoousios*, meaning "one and the same essence." The three Persons of the Trinity—Father, Son, and Holy Spirit—share the same divine nature. This is affirmed of Christ in relation to the Father in the Nicene Creed: "I believe in one Lord Jesus Christ... consubstantial with the Father."

### LAYING ON OF HANDS

The ritual act, going back to the Old Testament, whereby men were consecrated for sacred duties. From the New Testament onward, it has been the action used to ordain men to the priesthood, as well as to confer Confirmation.

## STUDY QUESTIONS

1. In one sentence, who is the Holy Spirit?
2. Where do we find the Holy Spirit at work in the Old Testament?
3. What was the meaning of *anointing* in the Old Testament?
4. What event revealed the three Persons of the Blessed Trinity for the first time?
5. How did the events of Pentecost change the Apostles?
6. What does the name "Counselor" reveal about the Holy Spirit?
7. What are the three principal ways the Holy Spirit guides the Church?
8. What does the title "Spirit of Truth" reveal about the Holy Spirit?
9. Why is the Holy Spirit sometimes called the "soul of the Church"?
10. Choose one of these symbols of the Holy Spirit: a cloud, wind, fire, or breath. Describe one event in which the Holy Spirit manifested himself this way.

## PRACTICAL EXERCISES

1. What symbol of the Holy Spirit is the most meaningful to you, and why? What does this symbol tell you about the Third Person of the Holy Trinity?

2. Think of a time that you asked the Holy Sprit to help you. (If you have not asked him to help you, set aside some time today to talk with him in prayer.) What did you request? Think of at least three ways you can call on the Holy Spirit in your daily life.

# You and Your Sponsor

***Talk to your sponsor about the symbols of the Holy Spirit.***

In this Chapter we read about the different symbols of the Holy Spirit, and we can better understand the role of the Holy Spirit in our Christian lives through some of the symbols associated with him: dove, cloud, light, water, anointing with oil, and others. Get together with your sponsor and talk about which symbols appeal most to each of you. Find passages in the Bible that use that symbol for the Holy Spirit and read them. In your discussion with your sponsor, consider the following questions:

1. What symbol for the Holy Spirit most appeals to you? Why?
2. How is that symbol used in the Bible? Is it used for things other than the Holy Spirit?
3. How does that symbol help you better understand the Holy Spirit and his role in your life?
4. How can you incorporate that symbol in your prayer and/or daily life?

During the Chrism Mass, Pope Francis *breathes* the Holy Spirit into the Sacred Chrism which will be used in the administration of the Sacraments of Baptism, Confirmation, and Holy Orders.

"And there appeared to them *tongues as of fire*, distributed and resting on each one of them. And they were all filled with the Holy Spirit..."

THE SACRAMENT OF

# Confirmation

Chapter 4

# THE CHURCH AS SACRAMENT OF SALVATION

## INTRODUCTION

***Christ founded his Church to continue his plan of salvation in the world.***

In continuing to prepare for Confirmation, you have come to see that you are part of God's great plan of salvation. This plan began when God created the human race. Adam and Eve sinned and lost God's friendship, yet God continued to reach out to his people and began preparing the human race for the Redeemer. You understand now that the Son of God, Jesus Christ, is the fullness of Divine Revelation.

Yet most people living in Christ's time did not hear the Good News of salvation from Christ himself. And many people who did hear the Gospel message from Christ either did not respond to it or simply rejected it. So, although Christ's mission was "finished," God is not finished saving mankind.

God's plan of salvation continued even after Christ ascended into heaven. At Pentecost God sent his Holy Spirit to be the soul of the Church. Followers of Christ, empowered by the Holy Spirit, teach the Gospel to others in order to extend Christ's work. That is why Christ established his Church, appointed his Apostles to govern and direct it, and gave them the power to continue his mission of salvation throughout the world. That also is why every follower of Christ—every one of us—is called to be his disciple, bringing others to know Christ and enter his Church through word and example.

The Church is the means by which each person can become a disciple of Christ. Christ established his Church to continue his work in the world and to be the sign and instrument of salvation to all.

*Christ Handing the Keys to St. Peter* by Perugino. Christ established his Church, appointed his Apostles to govern and direct it, and gave them the power to continue his mission of salvation throughout the world.

After reading this chapter, you will be able to answer these questions:

- How did God regather his people as one, and why does he call you to be part of his people?
- What does it mean to call the Church the "Sacrament of Salvation"?
- Why are the Sacraments important?
- What are the four marks of the Church?
- What is the hierarchy of the Church?

*The Last Supper* by Vouet.
The Seven Sacraments are visible signs, instituted by Christ and entrusted to the Church, that give grace to the person who receives them.

## REDEMPTION COMES TO US THROUGH THE SACRAMENTS

***The sacred signs that Christ gave to the Church dispense his saving grace to us.***

Signs and symbols are all around us, and these signs and symbols have meaning. For instance, we all have seen a stop sign, which tells the driver he must stop his car. The sign does not itself stop the car, but the driver understands that it means that he must stop. Signs point to deeper realities that perhaps cannot be seen directly. For example, when we are happy, we might smile or laugh. When we are deeply hurt or sad, we might cry. When we accomplish great things, we express pride and happiness. A laugh, a frown, and a look of joy all communicate something deeper and unseen.

Signs and symbols can also represent spiritual realities, and God often uses them to express his will. In the Old Testament God used visible signs to indicate his presence. He also directed his people to use signs as part of their covenant with him. Here are some examples:

- When God made his covenant with Noah, he put a rainbow in the sky as a sign that he would never destroy the earth by water again.
- When God established the Passover meal with Moses and the Israelites, he directed them to sacrifice an unblemished lamb and to sprinkle its blood on their doorposts.
- With Moses and the Israelites, God spoke through peals of thunder, fire, and smoke on Sinai. He manifested his presence in the cloud that guided his people by day and the pillar of fire that led them at night.
- Aaron, the priests, and the great kings were anointed with holy oil as a sign that the Spirit was upon them.

### Christ as a Sign

The greatest of these visible signs from God is Jesus Christ himself. When Christ came in the flesh, he made visible the invisible God.

**[Christ] is the image of the invisible God. (Col 1:15)**

Throughout the course of his earthly ministry, Christ used things like light, water, and salt to express the love of the Father.

Many of Christ's healings were performed through physical signs. Here are some examples:

- Christ laid hands on people who were sick or crippled to heal them.
- He healed a blind man by spitting onto the ground, making clay, rubbing it in the man's eyes, and instructing him to wash it off. (Jn 9:1-7)
- He used several signs as he healed a deaf man who had a speech impediment:

**[Jesus] put his fingers into his ears, and he spat and touched his tongue; and looking up to heaven, he sighed, and said to him, *"Ephphatha,"* that is, "Be opened." And his ears were opened, his tongue was released, and he spoke plainly. (Mk 7:33-35)**

## Sacraments as Signs

**The Church in this world is the sacrament of salvation, the sign and the instrument of the communion of God and men. (CCC 780)**

When we speak of God using physical signs to express spiritual realities, we say that God is acting "sacramentally." Broadly speaking, all of reality is sacramental in that God uses creation to direct people to himself. In this sense, the signs God gave in the Old Testament were sacramental.

God's greatest sacramental sign occurred when the Son of God took on flesh and became man. Jesus Christ is the living, ever-present Sacrament of God.

But we usually use the word "sacrament" in a more specific sense, meaning the seven specific signs which Christ left to his followers to express spiritual realities we cannot see. These are the Seven Sacraments. The Seven Sacraments are efficacious signs, instituted by Christ and entrusted to the Church, that give grace to the person who receives them.

**The sacraments are efficacious signs of grace, instituted by Christ and entrusted to the Church, by which divine life is dispensed to us. The visible rites by which the sacraments are celebrated signify and make present the graces proper to each sacrament. They bear fruit in those who receive them with the required dispositions. (CCC 1131)**

A Sacrament is a "sign" that not only can be seen and experienced but also actually gives the grace that it signifies. Put another way, a Sacrament is both a sign and an instrument of divine grace. Unlike a stop sign, which can only suggest what it symbolizes, a Sacrament performs what it symbolizes.

Every Sacrament includes a material sign (the *matter* of the Sacrament) and a spoken sign (the *form* of the Sacrament) that signify that Sacrament's spiritual effect on the soul. For example, water is the physical matter in Baptism—without water, you can't have a Baptism. This matter—water—is a sign of being cleansed of sin, for just as water cleanses the body, Baptism cleanses the soul of sin. The spoken form—"I baptize you in the name of the Father, and of the Son, and of the Holy Spirit"—signifies that the baptized person is entering into the Family of God. These signs show through our senses (sight, touch, hearing, etc.) what God does spiritually through the sign.

The Holy Spirit continues Christ's work through the Sacraments of the New Covenant he established.

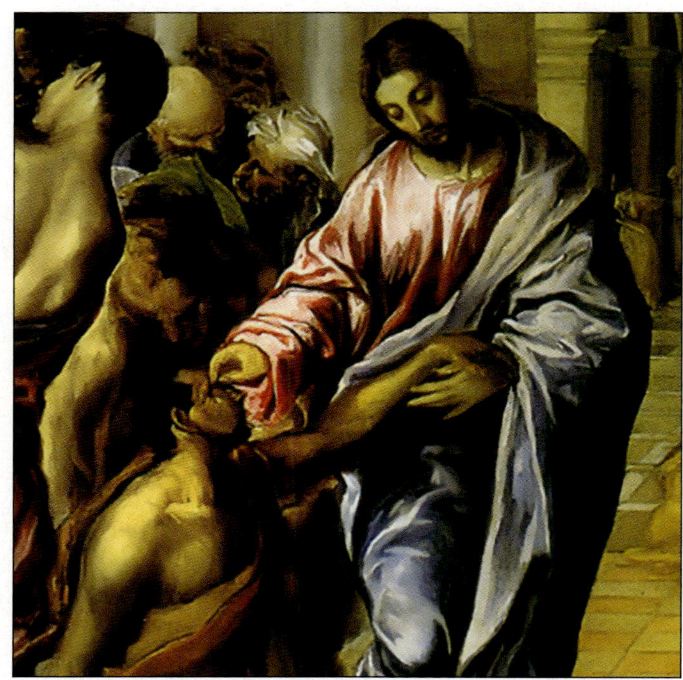

*Christ Healing the Blind Man* by El Greco.
Throughout the course of his earthly ministry, Christ used things like light, water, and salt to express the love of the Father.

Through the use of earthly things such as water, oil, bread, and wine, Christ infused these everyday signs with his very grace and power. By giving us the grace that they signify, the Sacraments help us increase in holiness, heal us, and give us spiritual nourishment to be faithful disciples.

Every one of the Seven Sacraments is an encounter with Christ, and each brings about an action Christ wants to perform in our lives. He brings us into the Church by the Sacrament of Baptism and later seals us with the Holy Spirit in Confirmation. He gives us his true Body and Blood as our spiritual food in the Sacrament of the Eucharist. He forgives our sins in the Sacraments of Penance and the Anointing of the Sick. He consecrates spouses in the Sacrament of Matrimony and ordains bishops, priests, and deacons in the Sacrament of Holy Orders. This is how Christ works through his Church to offer all people a participation in his divine life.

> **Sacraments are "powers that comes forth" from the Body of Christ, which is ever-living and life-giving. They are actions of the Holy Spirit at work in his Body, the Church. They are "the masterworks of God" in the new and everlasting covenant. (CCC 1115-1116)**

Each one of the Seven Sacraments carries with it unique gifts for the believer. Through the power of the Holy Spirit, physical signs like water, oil, bread, and wine are made into signs that give us divine life. Through the Holy Spirit, the Sacraments give us God's grace.

> **The mysteries of Christ's life are the foundations of what he would henceforth dispense in the sacraments, through the ministers of his Church, for "what was visible in our Savior has passed over into his mysteries." (CCC 1115)**

Christ brings us into the Church by the Sacrament of Baptism and later seals us with the Holy Spirit in Confirmation.

## NATURAL LIFE AND SUPERNATURAL LIFE

| | NATURAL | SUPERNATURAL |
|---|---|---|
| **Individuals** | Birth | Baptism |
| | Food for nourishment | Eucharist |
| | Strength for adulthood | Confirmation |
| | Medicine for healing | Reconciliation |
| | Serious illness needs special care | Anointing of the Sick |
| **Church** | Community leaders | Holy Orders |
| | Families / communities; new generations: Marriage was instituted by God in the natural order of creation, and Christ elevated it to the level of a Sacrament and therefore to the supernatural life | Matrimony |

## LITURGY

At church or in your reading you have probably heard or read the word ***liturgy***. The Mass is also sometimes called the Eucharistic Liturgy, and Eastern Catholics call it the Divine Liturgy. Further, the two parts of the Mass are called the Liturgy of the Word and the Liturgy of the Eucharist. Priests in the Church are obligated to pray the Liturgy of the Hours, which are psalms and other prayers that are compiled together and said many times daily.

But what is ***liturgy***?

> **The mission of the Holy Spirit in the liturgy of the Church is to prepare the assembly to encounter Christ; to recall and manifest Christ to the faith of the assembly; to make the saving work of Christ present and active by his transforming power; and to make the gift of communion bear fruit in the Church. (CCC 1112)**

The word liturgy comes from the Greek word for "public work" or "service done on behalf of the people." Christians use it to refer to the participation of the faithful in the "work of God." In the early Church it referred not only to the worship of the faithful but also to the preaching of the Gospel and to performing acts of charity. All of these actions are the work of God because Christ mandated that his Church do these things in his name after the Ascension and his sending of the Holy Spirit at Pentecost.

Today, "liturgy" is applied to the worship of the Church: the Mass, celebrations of the Sacraments, and other formal prayers. In every liturgy Christ works and acts through his Church using signs and rites. The liturgy is an exercise of the priesthood of Christ, who continues the work of our redemption in and through his Church.

> **"In the earthly liturgy we share in a foretaste of that heavenly liturgy which is celebrated in the Holy City of Jerusalem toward which we journey as pilgrims, where Christ is sitting at the right hand of God, Minister of the sanctuary and of the true tabernacle. (CCC 1090)**

> **In this sacramental dispensation of Christ's mystery the Holy Spirit acts in the same way as at other times in the economy of salvation: he prepares the Church to encounter her Lord; he recalls and makes Christ manifest to the faith of the assembly. By his transforming power, he makes the mystery of Christ present here and now. (CCC 1092)**

Another word often used in conjunction with liturgy is the word ***rite***. This word has two meanings:

- Rite can refer to an approved and official form that a liturgy takes. In this sense, the ***Rite*** of Confirmation includes the Renewal of Baptismal Promises, the Laying on of Hands, the anointing with Chrism, and so on.
- Rite can also refer to one of the groups of the Church's rich liturgical tradition. In this sense, the Antiochian ***Rite*** is based on the forms of worship and spirituality that developed around the ancient city of Antioch. (See "Different Ways to Celebrate the Sacraments," p. 78)

The Mass is sometimes called the Eucharistic Liturgy. Eastern Catholics call it the Divine Liturgy.

## THE SACRAMENT OF SALVATION

***The Church is a sign and instrument of the communion between God and humankind.***

One of the primary consequences of the Fall was that **communion** between God and mankind was severed. No longer did men and women have a direct relationship with God. We read in the previous chapter how God, through a series of covenants, worked to restore this communion. In each successive covenant, he regathers a larger group of people into union with him:

| Covenant Mediator | Covenant Group |
|---|---|
| Adam | Marriage |
| Noah | Household |
| Abraham | Family |
| Moses | Nation |
| David | Kingdom |

Through the final covenant, in which Christ himself is the covenant mediator, God himself restores and even elevates the communion between himself and the whole human race through the **Church**. The Church that he established fulfills all the Old Testament promises and prophecies about God gathering his people together as one. For this reason, the Church is also called the "new Israel" (CCC 877). She is God's people of the New Covenant in Christ.

The Church is where our communion with God is restored and even elevated to a new level. The Church becomes the sign and instrument of salvation for the world. For this reason the *Catechism* calls the Church "the great sacrament of divine communion which gathers God's scattered children together" (CCC 1108). Another term for the Church, in fact, is the **Sacrament of Salvation**.

We are familiar with the Seven Sacraments, which include Baptism and Confirmation. But why do we call the Church herself a "sacrament"?

Let us remember our definition of "sacrament"—it is an efficacious sign instituted by Christ to give grace to the one who receives it; it is both a sign and an instrument of divine grace.

### DIFFERENT WAYS TO CELEBRATE THE SACRAMENTS

The Catholic Church is blessed with many liturgical rites, all of which contribute to the richness of the Church as a whole. Most Catholics worldwide worship according to the Roman (or Western) Rite, which has its origins in the city of Rome. There are also many Eastern rites of the Church, celebrated by Catholics primarily in Eastern Europe, the Middle East, India, and Northern Africa.

> **These individual Churches...are consequently of equal dignity, so that none of them is superior to the others as regards rite. (*Orientalium Ecclesiarum* 3)**

The liturgical practices of both the West and the East have ancient traditions that go back to the Apostles. The devotions, customs, and culture of the Roman Rite developed in Western Europe around Rome. The devotions, customs, and culture of the Eastern rites developed in Eastern Europe, the Middle East, and the Near East around cities such as Constantinople, Antioch, Alexandria, and Jerusalem.

All the rites of the Church are fully legitimate. Individual Catholics, no matter their primary rite, are free to receive the Eucharist, the Sacrament of Confession, and the Anointing of the Sick in any of these Catholic rites. The other Sacraments should be received in the rite to which a person belongs.

> **Eastern Catholics refer to the Sacraments as the "Holy Mysteries." The word *mystery* emphasizes Christ's saving action that is effected through each Sacrament, while the word *sacrament* emphasizes the visible sign that houses Christ's action. (CCC 774)**

*The Divine Liturgy in a Greek-Catholic church in Slovakia.* The liturgical practices of both the West and the East have ancient traditions that go back to the Apostles.

The Church, too, is both a *sign* and an instrument. She is a sign of our communion with God because within the Church we are gathered and united as one in communion with him and with one another. She is an *instrument* of our communion with God because through her we receive the Seven Sacraments, which give us divine life.

The Church is the means by which Christ dispenses his grace through the Holy Spirit, because Christ entrusted the Sacraments to his Church. Although not counted as one of the Seven Sacraments, the Church is a sacrament herself—a sign and instrument of God's grace. It is through the Church that our communion with God is restored.

> **The Holy Spirit, whom Christ the head pours out on his members, builds, animates, and sanctifies the Church. She is the sacrament of the Holy Trinity's communion with men. (CCC 747)**

## APOLOGETICS 101:

### THE SACRAMENTS

(Adapted from the *Didache Bible*)

#### *Why did Christ institute the Sacraments as a means of conveying grace?*

> **Jesus came and said to [the eleven disciples]... "Go therefore and make disciples of all nations, baptizing them in the name of the Father and of the Son and of the Holy Spirit." (Mt 28:19)**
>
> **[Jesus] took bread, and when he had given thanks he broke it and gave it to them, saying, "This is my body which is given for you. Do this in remembrance of me." (Lk 22:19)**

God surely can—and does—dispense his grace as he sees fit in countless ways, and he is by no means restricted to the Sacraments that he instituted. Yet Christ instituted Seven Sacraments that he directed his Church to use as special avenues of grace.

By nature every person is composed of two elements: body and soul—a material, visible body and a spiritual, invisible soul. As St. Thomas Aquinas explained, human beings are led by things that are physical, things that can be seen and experienced by the senses.

We thus have a fundamental need for ritual, for visible expressions of what cannot be seen. We also have a natural need to "ritualize" the significant events and realities in our lives. This is why we have graduation ceremonies, awards banquets, family dinners on holidays, and national days of remembrance. Each of these rituals celebrates something intangible but important in our lives: achievement, gratitude, or patriotism.

Utilizing this aspect of our humanity, Christ instituted the Sacraments to confer grace through physical signs. The Sacraments give form to spiritual "events" and serve as signs of deeper realities. The chief difference with the Sacraments is that, unlike merely human rituals, the very act of administering a Sacrament, body and soul, confers the grace that is signified by the act just as Christ intends. As St. Leo the Great explained, "What was visible in our Savior has passed over into his mysteries" (Sermo., 74, 2: PL 54, 398).

The Sacraments also serve to express the faith that is within us—both individually and as a community—and to provide a model and instruction to help us grow in faith. Sacramental signs and rites convey something about what we believe, and their visible expression reinforces those beliefs in others and within ourselves.

## SANCTIFYING GRACE AND ACTUAL GRACE

Grace is a free and undeserved gift from God that allows us to participate in God's own life. It is necessary to receive grace to follow God and be with him forever in heaven.

> **Grace is *favor,* the free and undeserved help that God gives us to respond to his call to become children of God, adoptive sons, partakers of the divine nature and of eternal life. (CCC 1996)**

Through grace:

- We have forgiveness of our sins and are made holy.
- We become a new creation.
- We are able to participate in the life of the Blessed Trinity.
- We are able to call upon God as Father.
- We are led through this world and into eternal life.

Grace comes to us in two primary forms: sanctifying grace and actual grace.

**Sanctifying grace** is received in the Sacraments through the power of the Holy Spirit. The *Catechism* describes sanctifying grace as a "stable and supernatural disposition that perfects the soul itself to enable it to live with God, to act by his love" (CCC 2000). This divine life is so different from human experience that St. Paul calls it a "new creation" (2 Cor 5:17).

> **Sanctifying grace is the gratuitous gift of his life that God makes to us; it is infused by the Holy Spirit into the soul to heal it of sin and to sanctify it. (CCC 2023)**

Sanctifying grace is necessary for salvation. It is sometimes called ***habitual grace*** because it helps us build up virtues (holy habits) to choose good over evil. Having sanctifying grace, however, does not mean that we are unable to sin. In spite of the grace we receive in the Sacraments, we continue to sin and experience difficulties and doubts about our faith. But sanctifying grace helps us to battle against these temptations.

Sanctifying grace is weakened in the soul by minor sins against God, called ***venial sins***. Sanctifying grace is lost through ***mortal sins***, which are serious sins against God. A person who chooses mortal sin separates him- or herself from God and his divine love.

The Sacrament of Penance restores sanctifying grace in our souls and repairs our relationship with God. The Church recommends frequent Confession to keep grace in our souls and to avoid future sins. This Sacrament also keeps smaller sins from growing into more serious ones.

**Actual grace** is the grace that God gives us to strengthen us at particular moments when we are tempted to do evil—to commit an actual sin—or when we want to do something virtuous. Like sanctifying grace, actual grace is received in the Sacraments, but it can also be received in many other ways, such as through praying, performing good works, or asking for it.

> **God also acts through many actual graces, to be distinguished from habitual grace which is permanent in us. (CCC 2024)**

Actual grace does not force us to choose good over evil; rather, it helps us to choose the good.

It is necessary to receive grace to follow God and be with him forever in heaven. *Sanctifying grace* is received in the Sacraments through the power of the Holy Spirit.

## GRACE *Continued*

Actual grace can be received by performing good works.

Actual grace is freely given and is available to every person. When we rely on God's help, especially when we are tempted, he will give us the grace that we need when we encounter larger temptations.

Sanctifying grace is permanent; it can only be lost by sin. Actual grace is a help from God, a boost. It's temporary, but constantly renewable.

Sanctifying and actual graces are sent to us through a variety of means. Primary among them are ***sacramental graces***, which are gifts proper to each Sacrament.

> **The Church affirms that for believers the sacraments of the New Covenant are necessary for salvation. "Sacramental grace" is the grace of the Holy Spirit, given by Christ and proper to each sacrament. The Spirit heals and transforms those who receive him by conforming them to the Son of God. The fruit of the sacramental life is that the Spirit of adoption makes the faithful partakers in the divine nature by uniting them in a living union with the only Son, the Savior. (CCC 1129)**

For example, one first receives sanctifying grace through the Sacrament of Baptism. If sanctifying grace is later lost through mortal sin, one can have it restored through the Sacrament of Penance. Through other Sacraments, one can receive actual graces to live a good and holy life.

Further, God gives graces through prayer, our good works, and other means. In a wonderful mystery, God gives us the grace to be holy, and by being holy, we receive more grace!

# THE MARKS OF THE CHURCH

***The Church of Christ can be recognized by its four defining characteristics.***

Christ founded one Church nearly 2,000 years ago, which by God's grace has spread throughout the world. Unfortunately, since then divisions among Christians have arisen over matters of doctrine or leadership. Because of these disagreements, groups of Christians over the years have broken away from the Church. They established other communities of faith that reflect their own beliefs.

Here are examples of two of the largest groups of non-Catholic Christians:

- The Eastern Orthodox Churches broke away from the Catholic Church in the eleventh century. Although separated from the Catholic Church, these churches have the Seven Sacraments. The Catholic Church recognizes these Sacraments as valid. However, these Churches differ from the Catholic Church in that they do not fully accept Catholic teaching regarding the authority of the Pope.
- The Protestant ecclesial communities broke away from the Catholic Church beginning in the sixteenth century. They rejected most of Catholic doctrine, and some of the Sacraments, and also rejected the authority of the Pope and the Catholic bishops.

Do you think Christ wants his followers to be divided like this? To find the answer, consider Christ's prayer the night before he died:

> **Jesus lifted up his eyes to heaven and said… "Holy Father, keep them in thy name, which thou hast given me, that they may be one, even as we are one." (Jn 17:1, 11)**

Christ founded one Church, and he wants all people to become part of that communion. But with all the different Christian groups in the world today, how can we know which is the true Church founded by Christ? The early Christians distinguished four marks, or defining characteristics, of Christ's Church: the Church is *One*, *Holy*, *Catholic*, and *Apostolic*. These are called the **marks of the Church**.

### "Church" in the New Testament

In the New Testament the original Greek word often used to refer to the Christian community is *ekklesia*, which means "assembly" or "what is called together." Its root means "to call out [from a larger group]." This was the same word that those who translated the Old Testament into Greek used to describe the assembly of the Israelites at Mt. Sinai when God made his covenant with Moses.

*Ekklesia* expresses the Church's mission to "call out" all peoples of all nations in order to gather them into the kingdom. This Old Testament prophecy expressed well the idea of "calling out":

> **It shall come to pass in the latter days**
> **that the mountain of the house**
> **of the Lord**
> **shall be established as the highest of the**
> **mountains,**
> **and shall be raised up above the hills;**
> **and peoples shall flow to it,**
> **and many nations shall come, and say:**
> **"Come, let us go up to the mountain**
> **of the Lord,**
> **to the house of the God of Jacob;**
> **that he may teach us his ways**
> **and we may walk in his paths." (Mi 4:1-2)**

Another Greek word was used to refer to the Christian community: *kyriake* ("belongs to the Lord"). This is the source of our modern words for the Family of God: in Scottish, *kirk*; in German, *kirche*; and in English, *church*.

These four marks of the Church should sound familiar to you. They are in the Nicene Creed, which is the creed usually prayed at Mass on Sundays. "I believe in one holy, catholic, and apostolic Church" (*Roman Missal*, The Order of Mass, no. 18). The marks of the Church describe some of the essential elements of the Church and her mission.

The Church is One, Holy, Catholic, and Apostolic because of Christ her founder, who gives her these traits and calls her to perfect them, and the Holy Spirit empowers the Church to do so.

> **The Church is ultimately one, holy, catholic, and apostolic in her deepest and ultimate identity, because it is in her that "the Kingdom of heaven," the "Reign of God" (Rev 19:6), already exists and will be fulfilled at the end of time. (CCC 865)**

Let us look at each of the marks of the Church.

## The Church Is One

> **Unity is of the essence of the Church. (CCC 813)**

Christ established one Church, and he desires that all people be united in it. As he prayed to his Father at the Last Supper: "Holy Father, keep them in thy name, which thou hast given me, that they may be one, even as we are one" (Jn 17:11).

What is this *oneness*? It means the members of the Church are united with one another and with the Blessed Trinity. It does not mean that every member of the Church agrees with every other member on every possible subject. But it does mean that there is one set of teachings on faith and morals that are considered "Catholic," and there is only one hierarchy of bishops and one Pope to whom we are all united.

> **There is one body and one Spirit, just as you were called to the one hope that belongs to your call, one Lord, one faith, one baptism, one God and Father of us all, who is above all and through all and in all. (Eph 4:4-6)**

## The Church Is Holy

> **The Church…is "the holy People of God," and her members are called "saints." (CCC 823)**

When we say "the Church is Holy," does that mean we think every person in the Church is holy? No.

The Church is called "Holy" because she is the Mystical Body of Christ, and Christ is the source of all holiness. Further, it is through the Church, particularly the Sacraments, that men and women have the ability to become holy—to become saints.

## The Church Is Catholic

> **First, the Church is catholic because Christ is present in her...In her subsists the fullness of Christ's body united with its head...Secondly, the Church is catholic because she has been sent out by Christ on a mission to the whole of the human race. (CCC 830-831)**

The word "catholic" was used to describe the Church very early in her history—it means "universal." What does it mean that the Church is universal? First, the Church is universal in that she is the means to salvation for all people, no matter their race, sex or nation. Also, the Church is universal because she contains the complete Deposit of Faith—the full means to salvation. There is nothing that one needs for salvation that must be found outside the Catholic Church.

## The Church Is Apostolic

> **The whole Church is apostolic, in that she remains, through the successors of St. Peter and the other apostles, in communion of faith and life with her origin: and in that she is "sent out" into the whole world. (CCC 863)**

Christ founded the Church on the Twelve Apostles. He called them to go and preach the Gospel to all nations. "As the Father has sent me, even so I send you" (Jn 20:21).

The foundation and authority that Christ gave to his Apostles did not end with the death of the last Apostle. This authority was "handed on" to their successors, the bishops. One example of this is when St. Peter stood up among the disciples and declared that another disciple must take the office that had been held by Judas. Through the casting of lots, St. Matthias was chosen to fill Judas's place. He received the same authority that the other Apostles possessed.

This **Apostolic Succession** will continue until Christ's return.

# THE CHURCH IS THE BODY OF CHRIST

***Members of the Church make up the one Body of Christ.***

Over the years Christians have used many images and symbols to describe the Church. Some of them come from Jesus himself. The "People of God," the "sheepfold," the "temple of God," or the "vineyard" are some examples. One of the most common images is the "Body of Christ." Amazingly, the phrase "Body of Christ" is more than just a way of speaking. It is a reality, one that is a mystery. A mystery, in this sense, is something that is real, but cannot be fully understood.

By entering into profound communion with Christ through Baptism by the power of the Holy Spirit, we become part of his Body:

> **Just as the body is one and has many members, and all the members of the body, though many, are one body, so it is with Christ. For by one Spirit we were baptized into one body—Jews or Greeks, slaves or free—and all were made to drink of one Spirit. (1 Cor 12:12-13)**

## ECUMENISM

On the night of the Last Supper, Christ prayed for his disciples: "Holy Father, keep them in your name, which you have given me, that they may be one, even as we are one" (Jn 17:11). Sadly, this unity has been splintered through sin on the part of her members.

In keeping with the will of Christ, the Church seeks to reunite all Christian communities in the one Church. The effort to achieve Christian unity is called ***ecumenism***. It is part of our obligation as Christians to work toward the unity desired by Christ.

There are many things the Church can do in order to help make Christian unity a reality. Among these are personal conversion, prayer, mutual respect and knowledge, formation in Christian unity, theological dialogue, and collaboration with other Christians in works of service.

*The Last Supper* by Bloch.
The Holy Spirit is the lifeblood, the inner driving force, of the Body of Christ.

The image of the Body of Christ emphasizes our unity with Christ and with our fellow believers. Christ is the Head of this Body, and we are its parts, or members. Just as each part of a body has a different function—hand, ear, foot, lung, and so on—every member of the Church has a role to play in the work of the Church. Christ, as Head, directs this work. The Holy Spirit is the lifeblood, the inner driving force, of this Body. Further, because the Church is the Body of Christ, we should love the Church as we love Christ.

When we use our gifts according to the will of the Father, we allow the kingdom to become more visible in the world. We, as followers of Christ, thereby become signs of his love and presence in the world. We become, in a sense, "sacraments" ourselves!

In the Eucharist we share in the true Body, Blood, Soul, and Divinity of Christ, which unites us more closely with Christ and with the rest of the Church. As St. Paul wrote:

> **Because there is one bread, we who are many are one body, for we all partake of the one bread. (1 Cor 10:17)**

## THE HIERARCHY OF THE CHURCH

***The Pope, bishops, and priests lead by their service to the People of God.***

The word "church" can mean different things in different contexts. The building in which the liturgy is celebrated is a *church*, we call our parish "our *church*," and the diocese is considered the local *church*.

But when we speak of "the Church," we mean the universal Catholic Church, the entire Body of Christ throughout the world. When we speak of what "the Church" teaches, we refer to the teaching authority given by Christ to that universal Church.

This authority rests on the Deposit of Faith—Sacred Scripture and Sacred Tradition. It is communicated to the faithful by the Pope and the bishops of the Catholic Church in union with him, who are the successors of St. Peter and the Apostles. They, along with the priests, constitute the **hierarchy** (governing authority) of the Catholic Church.

The bishops of the Church, with the Pope as their head, constitute the Magisterium, or teaching authority of the Church. As we learned in Chapter 1, the Magisterium preserves the Deposit of Faith and teaches with Christ's own authority, carrying out his mission of preaching the Gospel throughout the world.

Christ established the hierarchy of his Church during his earthly ministry. He selected the Twelve Apostles as his "inner circle" of disciples. He taught them and invited them to travel with him as he ministered to many people. He sent them out to preach and heal, and he gave them the power and authority to baptize, forgive sins, and consecrate the bread and wine that become his own Body and Blood in the Eucharist. He gave them the mission to make disciples of all nations. He guaranteed that the Holy Spirit would always be with the Church ensuring that she would always teach the truth.

Christ also appointed St. Peter to be the head of the Apostles and chief shepherd of the flock. Christ said to him:

> **"I tell you, you are Peter, and on this rock I will build my church, and the powers of death shall**

**not prevail against it. I will give you the keys of the kingdom of heaven, and whatever you bind on earth shall be bound in heaven, and whatever you loose on earth shall be loosed in heaven." (Mt 16:18-19)**

St. Peter is the first Pope of the Catholic Church. The Pope has been the visible source of unity among the bishops and all the Catholic faithful throughout the centuries.

## A Hierarchy of Service

Because men who have received the Sacrament of Holy Orders comprise the Catholic hierarchy, each of them has particular powers and authority. The Catholic hierarchy, however, is not about power. It is about serving the Church and the world. Bishops and priests exist to govern and administer the Church, to help lead the people to holiness, and to teach and preach the truths of the faith. They are at the service of the faithful. In fact, one of the titles of the Pope is "Servant of the Servants of God."

Remember the image of the Church as the Body of Christ. Every part of the body has a role to play for the good of the entire body. Even when roles are different, they all are essential and must cooperate toward their common mission. As the *Catechism* teaches:

**There exists among all the Christian faithful a true equality with regard to dignity and the activity whereby all cooperate in the building up the Body of Christ in accord with each one's own condition and function. (CCC 872)**

Every Christian must use the gifts and circumstances that God gives him or her to seek holiness and serve others. Everyone has a part to play in helping to build up the Kingdom of God.

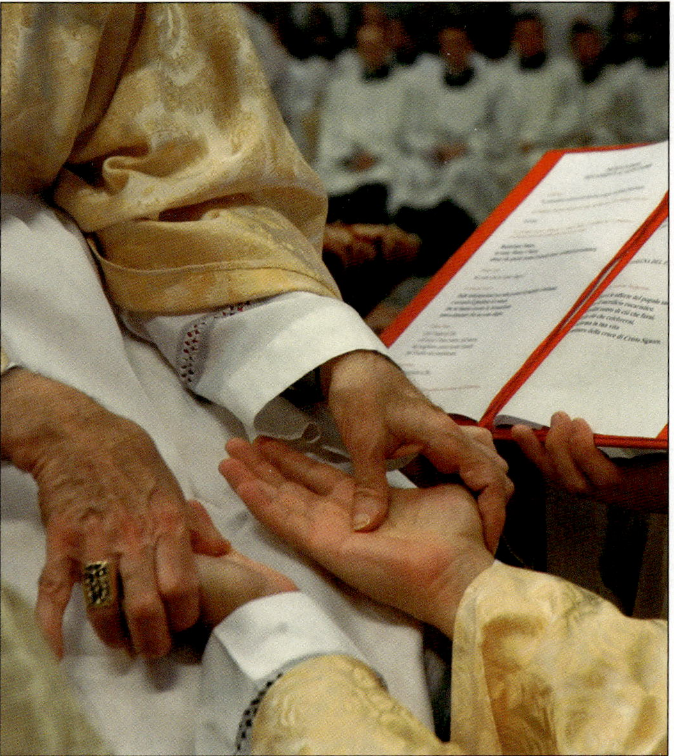

*The Sacrament of Holy Orders…a new priest is ordained.* Christ guaranteed that the Holy Spirit would always be with the Church ensuring that she would always teach the truth.

### THE CARDINALS OF THE CHURCH

**A cardinal is a bishop or priest appointed by the Pope to be his special advisor and to carry out certain special duties. The Pope may consult his cardinals on issues of importance to the whole Church. Oftentimes a cardinal is also an archbishop of an archdiocese or is given a position at the Vatican, the central administrative center for the Church.**

**One important task of the cardinals is to meet to elect a new Pope whenever a Pope dies or resigns. After Pope Benedict XVI resigned in 2013, the cardinals gathered in solemn prayer and discussion to elect Cardinal Jorge Bergoglio as Pope Francis.**

In 2013, the cardinals gathered to elect Cardinal Jorge Bergoglio as Pope Francis.

## CONCLUSION

**Since the Church is in Christ like a sacrament or as a sign and instrument both of a very closely knit union with God and of the unity of the whole human race, it desires now to unfold more fully to the faithful of the Church and to the whole world its own inner nature and universal mission. (*LG* 1)**

The Church is called the Sacrament of Salvation because she is both a sign and an instrument of grace. Through her sacred mission, the Good News is communicated throughout the world. Until the end of time she will, by the power of the Holy Spirit, continue that mission of inviting every person to enter the Church by accepting the gift of redemption won for us through Jesus Christ. By entering into the Church, the believer enters into the Body of Christ.

The Church is One, Holy, Catholic, and Apostolic. These marks of the Church direct our attention to the unity and holiness that we are all called to share in the Kingdom of God. United to Christ, the Church is a visible witness of the love of the Father.

Christ commissioned his Apostles to go out and preach the Gospel to all nations. Through the celebration of the Sacraments we encounter Christ and have access to his sanctifying grace. In this manner, Christ's saving work is continued in the world today.

We might tend to limit our idea of the Church as only the visible Church on earth. In reality, the Church is currently made up of members in three different states or conditions:

- The ***Church Militant*** is comprised of Christ's faithful here on earth.
- The ***Church Suffering*** is comprised of the souls in purgatory who have died in communion with God, but have not been fully purified.
- The ***Church Triumphant*** is comprised of the glorified members in heaven, enjoying the beatific vision forever.

Yet the Church is one. Christ unites each member of the Church to himself and all to one another. This is what is called the ***Communion of Saints***.

United to Christ, the Church is a visible witness of the love of the Father.

## POINTS TO REMEMBER

1. Redemption comes to us through the Church, who administers the Sacraments, which uses efficacious signs to communicate grace and draw us into communion with God.
2. The Church is called the Sacrament of Salvation because the saving mission of Christ continues through her.
3. The Church is One, Holy, Catholic, and Apostolic. These are called the marks of the Church.
4. When Christ established his Church, he chose the Apostles, with St. Peter as their head, to lead it. Their successors, the bishops, as well as those clerics who assist them—priests and deacons—make up the hierarchy of the Church.

# Witness of Christ

## St. John Paul II

Karol Wojtyla was born in Poland in 1920, the youngest of three children. In his early life, Wojtyla had to face many hardships. His mother died when he was only 8 years old. When he was 19, his country was invaded by Nazi Germany. After World War II was over, Poland was under the control of the atheist communist Soviet Union, which restricted the freedom of Catholics.

In spite of this, Wojtyla secretly studied to become a priest, and was ordained in 1946 at the age of 26. As a priest he worked both in a parish and at a university as a professor. After just twelve years he was ordained a bishop at the age of 38, making him the youngest bishop in Poland at the time. He participated in the Second Vatican Council, a worldwide gathering of bishops intended to express the truths of the Catholic faith to the modern world. Even though he was one of the youngest bishops in attendance, he was influential in many of the Council's decisions and writings.

Wojtyla continued as bishop in Poland, becoming the Archbishop of Krakow in 1964. In 1968 he was elevated to cardinal. However, his rise in the Church was not yet complete.

In August 1978 Pope St. Paul VI died, and Wojtyla was part of the conclave that elected the new Pope, John Paul I. However, Pope John Paul I died after only 33 days in office, and Wojtyla had to return to Rome to elect another Pope. This time, however, he was elected Pope! In honor of his predecessor, he chose the name John Paul II. He became the first non-Italian Pope in over 450 years.

As Pope, John Paul II was known for traveling the world to preach the Gospel to all peoples.

Possessing a great intellect, he wrote many important philosophical and theological works. This great intellect did not hinder him from relating to others; instead it allowed him to understand others and identify with them. He particularly cared for youth, establishing World Youth Days so that young people from around the world could gather together and celebrate their Catholic faith. When he went to the World Youth Day in the Philippines in 1995, over 5 million people attended!

Pope John Paul II worked tirelessly to teach the world a better way to live. He condemned Nazism and the atheist system of communism which made people objects of the State. He also warned of the dangers of an unchecked capitalism which could lead people to value possessions more than the good of their fellow man. He vigorously struggled against what he called the "culture of death," which promotes abortion, euthanasia, contraception, and other sins against life. In opposition to the culture of death he preached a "Gospel of Life." He showed how to live with courage and have a Christian attitude toward suffering, especially during the last years of his life.

Pope John Paul II reigned for more than 26 years, making him one of the longest-reigning Popes in history. When he died in 2005, people from around the world and of many religions mourned his death, and many in Rome chanted "*Santo Subito!*" meaning "[Make him a] saint now!" He was canonized a saint on April 27, 2014 by Pope Francis.

# VOCABULARY

### ACTUAL GRACE

This supernatural, free, and undeserved help from God is given for specific circumstances to help us choose what is good and avoid what is evil.

### APOSTOLIC SUCCESSION

The truth that the bishops today can trace their authority in a direct line back to the Apostles and ultimately from Christ himself, each consecrated a bishop by another bishop by the laying on of hands.

### COMMUNION

From the Latin *communio,* "mutual participation" or "oneness together," a translation of the Greek *koinonia*. In the sense of Holy Communion, the reception of the Body and Blood of Christ in the Eucharist; in the sense of fellowship, the bond of union with Christ and all baptized, faithful Christians in the Church.

### ECUMENISM

The task of healing the divisions and separations that afflict Christianity and restoring true unity as one Church. Also, cooperation among Christian faith traditions in achieving common goals.

### HABITUAL GRACE

An infused gift of the Holy Spirit by which a person receives the divine life of God in one's soul. This grace is also called "sanctifying" grace and through it a person receives the three theological virtues of faith, hope, and charity. Habitual grace enables one to live as a true disciple of Christ.

### HIERARCHY

From the Greek *hierarchia* ("sacred order"), the order of teaching authority in the Church, given by Christ himself, with the Pope as its head, followed by bishops, priests, and deacons.

### MARKS OF THE CHURCH

The four identifiable characteristics of the Church: unity, holiness, catholicity, and apostolicity. We affirm this when we pray in the Nicene Creed at Mass, "We believe in one, holy, catholic, and apostolic Church."

### MORTAL SIN

A grave offense against God that destroys a person's relationship with him by severing him or her from divine love. It destroys charity in the heart of man; it turns man away from God, who is his ultimate end and his beatitude, by preferring an inferior good to him.

### SACRAMENT OF SALVATION

Describes the Church as Christ's instrument of grace in the world through which God offers his redemption. The Church is the visible plan of God's love for humanity, and promotes the inner union of humanity with God.

### SANCTIFYING GRACE

The free and unmerited favor of God given through the Sacraments. This heals human nature wounded by sin by giving man a share in the divine life infused into the soul by the Holy Spirit. This grace is also called "habitual" grace, and through it a person received the three theological virtues of faith, hope, and charity. Such grace enables one to live as a true disciple of Christ.

### VENIAL SIN

An offense against the law and love of God that does not deprive the soul of sanctifying grace. It does, however, weaken a person's love for God and neighbor.

## STUDY QUESTIONS

1. What is a Sacrament?
2. What is sanctifying grace, and what is actual grace?
3. How does the Church relate to the people of Israel?
4. What does it mean to say that the Church is the Sacrament of Salvation?
5. What does it mean to say that the Church is *One*?
6. What does it mean to say that the Church is *Holy*?
7. In what two ways is the Church *Catholic*?
8. What does it mean to say that the Church is *Apostolic*?
9. How do the baptized make up Christ's Body?
10. Explain the role of St. Peter in the Church.

## PRACTICAL EXERCISES

1. Your friend, a non-Catholic Christian, has questions about the Catholic Church. She wants to know why Catholics think that the Catholic Church is the one Church that Christ established. How would you explain the four marks of the Church to her?

2. Do some research and find out when the current Pope was elected. How long were the cardinals in conclave deciding on the new Pope? Learn what the Pope's name was before his election, and why he chose the name he did after his election. Where was he a bishop before becoming Pope?

"The grace operating in young people paves the way for the Church's progress as regards both her expansion and her quality." —St. John Paul II

# Sealed in the Spirit

***Confirmation deepens your communion with God and with the Church.***

What is your status as a member of the Catholic Church? By receiving the Sacrament of Confirmation, you will be sealed in the Holy Spirit. Some people make the mistake of thinking that being a member of the Church is similar to being a member of a sports team or a choir. But to be a baptized member of the Church is something much more than that. It is part of your identity. Being Catholic is not something you *do* but something you *are*.

This is the difference. If you are on a basketball team, then you are a person who plays basketball. You could just as easily play another sport, plant a garden, or work at a restaurant. These are things that you might choose to do, but they do not define you as a person. However, if you are a member of the Catholic Church, you are not a person who happens to be Catholic. *You are a Catholic*. It is part of your identity. It is who you are.

Baptism changed you in a fundamental way. You are marked for Christ, and you now belong to him.

In the Sacrament of Baptism, you became a member of the Church, which is the Mystical Body of Christ. By receiving the Eucharist, you affirm that you are in communion with the Catholic Church. Moreover, by receiving the Eucharist, you are incorporated more fully into the Body of Christ.

The Sacrament of Confirmation deepens your communion with the Church. The seal of the Gift of the Holy Spirit further empowers you to live out your Baptism. It strengthens that unique and special relationship you have with Christ.

How should you live now that you recognize the importance of your initiation into the Church?

Strive to live your life in keeping with your identity as a Catholic. Throughout this book you will read about how to lead an authentically Catholic life—through prayer, obeying the commandments, witnessing to others about God's love, and loving and serving God and others. By living in this way your life and your identity become more fully integrated.

The Sacrament of Confirmation, the seal of the Gift of the Holy Spirit, deepens your communion with the Church.

# YOU AND YOUR PARENTS

***Living your Catholic identity means practicing your faith seriously as a family.***

Sometimes it is easy to tell who is a Catholic. When someone talks about something that happened "on the way home from Mass" or someone's forehead is marked with ashes on Ash Wednesday, that person is probably Catholic. When you walk into someone's home and see a crucifix or a statue of the Blessed Virgin Mary, that family might be Catholic. These are just a few of the "outward signs" of a person's Catholic identity.

Christ wants us to be proud of our Catholic faith and to live it to the fullest, and that includes outward signs that are true expressions of our love and faith.

Talk about the following questions with your parents. If you find that that answer is *no* or *not really*, talk about why not and how willing all of you are to make the answer yes.

1. Does our family attend Mass on Sundays (or Saturday evenings) and on Holy Days of Obligation?
2. Do we pray as a family, asking God to bless our food ("say grace") before meals, saying nightly prayers, praying a daily or weekly Rosary, or practicing other devotions?
3. When we eat meals in public places such as a restaurant or another person's home, do we say grace?
4. Does our home reflect our Catholic faith with a crucifix, statues, icons, and other tasteful Catholic artwork?
5. Do we spend time learning more about the Catholic faith?
6. Do we read good spiritual texts regularly such as the Bible and stories about the saints?

Be prepared to report back to the class on your talk with your parents and any decisions that resulted from it.

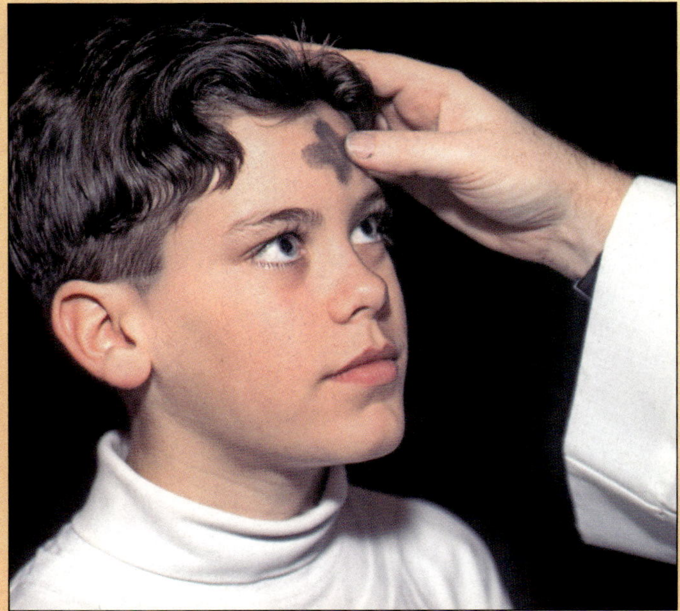

Christ wants us to be proud of our Catholic faith and to live it to the fullest, and that includes outward signs that are true expressions of our love and faith.

Do we pray as a family, asking God to bless our food ("say grace") before meals, saying nightly prayers, praying a daily or weekly Rosary, or practicing other devotions?

# YOU AND YOUR SPONSOR

### *What it means to be a member of the Mystical Body of Christ.*

One of the images of the Church is the Body of Christ. Spend some time discussing this image with your sponsor using the Scripture passages and questions below.

**Read 1 Corinthians 12:12-26. Consider St. Paul's analogy while you talk about these questions:**

1. Give examples of gifts you have noted in certain members of the Body of Christ that they use to build up the Church.
2. What gifts do you have that can build up the Church? How have you done this, and how might you do this in the future?
3. How is the dignity of every human person shown in this passage?
4. This passage ends with the sentence "If one member suffers, all suffer together; if one member is honored, all rejoice together."
How have you seen this within the Church?

**Now read 1 Corinthians 10:16-17 and talk about these questions:**

1. What does this passage reveal about the Real Presence of Christ in the Eucharist?
2. What does this passage reveal about the communion that exists among the faithful when we receive the Body of Christ together in Holy Communion?

"For by one Spirit we were all baptized into one body... and all were made to drink of one Spirit." (1 Cor 12:13)

THE SACRAMENT OF

# Confirmation

## Chapter 5
## THE SACRAMENTS OF INITIATION: BAPTISM

### INTRODUCTION

***We are separated from God by sin, but Baptism restores us to divine friendship.***

In the previous chapter we discussed why the Church is called the Sacrament of Salvation. She is the instrument through which Christ gives his grace in order to invite and lead every human person to perfect happiness. This grace is primarily given through the Church by the power of the Holy Spirit by means of the Seven Sacraments. It is through the Seven Sacraments that we come to salvation.

Our relationship with God has been damaged by sin. Salvation is a restoration of that relationship. The Sacrament of Baptism cleanses us from sin, brings us back into friendship with God, and makes us members of the Church. Before his Ascension, Christ commanded his Apostles to make disciples of all nations, teaching and baptizing them (Mt 28:19-20).

The cleansing from Baptism opens the gates of salvation, making us part of God's family—as true children of God.

Three of the Seven Sacraments—Baptism, the Eucharist, and Confirmation—are called the Sacraments of Initiation. They bring us into the life of Christ and his Church. They give us the strength to continue Christ's mission in the world today. The seven gifts of the Holy Spirit, which you will receive in Confirmation, will strengthen you in your baptismal commitment. They will help you live as a true son or daughter of God.

In the next few chapters, you will learn about the Sacraments of Initiation.

The cleansing from Baptism opens the gates of salvation, making us part of God's family—as true children of God.

After reading this chapter, you will be able to answer these questions:

- What is original holiness and justice?
- Why did we inherit Original Sin?
- What does sanctifying grace do for us?
- Why is the Sacrament of Baptism necessary for salvation?
- How is Baptism identified with Christ's Death and Resurrection?
- How is Baptism related to Pentecost?
- What are the form, matter, and minister of Baptism?
- What are the effects of the Sacrament of Baptism?

# THE EFFECTS OF ORIGINAL SIN

***The Fall of our first parents left us vulnerable to sin and in need of redemption.***

The familiar Bible story of Adam and Eve, as we read earlier, teaches us certain truths about God's creation and our first parents' Fall:

- Human beings are created in God's image and likeness, with a rational intellect, free will, and an immortal soul.
- Our first parents lived in complete harmony with God, sharing a personal and intimate friendship with him.
- God does not force human beings to love or obey him. He wants them to choose his love freely.
- Tempted by the serpent, Adam and Eve sinned by disobeying God's will.
- This **Original Sin** lost God's friendship. This had many specific consequences. Human beings lost sanctifying grace. They became subject to suffering and death and lost harmony with nature. They were weakened in their will and intellect, and became susceptible to further sin.
- The effects of Original Sin were passed on to all their descendants, except Jesus and, by a special grace from God, the Blessed Virgin Mary.

**By his sin Adam, as the first man, lost the original holiness and justice he had received from God, not only for himself but for all human beings. Adam and Eve transmitted to their descendants human nature wounded by their own first sin and hence deprived of original holiness and justice; this deprivation is called "original sin". (CCC 416-417)**

The *Catechism* tells us that human beings were created in a state of original holiness and justice. Original holiness means that at the very beginning they shared in God's divine life. Original justice means that there was harmony in three different spheres. There was harmony within the human person; harmony between Adam and Eve; and harmony between them and the rest of creation. This was all lost with Original Sin. Since the Fall, human beings have had to struggle against being mastered by sin. St. Paul writes, "by one man's disobedience many were made sinners" (Rom 5:19).

Original Sin is not a personal sin that we freely choose to commit but rather a condition we inherit. One of the primary effects of Original Sin is concupiscence. Concupiscence means that we are attracted to sin, even though it is never good for us.

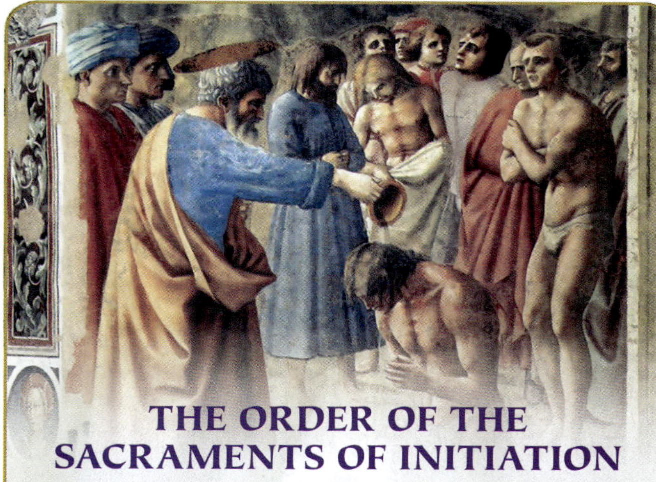

## THE ORDER OF THE SACRAMENTS OF INITIATION

In the early Church, converts to Christianity had to receive the three Sacraments of Initiation to enter the Church. These were usually received in one ceremony at Easter. First, the converts would be baptized, then they would receive Confirmation, then, during Mass, they would receive the Eucharist for the first time. Eventually, however, this practice changed in some parts of the Church. The Sacraments of Initiation were not necessarily received by all at once. By this time the majority of those being baptized were infants instead of adults. This led to the order of reception being changed. It came to be that a child would be baptized soon after birth, receive First Communion around the age of seven, then receive the Sacrament of Confirmation several years after that—usually by the age of 16 or so. This is most likely the order in which you are receiving the Sacraments of Initiation.

In some dioceses in the United States, bishops are restoring the order of the Sacraments of Initiation to the ancient practice by having children receive Confirmation before their First Communion. However, in this book, the order in which the Sacraments of Initiation are discussed will follow the order that Catholics in the West more commonly receive them: Baptism, then the Eucharist, and then Confirmation.

## ORIGINAL SIN AND THE BLESSED VIRGIN MARY

Because of the Fall of our first parents, all their descendants were impacted by Original Sin. But there were two exceptions: Jesus and Mary. Jesus was not born with Original Sin because, as the Son of God, he is a divine Person. Although Christ could be tempted by sin, he never gave in to that temptation. Further, he did not have the attraction to sin (i.e., concupiscence) that all those affected by Original Sin have.

The Blessed Virgin Mary, although a human person like us, was preserved from the effects of Original Sin. Through a special grace, she was "immaculately conceived." She was created in her mother's womb without the stain of Original Sin on her soul. This was a unique grace that she was given as the Mother of God. It made her a pure and holy vessel through which Christ entered the world. Mary's Immaculate Conception was not due to any merit of her own, and her salvation was still dependent on the merits of Christ.

> In the sixth month the angel Gabriel was sent from God to a city of Galilee named Nazareth, to a virgin betrothed to a man whose name was Joseph, of the house of David; and the virgin's name was Mary. And he came to her and said, "Hail, full of grace, the Lord is with you!" But she was greatly troubled at the saying, and considered in her mind what sort of greeting this might be. And the angel said to her, "Do not be afraid, Mary, for you have found favor with God. And behold, you will conceive in your womb and bear a son, and you shall call his name Jesus. He will be great, and will be called the Son of the Most High; and the Lord God will give to him the throne of his father David, and he will reign over the house of Jacob for ever; and of his kingdom there will be no end."
>
> And Mary said to the angel, "How can this be, since I have no husband?"
>
> And the angel said to her,
> "The Holy Spirit will come upon you,
> and the power of the Most High will
> overshadow you;
> therefore the child to be born will be
> called holy,
> the Son of God.
> And behold, your kinswoman Elizabeth in her old age has also conceived a son; and this is the sixth month with her who was called barren. For with God nothing will be impossible." And Mary said, "Behold, I am the handmaid of the Lord; let it be to me according to your word."
>
> And the angel departed from her.
> (Lk 1:26-38)

Because of her cooperation with the immense grace God gave her, she alone among all human persons withstood the temptations of sin to which Eve first succumbed.

The Church celebrates the Feast of the Immaculate Conception on December 8.

## ATONING FOR SIN

***Sacrifice is necessary to make up for sin.***

As we read earlier in this book, God calls people back into communion with him. His Revelation through the patriarchs, the Old Covenant, the Law, and the prophets invited sinful human beings to repent and be faithful. God also gave his chosen people guidelines for worship and sacrifices that would allow them to atone for their sins.

Yet while God's Revelation helped people understand what was sinful, and the Old Testament sacrifices helped people *atone* for their sins, they did not *cleanse* people from their sins. "It is impossible that the blood of bulls and goats [common sacrifices in the Old Testament] should take away sins" (Heb 10:4). That is why the Son of God became man and "offered for all time a single sacrifice for sins…For by a single offering he has perfected for all time those who are sanctified." (Heb 10:12, 14)

*The Crucifixion* by Tiepolo.
Our sins are forgiven through Christ's redemptive work—his Passion, Death, Resurrection, and Ascension.

Christ's Sacrifice was not only **atonement**, or "making up," for our past sins. It also atoned for every sin by every human person throughout time. Our sins are forgiven through Christ's redemptive work—his Passion, Death, Resurrection, and Ascension. In response, we must accept his mercy and forgiveness. Fortunately, he gives us his help to accept it! His Sacrifice provides us with grace, which is the divine help we need to respond to him in faith. The first response to his grace is to receive the Sacrament of Baptism.

## OLD TESTAMENT TYPES OF BAPTISM

***As God regathered his people, he left signs of Baptism's cleansing power.***

Long before Christ instituted the Sacrament of Baptism, it was foreshadowed in the Old Testament. The foreshadowings are called "types." They helped prepare God's people for the Sacrament.

***Noah and the flood.*** Noah and his family, who were faithful to God, were saved by entering the Ark while the floodwaters washed sin from the earth. In the First Letter of St. Peter, the Apostle explains that the story of Noah is a type of Baptism. Just as the flood waters wipe away sinful mankind and cleanse the earth, so also the waters of Baptism wipe away our sins and make us clean (1 Pt 3:20-21).

***Crossing the Red Sea.*** Moses led the Israelites across the Red Sea from slavery to freedom. When the priest blesses the water at the Easter Vigil, his prayer explains that this event is a type of Baptism:

> **[You] caused the children of Abraham**
> **to pass dry-shod through the Red Sea,**
> **so that the chosen people,**
> **set free from slavery to Pharaoh,**
> **would prefigure the people of the baptized.**
> (*Roman Missal*, The Easter Vigil, no. 44, Blessing of Baptismal Water)

Baptism frees us from slavery to sin and death and frees us to live a new life in Christ.

***Crossing the Jordan River.*** When the chosen people came into the Promised Land, they passed through the Jordan River into the land of Canaan. There they finally received the promises of God.

When we are led to receive Baptism, we pass through its waters and are marked for eternal life.

***The story of Naaman.*** Naaman, an enemy of Israel, was a leper. He had a fatal disease which slowly tore away at his skin. He asked Elisha, a prophet of God, to help him, and Elisha told him to bathe seven times in the Jordan River. Naaman was met with the healing power of God:

> **[Naaman] went down and dipped himself seven times in the Jordan, according to the word of the man of God; and his flesh was restored like the flesh of a little child, and he was clean. (2 Kgs 5:14)**

The waters of the Jordan are a type of the waters of Baptism, which restore our souls and make us new creations.

*The Baptism of Christ* by Corot.

## THE BAPTISM OF CHRIST IN THE JORDAN RIVER

***Christ chose to receive baptism from St. John the Baptist.***

Before Christ began his public ministry, John the Baptist publicly preached to the people, calling them to repent of their sins, and in a sign of that repentance, to be baptized by him in the Jordan River. One day, Jesus approached John the Baptist to be baptized, but John, knowing who Christ was, wanted Christ to baptize him. Christ explained: "Let it be so now; for thus it is fitting for us to fulfil all righteousness" (Mt 3:15). St. John in obedience then baptized Christ. The people who were present at this baptism heard the voice of God the Father and saw the Holy Spirit descend in the form of a dove.

Unlike the Sacrament of Baptism, which Christ instituted later, the baptism of St. John did not give sacramental grace. It did not wash away Original Sin (of course, Our Lord was sinless and had no need for cleansing). It was simply a sign of repentance and a foreshadowing of the later Sacrament of Baptism. St. John himself taught this:

> **"I baptize you with water for repentance, but he who is coming after me is mightier than I, whose sandals I am not worthy to carry; he will baptize you with the Holy Spirit and with fire." (Mt 3:11)**

Christ was sinless, formed in his mother's womb by the Holy Spirit. Although he was truly human and experienced temptation, he never sinned, so he did not need to repent for anything. Why, then, did Christ request to be baptized by St. John the Baptist? St. Paul gives us the answer:

> **Though he was in the form of God, [Christ] did not count equality with God a thing to be grasped, but emptied himself, taking the form of a servant, being born in the likeness of men. And being found in human form he humbled himself and became obedient unto death, even death on a cross. (Phil 2:6-8)**

Christ allowed himself to be baptized by John to announce the beginning of his public ministry as well as to mark the beginning of the decline of John the Baptist's ministry. John himself had said of Jesus, "He must increase, but I must decrease" (Jn 3:30). Further, by being baptized in the waters of the Jordan River, Christ cleansed all waters for use in sacramental Baptism. In other words, in some mysterious fashion, the process of Baptism was "reversed" when Christ was baptized. Instead of Jesus being cleansed by the waters, he cleansed the waters for us!

When Christ preached the Gospel, he taught about the Baptism that was not just a symbol of repentance but rather a rebirth into new life through water and the Holy Spirit.

# WHY WE NEED BAPTISM

***Baptism is linked to Christ's Death and Resurrection and grants us new life in the Holy Spirit.***

Christ remade the practice of baptism as a Sacrament that marks a person indelibly, which means for all eternity. Baptism makes it possible for him or her to be in communion with God in heaven. Baptism is never simply a symbolic action. It is always a life-changing and necessary action of God.

**Christ taught that the Sacrament of Baptism is necessary for salvation.** During Christ's public ministry, Nicodemus, a Pharisee, visited him in secret to learn more about his message. Christ told him that a person must be "born anew" in order to "see the kingdom of God" (Jn 3:3). When a perplexed Nicodemus asked how an old man could be born again, Christ explained that the rebirth of which he spoke was not physical. "Unless one is born of water and Spirit, he cannot enter the kingdom of God" (Jn 3:1-5).

Before Christ ascended into heaven, he instructed his Apostles to "make disciples of all nations, baptizing them in the name of the Father and of the Son and of the Holy Spirit" (Mt 28:19). He taught them also about why we need Baptism. "He who believes and is baptized will be saved; but he who does not believe will be condemned" (Mk 16:16).

> **Baptism is necessary for salvation for those to whom the Gospel has been proclaimed and who have had the possibility of asking for this sacrament. (CCC 1257)**

**Baptism is a sharing in the Death and Resurrection of Christ.** The New Testament reveals that Baptism is a share in the Death of Christ as we die to sin in the baptismal waters:

> **Do you not know that all of us who have been baptized into Christ Jesus were baptized into his death? We were buried therefore with him by baptism into death. (Rom 6:3-4)**

Just as Baptism brings one into the Death of Christ, so also does it allow a person to share in the Resurrection of Christ.

> **If we have been united with him in a death like his, we shall certainly be united with him in a resurrection like his. (Rom 6:5)**

*The Resurrection* by Bloch.
Just as Baptism brings one into the Death of Christ, so also does it allow a person to share in the Resurrection of Christ.

Through Baptism, the salvation that Christ won through his Death and Resurrection are *applied* to us. We are not simply observers of the events of the Paschal Mystery, but through Baptism, we become part of them as we unite ourselves to Christ.

**At Baptism, we receive the Holy Spirit.** When the Holy Spirit came to the Apostles at Pentecost, they were filled with strength and courage. They left the Upper Room and went into the streets of Jerusalem to preach the Gospel of Christ. Many of the people were moved by St. Peter's preaching and asked what they should do. He said:

> **"Repent, and be baptized every one of you in the name of Jesus Christ for the forgiveness of your sins; and you shall receive the gift of the Holy Spirit." (Acts 2:38)**

Confirmation completes this process by giving us the gifts of the Holy Spirit so we can faithfully live as disciples of Christ.

## EFFECTS OF BAPTISM

***Baptism is so profound that it changes us permanently.***

Throughout this chapter you have read about several effects that the Sacrament of Baptism has on those who receive it. This is a more complete list of what this Sacrament does for us:

**Baptism cleanses us from Original Sin.** The stain on our soul left by the sin of our first parents is erased. We still suffer the *effects* of Original Sin—concupiscence, sickness, suffering, death. However, the sin itself is gone. The cleansing of Original Sin makes entry into heaven possible for us.

**Baptism cleanses us from all actual sins.** An *actual sin* is any sin we commit by our own free will in our thoughts, words, actions, or failure to act. Infants and very young children may not be capable of actual sin, but older children and adults who receive Baptism are forgiven all actual sins along with Original Sin. Further, every sin has a negative impact on one's soul (called "temporal punishments"), and Baptism also removes these temporal punishments from the soul.

**Baptism fills us with sanctifying grace, making us adopted children of God.** The gift of grace is poured

### DYING AND RISING WITH CHRIST IN BAPTISM

The act of baptizing illustrates the dying and rising one shares with Christ in the Sacrament. The word "baptism" comes from the Greek *baptizein*, meaning "to plunge" or "to immerse." In the time of Christ and in the early Church, Baptism was practiced by immersion into water. The person being baptized is submerged in the water three times. To go under the cleansing waters of Baptism is a sign of dying to sin and dying with Christ. To come back out from under the water is a sign of rising again to new life and our hope of resurrection. Baptism by immersion is not necessary—often today a priest or deacon will simply pour water over a child's forehead—but the act of immersion does more fully symbolize what is occurring in Baptism.

### THE EARLY CHRISTIANS HAD A FORMATION PROCESS FOR NEW CHRISTIANS

Baptism has always been preceded by the preaching of the Gospel. Before a person can be baptized, he or she has to learn about the Good News of salvation and the life of Christ. That way he or she can accept the gift of faith freely. The teaching of the Gospel prepares people for initiation into the Church, much like this book and your Confirmation program is preparing you to receive the Sacrament of Confirmation.

As the early Church grew in numbers, a process developed for welcoming new people to receive the Sacraments of Initiation. Eventually it became a three-year formation program which taught Christian doctrine, morality, and spirituality. Those who were preparing were called **catechumens**, and the process was called the **catechumenate**. These were some elements of the catechumenate:

- The candidate, in order to be accepted into the catechumenate, had to be recommended or sponsored by a practicing Christian.
- Catechumens prayed, did works of penance, and received instruction in the faith.
- Catechumens demonstrated to the Christian community that they were living good Christian lives.
- Catechumens entered into deeper preparation during Lent to prepare for Baptism at the Easter Vigil.

Today the Rite of Christian Initiation of Adults (RCIA) is based on this ancient catechumenate and is the primary means by which converts of all ages are brought into the Church.

into us by the Holy Spirit. It is called *sanctifying* grace because it makes us holy and restores us to full communion with the Blessed Trinity. This grace makes us sons and daughters of God—part of God's family.

**Baptism infuses us with the theological virtues of faith, hope, and love.** Baptism helps us to believe in God, hope in God, and love God even more. These gifts of Baptism help us to listen to the Holy Spirit and heed what he tells us. They assist us in growing in holiness and moral virtue.

**The Holy Spirit makes us a new creation in Christ.** Not only are we restored to God's friendship in Baptism, we also are made to share in his divine life, becoming his adopted sons and daughters. We become new creations, temples of the Holy Spirit.

**We are sealed for Christ.** Baptism leaves what is called a "character" on the soul. This is a special term which means an indelible mark on the soul that cannot be removed. This mark shows that a person belongs to Christ from then onward—not just for a time, but forever. We cannot lose this mark, no matter how badly we sin. Baptism is our seal for redemption, which marks us for eternal life.

> **Baptism imprints on the soul an indelible spiritual sign, the character, which consecrates the baptized person for Christian worship. (CCC 1280)**

### THE EASTER VIGIL

Once adults have completed the catechumenate, they usually receive their Sacraments of Initiation at the Easter Vigil.

The Easter Vigil is the Mass that is celebrated the night before Easter. Starting after dark, the Easter Vigil celebrates the greatest event in human history: the Resurrection of Jesus Christ from the dead. During the Easter Vigil, there are extra Scripture readings, many of which point to Old Testament types of Baptism. During the Liturgy, catechumens are baptized and confirmed, and then receive the Eucharist for the first time. The Easter Vigil demonstrates the unity of the three Sacraments of Initiation, as catechumens receive all three during one liturgy.

**Baptism makes us members of the Mystical Body of Christ.** Baptism brings us into Christ, making us members of his Body, the Church.

**Baptism gives us a share in Christ's mission as priest, prophet, and king.** Because we have been baptized into the Death and Resurrection of Christ, we have died to sin and risen to new life. Now we are called to continue Christ's mission on earth of taking the Good News of salvation throughout the world.

## THE BAPTISMAL LITURGY

***The richly symbolic baptismal liturgy helps express the meaning of Baptism.***

The celebration of the Rite of Baptism includes rich symbols that emphasize what the Sacrament accomplishes.

### Form, Matter, and Minister

Every Sacrament includes three essential elements: a minister who performs it, as well as its form and matter. These are special terms that have precise definitions. These definitions might be different from how you use these words in daily life.

The *form* is composed of the liturgical words used to give sanctifying grace. At Baptism the form requires that the person be baptized "in the name of the Father, and of the Son, and of the Holy Spirit." This is called the Trinitarian Formula because it names each of the three Persons of the Blessed Trinity, just as Christ instructed (Mt 28:19).

The *matter* is the physical sign that gives sanctifying grace. At Baptism the matter is water. The person can either be immersed in water three times, or the minister can pour or sprinkle water on his head three times.

The *minister* is the person who uses the form and matter to give sanctifying grace. The ordinary minister of Baptism is a bishop, priest, or deacon. However, in an emergency, any person—even someone who is not baptized—can baptize someone. As long as he or she uses the correct form and matter and has the intention to do what the Church does in conferring the Sacrament of Baptism, the baptism would be valid. The Church requires that the same person who performs the action of baptizing also pronounces the words.

**The ordinary ministers of Baptism are the bishop and priest and, in the Latin Church, also the deacon. In case of necessity, anyone, even a non-baptized person, with the required intention, can baptize, by using the Trinitarian baptismal formula. The intention required is to will to do what the Church does when she baptizes. The Church finds the reason for this possibility in the universal saving will of God and the necessity of Baptism for salvation. (CCC 1256)**

## The Rite of Baptism

The Rite of Baptism uses other symbols and gestures to represent the meaning of the Sacrament. These are not necessary if a person, for example, needs to be baptized quickly because of the danger of death, but they should be included whenever there is time. These are four symbols and gestures:

- The minister, parents, and godparents make the Sign of the Cross on the baptismal candidate's forehead, emphasizing that he or she is "marked for Christ." Christ's Sacrifice on the Cross allows the person to die to sin and enter eternal life.

### GRAFTED ONTO CHRIST

Christianity is not primarily about becoming a good person or doing the right thing. Anybody—pagan, Muslim, Jew, or nonbeliever—could be any of those things...but none of that is distinctive to Christianity.

To be a Christian is to be grafted onto Christ and hence drawn into the very dynamics of the inner life of God.

Doing good things [or] being ethically upright is great. It will flow from...following Jesus. [R]ather we speak of becoming a member of his mystical body and therefore sharing in his own relationship to the Father. Jesus is the son of God by nature and we become, by baptism, [adopted] sons and daughters of God. And that is why it is so important to say that we are baptized in the name of the Father and of the Son and of the Holy Spirit.

(Bishop Robert Barron, *Sermon 679: Priest, Prophet, and King: The Baptism of the Lord*, January 11, 2014)

At Baptism the *form* requires that the person be baptized "in the name of the Father, and of the Son, and of the Holy Spirit."

- The newly baptized person is clothed in a white robe. This symbolizes that he or she has "put on Christ" (Gal 3:27). To put on Christ means to have been made holy, so as to share in his Resurrection.
- The candidate is given a candle, symbolizing Christ as the "light of the world" (Jn 9:5). Christ told his followers, "You are the light of the world" (Mt 5:14). Christians are to shine forth and bring the light of faith to others.
- The candidate is anointed with Sacred Chrism. This shows that he or she has received the gift of the Holy Spirit and is now incorporated into Christ, who was anointed priest, prophet, and king.

There are three other elements of the Rite of Baptism that are related to what you have read so far in this book:

- Reading of the Word of God. This is a sign that Baptism is a response to faith.
- Renunciation of Satan and his works. This is a sign that Baptism frees us from slavery to sin.
- Profession of Faith (Creed). This is a sign that Baptism is our response to God's gift of faith and is a public act.

## BAPTIZING INFANTS

Baptism is a person's response to God's gift of faith. Then why does the Church baptize infants and children who are too young to choose for themselves to believe in Christ and follow him?

When an infant or small child is baptized, his or her parents and godparents provide the choice for the child. Imagine an infant who has a life-threatening sickness. The child cannot consent to treatment, so the parents consent for him. Likewise, at Baptism an infant's parents and godparents choose for the child the life-saving gift of sanctifying grace through Baptism. Because they are born with the effects of Original Sin, children need the rebirth of water and the Spirit in order to be freed from slavery to sin.

Scripture suggests that it was the custom to baptize babies and infants even from the earliest days of the Church. The New Testament records several instances of entire households receiving Baptism. A household was composed of parents, children, other relatives, and sometimes servants.

The precedent goes back even further than the early Church. The requirement of the Law God gave to Abraham is that newborn males undergo a rite of circumcision eight days after birth. For the Jews, circumcision is a visible sign of belonging to God's covenant. An infant eight days old cannot choose circumcision, but his parents brought him forth for this ritual. St. Paul calls Baptism the new, spiritual "circumcision":

> **In him also you were circumcised with a circumcision made without hands…and you were buried with him in baptism, in which you were also raised with him through faith in the working of God. (Col 2:11-12)**

The Tradition of the Church has always been to bring children to Christ through the Sacrament of Baptism.

# CAN THOSE NOT RECEIVING THE SACRAMENT OF BAPTISM BE SAVED?

***The Church hopes for the salvation of those who do not receive the Sacrament of Baptism, but who also desire to be saved.***

The Sacrament of Baptism is necessary for salvation "for those to whom the Gospel had been proclaimed and who have had the possibility of asking for the Sacrament" (CCC 1257). Christ taught that Baptism is the path to salvation. "Truly, truly, I say to you, unless one is born of water and the Spirit, he cannot enter the kingdom of God" (Jn 3:5).

However, God himself is not bound by his Sacraments. He can save a person through means that are known to him only. We should never conclude that an unbaptized person is in hell. We should pray for the soul of everyone who dies without Baptism. Because we know that God is both just and merciful,

> **those who die for the faith, those who are catechumens, and all those who, without knowing of the Church but acting under the inspiration of grace, seek God sincerely and strive to fulfill his will, can be saved even if they have not been baptized. (CCC 1281)**

The Church affirms two kinds of "baptism" by which a person could be saved without receiving the formal Sacrament of Baptism:

- Baptism of Blood refers to the salvation of people who die as witnesses for Christ but have not received the Sacrament of Baptism. Often in the early Church, catechumens were arrested alongside Christians and martyred when they refused to renounce Christ. The unbaptized catechumens were recognized as obtaining salvation. As Christ proclaimed, "Every one who acknowledges me before men, I also will acknowledge before my Father who is in heaven" (Mt 10:32).
- Baptism of Desire refers to salvation for those who desire to be baptized, but die before receiving the Sacrament. For example, an unbaptized adult might be preparing to be baptized at the Easter Vigil, but die suddenly

before that sacred night. Further, one who does not know of Christ, but desires to follow God faithfully, might be said to desire Baptism without realizing it. We can hope in the mercy of God to bring salvation to such persons.

> **Every man who is ignorant of the Gospel of Christ and of his Church, but seeks the truth and does the will of God in accordance with his understanding of it, can be saved. It may be supposed that such persons would have desired Baptism explicitly if they had known its necessity. (CCC 1260)**

However, it is important to remember that we cannot assume salvation for those who are unbaptized, and should do all we can to help people know the importance of being baptized.

Tragically, young children, born and unborn, sometimes die before reaching the waters of Baptism. The Church prays for them, trusting in the mercy of God. Christ's own words regarding children ought to console us. "Let the children come to me, do not hinder them; for to such belongs the kingdom of God" (Mk 10:14).

"Let the children come to me, do not hinder them; for to such belongs the kingdom of God."

## UNBAPTIZED BABIES WHO DIE

If Baptism is necessary for salvation, what happens to unbaptized babies who die? What about babies aborted in the womb? They have committed no actual sins, but they are afflicted with Original Sin. Where will they go after death?

One idea is that when unbaptized babies die, they go to limbo, where they will remain forever in a state of perfect natural happiness but without the full joy of heaven. The reasoning is that an unbaptized person does not have sanctifying grace, so he or she cannot be in heaven. Yet an unbaptized infant has not chosen to sin, so he or she cannot be in hell.

The concept of limbo was very popular among Catholics in the Middle Ages, as people wanted to resolve this apparent conflict, but it was never an official teaching of the Church. In modern times most theologians and members of the hierarchy no longer subscribe to it, emphasizing more our hope in the mercy of God in these situations.

The Church teaches that we can rely on the mercy of God for those babies who died or are aborted. No one knows exactly what happens to unbaptized infants because God has not revealed it. Scripture and Tradition do, however, reveal many reasons for us to hope that these innocent children enjoy the full happiness of communion with God in heaven.

> The great mercy of God who desires that all men should be saved, and Jesus' tenderness toward children...allow us to hope that there is a way of salvation for children who have died without Baptism. (CCC 1261)

A prayer used at the funeral of infants who died before Baptism asks God that their parents may be assured that their child "has been entrusted to your divine compassion."

### THAT ALL MAY BE SAVED

**I urge that supplications, prayers, intercessions, and thanksgivings be made for all men, for kings and all who are in high positions, that we may lead a quiet and peaceable life, godly and respectful in every way.**

**This is good, and it is acceptable in the sight of God our Savior, who desires all men to be saved and to come to the knowledge of the truth. (1 Tm 2:2-4)**

## CONCLUSION

The Sacrament of Baptism has the power to forgive sins—Original Sin and actual sin. It is called the "gateway to life in the Spirit" (CCC 1213). Through it we receive sanctifying grace and are reborn in the Holy Spirit. It is also the gateway to the other Sacraments, since Baptism must be received before any other.

**Baptism:**

- Cleanses us of all sin, including Original Sin.
- Opens the gates of heaven so that we each may enter into eternal life.
- Makes us members of the Church and the Mystical Body of Christ.
- Infuses us with theological and moral virtues.
- Makes us truly children of God.
- Enables us to participate in the inner (divine) life of God.
- Gives us sanctifying grace.

Baptism thus is a foundation for the Sacrament of Confirmation, which deepens and furthers our baptismal commitment. The gifts of the Holy Spirit that will come to you in Confirmation will help you live as a good, faithful disciple of Christ in the world.

## POINTS TO REMEMBER

1. Our first parents, Adam and Eve, were created in a state of original holiness and justice. They lost this state through the Original Sin and passed its effects on to their descendants. Baptism cleanses us from Original Sin and gives us new life in Christ, making us capable of being like him (holy).
2. The Sacrament of Baptism is necessary for salvation and opens heaven for us. Christ said a person must be born again of water and the Holy Spirit in order to enter the kingdom of God.
3. Baptism marks us as Christ's and fills us with sanctifying grace. It infuses us with the theological virtues and anoints us as priests, prophets, and kings. It makes us children of God, temples of the Holy Spirit, and new creations in Christ. Thus, we are made part of the Family of God because we are now part of the Mystical Body of Christ.
4. In the Sacrament of Baptism, the matter is water and the form is the Trinitarian formula ("I baptize you in the name of the Father, and of the Son, and of the Holy Spirit"). The ordinary minister is a bishop, priest, or deacon; however, in an emergency, anyone can be the minister of Baptism as long as he or she does what the Church intends to do in conferring Baptism.

A small candle lit during the Baptism symbolizes that the baptized has been given the light of Christ. The candle is given to the child to use throughout their lives at important events like First Communion and Confirmation.

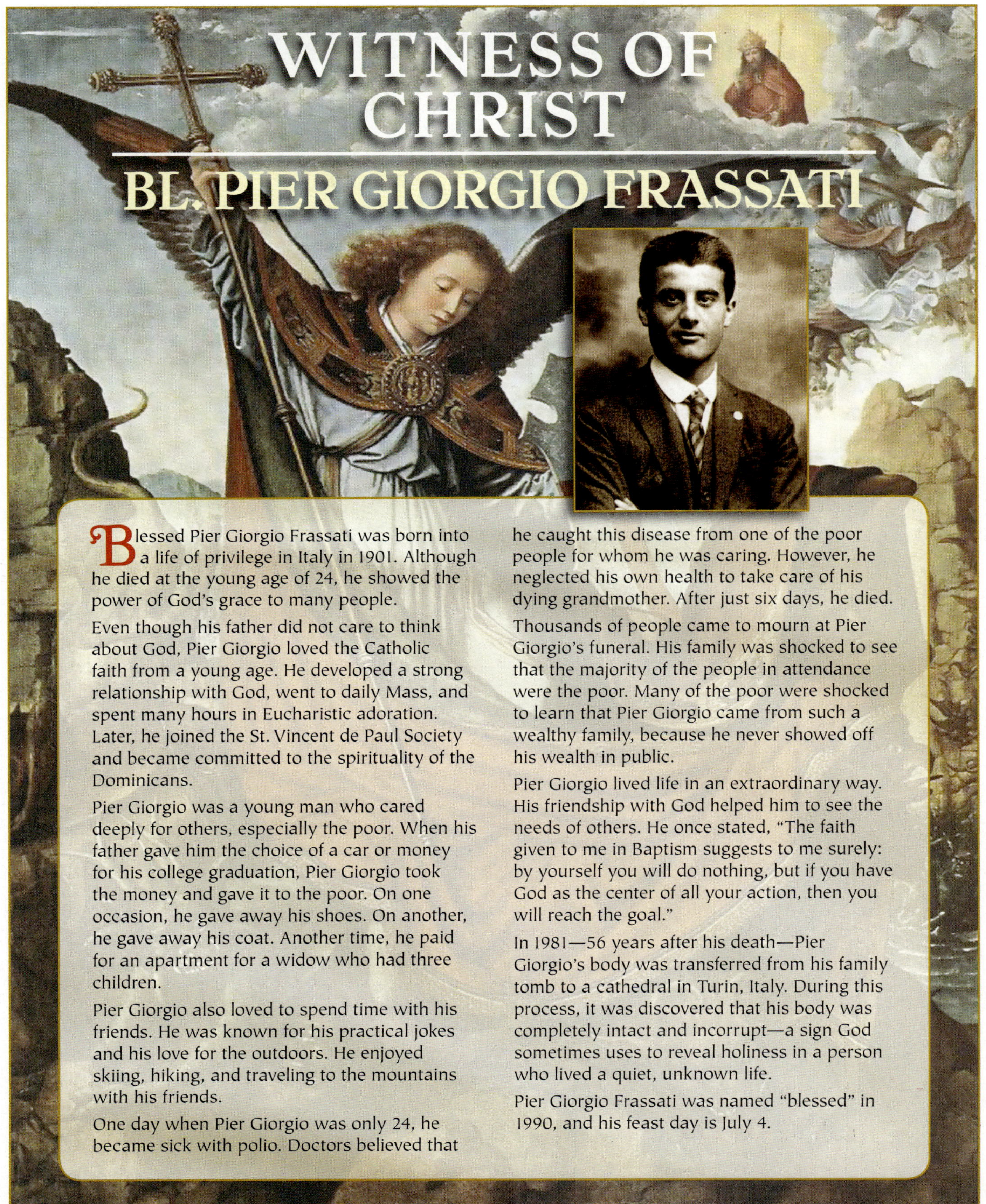

# WITNESS OF CHRIST

## BL. PIER GIORGIO FRASSATI

Blessed Pier Giorgio Frassati was born into a life of privilege in Italy in 1901. Although he died at the young age of 24, he showed the power of God's grace to many people.

Even though his father did not care to think about God, Pier Giorgio loved the Catholic faith from a young age. He developed a strong relationship with God, went to daily Mass, and spent many hours in Eucharistic adoration. Later, he joined the St. Vincent de Paul Society and became committed to the spirituality of the Dominicans.

Pier Giorgio was a young man who cared deeply for others, especially the poor. When his father gave him the choice of a car or money for his college graduation, Pier Giorgio took the money and gave it to the poor. On one occasion, he gave away his shoes. On another, he gave away his coat. Another time, he paid for an apartment for a widow who had three children.

Pier Giorgio also loved to spend time with his friends. He was known for his practical jokes and his love for the outdoors. He enjoyed skiing, hiking, and traveling to the mountains with his friends.

One day when Pier Giorgio was only 24, he became sick with polio. Doctors believed that he caught this disease from one of the poor people for whom he was caring. However, he neglected his own health to take care of his dying grandmother. After just six days, he died.

Thousands of people came to mourn at Pier Giorgio's funeral. His family was shocked to see that the majority of the people in attendance were the poor. Many of the poor were shocked to learn that Pier Giorgio came from such a wealthy family, because he never showed off his wealth in public.

Pier Giorgio lived life in an extraordinary way. His friendship with God helped him to see the needs of others. He once stated, "The faith given to me in Baptism suggests to me surely: by yourself you will do nothing, but if you have God as the center of all your action, then you will reach the goal."

In 1981—56 years after his death—Pier Giorgio's body was transferred from his family tomb to a cathedral in Turin, Italy. During this process, it was discovered that his body was completely intact and incorrupt—a sign God sometimes uses to reveal holiness in a person who lived a quiet, unknown life.

Pier Giorgio Frassati was named "blessed" in 1990, and his feast day is July 4.

# VOCABULARY

### ATONEMENT

Reparation for an offense through a voluntary action that compensates for the injustice done.

### CATECHUMEN

From the Greek for "one being instructed." A Catechumen is one being instructed in the Christian faith before Baptism.

### CATECHUMENATE

The instruction and formation of catechumens, those being prepared for membership in the Church. This also refers to the catechumens collectively and their position with respect to the Church.

### CONCUPISCENCE

The disordered state of human appetites or desires due to the temporal consequences of Original Sin. This situation remains even after Baptism, and constitutes an inclination to sin. This is often used to refer to desires resulting from strong sensual urges or attachment to things of this world.

### ORIGINAL HOLINESS

The supernatural and preternatural gifts enjoyed by our first parents before the Fall; these include sanctifying grace and exemption from sin, suffering, death, and concupiscence.

### ORIGINAL JUSTICE

The original state which our first parents enjoyed: harmony within themselves, with each other, and with all of creation.

### ORIGINAL SIN

Adam and Eve's abuse of their human freedom in disobeying God's command. As a consequence, they lost the grace of original holiness and justice, and became subject to the law of death; sin became universally present in the world, with every person being born into this condition. This sin separated mankind from God, darkened the human intellect, weakened the human will, and introduced into human nature an inclination toward sin. The term is also used to describe the fallen condition that affects all human beings as a result of that transgression.

*The Fall of Man* by Goltzius.
The sin of Adam and Eve separated mankind from God and introduced into human nature an inclination toward sin.

## STUDY QUESTIONS

1. What are the three Sacraments of Initiation?
2. What is Original Sin?
3. Why did Christ allow himself to be baptized by St. John the Baptist?
4. Why is the Sacrament of Baptism necessary for salvation?
5. How is Baptism identified with Christ's Death and Resurrection?
6. How is Baptism related to Pentecost?
7. What is the "remedy" to Original Sin?
8. What does sanctifying grace do for us?
9. What are the effects of the Sacrament of Baptism?
10. What are the form, matter, and minister of Baptism?

## PRACTICAL EXERCISES

1. Think of three ways you use water in your everyday life, for example, to clean, drink, and refresh. How do these three uses relate to what the waters of Baptism do for a person?

2. Consider the many signs, symbols, and gestures within the Rite of Baptism: water, oil, a candle, a white garment, the Sign of the Cross, and so on. All of these point to deeper, unseen truths. Now think about how we use certain signs, symbols, and gestures to celebrate other achievements in life, for example, a birthday, graduation, sports award, or ribbon-cutting ceremony for a new building. Pick one of these events and note at least three signs, symbols, or gestures and note what they signify.

Consider the many signs, symbols, and gestures within the Rite of Baptism: water, oil, a candle, a white garment, and the Sign of the Cross.

# SEALED IN THE SPIRIT

***Sanctifying grace given to us in Baptism restores the holiness lost through Original Sin.***

God, who is perfectly holy, calls us to himself, which means he calls us to holiness.

As you read in this chapter, the Sacrament of Baptism gives us sanctifying grace, which makes us holy. Yet we still must battle sin and temptation throughout our lives. The life of a true follower of Christ is a struggle to seek the will of God above all else, and to love and serve God and neighbor day by day. It is a call to seek holiness continually throughout our lives. Our goal, of course, is to enjoy communion and happiness with God in heaven forever.

The sanctifying grace given to us in Baptism restores the holiness lost through Original Sin. In fact, it not only restores that lost holiness, it pours forth even greater blessings than those which sin took from us. Made holy in Baptism, we are called to still greater holiness: the holiness of God, who is perfectly holy. This is what the Church refers to as the "universal call to holiness," which we will read more about in Chapter 10. All the baptized are called to holiness simply because we have been baptized. We have responded in faith, "put on Christ" (Gal 3:27), and now we are new creations and children of God.

The universal call to holiness is often described as a call to Christian perfection or to the perfection of charity. As you have read, Christ said that we "must be perfect, as your heavenly Father is perfect" (Mt 5:48). Does this seem like an impossible request, to be as perfectly holy as God?

It is true that we can never achieve true perfection in this life. Perfect holiness and perfect happiness are only possible in perfect communion with God. That comes only in heaven. But our lifelong mission as faithful disciples is to keep growing toward that perfection: to become more holy, more Christlike, more in communion with God. Simply put, seeking holiness means seeking to do what God wants us to do.

As St. Paul wrote, God wants us to be holy. "This is the will of God, your sanctification" (1 Thes 4:3), and only God can make us holy. He does this through his sanctifying grace. Only he, through the merits of the Death and Resurrection of Christ, can welcome us into heaven. But by our faith and by orienting our human will to God's will, we can receive the grace that he freely offers to us. We cannot "earn" holiness by what we do, but we can always choose to cooperate with God's grace to grow in holiness.

*The Sermon on the Mount* by Dore.
Our lifelong mission as faithful disciples is to keep growing toward Christian perfection: to become more holy, more Christlike, more in communion with God.

# YOU AND YOUR PARENTS

***Your Baptism marked the start of your new life in Christ, so it is a date to celebrate.***

Do you know the date of your Baptism? It was an important day in your life: the day that you became a child of God and were cleansed of all sin. You received the sanctifying grace of the Holy Spirit. You were sealed with Sacred Chrism, anticipating the Sacrament of Confirmation. You became a Christian and a Catholic.

It is even more important than your birthday. At your birth, you came into the world (even though you had already been alive for many months). At your Baptism, you began a new life in Christ!

With your parents, read the following words of Pope Francis about your baptismal date:

> **Many of us have no memory of the celebration of this Sacrament, and it is obvious why, if we were baptized soon after birth. I have asked this question two or three times already, here, in this square: who among you knows the date of your Baptism, raise your hands. It is important to know the day on which I was immersed in that current of Jesus' salvation. And I will allow myself to give you some advice...but, more than advice, a task for today. Today, at home, go look, ask about the date of your Baptism and that way you will keep in mind that most beautiful day of Baptism.**
>
> **To know the date of our Baptism is to know a blessed day. The danger of not knowing is that we can lose awareness of what the Lord has done in us, the memory of the gift we have received. Thus, we end up considering it only as an event that took place in the past—and not by our own will but by that of our parents—and that it has no impact on the present. We must reawaken the memory of our Baptism.**
>
> **We are called to live out our Baptism every day as the present reality of our lives. If we manage to follow Jesus and to remain in the Church, despite our limitations and with our weaknesses and our sins, it is precisely in the Sacrament whereby we have become new creatures and have been clothed in Christ.**
>
> **(Pope Francis, *General Audience*, January 8, 2014)**

Talk about your Baptism with your parents. What was the date? Who were your godparents? Who was there? What else can they tell you about that day? Do they have photos or video? Be prepared to share what you learned, and make an effort to observe the anniversary of your Baptism in some way. Ideas might include a special prayer of thanksgiving, lighting a candle, or a festive meal with your family.

Talk about your Baptism with your parents. What was the date? Who were your godparents? Who was there?

# You and Your Sponsor

***Through the Sacrament of Baptism, we are bearers of a new hope, and we are called to evangelize.***

You read about the powerful effects of the Sacrament of Baptism. With your sponsor, read the following words of Pope Francis:

> **It is by the power of Baptism, in fact, that, freed of original sin, we are inserted into Jesus' relation to God the Father; that we are bearers of a new hope, for Baptism gives us this new hope: the hope of going on the path of salvation our whole life long. And this hope nothing and no one can extinguish, for it is a hope that does not disappoint. Remember, hope in the Lord never disappoints.**
>
> **Thanks to Baptism, we are capable of forgiving and of loving even those who offend us and do evil to us. By our Baptism, we recognize in the least and in the poor the face of the Lord who visits us and makes himself close. Baptism helps us to recognize in the face of the needy, the suffering, and also of our neighbor, the face of Jesus. All this is possible thanks to the power of Baptism!**
>
> **(Pope Francis, *General Audience*, January 8, 2014)**

Let us look at what the Pope said. The call of the baptized is to be an example of Christian love in the world. Talk about these questions with your sponsor:

1. How does Baptism make us "bearers of a new hope"?
2. How does the "hope" in the previous question relate to the universal call to holiness (see this chapter's *Sealed in the Spirit*, p. 108)?
3. How can we, as baptized Christians, be better at forgiving and loving those who do evil to us?
4. How well do we recognize the face of Christ in the needy, the suffering, and our neighbors? How should we respond to that face?
5. When we enter or exit a church, we bless ourselves with holy water. Why do we do this? What should we remember as we are blessing ourselves with holy water?

What should we remember as we are blessing ourselves with holy water? Discuss this with your sponsor.

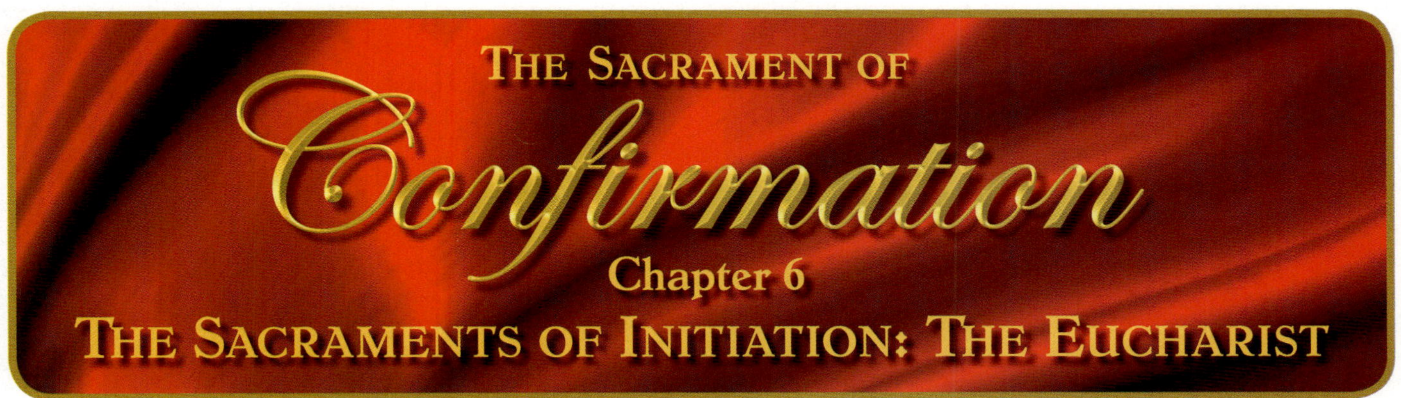


## INTRODUCTION

***The Eucharist is the "source and summit of the Christian life."***

Baptism is our entryway into the Church. It begins the process of becoming a disciple of Christ and our initiation into his Church. But our initiation is not yet complete, for we still need to receive the other two Sacraments of Initiation: the Eucharist and Confirmation. More than likely, you have already received your first Communion, and you are nearing the time that your initiation will be completed by your Confirmation. In this chapter we are going to learn more about the great gift of the Eucharist.

> **The Eucharist is "the source and summit of the Christian life." "The other sacraments...are bound up with the Eucharist and are oriented toward it. For in the blessed Eucharist is contained the whole spiritual good of the Church, namely Christ himself." (CCC 1324)**

We have seen how God prepared the world for thousands of years for the coming of Christ. We call this "salvation history." Part of this history also prepared his people for the gift of the Eucharist. In the Passover, the animal sacrifices, and the manna from heaven we see foreshadowings of the Eucharist.

Most importantly, the Eucharist is not just a commemorative meal. It is a true sacrifice, re-presenting Christ's Sacrifice on the Cross. The Lord told the prophet Malachi, centuries before the time of Christ, "For from the rising of the sun to its setting my name is great among the nations, and in every place incense is offered to my name, and a pure offering; for my name is great among the nations, says the Lord of hosts" (Mal 1:11). The Eucharist

By the action of the Holy Spirit through the prayers of the priest, bread and wine are transformed into the Body and Blood of Jesus Christ.

is that "pure offering," which is offered every day throughout the world.

> **Assemble on the Lord's Day, and break bread and offer the Eucharist; but first make confession of your faults, so that your sacrifice may be a pure one. Anyone who has a difference with his fellow is not to take part with you until he has been reconciled, so as to avoid any profanation of your sacrifice. For this is the offering of which the Lord has said, "Everywhere and always bring me a sacrifice that is undefiled, for I am a great king, says the Lord, and my name is the wonder of nations." (*Didache* 14 [AD 70])**

The Eucharist is central to our Christian life. It gives us strength to live as a disciple of Christ, and gives purpose to our Christian life. It is through the Mass that the Eucharist comes to us. By the action of the

"This is my body which is given for you. Do this in remembrance of me." (Lk 22:19)
Christ wanted to leave his followers a way to remember his work of salvation.

Holy Spirit through the prayers of the priest, bread and wine are transformed into the Body and Blood of Jesus Christ. When we receive Holy Communion, we are united to Christ and his Church, and we are given spiritual food for our pilgrimage to heaven.

After reading this chapter, you will be able to answer these questions:

- What do we mean when we call the Eucharist a memorial?
- Why is the Eucharist called a sacrifice?
- When did Christ institute the Sacrament of the Eucharist?
- What is transubstantiation?
- How can you participate in Mass and receive the Eucharist faithfully?
- What are the effects of receiving Holy Communion?
- Why do we have to go to Mass?

# THE OLD TESTAMENT PREPARED THE PEOPLE OF GOD FOR THE EUCHARIST

***God's actions in the Old Testament prefigure his gift of the Eucharist.***

## The Eucharist: The New Passover

> **The Eucharist is the memorial of Christ's Passover, the making present and the sacramental offering of his unique sacrifice, in the liturgy of the Church which is his Body. (CCC 1362)**

On the night of the Last Supper, Christ knew that the time of his Passion was approaching. He wanted to leave his followers a way to remember his work of salvation. He also desired that they would participate in it for all time.

Let's recall what we know about what happened at the Last Supper, which we hear in the Eucharistic Prayer at every Mass:

> **He took bread, and when he had given thanks he broke it and gave it to them, saying, "This is my body which is given for you. Do this in remembrance of me." (Lk 22:19)**

Then he did the same with a chalice of wine:

> **He took a chalice, and when he had given thanks he gave it to them, saying, "Drink of it, all of you; for this is my blood of the covenant, which is poured out for many for the forgiveness of sins." (Mt 26:27-28)**

Through these actions of consecrating the bread and wine and offering them to his Apostles, Christ instituted the Sacrament of the Eucharist.

Before the Last Supper, Jesus asked his disciples to prepare the traditional Passover meal for them to celebrate together. In Jewish tradition the Passover meal made the events of the Exodus—the Israelites' freedom from slavery in Egypt—present and real in their midst. It was a "memorial" of those historic events in salvation history.

The word "memorial" might remind you of a landmark of some great historic event or of a religious service for someone who has died. We build physical memorials to great political leaders, important moral leaders, and legendary sports figures. We celebrate memorial services at a chapel or cemetery so that we can reflect on the life of someone who has passed on to the next world, to mourn, and to pray for his or her salvation.

But for the Jews, a memorial is much more than just a memory of past events. It is a *participation* in them. It allows those who have come after the original Passover to become part of that pivotal event. The Passover celebration makes present that which happened in the past.

While adopting the rituals of the Passover meal, Jesus at the Last Supper gave it even more meaning. At the Last Supper Christ changed the bread and wine into his own Body and Blood, and told his Apostles to eat and drink. He also told them, "Do this in remembrance of me" (Lk 22:19). At Mass, when the priest changes the bread and wine into the Body and Blood of Christ, his actions are not just a reenactment or imitation of what Christ did at the Last Supper. Nor is this ritual just a symbol of what Christ did for us by dying on the Cross. Instead, the Eucharist *re-presents* the one Sacrifice of Christ in such a way that the Sacrifice is present among us. It is a historical event, yes, but it is also happening now in our presence.

*The Signs on the Door* by Tissot.
"For the LORD will pass through to slay the Egyptians; and when he sees the blood on the lintel and on the two doorposts, the LORD will pass over the door, and will not allow the destroyer to enter your houses to slay you." (Ex 12:23)

## The Mass: The Fulfillment of Old Testament Sacrifices

The Last Supper, when Christ instituted the Eucharist, was also the First Mass. By establishing the Mass, Christ made it possible for the Church, through the priest, to re-present his Sacrifice on the Cross. His Sacrifice is the fulfillment and perfection of the sacrifices found in the Old Testament.

Sacrifice was an essential element of the religious ritual established by the Old Testament Law. These sacrifices had four characteristics. They were each fulfilled in the Sacrifice of Christ on the Cross:

- **Old Testament sacrifices were offered by a priest.** Christ is the Eternal High Priest who offers the Sacrifice of himself on the Cross.
- **In the Old Testament the sacrificial victim was an unblemished male animal.** Christ was a sinless (i.e., unblemished) male, and he is the Victim of the one Sacrifice in the Eucharist. The Passover meal used a spotless lamb; Christ is called the Lamb of God because he is the Sacrifice of the new Passover.
- **Old Testament sacrifices were offered as remission for sin.** Christ's Sacrifice on the Cross atoned for all the sins of the world.
- **In the Old Testament the sacrificial victim was destroyed in some way.** The lamb or other animal being offered was slaughtered. Part of the remains would be cast into fire as a burnt offering to God, while the other part would be eaten by the priests or the people. To eat together was a sign of being in communion with one another and, therefore, offering themselves also in the sacrifice. When both God (through the fire) and man (through eating) "consume" the sacrifice, they are in communion. Christ sacrificed himself willingly on the Cross in obedience to the will of his Father; when we eat his Body and Blood in the Eucharist, we are in communion with God.

There is one important difference between the Old and New Testament sacrifices. *The Old Testament sacrifices had to be offered continuously.* Priests of the Old Covenant had to keep making sacrifices in order to make satisfaction for new sins (in other words, to satisfy the penalty due to those sins). In

*Miracle of the Bread and Fish* by Lanfranco.
"I am the living bread which came down from heaven; if any one eats of this bread, he will live for ever;..." (Jn 6:51)

the New Covenant, Christ's Sacrifice is eternal and has infinite value. It makes satisfaction for all sins for all time: past, present, and future. His one Sacrifice gives more than enough grace for everyone to be saved. The Mass does not *repeat* Christ's Sacrifice. It *re-presents* that one event that occurred on Calvary almost 2,000 years ago.

> **The sacrifice of Christ and the sacrifice of the Eucharist are *one single sacrifice*. (CCC 1367)**

## Holy Communion: Manna from Heaven

At the Last Supper, Jesus said to his disciples, "Take, **eat**; this is my body...**Drink** of it, all of you; for this is my blood of the covenant" (Mt 26:27-28, emphasis added)—he did not intend for his followers to simply witness the Mass, but to eat his Body and drink his Blood. Consuming the Eucharist gives us food for our spiritual journey through life. Receiving the Eucharist is called Holy Communion.

One of Christ's most famous miracles—one that is recorded in all four Gospels—is the feeding of the five thousand. The story is familiar to us. Christ had been preaching all day to the crowds in a remote location. As the day grew long, the Apostles urged him to send the people home so they could eat. Instead Christ took five loaves of bread and two fish and fed the entire multitude with them. But the next day, the people still demanded a sign! They said:

> **"Then what sign do you do, that we may see, and believe you? What work do you perform? Our fathers ate the manna in the wilderness; as it is written, 'He gave them bread from heaven to eat.'" Jesus then said to them, "Truly, truly, I say to you, it was not Moses who gave you the bread from heaven; my Father gives you the true bread from heaven. For the bread of God is that which comes down from heaven, and gives life to the world." (Jn 6:30-33)**

Instead of performing another miracle with physical bread, Jesus used this opportunity to teach them that he would give of himself in the Eucharist:

> **"Your fathers ate the manna in the wilderness, and they died. This is the bread which comes down from heaven, that a man may eat of it and not die. I am the living bread which came down from heaven; if any one eats of this bread, he will live for ever; and the bread which I shall give for the life of the world is my flesh." (Jn 6:49-51)**

Many of the people objected, wondering how this man could give them his flesh to eat. Christ made his meaning even more plain:

> **"Truly, truly, I say to you, unless you eat the flesh of the Son of man and drink his blood, you have no life in you; he who eats my flesh and drinks my blood has eternal life, and I will raise him up at the last day. For my flesh is food indeed, and my blood is drink indeed. He who eats my flesh and drinks my blood abides in me, and I in him." (Jn 6:53-56)**

For many of Christ's listeners this teaching was unacceptable, and they abandoned him because of it. Christ, however, did not soften his words for them. He reiterated that his followers would have to "eat his flesh and drink his blood." The Apostles began to understand his words better when they shared the Last Supper with him.

The Israelites needed manna from heaven for their journey to the Promised Land. So, too, we need Holy Communion on our journey to the final promised land, heaven.



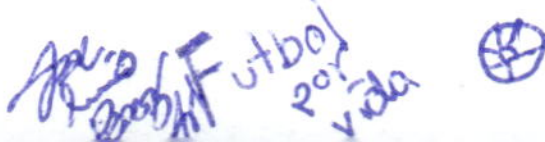

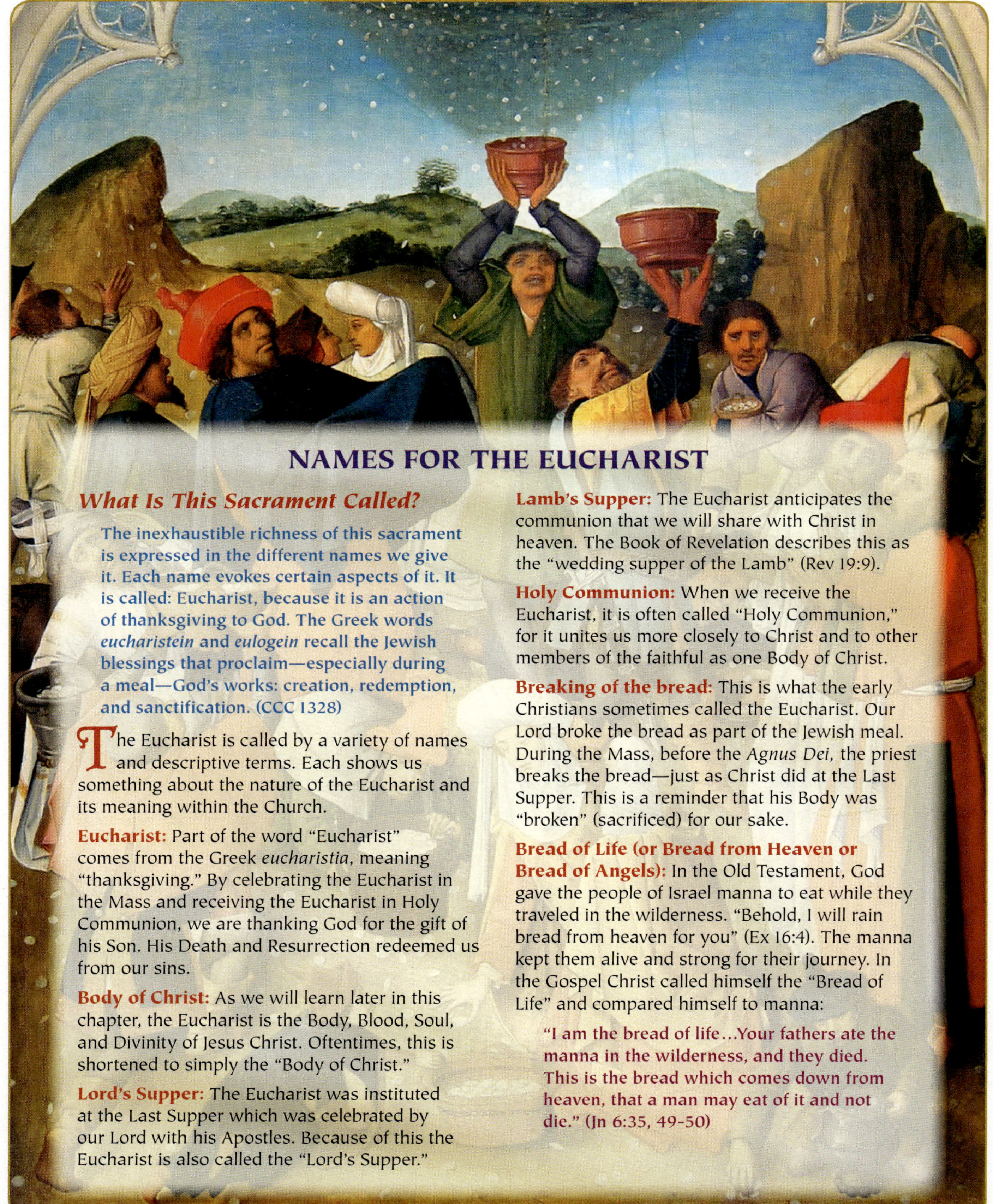

## NAMES FOR THE EUCHARIST

### *What Is This Sacrament Called?*

> The inexhaustible richness of this sacrament is expressed in the different names we give it. Each name evokes certain aspects of it. It is called: Eucharist, because it is an action of thanksgiving to God. The Greek words *eucharistein* and *eulogein* recall the Jewish blessings that proclaim—especially during a meal—God's works: creation, redemption, and sanctification. (CCC 1328)

The Eucharist is called by a variety of names and descriptive terms. Each shows us something about the nature of the Eucharist and its meaning within the Church.

**Eucharist:** Part of the word "Eucharist" comes from the Greek *eucharistia*, meaning "thanksgiving." By celebrating the Eucharist in the Mass and receiving the Eucharist in Holy Communion, we are thanking God for the gift of his Son. His Death and Resurrection redeemed us from our sins.

**Body of Christ:** As we will learn later in this chapter, the Eucharist is the Body, Blood, Soul, and Divinity of Jesus Christ. Oftentimes, this is shortened to simply the "Body of Christ."

**Lord's Supper:** The Eucharist was instituted at the Last Supper which was celebrated by our Lord with his Apostles. Because of this the Eucharist is also called the "Lord's Supper."

**Lamb's Supper:** The Eucharist anticipates the communion that we will share with Christ in heaven. The Book of Revelation describes this as the "wedding supper of the Lamb" (Rev 19:9).

**Holy Communion:** When we receive the Eucharist, it is often called "Holy Communion," for it unites us more closely to Christ and to other members of the faithful as one Body of Christ.

**Breaking of the bread:** This is what the early Christians sometimes called the Eucharist. Our Lord broke the bread as part of the Jewish meal. During the Mass, before the *Agnus Dei*, the priest breaks the bread—just as Christ did at the Last Supper. This is a reminder that his Body was "broken" (sacrificed) for our sake.

**Bread of Life (or Bread from Heaven or Bread of Angels):** In the Old Testament, God gave the people of Israel manna to eat while they traveled in the wilderness. "Behold, I will rain bread from heaven for you" (Ex 16:4). The manna kept them alive and strong for their journey. In the Gospel Christ called himself the "Bread of Life" and compared himself to manna:

> "I am the bread of life…Your fathers ate the manna in the wilderness, and they died. This is the bread which comes down from heaven, that a man may eat of it and not die." (Jn 6:35, 49-50)

## TRANSUBSTANTIATION

***The Body, Blood, Soul, and Divinity of Jesus Christ are made truly present in the Eucharist.***

**"It has always been the conviction of the Church of God...that by the consecration of the bread and wine there takes place a change of the whole substance of the bread into the substance of the body of Christ our Lord and of the whole substance of the wine into the substance of his blood. This change the holy Catholic Church has fittingly and properly called transubstantiation." (CCC 1376)**

Christ is present in many ways in his Church. The Catechism teaches that Christ is present:

- in his Word.
- in the Liturgy.
- in the Sacraments, which he instituted.
- in the poor, the sick and the imprisoned (see CCC 1373).

However, the presence of Christ in the Eucharist is distinctive. The substance (nature or essence) of the bread and wine, by the power of the Holy Spirit, becomes the substance of the Body, Blood, Soul, and Divinity of Christ, i.e., the whole Christ. This change is called **transubstantiation**. The appearances (which are traditionally called "accidents") of the bread and wine remain (color, taste, texture, and so on), while only the substance is changed.

The Eucharist is called the **Real Presence** because the fullness of Christ's presence resides in this Sacrament. The consecrated gifts are no longer bread and wine, despite what they look, taste, or feel like. They are the ultimate gift, the Body and Blood of Christ.

Because the Eucharist is truly the Body, Blood, Soul, and Divinity of Christ, we adore it and treat it with the utmost respect.

Adoration is reserved for God alone—it is man's acknowledgement that he is a creature and that God is the Creator. In **Eucharistic adoration**, we adore Christ, the God-man, in the Eucharist. During Eucharistic adoration, the host is placed in a special vessel called a **monstrance**, which allows adorers to view the Eucharistic host.

*The Mass of St. Gregory.*
The substance (nature or essence) of the bread and wine, by the power of the Holy Spirit, becomes the substance of the Body, Blood, Soul, and Divinity of Christ, i.e., the whole Christ.

Many parishes offer perpetual adoration where the Eucharist is exposed for twenty-four hours a day to be worshiped and adored. Parishes that offer this are a great gift because the faithful can visit Christ any time throughout the day or night.

Every Catholic church has a **tabernacle** where the Eucharist is reserved. Sometimes it is behind or near the altar, and other times it is in a side chapel that is suited to adoration. Catholics genuflect toward the tabernacle when entering or leaving a church. This outward expression of reverence shows our belief that Christ is truly present in the tabernacle.

Outside of Mass the faithful are invited to spend time with Christ present in the Eucharist. We as Catholics should make visiting Christ in the Blessed Sacrament a priority.

## THE MASS

***At the Mass, the priest consecrates the bread and wine, after which the bread and wine become the Body, Blood, Soul, and Divinity of Our Lord.***

At the Last Supper Christ instituted the Eucharist. Thus the Last Supper is considered the first Mass. It is at the Mass that bread and wine are transformed into the Eucharist. It is at the Mass that we can receive this wonderful gift.

Although a bishop or priest can be the celebrant at Mass, for the rest of this chapter we will refer to the *priest* since the parish priest as the celebrant is the common experience of most Catholics. Also, these sections will be describing the Roman Rite of the Church. The Eastern Rites have the same basic parts of the Mass, but are different in some of the particulars.

### WHAT THE SAINTS SAY ABOUT EUCHARISTIC ADORATION

**There is more sweetness in one hour of prayer before Jesus in the Blessed Sacrament than in all the world's crowded theaters, and brilliant drawing rooms, and giddy diversions, and social gatherings. (St. Gabriel Possenti)**

**Whenever I go to the chapel, I put myself in the presence of our good Lord, and I say to him, "Lord, I am here. Tell me what you would have me to do."...And then, I tell God everything that is in my heart. I tell him about my pains and my joys, and then I listen. If you listen, God will also speak to you, for with the good Lord, you have to both speak and listen. God always speaks to you when you approach him plainly and simply. (St. Catherine Laboure)**

**If we truly knew how to appreciate it [the Holy Eucharist], it alone would fortify and sustain us. (St. Theodore Guerin)**

## APOLOGETICS 101:

### CHRIST'S REAL PRESENCE IN THE EUCHARIST

(Adapted from the *Didache Bible*)

***How is Christ truly present in the Eucharist?***

> **Jesus said to [the Jews], "Truly, truly, I say to you, unless you eat the flesh of the Son of man and drink his blood, you have no life in you; he who eats my flesh and drinks my blood has eternal life...For my flesh is food indeed, and my blood is drink indeed." (Jn 6:53-55)**
>
> **[Jesus] took bread, and when he had given thanks he broke it and gave it to them, saying, "This is my body which is given for you. Do this in remembrance of me." (Lk 22:19)**

The Church teaches that Jesus Christ is truly, really, and substantially present—in his Body, Blood, Soul, and Divinity—in the Eucharist. The bread and wine consecrated by the bishop or priest in the Mass become the Body and Blood of Christ.

The Church has always recognized Christ's Real Presence in the Eucharist. Christ's words in instituting this Sacrament at the Last Supper were unequivocal: "This is my body...This is my blood" (Lk 22:19-20). In the Eucharist "the body and blood, together with the soul and divinity, of our Lord Jesus Christ and, therefore, *the whole Christ is truly, really, and substantially contained*" (Council of Trent). St. Paul condemns the unworthy reception of the Eucharist as a profanation of the very Body and Blood of Christ (see I Cor 11:27-29). Already in the fourth century, St. Cyril of Jerusalem exhorted, "Do not see in the bread and wine merely natural elements, because the Lord has expressly said that they are his Body and his Blood: faith assures you of this, though your senses suggest otherwise" (*Mystagogical Catecheses*, IV).

This change in the Eucharistic species in which the substance of the bread and wine become the Body and Blood of Christ is called *transubstantiation*. It occurs at the consecration during the Mass, when the bishop or priest pronounces the *words of consecration* over the bread and wine as Christ commanded.

In the Eucharist Christ remains truly and totally present under the appearances of bread and wine. He offers his Body and Blood to us in Holy Communion to be nourished by his divine life. The Eucharist is, therefore, not merely a symbol of Christ's presence but also the active presence of Christ himself, who gives himself to us unconditionally so our lives might be united to his intimately. The Eucharist is "the perfection of the spiritual life and the end to which all the sacraments tend" (*Summa Theologica* III, 73, 3c).

The Mass consists of two main parts: the *Liturgy of the Word* and the *Liturgy of the Eucharist*. In each part Christ becomes present and invites us to deepen our communion with him.

In the Liturgy of the Word, we hear readings from the Scriptures—usually both Old and New Testament readings. These readings tell of God's love for us. They detail how we are part of his plan of salvation. The high point of the Liturgy of the Word is the Gospel reading, during which we hear the actual words of Christ. We hear about his work to save us. This is so important that we stand as a sign of respect during the Gospel reading. After the Gospel, the priest's homily often explains the readings in more detail and tells how they relate to us.

After the Liturgy of the Word, the Mass continues in the Liturgy of the Eucharist. Just as we received Jesus in the reading of Scripture in the first part of the Mass, now we will receive him sacramentally in Holy Communion. The Liturgy of the Eucharist is centered on the **Eucharistic Prayer**, during which the priest prays for the Holy Spirit to come down and transform the bread and wine into the Body and Blood of Christ. Shortly after the conclusion of the Eucharistic Prayer, the congregation is called forward to receive Holy Communion. We received Jesus in the reading of Scripture in the first part of Mass, and now we receive him sacramentally in Holy Communion. The Mass ends with the priest encouraging all to take what they have received at Mass and live it out in their lives.

## PARTICIPATING IN THE MASS

***Everyone, from the celebrant to the faithful in the pews, has an active role in the Mass.***

**Mother Church earnestly desires that all the faithful should be led to that fully conscious, and active participation in liturgical celebrations which is demanded by the very nature of the liturgy. (*SC* 14)**

Every Sunday and on Holy Days of Obligation Catholics are required to go to Mass. The Church requires attendance at Mass on certain days to emphasize that attending Mass is central to the Christian life.

**The Sunday Eucharist is the foundation and confirmation of all Christian practice. For this reason the faithful are obliged to participate in the Eucharist on days of obligation, unless**

### CHRIST'S SACRIFICE ON THE CROSS AND THE MASS

| | ON THE CROSS | IN THE MASS |
|---|---|---|
| PRIEST | Jesus Christ | Jesus Christ. The priest stands in his place. |
| SACRIFICIAL VICTIM | His Body and Blood | His Body, Blood, Soul, and Divinity (under the appearance of bread and wine). |
| OFFERING | Christ's offering of himself | The same offering of Christ, offering himself through his minister, who acts "in the Person of Christ the Head." |

## INTRODUCTORY RITES

- **The Entrance.** The Mass opens with a procession to the altar.
- **The veneration of the altar.** The priest enters the sanctuary and kisses the altar as a sign of respect for Christ, whom the altar represents.
- **The Penitential Act.** The priest prompts the faithful to remember their sins and then ask for God's mercy and forgiveness.
- **The Gloria.** All sing the hymn "Glory to God in the highest...," which is a hymn of praise to the Blessed Trinity.
- **The Collect.** The priest offers an opening prayer that summarizes the intentions suggested by the liturgical time or feast day.

> **excused for a serious reason (for example, illness, the care of infants) or dispensed by their own pastor. Those who deliberately fail in this obligation commit a grave sin. (CCC 2181)**
>
> **Participation in the communal celebration of the Sunday Eucharist is a testimony of belonging and of being faithful to Christ and to his Church. The faithful give witness by this to their communion in faith and charity. Together they testify to God's holiness and their hope of salvation. They strengthen one another under the guidance of the Holy Spirit. (CCC 2182)**

During the Mass, every person participates, but in different ways. Just as each member of a sports team has a different role, so also each person at Mass has a different role.

> **Christians come together in one place for the Eucharistic assembly. At its head is Christ himself, the principal agent of the Eucharist... It is in representing him that the bishop or priest acting in the person of Christ the head (*in persona Christi capitis*) presides over the assembly, speaks after the readings, receives the offerings, and says the Eucharistic Prayer. All have their own active parts to play in the celebration, each in his own way: readers, those who bring up the offerings, those who give communion, and the whole people whose "Amen" manifests their participation. (CCC 1348)**

**Priests** act in the person of Jesus Christ the Head (*in persona Christi capitis*) at the celebration of the Mass as the visible representatives of Christ, who is the Eternal High Priest of the New Covenant. Pronouncing Christ's words, and doing as Christ commanded, a priest consecrates the Eucharist, by which bread and wine become the Body and Blood of Christ. Through the Eucharistic liturgy, he makes the one and eternal Sacrifice of Christ present. He unites the offerings of all the faithful to that Sacrifice.

**Deacons** assist the priest at the altar. A deacon serves by proclaiming the Gospel, sometimes giving the homily, assisting at the altar, and distributing Holy Communion. In doing so, the deacon acts in the Person of Christ the Servant.

**Members of the lay faithful** and those in consecrated life may serve in other auxiliary roles in the liturgy, such as altar servers, lectors, or cantors. Yet all the assembled faithful, like the members of the Body of

## THE LITURGY OF THE WORD

- **The readings from Scripture.** Two or three readings from Scripture are proclaimed, and one of these readings is always from one of the four Gospels.
- **The homily.** The faithful listen to the priest, or sometimes the deacon, comment on the readings or a related teaching of the Church.
- **The Profession of Faith.** The faithful recite the Nicene Creed (or the Apostles' Creed).
- **The Universal Prayer, or Prayer of the Faithful.** A series of prayers or petitions for the good of the world and the Church are then offered.

The Roman Missal (Latin: *Missale Romanum*) is the liturgical book that contains the texts and rubrics for the celebration of the Mass in the Roman Rite of the Catholic Church.

Christ that they are, are united in their participation in this one celebration of the Eucharist.

Your participation in the Mass includes your whole person: both your soul and your body. As with all the Sacraments, a good interior disposition and your commitment to prayer will make you more receptive to the grace that God gives freely in the Eucharist.

How can you do this? Preparation is important.

To prepare yourself for Mass, remind yourself that it is the most important event of your day. Think about it: the opportunity to be in the presence of Christ and to receive his Body and Blood is a unique privilege that is far greater than anything else you could possibly experience!

If you are in a **state of grace**—free of mortal sin—you may prepare to receive Holy Communion. If you are not in a state of grace, still go to Mass but do not receive the Eucharist until you have received the Sacrament of Penance and absolution for your sin. Use some of the silent parts of the Mass to reflect on your sins, think about ways to avoid them in the future, and ask God's help to remove any obstacles to receiving absolution. Remember that you are in the presence of Christ and with the loving Family of God, who are ready to celebrate your return to friendship with him!

Ask God to help you with these four things, and cooperate with his help:

- **Keep the Eucharistic fast.** The Church requires you to abstain from food and drink (other than water or medicine) for at least one hour before receiving Communion.
- **Pray on the way to Mass** and spend some time in prayer in church before Mass begins. Pray for the priest, the other members of the faithful, and for yourself and your own needs. Ask the Holy Spirit to help you to be receptive to the graces that are available by attending Mass and receiving Holy Communion.
- **Enter into the presence of God.** Arrive early, dress appropriately for Mass, and maintain reverence as you enter the sacred place. Bless yourself with the Sign of the Cross, using holy water from the font or baptistry. Before entering your pew, genuflect toward the tabernacle where the Blessed Sacrament is reserved. Kneel for a time in prayer, and make an examination of conscience. Continue praying as you wait for Mass to begin. If it helps you focus on the Mass, open a missal and read the readings of the day. Maintain a frame of mind that will help you to focus on the divine.
- **Stay attentive and engaged.** The Church calls us to "full, active, and conscious participation" in the Mass (CCC 1141). Listen to the prayers, readings, and homily. Join in the hymns, responses, *Gloria*, Creed, and prayerful silences.

## THE LITURGY OF THE EUCHARIST

- **The Preparation of the Gifts.** Members of the faithful might process to the sanctuary carrying the bread and wine that are to be consecrated on the altar.
- **The Eucharistic Prayer.** The priest now offers the primary prayer of the Liturgy of the Eucharist. See the sidebar "The Eucharistic Prayer."
- **The Lord's Prayer.** The priest asks everyone to pray in unison in the words that Christ taught: "Our Father, who art in heaven..."
- **The Rite of Peace.** The priest greets all the faithful, and asks them to give each other a sign of peace. This is a symbol of peace, communion, and charity exchanged before approaching the Eucharist in Holy Communion.
- **The Breaking of Bread (during the *Agnus Dei*).** The priest breaks the consecrated host, placing a small piece of it in the chalice. This signifies that the many faithful are made one body by receiving communion from the one Bread of Life, which is Christ.
- **The *Agnus Dei*.** The congregation acclaims the Sacrifice of Christ, their savior: "Lamb of God, you take away the sins of the world..."
- **Holy Communion.** The priest then distributes the Eucharist to the faithful who approach the altar to receive it.
- **Concluding Rite.** The priest prays the Prayer After Communion, thanking God and asking that the Eucharist may change lives. The deacon or priest dismisses the faithful, and a closing hymn may be sung.

If you are physically able to do so, sit, stand, and kneel. Make the Sign of the Cross and offer a sign of peace. The Mass is a solemn and joyful occasion, and so your heart, soul, and body should reflect this.

## RECEIVING HOLY COMMUNION

***The Eucharist gives us strength and increases our union with Christ.***

When you receive the Eucharist in a state of grace, the effects and fruits of this Sacrament in you can be profound. The better prepared you are, the more disposed you will be to receive its wonderful graces.

> **To prepare for worthy reception of this sacrament, the faithful should observe the fast required in their Church. Bodily demeanor (gestures, clothing) ought to convey the respect, solemnity, and joy of this moment when Christ becomes our guest. (CCC 1387)**

Receiving Holy Communion has many effects on your soul, including:

- **The Eucharist strengthens our union with Christ.** Through this union you are also brought into communion with the whole Church. You

### MINISTER, MATTER, AND FORM OF THE EUCHARIST

As in every Sacrament, there are certain essential elements in the celebration of the Eucharist:

- The *minister* of the Eucharist is a bishop or priest, who acts in the person of Jesus Christ (*in persona Christi*).
- The *matter* of the Eucharist is wheat bread and grape wine. The Roman Rite uses unleavened bread in the Eucharist. By ancient tradition, many of the Eastern Rites use leavened bread.
- The *form* of the Eucharist is the words of consecration.

### EUCHARISTIC PRAYER

> **With the Eucharistic Prayer—the prayer of thanksgiving and consecration—we come to the heart and summit of the celebration. (CCC 1352)**

- **Thanksgiving.** Especially in the preface to the Eucharistic Prayer, the priest gives thanks (Greek *eucharistia*) to the Father for all that he has done in Christ. He thanks God for Christ's work of salvation, often for the particular aspect of that work linked to the feast or time of year.
- **Acclamation.** Since the celebration of the Mass is a participation in the heavenly liturgy, the people join the choirs of angels in singing the *Sanctus* ("Holy, Holy, Holy Lord God of hosts…").
- ***Epiclesis* (invocation, or "calling down from on high").** The priest prays that the Holy Spirit will come down to change the bread and wine into the Body and Blood of Our Lord.
- **Institution Narrative and Consecration.** This central part of the Eucharistic Prayer recalls the Last Supper and the institution of the Sacrament of the Eucharist. With the words of consecration, the bread and wine become the Body and Blood of Our Lord Jesus Christ. After each consecration the priest silently elevates the host or chalice.
- ***Anamnesis* (Memorial Acclamation).** The assembled faithful recall the Death and Resurrection of Christ and our hope for his second coming.
- **Offering.** The whole Church offers through the priest the Sacrifice of Jesus Christ, asking that it be acceptable to God the Father. The Church asks that by the grace it brings we may be united to the Father, as joint members of the Body of Christ, by the working of the Holy Spirit.
- **Intercessions.** In communion with the whole Church in heaven and on earth, prayer is offered for all the faithful, both living and dead, so that they may share in the salvation won by Christ's sacrifice.
- **Final Doxology.** The Eucharistic prayer ends with a praise to God for all of his gifts and blessings.

were first incorporated into the Body of Christ at Baptism. This unity is strengthened in the Eucharist. Because it is a Sacrament, receiving the Eucharist in Holy Communion not only signals our communion but also works to deepen it.

The principal fruit of receiving the Eucharist in Holy Communion is an intimate union with Christ Jesus. Indeed, the Lord said: "He who eats my flesh and drinks my blood abides in me, and I in him." Life in Christ has its foundation in the Eucharistic banquet: "As the living Father sent me, and I live because of the Father, so he who eats me will live because of me" (CCC 1391).

Those who receive the Eucharist are united more closely to Christ. Through it Christ unites them to all the faithful in one body—the Church. Communion renews, strengthens, and deepens this incorporation into the Church, already achieved by Baptism. In Baptism we have been called to form but one body. The Eucharist fulfills this call (cf. CCC 1396).

- **The Eucharist builds and strengthens you in grace.** It "preserves, increases, and renews the life of grace you received at Baptism" (CCC 1392).
- **The Eucharist increases your ability to love.** Your tendency toward caring only about yourself is reduced, and you become more compassionate toward others. The Eucharist increases your love of God, of your neighbor, and of the poor. Ordinary food strengthens your body, restoring you when you are physically weak. This spiritual food restores and strengthens you in love.

## REQUIREMENTS FOR RECEIVING HOLY COMMUNION

The Eucharist offers you many graces to grow in holiness. You are limited only by your own capacity to receive these graces. For this reason, the more properly disposed—spiritually prepared—you are to receive Holy Communion, the more you will benefit from this Sacrament.

Going to Holy Communion is not a social event or a right; it is a gift from God and your response to his call.

St. Paul warns against receiving the Eucharist unworthily:

> **Whoever, therefore, eats the bread or drinks the cup of the Lord in an unworthy manner will be guilty of profaning the body and blood of the Lord. Let a man examine himself, and so eat of the bread and drink of the cup. For any one who eats and drinks without discerning the body eats and drinks judgment upon himself. (1 Cor 11:27-29)**

To help the faithful receive the Eucharist worthily, the Church sets a number of simple requirements for reception of Holy Communion:

- **You must be a baptized Catholic.** Holy Communion is a sign of unity with the Church that was founded by Christ and is headed by the successors to the Apostles. As a sign of unity, only those who are Catholic and believe what the Catholic Church teaches about the Eucharist can receive it.
- **You must be in a state of grace.** Being in a state of grace means that you are not conscious of having committed a serious sin. For this reason, you should always examine your conscience before receiving Holy Communion. If you have committed a mortal sin, receive the Sacrament of Penance before receiving Holy Communion.

  > **To respond to this invitation we must *prepare ourselves* for so great and so holy a moment... Anyone conscious of a grave sin must receive the sacrament of Reconciliation before coming to communion. (CCC 1385)**

- **You must fast for at least one hour before receiving the Eucharist.** You may take some water or medicine, but no other food or drink of any kind. Fasting helps to prepare you for the reception of Christ because it reminds you of your spiritual hunger for him.

Also, be sure to say a prayer of thanksgiving after you receive Holy Communion. The Eucharist is a tremendous gift, and we should always thank God for it!

Habits of daily prayer, a daily examination of conscience, and frequent reception of the Sacrament of Penance will help keep you on track so that you can always be prepared to receive Holy Communion.

- **The Eucharist strengthens you against sin and promotes good works.** The increase in love and communion pulls you away from worldly attachments and reduces concupiscence, which is your temptation to sin. This spiritual food helps you to practice good works and to avoid doing evil.

  To receive in truth the Body and Blood of Christ given up for us, we must recognize Christ in the poorest, his brethren:

  **You have tasted the Blood of the Lord, yet you do not recognize your brother...You dishonor this table when you do not judge worthy of sharing your food someone judged worthy to take part in this meal...God freed you from all your sins and invited you here, but you have not become more merciful. (St. John Chrysostom, *Hom. in 1 Cor.* 27, 4: PG 61, 229-230; cf. Mt 25:40)**

- **The Eucharist forgives venial sin.** Serious or mortal sins require the Sacrament of Penance. Lesser sins are absolved by worthy reception of the Eucharist when you are properly disposed and contrite for your sins. This is a result of being drawn more closely into the love and communion of Christ.

- **The Eucharist inclines you to foster unity with all Christians.** This Sacrament, which unites you to the Church and to Christ, increases your hope that all who believe in Christ will one day be united in one Church as Christ himself desires.

You probably have heard the expression that "you are what you eat." This can be said of the Eucharist. Receiving the Body of Christ incorporates you more fully into the Body of Christ, the Church. When you consume the Body and Blood of the risen Christ and allow the Holy Spirit to work within you, you become more like Christ himself.

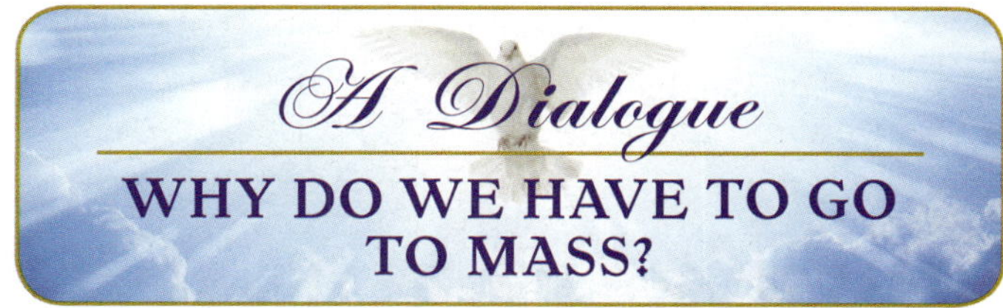

## A Dialogue
## WHY DO WE HAVE TO GO TO MASS?

**Mom:** "Maria, it's time to get up—we leave for Mass in half an hour!"

**Maria:** "But, Mom, I'm tired, do I have to go?"

**Mom:** "It's Sunday, what do you think?"

**Maria:** "I know we go to Mass on Sunday, can't I miss just this once?"

**Mom:** "Do you know why we go to Mass on Sundays?"

**Maria:** "Well, that's when they have Mass, so I guess that's why we go."

**Mom:** "Actually, St. John's has Mass every day, but Sunday is the day all Catholics are required to go to Mass. Do you know why?"

**Maria:** "Um...not really."

**Mom:** "Sunday is the day Jesus rose from the dead, and on every Sunday we celebrate his Resurrection—as well as remember his Death. Going to Mass helps us to remember these events, but also helps us to be part of them."

**Maria:** "How can we be part of something that happened 2,000 years ago?"

**Mom:** "This isn't the best analogy—but think of Mass as a time machine. When you go to Mass, you go back—not physically, but spiritually—back to Jerusalem when Jesus was on the Cross."

**Maria:** "That's kinda weird, Mom."

**Mom:** "I guess so, but it shows that you are part of God's great plan for everyone—you get to be part of the most important events that have ever happened. You know why else we go to Mass?"

**Maria:** "Cuz everyone else does?"

**Mom:** "Sure lots of other people do, but that's not why we go. We go in order to get strength to be good followers of Jesus. You know how hard it can be to be a Catholic today. Going to

Mass—and receiving Communion—helps us be better people, and better Catholics."

**Maria:** "That makes sense, I guess."

**Mom:** "So you think maybe you should get ready now?"

**Maria:** "Sure, Mom, I'll be ready in time—just make sure there's gas in the, uh, time machine."

## CONCLUSION

***The Christian life is centered around the Eucharist, which is its foundation.***

The Sacrament of the Eucharist is the Sacrament of Sacraments—the very foundation of Christian life. All that the Church is and does is centered on it. All the other Sacraments point to the Eucharist because it summarizes the entire plan of salvation for us. In celebrating the Eucharist, we proclaim Christ's Death, Resurrection, and Ascension. We anticipate his second coming and our own rising to eternal life.

Christ instituted the Eucharist at the Last Supper when he changed bread and wine into his own Body and Blood and gave it to his Apostles to eat and drink. He is the Bread of Life. Those who eat of this bread share in his divine life and enter into communion with him. At that first Mass, Christ transformed the Passover celebration and instituted the priesthood. The Church has been celebrating the Mass for the faithful ever since. Through the Eucharist Christ fulfills his promise that he will always be with us, even to the end of the world.

The Eucharist is a Sacrifice because it re-presents the one Sacrifice of Christ, which brought about our redemption by atoning for all sins past, present, and future. It is a memorial in the sense that the one Sacrifice of Christ is made present among us in the Eucharistic liturgy. We can unite our own sacrifices and sufferings to his and thereby share in his redemption.

On Sundays and Holy Days of Obligation, Catholics are required to go to Mass. And the Mass requires our active participation. Good interior and external preparation, assisted by the Holy Spirit, will make our participation more fruitful. Regular Confession and examination of conscience help prepare us for worthy reception of the Sacrament of the Eucharist. The Church requires us to participate in the Mass and to receive the Eucharist because it is essential to the Christian life.

If we are properly disposed, receiving Holy Communion will have many beneficial effects. It will bring us into closer union with Christ, build and strengthen us in baptismal grace, increase our ability to love, forgive our venial sins, strengthen us against sin and concupiscence, and lead us to seek and hope for greater unity with other Christians.

## POINTS TO REMEMBER

1. Throughout salvation history God prepared his people for the Eucharist. In the Passover, the animal sacrifices, and the manna from heaven, God gave hints as to the great gift he would bestow in the Eucharist.
2. When the priest acting in the person of Christ the Head (*in persona Christi capitis*) says the words of Consecration at the Mass, bread and wine are transformed into the Body, Blood, Soul, and Divinity of Christ. This process is called "transubstantiation."
3. The Mass consists of two main parts: the Liturgy of the Word, and the Liturgy of the Eucharist. In the first part, Scripture readings dominate as we encounter Christ in the Bible. In the second part, Christ becomes present to us sacramentally in the Eucharist.
4. When we are properly disposed in receiving Holy Communion, we are given strength for our Christian life, we enter into a deep communion with Christ, our ability to love is increased, our venial sins are forgiven, and we are united to our fellow Catholics.

# WITNESS OF CHRIST

## THE MIRACLE OF LANCIANO

We often struggle to believe what our Lord has revealed. God realizes that we experience doubts and have questions. He realizes that believing can be hard. He gives us supernatural faith to help us overcome these doubts and difficulties. Also, God has provided the Church with miracles through the centuries. These miracles are not meant to surpass the truths that Christ revealed. They are designed to help strengthen our faith in the Revelation of Christ. One such extraordinary event took place in Lanciano, Italy in the eighth century.

A monk in Lanciano was plagued by doubts over the Real Presence of Christ in the Eucharist. This caused him to have little peace. However, God intervened dramatically to help this monk's faith as well as strengthen the faith of generations to come.

One day when he was celebrating Mass, the monk suddenly stood silent. He was confused and scared at what he witnessed. But his fear was quickly replaced by happiness and peace. He turned to the people at Mass and told them to come forward and view an extraordinary miracle. The bread had been changed into human flesh, and the wine had been changed into human blood.

In 1970, with approval from the Vatican, the Archbishop of Lanciano handed over the flesh and the blood to be scientifically tested. The Church had safeguarded these relics for centuries. In 1971 the results of the scientific tests were published: the flesh is tissue from a human heart, and the blood is human blood. There was no evidence of any preservatives or mummification. There was nothing found that would suggest a hoax or any sort of deception.

In 1973 the World Health Organization and the United Nations appointed a group of scientists to see if they could come to the same conclusion as the first researchers. The researchers concluded that the first study was correct and accurate in its report. Most extraordinarily, the second group of scientists declared that the flesh is *living* tissue and reacts and responds like living human flesh.

Pilgrims still travel to Italy to see this great miracle. Yet a similar miracle happens at each and every Mass when the bread and wine are transformed into Christ's Body and Blood. The appearance of the Eucharist may seem quite ordinary, but with the eyes of faith we are assured that we are receiving the Body, Blood, Soul, and Divinity of our Savior, Jesus Christ.

# VOCABULARY

### EUCHARISTIC ADORATION

Adoration of the Blessed Sacrament when the sacred host is exposed in a monstrance.

### EUCHARISTIC PRAYER

The primary prayer of the Mass, the Eucharistic Prayer is said by the bishop or priest, and during it the bread and wine are transformed into the Body, Blood, Soul, and Divinity of Jesus Christ.

### MONSTRANCE

A vessel of precious metal used for exposing the Blessed Sacrament for adoration. At the center of the monstrance is a glass lunette, which allows the faithful to view the Blessed Sacrament during exposition.

### REAL PRESENCE

The true, real, and substantial presence of Christ—Body, Blood, Soul, and Divinity—under the appearance of the consecrated bread and wine of the Eucharist. The Church invites the faithful to deepen their faith in the Real Presence of Christ through worship and communion in the Eucharistic liturgy, and through acts of adoration outside of Mass.

### STATE OF GRACE

The condition whereby one enjoys the friendship of God. One who possesses "sanctifying grace" or "habitual grace" is enabled to know, love, and serve God and others in reference to him. The state of grace is lost by committing mortal sin but may be regained through the Sacrament of Penance or by an act of perfect contrition.

### TABERNACLE

The receptacle in a Catholic church were the Eucharist is reserved. The hosts are kept there to later take to the sick and other people who are unable to attend Mass, and also for people to pray silently in the presence of Christ.

### TRANSUBSTANTIATION

The term used to designate the unique change, in a true, real, and substantial manner, of the entire substance of the Eucharistic bread and wine into the Body and Blood of Christ, with his Soul and Divinity, leaving intact the "accidents" (the qualities, or attributes, of bread and wine).

A monstrance is a vessel of precious metal used for exposing the Blessed Sacrament for adoration.

## STUDY QUESTIONS

1. What did Passover celebrate in the Old Testament?
2. Why is the Eucharist called the new Passover?
3. How is Holy Communion a fulfillment of the miracle of the manna in the desert?
4. What does the word *Eucharist* mean?
5. What is transubstantiation?
6. What is the *epiclesis*?
7. What is the role of a bishop or priest in the Mass?
8. What are the four things you can do to help prepare to participate in the Mass?
9. What is the matter, form, and minister of the Eucharist?
10. If we have mortal sin on our soul, what must we do before receiving Holy Communion?

## PRACTICAL EXERCISES

1. Imagine you have a Catholic friend who does not believe in the Real Presence of Christ in the Eucharist. He says, "The bread is a symbol of Christ, but it's not really his Body and Blood." How would explain to him that the Eucharist is not just a symbol?

2. If you have the opportunity, participate in the Divine Liturgy at an Eastern Catholic church. Some of the prayers, symbols, and gestures may seem different, but you will recognize certain common elements: the structure of the Liturgy of the Word and the Liturgy of the Eucharist as well as reverence for the Body and Blood of Christ. If there are no Eastern Catholic churches in your area, watch a video of a Divine Liturgy online.

If you have the opportunity, participate in the Divine Liturgy at an Eastern Catholic church.

# Sealed in the Spirit

***To get to know Christ better, spend time with him in Eucharistic adoration.***

Do you believe in the Real Presence of Christ in the Eucharist? Think about it for a moment. Christ is really present, even though we only perceive what seems to be bread and wine.

Since the beginning of the Church, Christians have had a deep reverence for the consecrated bread and wine. Let's read again what St. Paul wrote about receiving the Eucharist worthily:

> **Whoever, therefore, eats the bread or drinks the cup of the Lord in an unworthy manner will be guilty of profaning the body and blood of the Lord. Let a man examine himself, and so eat of the bread and drink of the cup. For any one who eats and drinks without discerning the body eats and drinks judgment upon himself. (1 Cor 11: 27-29)**

Everyone shares in the one bread, which is the Body of Christ. In doing so, we are drawn more deeply into the Body of Christ, the Church.

In the early Church the priests set aside some Eucharistic hosts so that they could be taken to Christians who were not able to attend the liturgy. This way they too could share in the one bread of the Christian community. In later centuries the tabernacle became a focus of prayer because of the presence of Christ. The practice then developed of displaying a host in an ornate container, called a monstrance, so that people could see the Body of Christ as they prayed in his presence.

Many blessings and graces can come from praying in the presence of the Eucharist. These steps can help you make it a habit:

- Spend a few minutes praying in view of the tabernacle before or after Mass.
- When you pass a church, stop in and spend a few minutes in silent adoration in the presence of Christ.
- Check your parish bulletin for Benediction, exposition, and other Eucharistic events. These are opportunities for prayer before the Blessed Sacrament with the wider Catholic community.
- Learn which churches or chapels in your area have perpetual adoration, and visit regularly. Many of these churches and chapels ask people to sign up to pray at a certain time every week or month. Consider making such a commitment.

Learn which churches or chapels in your area have perpetual adoration, and visit regularly.

# You and Your Parents

***Family members can help each other prepare to receive the Eucharist worthily.***

Are you in the habit of preparing well to receive the Eucharist at Mass?

We easily slip into bad habits that take away from our experience of the Sacraments. Maybe you get distracted during Mass and go through the motions without a lot of thought. Maybe you do not take the Eucharistic fast seriously, grabbing a snack on the way to Mass. Maybe you do not take time to think about the great privilege of receiving the Body and Blood of Christ.

It is up to you to cooperate with God's grace, which helps you prepare yourself as best you can to receive Christ. You can also ask your family to help you. By making just a little more effort, family members can make it easier for everyone to get ready for Mass, both on the inside and outside.

Here are some thoughts that may help your family members get ready for Mass:

- Does your family arrive for Mass in plenty of time (ten minutes before Mass begins, for example), or do you arrive just in time for the opening hymn or even a little late? Talk to your parents about how important it is to have some time for quiet prayer in church before Mass begins. Suggest that the family leave home earlier. Remember to do your part, too. Make sure you are ready to go on time, and help your siblings get ready, too. In the car, try turning off the radio and leaving your earbuds at home. The quiet will help your frame of mind for Mass.
- Does your family dress appropriately for Mass? The Mass is something special: an occasion to talk with and receive God in a special way. So it might not be appropriate to wear the same clothes that you wear to walk through a park or relax with friends. Participating in the Mass is like being invited to have supper in God's own house, so your clothes—like your words and actions—should show respect for your Creator and Redeemer.
- Do you stay after Mass a few minutes to pray in thanksgiving and meditate on the Sacrament that you have just received? Christ's Body and Blood are really present inside you. Spend some time thanking God the Holy Spirit for this great gift, asking him to allow the grace of this Sacrament to make you a stronger, better Catholic. Talk to your parents about how important it is to have a little time for quiet prayer in church after the end of Mass. It is a good habit that helps you appreciate the great gift that you have received.

Participating in the Mass is like being invited to have supper in God's own house, so dress appropriately.

# YOU AND YOUR SPONSOR

***Receiving the Eucharist is a privilege that you should seek by attending Mass more often.***

Years ago some Catholics were meeting with the twentieth-century Indian spiritual leader Mahatma Gandhi. They explained to him our belief in the Real Presence of Christ in the Eucharist. Gandhi said he doubted that Catholics really believe it. "If I really believed that my Lord and my God were truly present in the tabernacle as you say he is," he said, "I would crawl on my belly to church every day to worship and adore him."

His point is very good. If you really believe that Christ is present in the Eucharist, then it only makes sense that you would desire to adore and receive him often.

How often do you participate in Mass? Surely you make the effort to go to Mass every Sunday (or on the preceding Saturday evening) and on every Holy Day of Obligation.

But do you participate in Mass more often than that?

If you are a student in a Catholic school, you might have the opportunity to participate in Mass as a class or with the entire student body on a regular basis. This is a good thing. When you do not feel like participating in Mass on a weekday, ask God to help you make an effort to get the most you can out of Mass. It is a tremendous privilege to receive the Eucharist in Holy Communion.

Do you participate in other weekday Masses, of your own free will? It is a good practice to do so. Think about it. In the Eucharist we receive the Body and Blood of Christ. Why would we not want to receive the Eucharist as often as possible?

Talk about the Real Presence with your sponsor. These questions for your sponsor might help begin a discussion:

1. Was there a time when you struggled with belief in the mystery of the Real Presence?
2. How do you prepare to receive the Eucharist in Holy Communion? What advice can you offer me for my own preparation?
3. Do you attend Mass more often than is required? Why or why not?

If weekday Masses are available in your area, try to participate in Mass at least one additional day per week, whether with your sponsor, on your own, or with your family.

If you are a student in a Catholic school, you might have the opportunity to participate in Mass on a regular basis. This is a good thing.

The Sacrament of

# Confirmation

Chapter 7

# The Sacraments of Initiation: Confirmation

## INTRODUCTION

***The Sacrament of Confirmation is linked to the Sacraments of Baptism and the Eucharist.***

In the previous two chapters you learned about two Sacraments of Initiation: Baptism and the Eucharist.

Baptism is the first of the Sacraments of Initiation and the gateway to all the other Sacraments. It cleanses us from all sin and fills us with sanctifying grace. Baptism also makes us adopted sons and daughters of God and infuses us with the theological virtues of faith, hope, and charity. The Eucharist is our "food of eternal life." Through the Eucharist we are spiritually nourished by the Body and Blood of Christ and are given a share in his life, participating in his Death and Resurrection. "He who eats my flesh and drinks my blood abides in me, and I in him" (Jn 6:56).

Confirmation is the third Sacrament of Initiation. It is the Sacrament which increases and deepens our baptismal graces and allows us to receive the fullness of the gifts of the Holy Spirit. But what does that mean? How do we receive the Holy Spirit? These are questions we will address in this chapter.

All three of these Sacraments are necessary for a person to be fully initiated into the Body of Christ. Together, these Sacraments form the foundation for living out your Christian mission, your call to holiness, which is your path to happiness.

All three of the Sacraments of Initiation are necessary for a person to be fully initiated into the Body of Christ.

After reading this chapter, you will be able to answer these questions:

- How did the Sacrament of Confirmation develop in Church history?
- What are the form, matter, and minister of Confirmation?
- What are the effects of the Sacrament of Confirmation?
- How is the Sacrament of Confirmation celebrated?
- Who can receive the Sacrament of Confirmation?
- Why is it important to receive it?

The Apostles, after receiving the Holy Spirit on Pentecost, went out to make disciples just as Christ had commanded.

## THE ORIGINS OF CONFIRMATION

***The Apostles prayed and laid hands on the newly baptized.***

Pentecost marked the beginning of the Holy Spirit's ministry in the Church. It will be helpful to take a moment now to review the complete account of Pentecost in your Bible. Read Chapter 2 of the Acts of the Apostles, which is the first book after the four Gospels.

Before the outpouring of the Holy Spirit at Pentecost, the Apostles experienced a time of waiting. They were confused, doubtful, and frightened. The risen Christ had appeared to them, and they had come to understand the plan of God more deeply. However, the Holy Spirit had not yet anointed them. They did not have the courage necessary to preach the Gospel to the unbelieving world.

The disciples needed the gifts of the Holy Spirit. They needed God's strength to bring Christ to others. Just as Christ did not begin his ministry until the Holy Spirit descended upon him at his baptism, the disciples, too, were waiting for the Holy Spirit. On Pentecost their wait ended.

The Apostles, after receiving the Holy Spirit, went out to make disciples just as Christ had commanded. They preached repentance and renewal in Jerusalem, then to neighboring towns, and eventually to the whole world. When people believed in the Gospel, they were baptized, and thus received the Holy Spirit as well.

> **Filled with the Holy Spirit the apostles began to proclaim "the mighty works of God," and Peter declared this outpouring of the Spirit to be the sign of the messianic age. Those who believed in the apostolic preaching and were baptized received the gift of the Holy Spirit in their turn. (CCC 1287)**

The Apostles even went into regions that were traditionally hostile to the Jewish people. One example of this was Samaria:

> **When the apostles at Jerusalem heard that Samaria had received the word of God, they sent to them Peter and John, who came down and prayed for them that they might receive the Holy Spirit; for it had not yet fallen on any of them, but they had only been baptized in the name of the Lord Jesus. Then they laid their hands on them and they received the Holy Spirit. (Acts 8:14-17)**

*St. Peter and St. John laying on hands in Samaria.* "and they received the Holy Spirit."

*St. Paul Preaching in Athens* by Raphael.
The Apostles understood that the outpouring of the Holy Spirit was not a gift reserved just for them.

In the town of Ephesus, St. Paul came across some believers who had received only the baptism of St. John the Baptist:

> **Paul said, "John baptized with the baptism of repentance, telling the people to believe in the one who was to come after him, that is, Jesus." On hearing this, they were baptized in the name of the Lord Jesus. And when Paul had laid his hands upon them, the Holy Spirit came on them. (Acts 19:4-6)**

The Apostles understood that the outpouring of the Holy Spirit was not a gift reserved just for them but was intended for all who believe in Christ. They gave the gift of the Holy Spirit to others, enabling Christians to live and proclaim the Gospel. The outpouring of the Holy Spirit was, from the beginning of Christianity, vital to the completion of a person's initiation into the Church.

### CONTINUING THE GRACE OF PENTECOST

**From that time on the Apostles, in fulfillment of Christ's will, imparted to the newly baptized by the laying on of hands the gift of the Spirit that completes the grace of Baptism....This laying on of hands is rightly recognized by Catholic tradition as the beginning of the sacrament of Confirmation, which in a certain way perpetuates the grace of Pentecost in the Church. (St. Paul VI, *On the Sacrament of Confirmation*)**

## A Brief History of Confirmation: FIRST CENTURIES OF THE CHURCH

***The Rite of Confirmation developed to serve a rapidly growing number of Christians.***

In the early centuries of the Church, the three Sacraments of Christian Initiation were generally received in one liturgical celebration. As you read in Chapter 4, a person who wanted to be a Christian entered the catechumenate. This was a time of instruction, prayer, and discernment. The catechumen learned about the faith and prepared to commit to a life in Christ and in the Church.

When the bishop determined that a catechumen was ready to be received into the Church, he would give the Sacraments of Initiation. The initiation took place usually at the Easter Vigil and included all the catechumens from the same diocese. After questioning the catechumens and hearing their profession of faith, the bishop would baptize them with water, confirm them through the laying on of hands, anoint them with oil, and then pray for the Holy Spirit to come upon them. The new Christians would then be clothed in white garments and led in procession into the Church. They would take part in the liturgy and receive the Eucharist in Holy Communion for the first time.

### Great Numbers of Christians

The earliest growth of Christianity was mainly in larger cities; beginning in the fourth century, the number of Christians grew quickly, especially in rural areas. There were so many catechumens and so many Christian communities that the bishops simply could not baptize and confirm everyone by themselves. A bishop's diocese might be large, and travel was relatively slow. The bishops needed a way to administer the Sacraments to all the catechumens of the rapidly growing Church. The Church in Western Europe and North Africa came up with a different solution to these problems than the Church in Eastern Europe and Asia Minor.

In the West, around the fifth or sixth century, bishops authorized their priests to baptize and give First Communion. Every few years the bishop would visit different regions of his diocese to give the Sacrament of Confirmation to the newly baptized.

In the East bishops allowed their priests to give all three Sacraments of Initiation. When the bishop visited the local communities, he distributed the Sacred **Chrism** that he had blessed; this was used by the priests to confirm new Christians.

## The Age of Confirmation and First Communion

In time, the practice of giving the Eucharist to baptized infants faded in the West, and it was given at a later age. The order of Confirmation and the Eucharist sometimes varied from region to region, but Baptism was always given first.

In 1215 the Pope called together a great council and it was decided that the Eucharist should be postponed in the Latin Church until the child was older and understood it better. Confirmation was given about the "age of reason" (when a child can understand right from wrong—usually about seven years old), and the Eucharist was given as First Communion about age eleven or twelve. This practice continued into the twentieth century.

In 1910 Pope St. Pius X decreed that children should receive the Eucharist at a younger age.

Most Catholics in the United States receive First Communion about age seven.

The Eucharist should be given beginning around the age of reason. He wanted young people to have the spiritual strength of the Eucharist to help them be faithful to Christ. However, this caused Confirmation to become postponed to a later age. Today most Catholics in the United States receive First Communion about age seven and then Confirmation between age thirteen and sixteen.

### WHEN SHOULD CONFIRMATION BE GIVEN?

When should a baptized Catholic receive the Sacrament of Confirmation? That is up to your bishop and the bishops in your country or region of the world.

The *Catechism* teaches:

> **In the Latin Church this sacrament is administered when the age of reason has been reached. (CCC 1318)**

For Catholics in the Latin Church, the Church's law states:

> **The sacrament of confirmation is to be conferred on the faithful at about the age of discretion [ability to tell right from wrong] unless the conference of bishops has determined another age. (CIC 891)**

## THE UNITY OF THE SACRAMENTS OF INITIATION

***Baptism, the Eucharist, and Confirmation together constitute initiation into the Church.***

Baptism, the Eucharist, and Confirmation, although they are three distinct Sacraments, are united in that all three are necessary to initiate a person into the Body of Christ.

> **Baptism, the Eucharist, and the sacrament of Confirmation together constitute the 'sacraments of Christian initiation,' whose unity must be safeguarded. (CCC 1285)**

Each of these Sacraments gives us "life"—the spiritual life we need to be Christ's disciples. We are born anew in the Sacrament of Baptism, opening us up to God's grace. In the Eucharist, we receive the food we need to live each day like Christ. And in Confirmation, we are given strength to battle temptation and witness our faith to others.

We can compare this to our natural (physical) life. We are all born into this world, thus beginning our life here on earth. But to survive, we need to eat food every day. But we don't just want to survive. We want to thrive and be the best we can be. We need to strengthen our bodies and keep them in good shape. These same things need to be done in the spiritual life, and are done through Baptism, the Eucharist, and Confirmation.

## THE LAYING ON OF HANDS

***In Scripture we find that the laying on of hands is deeply symbolic.***

Earlier in this book, you read about the events and people in the Old Testament that are *types* of the Sacrament of Confirmation in the New Testament. You read about people who were anointed for a sacred duty—primarily priests, prophets, and kings. The spirit of God "came upon" them so as to give them the power to teach, to prophesy, or to govern God's chosen people.

You also read of two of the physical signs that accompanied the conferring of the Spirit of God: the *laying on of hands* (sometimes called the "imposition of hands") and the *anointing* with oil. These two signs of the Sacrament of Confirmation find their origin in the Old Testament and their fulfillment in Christ.

### The Laying on of Hands

> **The imposition of hands is rightly recognized by the Catholic tradition as the origin of the sacrament of Confirmation, which in a certain way perpetuates the grace of Pentecost in the Church. (CCC 1288)**

The laying on of hands signifies the outpouring of the Holy Spirit. This gesture has been used by God's people since long before the time of Christ. For instance, Moses laid his hands on Joshua to show that he was the new leader of the people. Moreover, it was also a common ritual gesture in the Old Testament. A priest would lay his hands on a sacrificial animal, setting it apart for a sacred purpose.

The laying on of hands is present as well in the New Testament. Christ used this gesture when he raised someone from the dead, healed the sick, or gave a blessing. It was also used when the Apostles ordained the first deacons and consecrated people for missionary work. It is connected to the gifts that are received with the Sacrament of Holy Orders:

> **Do not neglect the gift you have, which was given you by prophetic utterance when the elders laid their hands upon you. (1 Tm 4:14)**

From the very beginning of the Church, laying on of hands has been an integral part of the Sacrament of Confirmation. The New Testament even calls the laying on of hands part of the "elementary doctrine of Christ" (Heb 6:1-2).

When you receive Confirmation, the bishop will lay his hands on your head, either directly, or by extending his hands over you and your fellow candidates.

## ANOINTING WITH OIL

***The use of Sacred Chrism reminds us that we are priests, prophets, and kings.***

Another element of the Sacrament of Confirmation is the anointing with Sacred Chrism, a perfumed oil that has been consecrated by the bishop. It signifies the beautiful and fragrant gifts of the Holy Spirit.

Oil was a rich symbol in the ancient world, representing joy and cleansing, as well as healing and strength. Oil would be rubbed on wounds and

The Sacred Chrism is a perfumed oil that has been consecrated by the bishop. It signifies the beautiful and fragrant gifts of the Holy Spirit.

injuries to refresh the skin. It was also used as a cosmetic and to anoint bodies before burial.

In the Old Testament, kings, priests, and prophets were anointed with oil to signify their consecration for a sacred mission. For example, David was anointed to show that he would be king:

> **Samuel took the horn of oil, and anointed [David] in the midst of his brothers; and the Spirit of the Lord came mightily upon David from that day forward. (1 Sm 16:13)**

The New Testament records similar uses of anointing. The Apostles anointed the sick with oil to heal them (Mk 6:13). The earliest Christians would request priests ("elders") for the Anointing of the Sick in times of illness:

> **Is any among you sick? Let him call for the elders of the church, and let them pray over him, anointing him with oil in the name of the Lord. (Jas 5:14)**

## Anointing in Confirmation

Traditionally, marking someone on the forehead identified the person with some group or person. In the Sacrament of Confirmation, the forehead is anointed with Sacred Chrism as a sign that the confirmand belongs completely to Christ. He or she has been set apart for him and is "sealed" with the Holy Spirit. For two reasons the marking is in the sign of the Cross. First, it shows that identifying with Christ can involve suffering. Second, it reminds the confirmand that he or she must conform to Christ and his Cross. This anointing gives strength and grace to face the challenges and temptations of life.

In the Sacrament of Confirmation, the forehead is anointed with Sacred Chrism as a sign that the confirmand belongs completely to Christ.

> **This anointing with Chrism aptly signifies the spiritual anointing of the Holy Spirit, who is given to the faithful. (St. Paul VI, *On the Sacrament of Confirmation*)**

Anointing with oil is a sign that is used in four of the Church's Sacraments: Baptism, Confirmation, Holy Orders, and the Anointing of the Sick. At the Chrism Mass during Holy Week, the bishop of a diocese blesses the holy oils that will be used to give the Sacraments throughout the year: the *Oil of the Catechumens*, the *Oil of the Sick*, and *Sacred Chrism*.

While the New Testament refers to the Sacrament as the "laying on of hands," the early Church added an anointing with Sacred Chrism to show the "anointing" of the Holy Spirit. Those who are anointed with Sacred *Chrism* are *Christians*. Christians are followers of *Christ*, the "Anointed One."

> **Very early, the better to signify the gift of the Holy Spirit, an anointing with perfumed oil (chrism) was added to the laying on of hands. This anointing highlights the name "Christian," which means "anointed" and derives from that of Christ himself whom God "anointed with the Holy Spirit." (CCC 1289)**

The name *Confirmation* was first used by St. Ambrose of Milan in the fourth century to describe the meaning of this anointing:

> **God the Father has sealed you, Christ the Lord has confirmed you and has given you the gift of the Spirit in your heart. (St. Ambrose, *On the Mysteries*, 7.42)**

The word *Confirmation* shows that the anointing "confirms" (completes) the faith that began at Baptism by "confirming" (strengthening) baptismal grace. Eastern Catholics call this Sacrament **Chrismation**. This word is derived from Chrism, the holy oil used in this anointing.

The ordinary *minister* of the Sacrament of Confirmation is the bishop.

# ESSENTIAL ELEMENTS OF CONFIRMATION

***The seal of Confirmation means that we belong completely to Christ and his service.***

As was mentioned previously, every Sacrament includes *matter* and *form*, and involves a *minister*. What are the matter, form, and minister of Confirmation?

## Matter, Form, and Minister

The ***matter*** of Confirmation—the physical sign used in the Sacrament—is the Sacred Chrism and the laying on of the hand, and the minister is a bishop or priest. Sacred Chrism is the oil with which the bishop anoints the confirmand. This is olive oil mixed with balsam (a fragrant substance) that has been blessed by the bishop. Oil is a sign of abundance and joy, and balsam is a symbol of the "aroma of Christ" (2 Cor 2:15). The candidate's forehead is anointed with Sacred Chrism.

The ***form*** of Confirmation is the words "Be sealed with the Gift of the Holy Spirit."

The ordinary ***minister*** of the Sacrament of Confirmation is the bishop. However, a Roman Rite bishop can give this power to a priest if there is a special need. This often happens when an adult is received into the Church at the Easter Vigil Mass, since the bishop cannot be at every parish at once. A priest is also authorized to confirm a baptized person who is in danger of death.

## The Seal of Confirmation

This seal is a character, or mark, on your soul that cannot be removed. Your soul will be marked with a sign that you belong totally to Christ and that he accepted your commitment to serving him throughout your life. It is a sign that Christ, through his Holy Spirit, will always give you the grace that you need to be his witness in the world, a living example of what it means to be a faithful Catholic.

The seal also means that the Holy Spirit will help you through whatever trials you face because of your faith. You will be given strength to defend your faith and hold on to it, even when you are persecuted for it. If you are faced with a serious threat—even a threat to your life—the Holy Spirit will help you hold fast to your faith no matter the circumstances.

# EFFECTS OF CONFIRMATION

***Many gifts and graces will come to you in Confirmation.***

You have already read about some of the many effects of the Sacrament of Confirmation. Remember that a Sacrament is an efficacious sign that gives the grace that it signifies. These effects will take place within you when you receive Confirmation.

As with any gift, however, we must make the free choice to cooperate with each effect in order to receive its benefits. It is up to you to use God's grace in your life as you seek his will and grow in holiness. Later chapters will focus more on how to live your Confirmation gifts and graces to the fullest.

> **Confirmation perfects Baptismal grace; it is the sacrament which gives the Holy Spirit in order to root us more deeply in the divine filiation, incorporate us more firmly into Christ, strengthen our bond with the Church, associate**

> us more closely with her mission, and help us bear witness to the Christian faith in words accompanied by deeds. (CCC 1316)

> A candidate for Confirmation who has attained the age of reason must profess the faith, be in the state of grace, have the intention of receiving the sacrament, and be prepared to assume the role of disciple and witness to Christ, both within the ecclesial community and in temporal affairs. (CCC 1319)

These are the major effects of Confirmation and what they do for you:

**Confirmation perfects baptismal grace.** *Perfects* in this sense means "completes." It completes your Baptism, and initiates you further into the Church.

**Confirmation seals us with the mark of the Holy Spirit.** A character, or mark, will be imprinted on your soul, marking you for Christ, and this mark cannot be removed. This mark is commonly called *indelible*, meaning "cannot be deleted." Because of this **indelible mark**, Confirmation, like Baptism, can be received only once.

> Confirmation…imprints on the soul an *indelible spiritual mark*, the "character," which is the sign that Jesus Christ has marked a Christian with the seal of his Spirit by clothing him with power from on high so that he may be his witness. (CCC 1304)

**Confirmation gives us special graces for defending and witnessing to our faith.** The Holy Spirit helps you know and understand the truth. He helps you pray and make good decisions. He strengthens you when you are attacked, insulted, mistreated, or questioned for your beliefs, helping you to be a true witness of Christ.

> Confirmation…gives us a special strength of the Holy Spirit to spread and defend the faith by word and action as true witnesses of Christ, to confess the name of Christ boldly, and never to be ashamed of the Cross. (CCC 1303)

**Confirmation roots us more deeply as adopted sons and daughters of God.** By adoption through Baptism you were welcomed as a child of God the Father. In Confirmation you will draw even closer to your heavenly Father. You will also be united more closely with the Son of God, who is a brother to you. Our status as sons and daughters of God is sometimes called **divine filiation** (from the Latin *filius* or *filia*, meaning "son" or "daughter").

Confirmation seals us with the mark of the Holy Spirit. A character, or mark, will be imprinted on your soul, marking you for Christ, and this mark cannot be removed.

**Confirmation infuses in us the gifts and fruits of the Holy Spirit.** The seven gifts of the Holy Spirit are wisdom, understanding, counsel, fortitude, knowledge, piety, and fear of the Lord. Through Confirmation these gifts will be increased in you. These are your primary "tools" for living your call to holiness and the path in life that God wants you to follow. These seven gifts in turn have effects: the twelve fruits of the Holy Spirit. These are love, joy, peace, patience, kindness, generosity, faithfulness, gentleness, self-control, modesty, chastity, and goodness. The fruits of the Holy Spirit are supernatural acts that flow joyfully from the Christian life. We will learn more about the gifts and fruits of the Holy Spirit in Chapter 8.

**Confirmation perfects our bond with the Church.** By becoming more united to Christ, you become more united to the Body of Christ, his Church. The connection between Confirmation and your bishop strengthens your unity with all the members of the Catholic Church throughout the world. You also gain a stronger unity with the Communion of Saints, which includes the saints in heaven and the Holy Souls in purgatory. As we learned in Chapter 3, the Holy Spirit is the "soul" of the Church, giving it life. Thus, when we receive the gift of the Holy Spirit at Confirmation, we become more united to this "soul" of the Church.

## RENEWING YOUR BAPTISMAL PROMISES

You have renewed your baptismal promises every year during the Mass of Easter Vigil or Easter Sunday. The holy water should remind you of your baptism, be a sign of your identity as a Catholic Christian, and strengthen you "as servants of Christ and stewards of the mysteries of God" (1 Cor 4:10). "The person baptized belongs no longer to himself, but to him who died and rose for us" (CCC 1269).

It is also a good practice to renew your baptismal promises privately—between you and God during your daily prayer—on the anniversary of your baptism or a day of great personal joy.

Renewing your baptismal promises is a necessary step to take your faith seriously. It puts your mind and heart on answering Christ's call to follow him, share his Gospel in words and actions, put the Eucharist into action, build up the communion of faith, and share Christ's peace with the world. Christ is risen and lives within you, calling you every day to follow him.

Your bishop will also ask you to renew your baptismal promises during the celebration of Confirmation. This will take the form of five questions:

1. Do you renounce Satan, / and all his works and empty promises?
2. Do you believe in God, / the Father almighty, / Creator of heaven and earth?
3. Do you believe in Jesus Christ, his only Son, our Lord, / who was born of the Virgin Mary, / suffered death and was buried, / rose again from the dead / and is seated at the right hand of the Father?
4. Do you believe in the Holy Spirit, / the Lord, the giver of life, / who today through the Sacrament of Confirmation / is given to you in a special way / just as he was given to the Apostles on the day of Pentecost?
5. Do you believe in the holy catholic Church, / the communion of saints, / the forgiveness of sins, / the resurrection of the body, / and life everlasting?

And you will answer each question, "I do."

Living your baptismal promises also inspires other people to be good stewards of God's gifts, and together you can build up the Family of God.

You have renewed your baptismal promises every year during the Mass of Easter Vigil or Easter Sunday. Holy water should remind you of your baptism and be a sign of your identity as a Catholic Christian.

**John:** Dad, our teacher told us today that when we are confirmed, we'll become "soldiers of Christ."

**Dad:** That's right.

**John:** But who are we fighting? I thought God loved everyone.

**Dad:** That's a great question, John. Can you think of anyone who's an enemy of God?

**John:** Well, I guess Satan is.

**Dad:** Right. The Devil wants us to follow him instead of God, and so he tempts us to do things God doesn't want us to do. So we fight against Satan. Are there any other enemies of God?

**John:** Um...really bad people?

**Dad:** Yes, but not just really bad people. Really anyone who wants us to do things that God doesn't want us to do. We sometimes call this the "world." It doesn't mean that everyone is an enemy of God, just that many times the world around us is against God. Does that make sense?

**John:** Kinda.

**Dad:** Well, sometimes we hear people on television or movies or the internet tell us to do things we shouldn't do. We can even hear that sometimes from our political leaders. But just because everyone around us says we should do something, all that matters is whether God wants us to do it. So sometimes the world is our enemy. There is another enemy as well. Can you think of it?

**John:** Not really.

**Dad:** Another enemy of God is harder to recognize. I'm talking about ourselves.

**John:** What? I'm not an enemy of God! I'm on his side!

**Dad:** I know, Son, so am I. But oftentimes we have to fight against our own bad desires. We often want things that aren't really good for us. Sometimes someone might make fun of another kid at school because he thinks it will make him more popular. Or someone might tell a lie if he thinks it will help him get what he wants. When we do these things, we go against God.

**John:** I never thought of it like that. So we fight against ourselves?

**Dad:** In a way. St. Paul called it "the flesh." He wrote, "walk by the Spirit, and do not gratify the desires of the flesh. For the desires of the flesh are against the Spirit, and the desires of the Spirit are against the flesh; for these are opposed to each other, to prevent you from doing what you would" (Gal 5:16-17). In other words, we have to fight against our own desires when they go against what God wants us to do.

**John:** That sounds hard.

**Dad:** It can be, but the great thing is that God is there to help us. In fact, that's why he gave us the Sacrament of Confirmation! When you receive Confirmation, you'll be given extra strength to fight against the Devil, the world, and your own bad desires. That's why we say you are becoming a soldier for Christ when you are confirmed. Welcome to being a soldier!

When you receive Confirmation, you'll be given extra strength to fight against the Devil, the world, and your own bad desires.

# THE ORDER OF CONFIRMATION

*Confirmation is rich in meaning and power.*

As you get closer to being confirmed, you are probably curious: what will the Confirmation ceremony itself be like? What will I have to do? What will the bishop do? The Rite of Confirmation is a sacred event, during which the miracle of Pentecost is continued in the life of the Church. The Holy Spirit will descend upon you in a way that you have never before experienced!

Signifying its link with the Sacrament of the Eucharist, Confirmation is celebrated within the Mass. Here is how it will proceed:

## THE ORDER OF CEREMONY

### *Opening Song*

Candidates and sponsors assemble at the back of the church and process in and stand together in their seats. The bishop and servers follow.

### *Welcome and Introduction*

The symbols of Confirmation are presented—the Paschal Candle, the Book of the Gospels, the Sacred Chrism and the Water of Baptism.

### *Opening Prayer*

The opening prayer is specially suited for Confirmation. One of the options, for example, says the following:

> **Fulfill for us your gracious promise,**
> **O Lord, we pray,**
> **so that by his coming**
> **the Holy Spirit may make us witnesses**
> **before the world**
> **to the Gospel of our Lord Jesus Christ.**
> **(*The Order of Confirmation*, no. 58)**

### *The Liturgy of the Word*

The Sacred Scriptures are proclaimed. The Scriptures are the inspired stories of how God has worked in this world.

"May God the Father almighty bless you, whom he has made his adopted sons and daughters."

## THE RITE OF CONFIRMATION

### *The Calling of the Candidates*

The name of each candidate for Confirmation is called, and each candidate responds by standing up.

### *The Instruction of the Candidates*

The bishop invites all the candidates to gather around him at the front of the altar and he speaks to them about the gift they are soon to receive. Sponsors remain in their seats.

### *Renewal of Baptismal Promises*

The bishop asks the candidates to profess their faith publicly.

### *Laying On of Hands*

The bishop lays his hands over the candidates—saying a prayer to ask the Holy Spirit to come upon them. After a short silence, the bishop will extend his hands over the candidates and pray:

> **Almighty God, Father of our Lord Jesus Christ,**
> **who brought these your servants to new birth**
> **by water and the Holy Spirit,**
> **freeing them from sin:**
> **send upon them, O Lord, the Holy Spirit,**
> **the Paraclete;**
> **give them the spirit of wisdom and understanding,**

**the spirit of counsel and fortitude,**
**the spirit of knowledge and piety;**
**fill them with the spirit of the fear of the Lord.**
**(*The Order of Confirmation*, no. 25)**

The candidates then return to their seats.

### *Anointing with Chrism*

1. The ceremony of anointing with the Sacred Chrism is prepared. The bishop's seat is placed in front, and he takes his seat.
2. Candidates and sponsors go to the back of the Church and stand together.
3. The ushers call them forward at an appropriate time to be anointed by the bishop.
4. The sponsor stands behind the candidate and places the right hand on the right shoulder.
5. The bishop says to the candidate: "Be sealed with the Gift of the Holy Spirit." And the newly confirmed person replies: "Amen."
6. The bishop continues: "Peace be with you." And the newly confirmed replies: "And with your spirit."
7. The sponsor leads the newly confirmed youth to his or her seat and offers congratulations.

### *Prayers of Intercession*

The bishop invites the assembly into a time of prayer for the candidates and the world.

### *Final Blessing*

After Communion, the bishop will bless the newly confirmed. This threefold blessing is then said:

**May God the Father almighty bless you,**
**whom he has made his adopted sons and daughters**
**reborn from water and the Holy Spirit,**
**and may he keep you worthy of his fatherly love...**
**May his Only Begotten Son,**
**who promised that the Spirit of truth would abide in his Church,**
**bless you and confirm you by his power**
**in the confession of the true faith...**
**May the Holy Spirit,**
**who kindles the fire of charity in the hearts of disciples,**
**bless you and lead you blameless and gathered as one**
**into the joy of the Kingdom of God.**
**(*The Order of Confirmation*, no. 49)**

### *Recessional*

The bishop and servers process out of the Church and the newly confirmed and sponsors follow.

## RITE OF CHRISTIAN INITIATION FOR ADULTS (RCIA)

If you are reading this book, then you are probably preparing to be confirmed as a young adult. You have already been baptized and received your First Communion, and now you will complete the Sacraments of Initiation by being confirmed. But what about adults who have never been confirmed, or even baptized? How do they receive these Sacraments?

Generally, most adults go through a process called the Rite of Christian Initiation for Adults, or RCIA for short. During RCIA, which usually lasts about a year, interested adults learn about Catholicism and what it means to be a Catholic. Some may have received Baptism but not Confirmation. Others may be unbaptized.

During the Easter Vigil, these candidates then receive the Sacraments of Initiation that they have not yet received. For example, catechumens will be baptized, confirmed, and then receive their First Communion. Baptized candidates will be confirmed and receive their First Communion.

## STRENGTHENED BY THE SPIRIT, CALLED TO ACTION

Confirmation enriches the baptized with the strength of the Holy Spirit so that they can better witness to Christ in word and deed (CCC 1285). Anointed by the Holy Spirit at Confirmation, Christians strengthen their bond with the Church and become better equipped to carry out the Church's mission of love and service.

### At Confirmation, our faith and membership in the Body of Christ is confirmed, or strengthened.

In the Rite of Baptism, we become new members of the Body of Christ, but our journey does not end there. The decision to be baptized is followed by continued growth, learning, and witness as members of the Body of Christ. Our desire to continue to grow and develop as Christians finds expression in Confirmation, when we renew our baptismal promises and receive in a new way the gift of the Holy Spirit, which strengthens our "bond" with the Church and its members (CCC 1316; St. John Paul II, *On the Permanent Validity of the Church's Missionary Mandate*, 26).

### Confirmation connects us to a larger community.

The relationship of the bishop (who presides over the Rite of Confirmation) with the church community in a given area reminds us of our connection to the larger community of the Church, which is global. Thus, Confirmation reminds us that we belong to the Universal Church and to a local parish community (CCC 1309). The Sacred Chrism oil used during Confirmation points to the community's sharing of the Spirit, since the same oil is used during Baptism and to anoint bishops and priests during the Sacrament of Holy Orders. Oil for the Anointing of the Sick is also consecrated during Holy Week. The symbol of oil reminds us of the action of the Holy Spirit upon us as members in the Church family.

### At Confirmation, we receive the gifts of the Holy Spirit.

In the Gospels, the same Spirit that descended on Jesus during Baptism descends on the Apostles at Pentecost (CCC 1285-1287). The readings and homily we hear at Confirmation remind us that this same Spirit is present to us today. At Confirmation, we receive diverse spiritual gifts that work together for the "common good" and "the building up of the Church, to the well-being of humanity and to the needs of the world" (St. John Paul II, *The Vocation and the Mission of the Lay Faithful in the Church and in the World*, 24). At Confirmation, we pray for an increase of the gifts of the Spirit in our own lives in order to serve the cause of justice and peace in Church and world.

### The Spirit moves us to imitate the love and service of Christ and the saints.

In preparation for the Sacrament of Confirmation, we often perform many hours of service to help those in need. In doing so, we practice love and service in imitation of the saints whose names we often take at Confirmation. Anointed at Confirmation, we are further strengthened to live lives that give off "the aroma of Christ" as did the holy saints (CCC 1294). The Sacred Chrism is mixed with fragrant spices precisely to symbolize this "aroma."

The Holy Spirit pours love into our hearts so that we can become "instruments of grace" in order to "pour forth God's charity and to weave networks of charity" in the world (Pope Benedict XVI, *Charity in Truth*, no. 5). The Holy Spirit "harmonizes" our hearts with Christ's heart and moves us to love others as Christ loved when he washed the disciples' feet and gave his life for us (Pope Benedict XVI, *God Is Love*, no. 19).

Confirmation is not only an anointing, but also a commissioning to live out our faith in the world.

## STRENGTHENED BY THE SPIRIT *Continued*

**At Confirmation, we recommit to participate in the Church's work and mission.**

Sealing with the gift of the Spirit at Confirmation strengthens us for ongoing service in the Body of Christ in the Church and in the world. It prepares us to be active participants in the Church's mission and to "bear witness to the Christian faith in words accompanied by deeds" (CCC 1316). Finally, the Spirit sends us as workers in the vineyard and instruments of the Holy Spirit in renewing the earth and promoting God's Kingdom of justice and peace.

Thus, Confirmation is not only an *anointing*, but also a *commissioning* to live out our faith *in the world*. We are already called to mission by virtue of our Baptism, but at Confirmation we are endowed with gifts of the Spirit (like the Apostles in Acts 2) to be "ever greater witness[es] to the Gospel in the world" (Pope Benedict XVI, *Sacrament of Charity*, no. 17). As disciples and witnesses to Christ in both Church and world (CCC 1319), we are sent out to act on behalf of the poor and vulnerable, promoting the life and dignity of every human person.

**The Holy Spirit inspires us to Gospel action that includes human development and work to end injustice.**

The Holy Spirit inspires the work of evangelization, which includes work not only for all peoples' spiritual well-being, but also the evangelization of systems and cultures (St. John Paul II, *On the Permanent Validity of the Church's Missionary Mandate*, nos. 42, 65). The Church's missionary activity includes a "commitment to peace, development and the liberation of peoples; the rights of individuals and peoples, especially those of minorities; the advancement of women and children; safeguarding the created world," and many other areas of action in the world (*On the Permanent Validity of the Church's Missionary Mandate*, no. 37).

In addition, action inspired by the Holy Spirit calls us to "bear witness to Christ by taking courageous and prophetic stands in the face of the corruption of political or economic power." The Spirit also "overcomes barriers and divisions of race, caste, or ideology" and makes the Christian-on-mission into "a sign of God's love in the world—a love without exclusion or partiality" (*On the Permanent Validity of the Church's Missionary Mandate*, nos. 43, 89).

**Confirmation calls us to share Christ's mission to promote life and dignity.**

The baptized, anointed by the Holy Spirit, are incorporated into Christ, who is priest, prophet, and king, and called to share in his mission (CCC 1241). We share Christ's priestly mission by giving of ourselves daily in union with Christ's supreme sacrifice on the Cross. As prophets, we announce the Kingdom of God in both word and deed and we witness to the Gospel in family, social life, and community, and in our commitment to human life and dignity. We share the kingly mission by seeking God's Kingdom of justice in the world. We do this when we overcome the kingdom of sin, give of ourselves, recognize Jesus in "the least of these" (Mt 25:40), and work for justice and peace.

All those anointed by the Spirit at Baptism and Confirmation share Christ's mission in Luke 4:18-19: "The Spirit of the Lord is upon me, / because he has anointed me / to bring glad tidings to the poor. / He has sent me to proclaim liberty to captives / and recovery of sight to the blind, / to let the oppressed go free, / and to proclaim a year acceptable to the Lord" (see also *The Vocation and the Mission of the Lay Faithful in the Church and in the World*, nos. 13-14).

### QUESTIONS FOR REFLECTION

***Membership in the community.*** What does it mean to be part of the Body of Christ?

***Gifts of the Spirit.*** What gifts have you been given? How are you called to use those gifts to benefit others?

***Listening to God's call.*** Who are you called to be? What are you called to do with your life?

***Mission in the world.*** What is the mission of the Church? What is your role in carrying it out? To what are you commissioned?

***The witness of the saints.*** How do the lives of the saints inspire you to "give off the aroma of Christ"?

## CONCLUSION

***We need Confirmation and the gifts of the Holy Spirit to live as witnesses to Christ.***

The Holy Spirit has been at work in the world since its creation. He has anointed priests, prophets, and kings in the time of the Old Testament. He came upon those whom were chosen to be leaders of God's People. Christ revealed the Holy Spirit as the Third Person of the Trinity, and he descended upon the Apostles at Pentecost, ushering in the age of the Church.

In the Sacrament of Confirmation, the Holy Spirit will come to you in a particular way. Along with Baptism and the Eucharist, it is one of the Sacraments of Initiation. You are not fully initiated into the Church until you have received all three. Confirmation gives each person an increase in sanctifying grace, which makes us more holy and gives us the potential and desire to increase in holiness. Furthermore, Confirmation is a prerequisite to answering God's call in the vocations of Holy Orders, marriage, and the consecrated life, for Confirmation gives us the grace to respond to our vocation.

The essential effect of Confirmation is to perfect the grace received in Baptism. It strengthens the already existing bond between the baptized person and the Church through the power of the Holy Spirit. It graces the confirmed person to witness to Christ by word and deed. Divine filiation is the key to understanding the mission of a person confirmed in Christ. As sons and daughters of God, we are called upon to act in every situation as Christ himself would act. When tempted to deny the faith or to sin, we should rely on the great spiritual strength given us by God in the Sacrament of Confirmation.

Further, through Confirmation, you will receive the gifts and fruits of the Holy Spirit. You will be fully initiated into the Church. In the following chapters we will learn more about how to respond to the graces received in this great Sacrament.

Confirmation gives each person an increase in sanctifying grace, which makes us more holy and gives us the potential and desire to increase in holiness.

## POINTS TO REMEMBER

1. Baptism, the Eucharist, and Confirmation are united because they all are essential to full Christian initiation.
2. The matter of Confirmation is Sacred Chrism and the laying on of the hand; the form is the words "Be sealed with the Gift of the Holy Spirit," and the minister is a bishop or priest.
3. Confirmation has many effects. It roots us more deeply as children of God and members of the Church. It perfects our baptismal graces. It seals us with the Holy Spirit and grants us his gifts. It empowers us to be faithful witnesses of Christ.
4. To be sealed with the gift of the Holy Spirit means to have an indelible mark on our souls that shows that we belong to Christ.

# Witness of Christ

## St. Josephine Bakhita

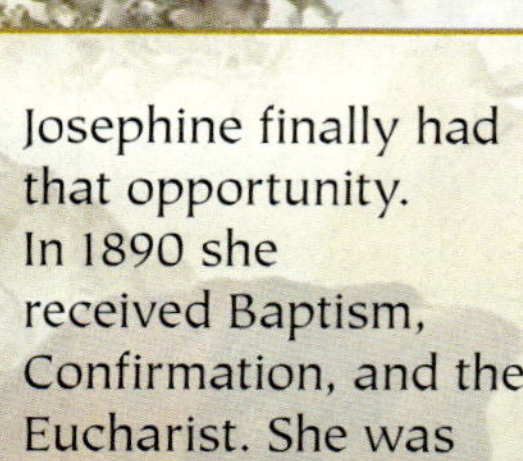

In every saint's life there is a common thread: the importance of the Sacraments. Their stories show how the Sacraments have power over any evil or darkness. The Sacraments bring hope, peace, and healing. The story of St. Josephine Bakhita shows the impact the Sacraments can have on a person's life. Through them God's love can break through the strongest oppression and lead us into his loving arms.

St. Josephine Bakhita was born in 1869 in Sudan in Africa. At a young age she was kidnapped and sold into slavery. Treated merely as property, she eventually forgot her own name. *Josephine* was the name given to her by one of her owners much later. As a child she was beaten and whipped many times. However, her life would change when she was bought by an Italian man who belonged to the Italian Consulate in Sudan.

Josephine was amazed when the Italian treated her with kindness and dignity, and she began to feel peace and joy. When the family left the Sudan, she traveled with them to Italy.

There Josephine was owned by Augusto Michielli, and she cared for his daughter Mimmina. When Augusto and his wife had to go back to Africa, Josephine and Mimmina were placed in the care of the Canossian Sisters in Venice.

Josephine's joy blossomed when she was with the sisters. She later said:

> **Seeing the sun, moon and the stars, I said to myself: who could be the Master of these beautiful things? And I felt a great desire to see him, to know him and to pay him homage.**

Josephine finally had that opportunity. In 1890 she received Baptism, Confirmation, and the Eucharist. She was so overjoyed at the reception of the Sacraments of Initiation that she was seen kissing the baptismal font saying, "Here, I became a daughter of God."

Eventually Mr. Michielli came back to Italy to take Mimmina and Josephine with him to Africa. However, since she had been given the Sacraments, Josephine was filled with a new courage. She said that she wanted to stay with the Canossian Sisters so she could worship and serve God. Mr. Michielli released her from slavery. In 1893 she became a religious sister at the Institute of St. Magdalene of Canossa. She served as a sister for fifty years.

Sister Josephine had various duties, including cooking, sewing, and greeting visitors. She did these ordinary things with dedication and cheerfulness. She showed tremendous love for the children who attended the sisters' school. She was soothing and gentle, even with the children who misbehaved. She comforted poor or troubled people who passed by the Institute. She was known so much for her kindness and pleasant nature that the local people referred to her lovingly as their "Black Mother."

St. Josephine died in 1947 with a smile illuminating her face; she had lived a true fear of the Lord. Her feast day is February 8.

## VOCABULARY

### CHRISM
Greek for "anointing." It is oil mixed with balsam, signifying the gift of the Holy Spirit, that is consecrated by a bishop. Chrism is used in the Sacraments of Baptism, Confirmation, and Holy Orders.

### CHRISMATION
This alternative name for the Sacrament of Confirmation, named for the Sacred Chrism used, is often used in the Eastern Churches.

### DIVINE FILIATION
The unique Sonship of Jesus Christ in relation to God the Father; also, Christians' unique status as adopted sons and daughters of God by virtue of Baptism. This consoling mystery brings each Christian a spirit of sincerity and trust while filling him or her with love for and wonder towards God; see the Parable of the Prodigal Son (Lk 15:11-32).

### INDELIBLE MARK
A permanent mark conferred by the Sacraments of Baptism, Confirmation, and Holy Orders that configures the Christian to Christ and his Church, remains within him or her as a positive disposition for grace, promises and guarantees divine protection, and grants him or her a vocation to divine worship and to the service of the Church; therefore, these Sacraments can be received validly only once.

The rites employed in consecrating the Sacred Chrism illustrate that it is a ceremony of the highest importance. It must be blessed during the solemn high Mass of Holy Thursday. The Chrism, being perfected with a final prayer, receives the homage of all the sacred ministers present, each making a triple genuflection towards it, and each time saying the words, *Ave sanctum chrisma* ("Hail, Sacred Chrism").

## STUDY QUESTIONS

1. After Christ's Resurrection and Ascension, why did the Apostles still need the gifts of the Holy Spirit?
2. How was Confirmation conferred in the New Testament?
3. At what age may Confirmation be given?
4. How are Baptism, the Eucharist, and Confirmation closely united?
5. Describe an example of the laying on of hands that was associated with the Holy Spirit in the New Testament.
6. What did oil symbolize in the ancient world?
7. What are the *form* and *matter* of Confirmation?
8. Name and describe three effects of the Sacrament of Confirmation.
9. What does it mean to be *sealed* with the gift of the Holy Spirit?
10. Why may Confirmation only be received once?

## PRACTICAL EXERCISES

1. Imagine that your cousin, who was raised and lived his life without any religion, is thinking about becoming Catholic. Since he knows you are preparing for Confirmation, he emails you asking what he would have to do to become Catholic. Write your cousin back, explaining to him what the Sacraments of Initiation are and, in general, what their effects are. Be sure to get him excited about them!

2. Imagine that your aunt, while having dinner with your family, asks what is happening in your life these days. You mention school, your hobbies, and that you are preparing for Confirmation. She is happy to hear this, and she congratulates you on becoming an adult in the Church. Explain to your aunt two things: first, why Confirmation is not "becoming an adult" and, second, the real meaning of this Sacrament.

In Confirmation, we are given strength to battle temptation and witness our faith to others.

# Sealed in the Spirit

***The gifts of the Holy Spirit will help you stand up for your faith in the face of opposition.***

The gifts of the Holy Spirit that you will receive in Confirmation will help you stand up for your faith in the face of opposition. The supreme example of Christians standing up for their faith are the martyrs—those who were killed for their Christian discipleship. These heroic men and women were able to make the ultimate sacrifice—death—and, through the power of the Holy Spirit, remain faithful in spite of the danger they faced. Through Confirmation, you, too, will be given the strength to witness to Christ even in the face of persecution or death.

Are you ready for that?

You might be interested to know that the extraordinary form of the Rite of Confirmation includes a light slap on the cheek. Perhaps some of the older members of your family remember it. (It was not so much of a *slap* as a *light tap* with the fingers.) This reminds us that service of Christ is difficult and can even be dangerous. It developed from a gesture of peace and affection between the bishop and the confirmand, but as the Church went through troubling times and persecution, the gesture became a sign of being strengthened to stand up for the faith.

This slap is symbolic of the need for strength in times of persecution, even to the point of martyrdom, and is a reminder that the Christian needs to be a "soldier of Christ" (2 Tm 2:3). Paul encourages his friend and son in the Lord, Timothy, to remain strong in the faith:

> **You then, my son, be strong in the grace that is in Christ Jesus...Take your share of suffering as a good soldier of Christ Jesus. (2 Tm 2:1, 3)**

To be a *soldier of Christ*, then, means to find strength through grace, share and teach the Good News, and be willing to suffer for the sake of Christ.

Even if these days the bishop is not going to give you a slap on the cheek, you can be confident that Confirmation will give you the strength to be a soldier of Christ. Sometimes you might struggle to remain faithful to Christ. You may find it hard to remain a good witness to him when other people look down on your faith. You might even be threatened with physical harm because of your faith. But the gifts of the Holy Spirit will give you strength to overcome any obstacle to God throughout your life.

To be a soldier of Christ means to find strength through grace, share and teach the Good News, and be willing to suffer for the sake of Christ.

# SEALED IN THE SPIRIT

## A LETTER FOR YOUNG PEOPLE AT CONFIRMATION*

"You will receive power when the Holy Spirit has come upon you. And you will be my witnesses." (Acts 1:8)

**Dear Friend of Jesus,**

Confirmation is very near and you should feel excited. You will soon receive a most precious gift—the gift of the Holy Spirit. Your family and your parish family are so proud of you. This year is a special year, because you will be confirmed.

The preparation is being done, and the bishop will soon anoint you with the Sacred Chrism, confirming and sealing you with God the Holy Spirit.

Without the Holy Spirit, every Christian is like a sailing ship without the wind, a candle without a flame, a body without a breath. Without the Holy Spirit you can look good, but never fulfill your potential to be the good person God created you to be.

God, who created you in love to be a person of love, never wants to lose this special relationship with you given at your Baptism. The Holy Spirit is given as a gift from God the Father to draw you closer to Jesus, who is God the Son. When you come close to Jesus, then you become the real person of love God created you to be.

To understand how the Holy Spirit might work in your life, look at the life of Jesus and see how he lived his life full of God's Holy Spirit. This gift can and will make a difference in your life if you allow the Holy Spirit to guide your thoughts and actions.

Whenever you are in need, please say the prayer: "Holy Spirit, help me!" The Holy Spirit is not only there to bring you close to Jesus. He also helps you to act like Jesus.

After Confirmation, you will be expected to do things for your family and for your Church family and for the poor and needy to help bring more love to the world. To help you do this, you have chosen a sponsor, a special spiritual friend who stands with you to support you so that you can live more like Jesus.

Please thank your sponsor for being there for you, and thank God every day for sending you this sponsor. When you are anointed with the Sacred Chrism, your sponsor will place his or her right hand on your shoulder. This is an ancient practice by which the sponsor symbolically tells everyone that you are ready in faith to receive this gift, and that he or she is there to support and sustain you in your journey of faith. That hand on you is a reassurance, a blessing, a commitment, a faithful relationship, a comfort, and a support.

Do not forget to keep in touch with your sponsor and invite him or her to help you to do things as Jesus would have done, and to help strengthen your own spiritual practices.

Above all, please be relaxed. The bishop will enjoy being here with you on that holy day.

Do not forget to thank your family for preparing you. They love you very much. Get ready for a wonderful celebration!

God Bless you, and thank you for taking this important step in your Catholic faith.

When you come to be anointed, the bishop will say to you: "Be sealed with the Gift of the Holy Spirit." Please respond to the bishop in a strong voice with: "Amen."

* Adapted from "A Letter for Children at Confirmation" by Fr. John Hodgson, CSsR, St. Mary of the Cross MacKillop, Warnervale, NSW, Australia.

# YOU AND YOUR PARENTS

***The Holy Spirit works in our lives, even when we do not realize it.***

How do you know that the Holy Spirit is working in your life? How do you know that the Holy Spirit is working in the life of someone you know?

It is not always easy to know how the Holy Spirit is working. He is pure spirit, so he cannot be sensed: seen, touched, smelled, measured, and so on. This list gives you a few ways to learn how the Holy Spirit is working in your life and in the lives of people around you:

- The Holy Spirit leads us to Christ. Do you put Christ first in your life, and serve him before all others?
- He leads us to truth. Have you learned the teachings of the Church? Can you explain them to others?
- He leads us to pray. Do you spend time in prayer every day?
- He leads us to serve. Do you have a desire to help the poor, visit the elderly, or volunteer for a crisis pregnancy center?
- He leads us to forgive and to seek forgiveness. When you are hurt, do you want to retaliate, or do you forgive?

Talk about these ideas with your parents. Ask about their experience of the Holy Spirit in their lives, and share some of the experiences of him in your life.

You might want to use these questions to help your discussion:

1. How have you experienced the Holy Spirit working in your life?
2. How has the Holy Spirit inspired you in what to say or what to do in a particular situation?
3. How have you seen the Holy Spirit at work in another person?
4. How do you know when the Holy Spirit is working in your life?

Be prepared to report back to the class on your talk with your parents.

Christ leads us to truth.
Have you learned the teachings of the Church?
Can you explain them to others?

# YOU AND YOUR PARENTS

## A LETTER FOR PARENTS OF A CANDIDATE FOR CONFIRMATION*

**Dear Parents,**

Congratulations!

You must be proud of your commitment and love for your child, assuring him or her to receive all the spiritual blessings that God gives the Catholic community in the Sacraments.

Thank you for preparing your child through your own example of Christian living—the time spent to go through the lessons, your attendance at Sunday Mass, and helping him or her choose a sponsor.

There is a letter on the previous page addressed to your child. Please read this letter out loud with him or her. Read slowly as it may help a little to prepare your child for the big event. Please explain to your child how much the parish family also values him or her as you do.

When your child comes to be anointed, the bishop will say: "Be sealed with the Gift of the Holy Spirit." Please practice with your child to respond to the bishop in a strong voice: "Amen." Then the bishop will continue: "Peace be with you," to which your child will reply: "And with your spirit."

There is also a note on the next page for your child's sponsor. Encourage your child to read this with him or her well before the ceremony, to help in the preparation and the celebration.

After the celebration of Confirmation, help your child to keep in touch with his or her sponsor. This relationship can be special, but may need nurturing.

The time after Confirmation is very important. It is a time to let your child know of the expectation of the Holy Spirit to grow closer to Jesus by doing things that help others, especially those less fortunate. Any help to reinforce this message and the Christian value of service will develop your child's faith enormously.

The responsibility to developing your child's faith is always a big task. May you know how much your parish family admires you and how keen it is to support you.

Your parish family never wishes to take this primary responsibility away from you, but they are very willing to offer all the help they can. The catechists have enjoyed the opportunity to work with you.

If, after the ceremony, there are suggestions you have on how to help next year's candidates experience Confirmation better, please let the catechist or your priest know. Suggestions are always welcome.

Thank you once again for trusting in God's love and care for you and your family. Enjoy your after Confirmation celebrations!

As sons and daughters of God, we are called upon to act in every situation as Christ himself would act.

* Adapted from "A Letter for Parents of Confirmation Children" by Fr. John Hodgson, CSsR, St. Mary of the Cross MacKillop, Warnervale, NSW, Australia.

# You and Your Sponsor

***The Holy Spirit makes it possible for Christ to live in your soul.***

**"I have been crucified with Christ; it is no longer I who live, but Christ who lives in me." (Gal 2:20)**

Think about your experience of playing a team sport. If you have not played a sport, think about a group activity that needs a leader: a choir, a stage production, a charity drive, or anything similar. Remember all the things that a coach or leader has to do for everyone in the group. A coach will teach every person, encourage every person, train every person, and push every person to be better today than he or she was yesterday. If someone stops improving or practicing, the coach will change strategies or remind everyone of the importance of practice. A coach can sometimes be hard on people, but he or she is looking out for the best interests of the team members and making sure that everyone takes the commitment seriously .

Your sponsor can be like your coach as you prepare for Confirmation. Your sponsor can also be a coach to you after Confirmation by making sure that you use the gifts of the Holy Spirit, practice your faith, and continue to learn about the Catholic faith.

Talk about the idea of your sponsor as a kind of coach. You might want to use these tips to help your discussion:

- Ask your sponsor to serve as your "coach" as you prepare for Confirmation.
- Show that you are thankful for the support, tell your sponsor about ways that he or she has been helpful so far, and encourage your sponsor to continue.
- Talk about areas of your life where your practice of the faith is not as full. Ask your sponsor to be more assertive in checking up on your progress.
- Ask your sponsor to stay active as your "coach" even after your Confirmation. Tell your sponsor that you will need help to grow in faith and holiness.

You are counting on your sponsor to be a lifelong friend and mentor in the faith. Your sponsor will appreciate that trust, and he or she will take that role seriously.

You are counting on your sponsor to be a lifelong friend and mentor in the faith. Your sponsor will appreciate that trust, and he or she will take that role seriously.

# You and Your Sponsor

## A Note for Sponsors at Confirmation Time*

"You will receive power when the Holy Spirit has come upon you. And you will be my witnesses." (Acts 1:8)

### Dear sponsor,

Congratulations, and thank you for being involved in the life of the young adult about to be confirmed. May you receive a great blessing through this relationship.

The young adult in your care is about to receive a most precious gift—the gift of the Holy Spirit to draw each Christian closer to Jesus Christ. When we think of how the Holy Spirit might work in our life, we look to Jesus and see how he lived his life full of God's Holy Spirit. This gift can and will make a difference in this child's life if he or she allows the Holy Spirit to guide every thought and action.

In order to help him or her appreciate and live out the enormity of this gift, you have been chosen to be a sponsor. If you were also his or her baptismal godparent, then you continue a special bond begun at baptism.

The young adult to be confirmed sees in you a profound faith commitment, finds trust, and knows you are someone who will care about his or her growth in the faith. It is not all that complicated, but it does take time, a caring heart, and a listening ear. The young adult's parents are calling you to be someone special for their child: to set an example; help teach their young adult about the Catholic faith; and have a lifelong relationship of prayer, faith sharing, and love. Take some time to pray for God's blessing on your ability to do this.

Another symbolic action of the sponsor is the placing of your right hand on the right shoulder of the young adult to be confirmed. This is an ancient practice in which the sponsor symbolically tells everyone that the young adult is ready in faith to receive this gift and that you are there to support and sustain him or her throughout the journey of faith. Your hand is a reassurance, a blessing, a commitment, a faithful relationship, a comfort, a support.

Here are a few suggestions on how to be the best possible sponsor:

### ✧ Be a living model of faith

At least a part of what this young adult admires in you is your faith! If the way you practice your faith is not what it should be, do not forget that conversion is a daily choice. Your life should not become artificially pious, but your faith should be authentic and sincere.

### ✧ Pray for your candidate and yourself

As the candidate decides to be confirmed, he or she needs spiritual strength. Your prayers are important, but don't forget to pray for yourself also, that you can share why you value and practice your Catholicism. Attend Mass together, or even exercise the fortitude to come to Reconciliation together.

### ✧ Give of your time and share your gifts

Once confirmed, the young adult is ready to put his or her faith into action. So help and work on a project together that helps the poor and needy or those less fortunate. Let him or her see how we choose right from wrong, and how we care. You could also share your own experiences or write a letter of encouragement. Let your unique God-given talents shine!

### ✧ An appropriate gift

Offer a gift of spiritual significance—a new Bible, prayer book, rosary, or book about our faith or about the saint the candidate has chosen as a Confirmation name—but be creative and relevant!

### ✧ Don't miss the ceremony

Participating in the ceremony is the easiest part of being a sponsor. Your basic job will be to place your hand on your candidate's shoulder. You are there to be a support, but your role will only just be beginning.

### ✧ Don't forget this newly confirmed Catholic

After Confirmation day, remember and participate in special days in this young adult's life: his or her birthday, the anniversary of this Confirmation, Church holy days, and the anniversary of other Sacraments like his or her Baptism, Matrimony, or Holy Orders. At least send a card or make a phone call. Continue to go to Mass together if possible, or from time to time do some service to the community. Put those "gifts of the Spirit" into practice. Please enjoy this special relationship for the rest of your lives.

* Adapted from "A Note for Sponsors at Confirmation Time" by Fr. John Hodgson, CSsR, St. Mary of the Cross MacKillop, Warnervale, NSW, Australia.

THE SACRAMENT OF

# Confirmation

## Chapter 8

# THE GIFTS AND FRUITS OF THE HOLY SPIRIT

## INTRODUCTION

***In Confirmation the gifts and fruits of the Holy Spirit will increase and deepen in your life.***

**Saint Thomas compares the Gifts [of the Holy Spirit] to the sails of a boat and the virtues to the oars of a boat. Let us imagine a couple sailing in a small boat that also has oars. If there is no wind and they want to return to the port, they have to row with the oars; the virtues are like that. If the wind fills the sails, then they return to port easily without having to row; Saint Thomas likens the sails to the Gifts—just as the sails catch the wind and move the boat, so the Gifts catch or receive impulses from the Holy Spirit which perfect the acts of virtue and help us to grow in love of God and holiness of life. In this regard Saint Thomas says: "The gifts are perfections of man, whereby he is disposed so as to be amenable to the promptings of God." (Kenneth Baker, SJ, *The Seven Gifts of the Holy Spirit: Sails of the Soul*)**

One of the primary purposes of the Sacrament of Confirmation is to strengthen those who receive it to be disciples of Christ in the world. But how does that happen? What exactly does Confirmation give a person that helps him or her follow Christ more faithfully?

Confirmation increases and deepens the ***gifts*** of the Holy Spirit you first received at Baptism. These gifts give the one who receives them the power to live out the commands of God, and to bring others to him. Furthermore, these gifts have certain effects on the person, called ***fruits***. These fruits of the Holy Spirit are supernatural acts that flow from living out the gifts of the Holy Spirit.

*Battle of Lepanto* by Cambiaso.
The Battle of Lepanto was a crucial naval battle on October 7, 1571 where the Christian Holy League defeated a much larger invading Turkish fleet. Pope St. Pius V had urged every Christian to prepare for the battle by praying the Rosary. St. Pius V added "Help of Christians" to the Litany of Loreto in thanksgiving for the victory.

After reading this chapter, you will be able to answer these questions:

- What are the gifts of the Holy Spirit, and what can they do for us?
- Why are the gifts of the Holy Spirit necessary?
- What are the fruits of the Holy Spirit?
- What is the difference between the gifts and fruits of the Holy Spirit?

## GIFTS OF THE HOLY SPIRIT

***Wisdom, Understanding, Counsel, Fortitude, Knowledge, Piety, and Fear of the Lord.***

**The moral life of Christians is sustained by the gifts of the Holy Spirit. These are permanent dispositions which make man docile in following the promptings of the Holy Spirit. (CCC 1830)**

At Baptism we receive the seven gifts of the Holy Spirit. At Confirmation, these gifts are increased and strengthened in us. The gifts of the Holy Spirit help us live our Catholic faith in a bolder, more powerful way. If we cooperate with them, we can become faithful disciples of Christ.

The gifts of the Holy Spirit are not only for certain "holy" people—they are for everyone. They are habits that exist in any soul in the state of grace. However, only those who are sincerely trying to follow Christ will be able to make use of these graces. For those baptized as infants, the actual exercise of these gifts begins only after the person has reached a certain age of reason, even though these gifts were already present in the soul. The greater the personal holiness of the soul, the more productive the exercise of the gifts of the Holy Spirit can be. In short, these gifts help the intellect and the will to receive effectively the inspiration of the Holy Spirit.

*Nativity: Birth of Christ* by Giotto.
Jesus Christ is the model of the gifts of the Holy Spirit.

The gifts of the Holy Spirit work within us. They are interior characteristics, or dispositions, that make us more attentive to the promptings of the Holy Spirit. Because our human nature has been wounded by sin, we are incapable of achieving holiness on our own. These gifts provide us with God's help to lead a good moral life of faith. At Baptism we received the theological virtues of faith, hope, and charity. The gifts of the Holy Spirit will help us complete and perfect the virtues that we already possess from our Baptism. In other words, the gifts of the Holy Spirit have the ability to increase our faith, make our hope for salvation stronger, and help us shine forth with the love and compassion of Christ.

Jesus Christ is the model of the gifts of the Holy Spirit. Isaiah prophesied that the Messiah would receive the fullness of the Holy Spirit and be filled with his divine gifts:

**The Spirit of the LORD shall rest upon him,**
**the spirit of wisdom and understanding,**
**the spirit of counsel and might,**
**the spirit of knowledge and the fear of the LORD.**
**And his delight shall be in the fear of the LORD.**
**(Is 11:2-3)**

As Isaiah prophesied, Christ possessed these gifts perfectly, and he showed us how to live them out in their fullness. This same Holy Spirit is also given to Christ's followers. At the Last Supper, he told the Apostles about the Holy Spirit. "All that the Father has is mine; therefore I said that he will take what is mine and declare it to you" (Jn 16:15). He also promised that "the Counselor, the Holy Spirit, whom the Father will send in my name, he will teach you all things, and bring to your remembrance all that I have said to you" (Jn 14:26).

**On the day of Pentecost when the seven weeks of Easter had come to an end, Christ's Passover is fulfilled in the outpouring of the Holy Spirit, manifested, given, and communicated as a divine person: of his fullness, Christ, the Lord, pours out the Spirit in abundance. (CCC 731)**

Christ gave the Holy Spirit to his Apostles on the day of Pentecost, and they, in turn, passed on the Holy Spirit to everyone who believed and was baptized. As you read previously, the Apostles laid hands on the baptized and prayed that they would receive the Holy Spirit.

*The Disciples of Jesus Baptize* by Tissot.
Christ gave the Holy Spirit to his Apostles on the day of Pentecost, and they, in turn, passed on the Holy Spirit to everyone who believed and was baptized.

## The Gifts Are Yours to Use

Think for a moment about the gifts that you received for your birthday or Christmas. You were probably given a number of presents, all boxed up and wrapped attractively with paper and ribbon. A gift tag confirmed that each gift was for you. You probably thanked the person who gave you these things.

Imagine that, instead of opening your presents, you stored them in the back of a closet. What good can those gifts do you? The wrapped boxes are still gifts, still yours, and still look nice...but you may not even know what is inside those boxes. You cannot enjoy or benefit from your gifts unless you unwrap them and use them. If you received a shirt, you must wear it to benefit from it. If you received a book, you must read it to benefit from it. If you received a football, you must play with it to benefit from it.

Although you will receive the seven gifts of the Holy Spirit at Confirmation, you must "unwrap" and "use" them by cooperating with God's grace. This will help you grow in happiness and holiness, allowing the Holy Spirit to make you more like Christ. Fortunately, God is always ready to give you actual graces to help you use his gifts.

In this chapter, you will read about each of the seven gifts individually and learn how you can apply them in your own life.

**The seven gifts of the Holy Spirit are wisdom, understanding, counsel, fortitude, knowledge, piety, and fear of the Lord. They belong in their fullness to Christ, Son of David. They complete and perfect the virtues of those who receive them. (CCC 1831)**

# WISDOM

***Wisdom helps us to see things from God's perspective.***

The first of the gifts of the Holy Spirit is wisdom. Most of us have a vague understanding of what "wisdom" is, even if we can't exactly define it. We might think of it as being smart or picture a wise old man with a long white beard. The gift of wisdom that comes from the Holy Spirit is a very special gift: it directs the mind to judge things from God's perspective. It allows us to see things from his better, more accurate, perspective. It also leads us to value things of God above all earthly things.

Imagine being at the bottom of a deep valley. Your view is limited, because you can't see the whole valley from the bottom. But now imagine being in a helicopter flying above it. Now your perspective allows you to see more clearly the entire valley. Wisdom works a lot like this, which is why the older we get, the more human wisdom we acquire. We have a greater perspective, one that includes all our years here on earth.

The gift of wisdom allows us to see the world, ourselves, and our neighbor as God sees them. It enlightens the mind and directs the heart to a purer, deeper love for God. Because the gift of wisdom helps us see the world with God's eyes, we will become more capable of serving him by doing his will. We will listen to and be obedient to the Holy Spirit, who always leads us on the path of virtue and holiness.

## Using Your Gift of Wisdom

**Wisdom will help you recognize God's hand in your life.** You know that God is with you, that he loves you, and that he has a wonderful plan for your life. In everything that comes your way—success, disappointment, difficulty, joy, and sorrow—the gift of wisdom will allow you to have more trust in God and understand what he wants from you. Whether you are a star athlete, a benchwarmer, one who gets injured and cannot play, or one who gets cut during tryouts, you will be able to handle your situation in a virtuous way and grow in holiness through your experience.

**Wisdom will help you grow in other virtues.** For this reason it is the highest gift of the Holy Spirit. When you see things more from God's perspective, you will be more likely to practice patience, compassion, and kindness toward others. You will become more understanding of others and less focused on your own desires. You will want whatever God wills, and so you will more naturally seek to follow his will and act in the spirit of Christ.

### Models of the Gift of Wisdom

In the Old Testament, **Solomon**, who was aware of his great responsibility as King of Israel, prayed to God for wisdom so that he might be able to rule well:

> **"Give your servant therefore an understanding mind to govern your people, that I may discern between good and evil; for who is able to govern this great people of yours?" (1 Kgs 3:9)**

God was pleased with his prayer and granted him wisdom—so much so that "the whole earth sought the presence of Solomon to hear his wisdom, which God had put into his mind." (1 Kgs 10:24)

*Madonna with Angels* by Serra.
One of the Blessed Virgin Mary's traditional titles is "Seat of Wisdom" because in her womb she bore Christ, who is perfect wisdom.

The **Blessed Virgin Mary** is another example of a person who used the gift of wisdom. She was told she had been chosen to bear the Son of God because of her great love for God. She listened to and accepted the words of the Holy Spirit. She submitted herself completely to God's will.

One of her traditional titles is "Seat of Wisdom" because in her womb she bore Christ, who is perfect wisdom. Artistic representations of the Blessed Virgin Mary as the Seat of Wisdom usually depict the Christ child sitting on her lap. When we receive Christ in the Eucharist, we, too, become a sort of "Seat of Wisdom," as Christ takes his dwelling in us.

## UNDERSTANDING

***The grace by which we comprehend more deeply what God has revealed to us.***

We all have the ability to understand. If you didn't, you couldn't be reading this book, or be in school, or even know to eat or drink. So what is the gift of understanding the Holy Spirit gives us?

This gift of the Holy Spirit allows us to better understand God's Revelation. Through that better understanding, we will desire to have an active faith life. It won't help us to better understand math problems or how to speak French. But it will help us have a deeper understanding of what God has done in this world, and why he did it.

We can read the Bible, we can study the *Catechism*, and we can listen to the homily at Mass. But understanding what we read or hear is another matter entirely. Although we may have a human level of understanding without much effort, the gift of the Holy Spirit helps us comprehend the truths of our faith much more deeply. It also helps us realize the importance of the Catholic faith in everyday life. And it opens our mind so that we can comprehend the true meaning of Sacred Scripture and Tradition.

Once you understand God's revelations more clearly, you appreciate their goodness and rightness. You understand how to apply the Word of God to many situations. You see why God wants you to act in certain ways, and you are motivated to lead a more active life of faith.

*The Emmaus Disciples* by Bloemaert.
The gift of understanding helps you contemplate the mysteries of the faith such as the Blessed Trinity, the Incarnation, or the Real Presence of Christ in the Eucharist.

## Using Your Gift of Understanding

**Understanding helps you appreciate the mysteries of our faith.** A supernatural mystery cannot be fully understood by the human mind, not even with the help of the Holy Spirit. But the gift of understanding helps you contemplate the mysteries of the faith such as the Blessed Trinity, the Incarnation, or the Real Presence of Christ in the Eucharist. "Faith seeks understanding," St. Anselm said; likewise, understanding builds faith.

**Understanding enhances our reception of the Sacraments.** We do not have to be a genius to worthily receive the Sacraments, nor do we have to have a complete understanding of them. However, the gift of understanding can open our hearts more fully to the grace we receive in the Sacraments. It can help us understand the impact of that grace on our lives.

## Models of the Gift of Understanding

In Scripture, the story of **the disciples on the road to Emmaus** illustrates the gift of understanding. It was the very evening after Christ rose from the dead. As the two men walked and discussed their confusion over the Death of Jesus, Christ joined them. At first, the disciples did not know who he was. He began to explain all the Scriptures about the Messiah. When he "broke bread" with them, they came to understand that he was the Risen Christ. Afterward they said to one another, "Did not our hearts burn within us while he talked to us on the road, while he opened to us the scriptures?" (Lk 24:32).

**St. Jerome** translated the Bible into Latin in the fourth century. He possessed the gift of understanding, particularly in his ability to understand Scripture. Jerome had considerable human understanding, such as of human languages, but also had a deeper, divine, understanding of the meaning of God's Word.

## COUNSEL

***Aided by wisdom and understanding, this gift helps us make the choices that please God the most.***

Counsel helps us judge promptly, correctly, and in accordance with the mind and will of Christ.

We have seen that the Holy Spirit is also called the "Counselor." As Counselor, he offers us direction and advice for our lives. He counsels us in the truth in order to lead us on the path to God. The direction and advice he gives us is the gift of Counsel.

When you use the gift of Counsel, you know more than just how to tell right from wrong: you know how to choose the best action, the one that will lead you along the way to perfection and close union with God. You know how to ignore your own way of thinking and instead ask God what he wants you to do. Furthermore, you know when to act—neither too quickly or too slowly. When you accept the gift of Counsel, you hear God's will for you.

Yet counsel is more than the Holy Spirit speaking to you. It is also the Holy Spirit inspiring you as you speak to others. When a friend or family member has a particular need in his or her life, the gift of counsel—aided by wisdom and understanding—can give you the words and advice by which you can help. It won't come to you through some magical feeling, but you might find yourself offering counsel so good and wise that you know it is beyond your natural human ability.

*Joseph's Dream* by Gandolfi.
Counsel will help you recognize the voice of the Holy Spirit. St. Joseph had a very difficult decision to make, but he wisely took the counsel of an angel and "did as the angel of the lord commanded him" (Mt 1:24).

### Using Your Gift of Counsel

**Counsel will help you recognize the voice of the Holy Spirit.** Have you ever tried to pray about a decision but conflicting thoughts come into your head? It is tempting to think that the first idea that comes to mind must be the Holy Spirit talking to you, but that might not be the case. Pray that God will help you use the gift of counsel, and it will become easier to separate the thoughts that are of God from the thoughts that may be there to distract you from God.

**Counsel will make you a better friend to others.** Since this gift helps you speak to others, you can be of great service to them. The Holy Spirit will work through you to say what your friends and others need to hear. They may not realize it or appreciate it at first, but if they do they might continue to come to you for advice and counsel. With the Holy Spirit you will always speak the truth with love.

**Counsel will help you discern God's plan for your life.** With wisdom you have God's presence and can come to see things from his perspective. With understanding, you can have a deeper appreciation of what God has revealed. With counsel, you can apply that wisdom and understanding to making choices, both large and small.

### Models of the Gift of Counsel

**St. Joseph** had a very difficult decision to make. When the Blessed Virgin Mary was found to have conceived by the Holy Spirit, he knew it would bring her trouble. Everyone would think that Mary had been intimate with a man before marriage, and the Law prescribed a strict punishment for this sin. He considered breaking off their betrothal (which was like an engagement, but more binding). That way she could go away quietly and avoid the consequences. But an angel appeared to Joseph and said:

> **"Joseph, son of David, do not fear to take Mary your wife, for that which is conceived in her is of the Holy Spirit; she will bear a son, and you shall call his name Jesus, for he will save his people from their sins." (Mt 1:20-21)**

St. Joseph took this counsel and "did as the angel of the Lord commanded him" (Mt 1:24). Later, he learned that baby Jesus was in danger due to King Herod's plan to slay all the newborn male children. Joseph took advice from the angel again and fled with his family into Egypt.

**Pope St. Pius X** was the head of the Catholic Church for eleven years (1903-1914). One of his reforms was to invite children to receive the Sacrament of the Eucharist in First Communion at a younger age, around age seven. He had great trust in the will and guidance of God through the Holy Spirit. In his will, he wrote a prayer which said in part:

> **[God's] wisdom is infinite, and if I look to Him for counsel I shall not be deceived; His goodness is infinite, and if my trust is stayed on Him I shall not be abandoned. (Pope St. Pius X)**

## FORTITUDE

***The gift of fortitude makes you firm in professing and defending your Catholic faith despite all obstacles.***

When you think of the gift of fortitude, notice the first part of that word: *fort*. Ancient peoples built walls around their cities or settlements to protect themselves from attack. Later, military installations constructed with secure walls or other defensive measures were called forts. *Fort* and *fortitude* come from the Latin *fortis*, meaning "strong." These words carry the meaning of having strength against force or attack.

The gift of fortitude offers strength to your character and your will that can help you bear the struggles you face in life. Fortitude helps you to overcome human weakness, particularly fear. We all naturally fear danger, affliction, and suffering. But sometimes we have to endure such bad things for a greater good. For example, a parent might endure suffering in order to care for a disabled child. She does this lovingly, but it requires fortitude to overcome the temptation to avoid the suffering it involves.

The path to Christian perfection is not an easy one. You must overcome temptation, follow the lead of the Holy Spirit even when it is risky or difficult. You must be ready to stand up for the faith even when your friends and others mock you or reject you. Remember that many people rejected Christ himself, and he warned us to expect the same treatment. "If they persecuted me, they will persecute you" (Jn 15:20).

*The Martyrdom of St. Stephen* by Stella.
St. Stephen was the first Christian martyr. His preaching of the Good News angered the enemies of Christ so much that he was stoned to death. He had the strength of fortitude to stay faithful during his cruel death.

We can use the gift of fortitude not only when facing persecution but also in everyday situations. Temptation is sure to arise on a daily basis. The interior strength of the Holy Spirit helps you battle against sin and form good habits. This gift has great value as you grow in holiness.

### Using Your Gift of Fortitude

**Fortitude will help you deal with fear.** This gift does not eliminate fear from your life, but it does give you courage to deal with it. The saints and martyrs who faced ridicule, persecution, torture, and even death may well have experienced fear. However, they also had the strength of fortitude to endure it all. You will, too, in your life.

**Fortitude will help you combat temptation.** Even as you follow God's will in your life, you will continue to experience tests of your faith. St. Paul wrote:

> **No temptation has overtaken you that is not common to man. God is faithful, and he will not let you be tempted beyond your strength, but with the temptation will also provide the way of escape, that you may be able to endure it. (1 Cor 10:13)**

St. Bernadette Soubirous.
Her gift of fortitude led millions to come to accept her vision of the Blessed Virgin Mary as authentic.

**Fortitude will help you stand up to peer pressure.** Some of your temptations will come from friends and classmates. Some people do not respect you for your religious or moral beliefs, for going to Mass, for praying, and for believing in Christ. They might tease you about being a Catholic or ridicule your faith in other ways. Fortitude will help you handle such situations with love and stand up for your faith in spite of any attack.

## Models of the Gift of Fortitude

**St. Stephen** was the first Christian martyr. He was a deacon who was ordained to assist the Apostles, and he became a dynamic preacher of the Good News. His preaching angered the enemies of Christ so much that he was stoned to death. He proclaimed his faith even while enduring a cruel death:

> **As they were stoning Stephen, he prayed, "Lord Jesus, receive my spirit." And he knelt down and cried with a loud voice, "Lord, do not hold this sin against them." And when he had said this, he fell asleep. (Acts 7:59-60)**

"Fell asleep" is a way of saying that Stephen died. But he rose again to new life in heaven because he remained faithful to the end.

**St. Bernadette Soubirous** was a poor 14-year-old French girl to whom the Blessed Virgin Mary appeared. However, most people around her—including Church officials—were skeptical of her experience. Bernadette maintained the truth of what she had seen, and eventually people began to believe her. Later she entered a convent. She served as a nun joyfully, even though she endured terrible physical pains caused by tuberculosis. Her fortitude led millions to come to accept her vision as authentic, helping them to draw closer to Christ and his mother.

# KNOWLEDGE

***If we know God's plan, then we can use his gifts and creation to give him glory in everything.***

We read that the gift of wisdom allows us to see things from God's perspective. The gift of knowledge, on the other hand, enlightens our human perspective, allowing us to see God in creation. It also helps us to grasp, through creation, the greatness and love of God and his loving relationship with every creature.

Each of us accumulates human knowledge throughout our lives. We learn new things every day: how things work, current events, new theories and ideas, and information about the people we encounter. This learning happens both inside and outside the classroom as we experience the world and interact with others. Because everything comes from God, our knowledge of these things can help us, aided by the Holy Spirit, to know more about God himself.

The gift of knowledge is especially useful to you right now as a student. You are learning many subjects in school. Believe it or not, all of these subjects can help you know and love God more. As you learn more about math, for example, you can see the logic behind how God created the world. Knowing proper grammar can help you to express the truth about God and his creation to others. In a sense, through the gift of knowledge, every class becomes a religion class!

## Using Your Gift of Knowledge

**Knowledge helps us appreciate God's creation.** God created the world for human beings...for each of us. He did so beautifully: when he brought the world into being, "God saw that it was good" (Gn 1:10). This gift helps us recognize what is good around us.

**Knowledge helps us become better stewards of creation.** In the Old Testament, God put Adam and Eve in charge of creation, telling them to "fill the earth and subdue it" and to "have dominion" over it (Gn 1:26). He set them in the garden and told Adam to farm it and take care of it. Through the gift of knowledge, we can appreciate our role as caretakers of God's creation.

**Knowledge helps us to live a more detached life.** As we understand more fully the role of created things in this world, and how to use them as God intended, we will become more detached from things that don't matter. This will free us to become more attached to God.

## Models of the Gift of Knowledge

**St. Thomas Aquinas** is considered the greatest theologian in the Church's history. He took complex theological concepts and explained them using things everyone experiences and understands. In doing so, he used human knowledge as the basis for learning about God.

*The Apotheosis of St. Thomas Aquinas* by Zurbaran. The gift of knowledge enlightens our human perspective, allowing us to see God in creation. With the gift of knowledge, St. Thomas Aquinas formulated "The Five Ways" to prove the existence of God with logical arguments.

**St. Francis of Assisi** had a great love for creation, seeing it as the beautiful handiwork of God. He is usually depicted in harmony with nature, for example, surrounded by animals or preaching to birds. Toward the end of his life, he wrote the *Canticle of Creation*, a prayer that praises God for the created world. Pope Francis praised him for living the gift of knowledge. He "knew how to praise and laud his love through the contemplation of creation" (Pope Francis, *General Audience*, May 21, 2014).

# PIETY

***Because we are children of God, we come to know and love him intimately as our Father.***

Piety is a word we don't hear often. It is defined as the "quality of being religious or reverent." When we say someone is "pious," we usually mean that he is very religious. In other words, he might go to Mass frequently or spend a lot of time in prayer. Most people think piety is evident only in a person's external (visible) actions. But this is not really what is meant by the gift of piety.

Piety is our awareness that we are sons and daughters of God. It helps us to recognize the fact that God is our loving Father. When someone loves you, you want to respond to him or her in love. Whether it is a parent, friend, or spouse, being loved requires a response from you. If a friend helps you through a difficult time, then you will want to be kind to her in return. If your father takes you to all your practices and games, then you will want to show your appreciation to him for his sacrifices. Piety is the loving response we give to our heavenly Father, who has given us everything.

Jesus said, "Unless you become like children, you will never enter the kingdom of heaven" (Mt 18:3). Did he mean that we should act childish? No! He wants us to act like a little child should act toward his father: with complete trust and love, knowing that his father wants what is best for him. The gift of piety helps us to have that trust and love.

Through the gift of piety, we want to draw closer to God by attending Mass more often, praying more, and being faithful to God's commands in our life. These are outward signs of our inward devotion to God.

St. Josemaria Escriva used the gift of piety to see the love of Christ reflected in all of God's children.

## Using Your Gift of Piety

**Piety enriches our prayer life.** Recognizing that we should love God our Father in response to his love for us makes us want to draw closer to him in prayer. Christ taught us to call God our Father. He invited us to petition him for whatever we need. Like a good Father, God will answer our prayers in the way that is best for us.

**Piety makes us more gentle and compassionate with others.** Being a son or daughter of God brings a certain responsibility to uphold the family name. A loving child of God will imitate Christ, who is our brother and the perfect image of the Father. Especially when you are confronted with someone who is suffering or in some kind of need, God will help you remember Christ's gentleness and compassion so that you can respond like he did.

**Piety helps us become better witnesses for Christ.** When you speak and act as a true child of God, others will see the love of Christ reflected in you. Your actions are the most powerful witness you can give to the Gospel message.

## Models of the Gift of Piety

**St. Therese of Lisieux** was a young Carmelite nun of the late-nineteenth century who had a keen awareness of her role as a child of God. Knowing that she was unable to accomplish magnificent, heroic acts, she embraced the role of being "little before God," devoting herself to him in love and obedience as a small child would. Her spirituality came to be called her "little way of spiritual childhood." She committed herself to doing every task out of love for God and for others, whether she was cleaning the chapel, working in the convent laundry room, or tending to the sick and frail sisters. Her focus was always on recognizing that she was a daughter of God. "I tell you that it is enough to recognize one's nothingness and to abandon one's self like a child in the arms of God."

> **Jesus . . . said to them, "Let the children come to me, do not hinder them; for to such belongs the kingdom of God. Truly, I say to you, whoever does not receive the kingdom of God like a child shall not enter it." (Mk 10:14-15)**

**St. Josemaria Escriva** was a twentieth-century priest and founder of the religious group Opus Dei. He saw the fact that we are sons and daughters of God as the "foundation of the Christian life." We have a loving Father in heaven, and he cares dearly for his children. St. Josemaria taught that our proper response to being a child of God is to love God as our Father and work to please him in each moment of our lives.

*Vision of St. Teresa of Avila* by Chavarito.
St. Teresa of Avila understood the gift of Fear of the Lord and encouraged the faithful to examine their consciences often.

## FEAR OF THE LORD

***Reverence, wonder, and awe should be our response to the majesty and transcendence of God.***

"Fear of the Lord" is probably the most confusing of the gifts of the Holy Spirit. Although one might think so, it does not mean to be afraid of God. Being *afraid* describes the *emotion* that results from something dangerous or painful. *Fear* in the sense of this gift means to have awe and wonder as we ponder the greatness of God. There are no words adequate to describe God's majesty and power. We can try to speak of it, but for the most part we can only marvel.

We are in awe of God because he is beyond our ability to fully understand. He is both transcendent and immanent. His **transcendence** means that his greatness is without limit, far beyond our human capacity to understand him with the mind. His **immanence** means that he is present and active everywhere, sustaining all his creation. How he can be both is one of the mysteries of God.

The Fear of the Lord helps you to obey God in order to show him how much you love him. You do not follow his rules because you are afraid of harsh punishment. Instead, you fear offending him because you wish never to be separated from him. This gift helps you to keep your heart and mind focused on what God wants.

Fear of the Lord allows us to recognize the great difference between God and us, and how dependent we are upon him for everything. Further, fear of the Lord is a kind of "gateway" to the other gifts of the Holy Spirit, as these Scripture passages suggest:

> **The fear of the LORD is the beginning of wisdom;**
> **a good understanding have all those who practice it. (Ps 111:10)**
>
> **The fear of the LORD is the beginning of wisdom,**
> **and the knowledge of the Holy One is insight. (Prv 9:10)**

### Using Your Gift of Fear of the Lord

**Fear of the Lord makes us more aware of our sinfulness.** This gift will bring to mind your imperfections. This is a good thing. Imagine you are learning to play a musical instrument such as a guitar or piano. When you see an expert playing a difficult song, you are in awe of his or her talent and recognize how poorly you play by comparison. This recognition can inspire you to improve. In the same way, recognizing your sins can help you to grow in virtue and avoid future sins.

**Fear of the Lord strengthens our prayer life.** As you recognize God for who he is, you will become more thankful that your Father loves you as he does. You will praise him and have more trust in him. You will ask forgiveness for the ways you have offended him

*"And lo, I am with you always, to the close of the age."* (Mt 28:20)
The Fear of the Lord helps you to obey God in order to show him how much you love him.

through sin. Spending time in quiet prayer thinking about the greatness of God and his love for you is a great way to cultivate this gift of the Holy Spirit.

## Models of Fear of the Lord

**St. Teresa of Avila**, a sixteenth-century Carmelite nun, understood the importance of fear of the Lord when it comes to being prayerful. She asked people to meditate often on the beginning of Psalm 112: "Blessed is the man who fears the LORD." She also asked people to examine their consciences often:

> **If you want to gain this fear of the Lord, [it] is very helpful to understand the seriousness of an offense against God and to reflect on this frequently in your thoughts; for it is worth our life and much more to have this virtue rooted in our souls. (St. Teresa of Avila, *The Way of Perfection*)**

We see examples of fear of the Lord in the life of **St. Peter**, the head of the Apostles. When he first encountered Jesus and realized that he was the Messiah, he was humbled. He "fell down at Jesus' knees, saying, 'Depart from me, for I am a sinful man, O Lord.'" (Lk 5:8) St. Peter later wrote about how awe and wonder at the greatness of God should lead us to obey his will:

> **If you invoke as Father him who judges each one impartially according to his deeds, conduct yourselves with fear throughout the time of your exile. (1 Pt 1:17)**

*Domine quo vadis?* by Carracci.
St. Peter wrote about how awe and wonder at the greatness of God should lead us to obey his will.

## A Dialogue
### WILL I FEEL DIFFERENT AFTER I AM CONFIRMED?

**Lucy:** Mom, you know how I'm being confirmed next month?

**Mom:** It's on the calendar!

**Lucy:** I was wondering: will I feel any different after I'm confirmed?

**Mom:** What do you mean?

**Lucy:** Well, I've learned that the seven gifts of the Holy Spirit will be sealed in me at my Confirmation—will they make me different?

**Mom:** Yes and no. Receiving those gifts will make you different, but you probably won't feel any different afterwards, and people won't really notice a difference in you at first.

**Lucy:** Then what's the point?

**Mom:** Well, the gifts of the Holy Spirit are lifelong. They don't change you magically or instantly, but they *do* change you. Over time, if you are open to the Holy Spirit, you will be wiser, have greater fortitude, and have greater knowledge.

**Lucy:** But it seems like there are adults who are confirmed who don't really have those gifts.

**Mom:** That might be true, but it's not because they didn't receive them. If someone isn't practicing the gifts after their Confirmation, it's because they didn't *use* them. Instead of allowing the Holy Spirit to guide them, they do things on their own instead.

**Lucy:** Well, I'm gonna pray that I use all the gifts of the Holy Spirit after my Confirmation!

**Mom:** That's what Dad and I are praying too, Lucy.

# FRUITS OF THE HOLY SPIRIT

***The gifts that you will receive in Confirmation will form in you several good habits.***

> **By this power of the Spirit, God's children can bear much fruit. He who has grafted us onto the true vine will make us bear "the fruit of the Spirit:...love, joy, peace, patience, kindness, goodness, faithfulness, gentleness, self-control." "We live by the Spirit"; the more we renounce ourselves, the more we "walk by the Spirit." (CCC 736)**

The effects of the gifts of the Holy Spirit are called the **fruits of the Holy Spirit**. These are supernatural acts, or works, that flow joyfully from the Christian life. By living the fruits of the Holy Spirit, the soul begins to experience the peace and freedom that Christ won for us.

> **The fruits of the Spirit are perfections that the Holy Spirit forms in us as the first fruits of eternal glory. The tradition of the Church lists twelve of them: "charity, joy, peace, patience, kindness, goodness, generosity, gentleness, faithfulness, modesty, self-control, chastity." (CCC 1832)**

Although the Holy Spirit is mysterious, his presence in our souls is manifested in our actions and our demeanor. Even though we cannot see the Spirit, he transforms our lives so that we notice his effects.

As you prepare for Confirmation, contemplate these fruits of the Holy Spirit, and ask God to help them grow in you:

***Charity***, or ***love***, is a total dedication to God and love for him above all things. Charity also demands that we love our neighbor—our enemies as well as our friends. This love leads to our holiness and Christian perfection:

> **Love your enemies and pray for those who persecute you, so that you may be sons of your Father who is in heaven....For if you love those who love you, what reward have you? Do not even the tax collectors do the same? And if you salute only your brethren, what more are you doing than others? Do not even the Gentiles do the same? You, therefore, must be perfect, as your heavenly Father is perfect. (Mt 5:44-45, 46-48)**

Sts. Teresa of Calcutta and John Paul II lived their lives and vocations with total dedication to God and love for all his children. Their names are synonymous with *all* the fruits of the Holy Spirit listed in this chapter.

***Joy*** is gladness in the Lord, who is the source of our joy. Humanly speaking, joy usually springs from happy circumstances. But joy that comes from the Holy Spirit is not like that. Even in the midst of suffering and adversity the Christian is still joyful. He knows that God is in control of his life. St. Paul wrote that the early Christians "became imitators of us and of the Lord...with joy inspired by the Holy Spirit" (1 Thes 1:6).

***Peace*** is the abiding presence of God in our lives. No matter the situation, we are content in our relationship with God. We know that he cares for us always. "To set the mind on the flesh is death, but to set the mind on the Spirit is life and peace" (Rom 8:6).

***Patience*** helps us to understand that God has a time and a season for everything. We may have to suffer for a while, but God will be with us at all times. Further, we know we will eventually be with him in heaven if we are faithful to him.

***Kindness*** comes from recognizing Christ in every person and treating him or her accordingly. To slander others, to make cruel or sarcastic remarks at their expense, or to treat them discourteously is inconsistent with the life of a follower of Christ. The Holy Spirit can help us cultivate kindness in spite of our temptations to being selfish or short-tempered.

***Generosity*** is a measure of our response to all that God has given us. Whatever good we have is meant to be shared—whether it is our faith, our time, or our wealth. Carrying out the mission of Christ means having a generous spirit toward those in need.

***Faithfulness*** means following Christ in everything. We trust in God; we trust in what Christ teaches through his Church. We may not understand everything the Church teaches. However, we trust that the Church receives her teaching from God, and therefore we will follow it.

***Gentleness*** ensures that our strength is always softened by love. Christ emphasized this in his preaching. "Take my yoke upon you, and learn from me; for I am gentle and lowly in heart, and you will find rest for your souls" (Mt 11:29). The gentle person does not look for ways to disturb others, and does not desire conflict for conflict's sake.

***Self-control*** involves restraint of our desires in both thought and action. This means that we are not controlled by our passions and appetites. Instead, we allow the Holy Spirit to be our guide in our actions. This fruit allows us to be master of ourselves, instead of slaves to our desires.

***Modesty*** allows us to avoid the sin of pride, vanity, boasting, or seeking praise from others. It is also expressed by the care that we take in how we dress, act, and treat others.

***Chastity*** means practicing purity within one's state in life. For people who are not married, chastity means avoiding the marital acts and other lustful attractions. For married people, it means ensuring that every marital act is open to new life and is a true act of self-giving love shared exclusively between spouses.

***Goodness*** means having an essentially good nature. This fruit helps us consider the well-being of every person, the common good of the community, and our own pursuit of virtue in every decision. A person who lives a profound love for God will manifest goodness in all of his or her thoughts, words, and actions.

## CONCLUSION

***The gifts and fruits of the Holy Spirit are given for our good and the good of the Church.***

The Sacrament of Confirmation will give you the seven gifts of the Holy Spirit: wisdom, understanding, counsel, fortitude, knowledge, piety, and fear of the Lord. Each represents a deepening of your baptismal graces. These gifts will help you grow in holiness and Christian perfection. In order for the gifts of the Holy Spirit to benefit you, you must act upon them and allow them to draw you closer to God and others.

These gifts will inspire you to live as Christ lived: in complete dedication to the will of God and in service to others. They also create within you the virtues and dispositions that will be reflected in the fruits of the Holy Spirit. By these gifts and fruits you can draw closer to Christ and live your life in conformity to his, enabling you to become a strong Christian.

## POINTS TO REMEMBER

1. At your Baptism, you received the seven gifts of the Holy Spirit. At your Confirmation, they will be increased and strengthened in you. These gifts have effects in your life, called the fruits of the Holy Spirit.
2. There are seven gifts of the Holy Spirit: wisdom, understanding, counsel, fortitude, knowledge, piety, and fear of the Lord.
3. There are twelve fruits of the Holy Spirit: charity, joy, peace, patience, kindness, goodness, generosity, gentleness, faithfulness, modesty, self-control, and chastity.
4. A Christian life is made possible only through grace and virtues. The fullness of Christian life can be attained only by means of the seven gifts of the Holy Spirit.
5. The seven gifts of the Holy Spirit enable us to receive and readily obey the promptings of grace sent to us by the Holy Spirit.
6. The seven gifts of the Holy Spirit make us more attentive to the voice of God, and make it easier for us to follow his plan for our lives.

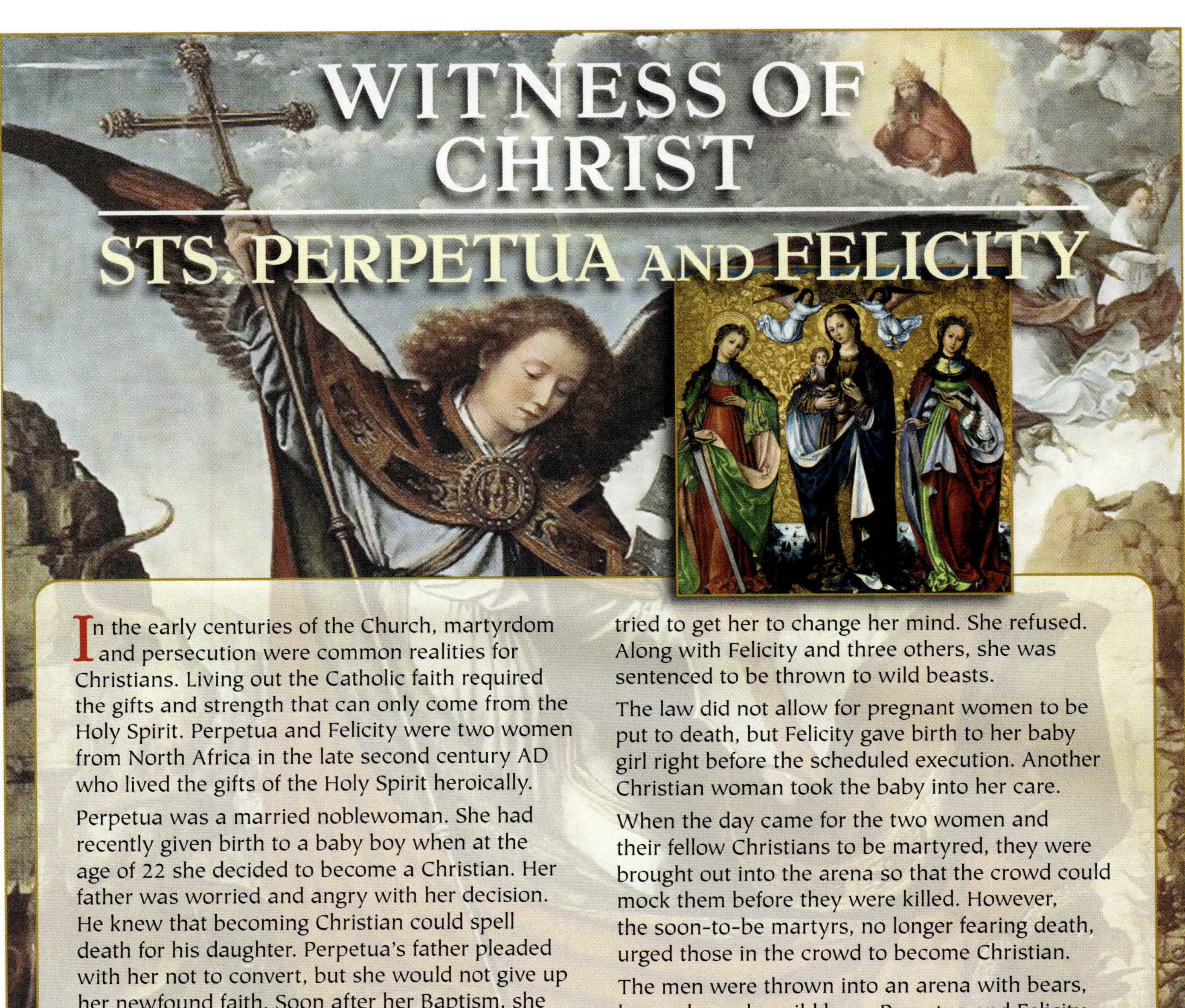

# Witness of Christ

## Sts. Perpetua and Felicity

In the early centuries of the Church, martyrdom and persecution were common realities for Christians. Living out the Catholic faith required the gifts and strength that can only come from the Holy Spirit. Perpetua and Felicity were two women from North Africa in the late second century AD who lived the gifts of the Holy Spirit heroically.

Perpetua was a married noblewoman. She had recently given birth to a baby boy when at the age of 22 she decided to become a Christian. Her father was worried and angry with her decision. He knew that becoming Christian could spell death for his daughter. Perpetua's father pleaded with her not to convert, but she would not give up her newfound faith. Soon after her Baptism, she was imprisoned, along with four catechumens.

Among the catechumens was Perpetua's servant, Felicity. Like Perpetua, Felicity was deeply dedicated to Christ and wanted to be baptized. At the time of her imprisonment she was eight months pregnant, but she was still treated cruelly and ridiculed by the guards.

The prison was overcrowded and completely dark. The prisoners had to endure sweltering heat and mistreatment. Perpetua's most difficult suffering was being separated from her baby. When Perpetua's father visited her, he threw himself at her feet and begged her to renounce her faith. However, Perpetua was steadfast and would not deny Christ. Even at her sentencing, the judge tried to get her to change her mind. She refused. Along with Felicity and three others, she was sentenced to be thrown to wild beasts.

The law did not allow for pregnant women to be put to death, but Felicity gave birth to her baby girl right before the scheduled execution. Another Christian woman took the baby into her care.

When the day came for the two women and their fellow Christians to be martyred, they were brought out into the arena so that the crowd could mock them before they were killed. However, the soon-to-be martyrs, no longer fearing death, urged those in the crowd to become Christian.

The men were thrown into an arena with bears, leopards, and a wild boar. Perpetua and Felicity were thrown before a wild cow. Although wounded by the wild animals, they survived the attacks. Eventually, the authorities cut the throats of all five of these Christians. Perpetua's last words were "Stand fast and love one another."

The Holy Spirit empowers us to be Christ's witnesses in the world. Filled with the Holy Spirit, Sts. Perpetua and Felicity endured martyrdom for Christ, preferring an early death to life outside of Christ. They lead lives marked by fortitude.

Their feast day is March 7, and they are remembered in the canon of the Mass in Eucharistic Prayer I.

## VOCABULARY

**CHARITY**
The fruit of the Holy Spirit which strengthens our ability to love God above all things for his own sake, and loves his neighbor as himself for the love of God. Also one of the theological virtues.

**CHASTITY**
The fruit of the Holy Spirit which gives the self-control necessary to live in purity and an inner unity of the bodily and spiritual being. Chastity is also a moral virtue.

**COUNSEL**
A gift of the Holy Spirit, Counsel helps one to hear the voice of the Holy Spirit and to judge promptly and rightly. This gift also allows one to assist others in determining the will of God for them.

**FAITHFULNESS**
A fruit of the Holy Spirit, faithfulness means that one is trustworthy and reliable.

**FEAR OF THE LORD**
One of the seven gifts of the Holy Spirit which ensures our awe and reverence before God.

**FORTITUDE**
The gift of the Holy Spirit that allows us to be strong in character and will in facing the struggles of life. It is sometimes called "courage." It is also a cardinal virtue.

**GENEROSITY**
One of the twelve fruits of the Holy Spirit, it is the virtue of giving beyond what is required by justice.

**GENTLENESS**
The fruit of the Holy Spirit which allows one to be submissive to God and considerate and humble towards others.

**GOODNESS**
A fruit of the Holy Spirit which helps one to think of the good of those around him at all times.

**IMMANENT**
Quality of God; he is present and active everywhere, sustaining all his creation.

**JOY**
A fruit of the Holy Spirit which gives a sense of gladness that comes not from external circumstances, but instead from trust in the Lord.

**KINDNESS**
A fruit of the Holy Spirit which allows one to avoid harshness and works to meet the needs of others.

**KNOWLEDGE**
A gift of the Holy Spirit, knowledge gives one the ability to see God in his creation, and to understand that creation more fully.

**MODESTY**
A fruit of the Holy spirit which gives one moderation, freedom from exaggeration, and self-control. This most often refers to propriety of behavior, chastity in thought and speech, and avoidance of revealing clothing that excites the senses and may lead others to sin.

**PATIENCE**
A fruit of the Spirit which allows us us to suffer the difficulties of life without complaint and for the good of others.

**PEACE**
One of the fruits of the Holy Spirit mentioned in Galatians 5:22-23. Peace is a goal of Christian living, as indicated by Jesus who said "Blessed are the peacemakers, for they shall be called children of God." The Fifth Commandment requires us to preserve and work for peace, which was defined by St. Augustine as "the tranquility of order," and which is the work of justice and the effect of charity.

## VOCABULARY Continued

### PIETY
One of the seven gifts of the Holy Spirit which leads one to devotion to God. Filial piety connotes an attitude of reverence and respect by children toward their parents. Piety also refers to the religious sense of a people, and its expression in popular devotions.

### SELF-CONTROL
A fruit of the Holy Spirit; it gives the ability to master your desire for pleasure for the sake of a greater good.

### TRANSCENDENT
Quality of God; his greatness is without limit, far beyond our human capacity to understand him with the mind.

### UNDERSTANDING
A gift of the Holy Spirit that helps us to better comprehend and appreciate God's Revelation.

### WISDOM
A spiritual gift which enables one to know the purpose and plan of God; one of the seven gifts of the Holy Spirit.

## STUDY QUESTIONS

1. How do the gifts of the Holy Spirit work within us?
2. Who is our model for living the gifts of the Holy Spirit, and why?
3. If we already possess wisdom, understanding, knowledge, and the other gifts of the Holy Spirit in Baptism, then why do we need to "receive" them at Confirmation?
4. What does it mean that we have "God's perspective" through the gift of wisdom?
5. How does the gift of counsel help both us and those around us?
6. How does the gift of fortitude relate to the idea of a "fort"?
7. What is the gift of knowledge, and how does it relate to the gift of wisdom?
8. What is the gift of piety, and how is it more than just being "religious"?
9. What is the gift of fear of the Lord, and how is it different than being *afraid*?
10. List the twelve fruits of the Holy Spirit, and explain two of them.

## PRACTICAL EXERCISES

1. Imagine a situation in which you might be called upon to use the gift of counsel. Write a brief story about how you hope that you might use it.
2. Think about the twelve fruits of the Holy Spirit, and ask yourself the following questions:
   a. Which two fruits do I show most strongly in my life? Give examples.
   b. Which two fruits are the weakest in my life? Give examples.
   c. What might I do to grow in the fruits that are the weakest in my life?

# SEALED IN THE SPIRIT

***Learn to follow Christ by reading about the saints who have received the Sacrament of Confirmation.***

Throughout this chapter, we have referred to various saints who lived out the gifts of the Holy Spirit. In order to give us clear guidance in how best to follow Christ, the Church puts forward the lives of the saints. By studying the lives of the saints, we can learn to see the action of the Holy Spirit within them. Through them we see how Catholics have followed him for the past 2,000 years.

An important benefit of studying the lives of the saints is discovering how many different ways there are to be Christ's disciple. It doesn't matter if you are a man or a woman, old or young, rich or poor. You can follow Christ faithfully in this life. People of every personality and circumstance have been holy disciples of Christ. Sainthood doesn't require changing who God made you to be.

As you read the lives of various saints, you will find that some of their stories really resonate with you, and some might not as much. That's okay. If certain saints are particularly attractive to you, then do more research to find out more about their lives. Work to model your own life after that of the saint who interests you, such as your Confirmation name saint. This will help you to become a saint yourself!

*Virgin and Child with Saints* by Boccaccino.
The saints represented in this painting are St. Catherine of Alexandria, St. Christine of Tyre, St. Peter, and St. John the Baptist. If certain saints are particularly attractive to you, then do more research to find out more about their lives.

# YOU AND YOUR PARENTS

***The gifts and fruits of the Holy Spirit involve things that your parents have taught you.***

The gifts and fruits of the Holy Spirit are not just special attributes we develop from scratch because of Confirmation. The Sacrament helps build them in us, to be sure, but if we are already developing virtue and growing in holiness, we will also be fostering these gifts and fruits.

The gifts and fruits of the Holy Spirit are attributes that your parents have probably tried to teach you at home. They want you to grow up to be wise, strong, pious, understanding, and knowledgeable. They want you to live in a spirit of kindness, generosity, patience, and all the other fruits of the Holy Spirit. It may be good to take a moment to recognize how these are worthy characteristics to have on a human level. Our parents, teachers, and other mentors have probably tried to instill them in us already. In Confirmation the Holy Spirit will provide us with a tremendous boost in the form of grace to help us live the gifts and fruits of the Holy Spirit more completely.

Ask your parents to read the sections in this chapter about the gifts and fruits of the Holy Spirit, and then talk about them with you. The following questions might help your discussion:

1. What gifts of the Holy Spirit do you think are most important for each of you right now?
2. How can your family show the fruits of the Holy Spirit?
3. How have your parents tried to foster these gifts in you?

*Parable of the Lost Sheep* by Soord.
In Confirmation the Holy Spirit will provide us with a tremendous boost in the form of grace to help us live the gifts and fruits of the Holy Spirit.

# YOU AND YOUR SPONSOR

***Your sponsor can help you live the gifts and fruits of the Holy Spirit.***

At the end of the last chapter, you invited your sponsor to act as a kind of coach, encouraging you in your preparation for Confirmation and in living your Confirmation afterward. Now it's time to put your sponsor to work!

Your sponsor has been confirmed and is probably familiar with the gifts and fruits of the Holy Spirit. Still, he or she might appreciate a refresher course. Review and discuss the sections in this chapter about the gifts and fruits of the Holy Spirit with your sponsor. The following questions might help you:

1. How has each of these gifts worked in your sponsor's life? Give examples.
2. How has your sponsor tried to live the fruits of the Holy Spirit?
3. How have the fruits of the Holy Spirit been evident in your sponsor's life? Give examples.
4. How would your sponsor advise you to grow in these gifts and fruits as you prepare for Confirmation?

*The Adoration of the Trinity* by Durer.
How would your sponsor advise you to grow in the gifts and fruits of the Holy Spirit as you prepare for Confirmation?

THE SACRAMENT OF

# Confirmation

Chapter 9

# LIFE IN THE HOLY SPIRIT: PRAYER

## INTRODUCTION

***Your path to holiness, your openness to grace, and your relationship with God rely on prayer.***

We have learned so far about God's plan for this world and for you. We have also learned about the Sacraments, especially the Sacrament of Confirmation and the gifts and fruits you receive from it. The rest of this book will focus on how one who has received the gift of the Holy Spirit in Confirmation should live as a disciple of Christ.

The foundation of a disciple's life is prayer. A disciple has a personal relationship with God, and it is only through prayer that this relationship with God can grow and be sustained. Through the bond that prayer nourishes, you can be strengthened in faith. Through this bond you can grow in communion with the Blessed Trinity. Prayer opens you up to the grace of the Holy Spirit. It helps you develop a good interior disposition. This makes you better able to use the gifts that you will receive in Confirmation.

After reading this chapter, you will be able to answer these questions:

- What is the "interior life"?
- What is prayer?
- How does the Holy Spirit help us in prayer?
- How can we strengthen our prayer life?
- What are the expressions and forms of prayer?

Through the bond that prayer nourishes, you can be strengthened in faith.

## THE INTERIOR LIFE

***Being a disciple of Christ means having a strong interior life.***

As human beings, we are made up of body and soul. If we want to be truly healthy then we need to make sure that both body and soul remain healthy. We probably know how to keep our bodies healthy: eat well, exercise, get enough sleep, etc. But how do we keep our souls healthy? Some parts of a healthy soul should be obvious to us by now, for example, living a moral life, attending Mass regularly, and going to Confession on a regular basis. Another important aspect of keeping a healthy soul is having a strong **interior life**. This is as important as breathing is to the body.

St. Francis by Tayler.
To have a strong interior life, we have to make prayer a fundamental part of our lives.

But what is the interior life?

The interior life consists primarily of two things. The first is a life of prayer—having a conversation with God. Second is recognizing the presence of God at all times. These two parts are related to each other. If you do not pray regularly, you will not recognize that God is always present with you. In addition, if you don't recognize God's presence, you will not be encouraged to pray regularly. Someone with a strong interior life lives every moment with the knowledge that God is with him. He can converse with God about anything, anytime. Instead of getting caught up in your surroundings, you can be at peace and know that God loves you and will always guide you.

**The Lord is near to all who call upon him,
to all who call upon him in truth. (Ps 145:18)**

But how do we acquire a strong interior life? The same way we get a strong body: discipline and perseverance. It is not enough to simply *want* a strong interior life; we have to work for it. This means making prayer a priority. Most of us pray at various times— such as before meals, before bedtime, or in a time of stress (such as before an upcoming test, or when someone close to you is sick). But to have a strong interior life, we have to make prayer a fundamental part of our lives. By doing so, we will come to see God as our companion in all we say and do.

As you get ready to be confirmed, consider your own interior life. Do you pray often? Do you just pray when you want God to do something, or because you want to talk to—and hear from—God? Do you recognize the presence of God in your daily life? Deepening your interior life by building a life of prayer is essential for living out the graces you will receive in Confirmation.

### *IMITATION OF CHRIST*
**by Thomas a Kempis**

Written centuries ago, *Imitation of Christ* is considered one of the most helpful books for deepening one's interior life. In fact, it is the most widely read devotional book in history other than the Bible. In this book the reader is helped along as he tries to imitate Christ. He learns how to pray and to live in the presence of God at all times. If you are looking for a way to deepen your own interior life, the *Imitation of Christ* is a great place to start!

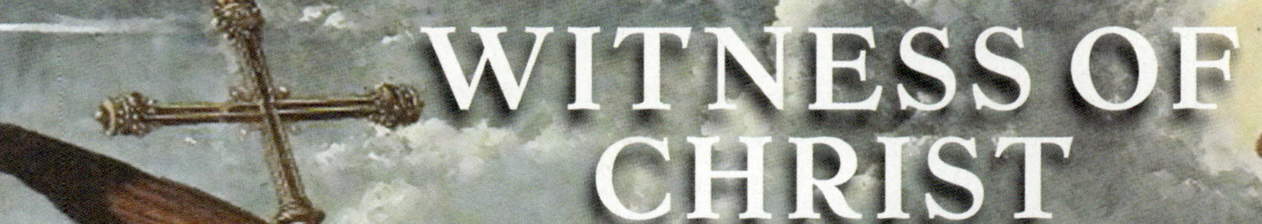

# Witness of Christ

## St. Maria Goretti

Maria Goretti, lovingly called "Marietta" by her family, was the daughter of poor Italian farm workers at the turn of the twentieth century. When she was nine her father died, compelling her mother to work in the fields to support the family. To Marietta fell the task of caring for her five younger siblings and cooking for the family as well as for their neighbors, Giovanni Serenelli and his nineteen-year-old son, Alessandro.

Alessandro developed an impure attraction to Marietta. He made advances toward her, but she resisted. Finding her alone at home one summer day in 1902, he tried to force himself on her; she protested, "No, Alessandro, it's a sin; you'll go to hell." He choked her, telling her that he would kill her if she did not give in. She said that she would rather die, and he stabbed her fourteen times with a metal file.

Marietta was taken to a hospital, and the doctors were surprised that she was still alive. She was begging for water, but this might have infected her pierced organs, which would lead to death. A nearby priest asked Marietta to think of Christ's thirst on the Cross; she agreed and did not ask for water again.

Because Marietta had lost so much blood, the doctors knew that her heart was too weak for anesthesia, but they still had to operate. Through several operations over the next twenty hours, she did not cry out at all; instead, she offered her silent pain for the salvation of souls and the conversion of sinners. When the priest asked Marietta if she might forgive Alessandro, she answered, "I forgive him with all my heart, and I hope he will be with me in heaven." She died from all this two days later.

Although Maria Goretti's death was heroic and remarkable, it was not the end of her story.

Alessandro was sentenced to thirty years in prison. He was so wild with rage and unrepentant that he had to be kept in solitary confinement for the first six years of his prison term. Then one night he had a dream in which he saw Marietta in a garden, picking fourteen lilies, which she gave to him. Afterward he asked for a bishop to hear his confession. He became a model inmate and was released from prison early for good behavior.

Once free from prison, Alessandro sought out Maria's mother and asked her to forgive him. "If she forgave you, how can I do otherwise?" she responded. Alessandro accompanied her to Christmas Mass and spoke before the congregation about his repentance and God's forgiveness. He spent the rest of his life in prayer and penance, working as a gardener for a Capuchin monastery.

Maria Goretti's canonization in 1950 drew the largest crowds that had ever attended a canonization; it was the first canonization that had to be held outside in St. Peter's Square instead of inside the basilica. At eleven years old, she was the youngest person ever to be canonized. Perhaps the most amazing sight at her canonization was her own mother seated beside Alessandro himself!

Maria Goretti is considered a martyr for purity because of her desire to die rather than commit a mortal sin. But what made her a saint even more was her forgiveness, which continues to witness to the love of Christ long after her death, even today.

*Good Friday Morning: Jesus in Prison* by Tissot.
As we learn about prayer, we need to ask the Holy Spirit to help us to pray.

## PRAYER AND THE HOLY SPIRIT

***Although you may encounter difficulties in prayer, the Holy Spirit is there to help you.***

Personal prayer is your conversation with God. Think about the many conversations you have throughout each day—with friends, teachers, your parents, and even strangers. Some of these conversations might come easily and seem to take no effort at all. Other conversations might be difficult and leave you worn out afterwards. Your conversations with God in prayer are similar. Sometimes they seem effortless, but other times they can be difficult and even feel like a chore.

As disciples of Christ we are to pray always, whether it comes easily or is difficult. When prayer is difficult, your mind may wander. You may be easily distracted and unable to focus for long. You may feel that no one is listening, that your prayer isn't "good enough," or that you simply do not have the words. All of these obstacles can frustrate and discourage you. Sometimes you might be tempted to give up on prayer entirely. But this is not an option if you really want a relationship with God—a friendship. Friends need to talk and communicate to keep their relationship strong.

Fortunately for us, God knows it can be difficult at times to converse with him in prayer, and so he gives us many helps. For example, he gave us the *Lord's Prayer*, also called the "Our Father," perhaps the most beloved prayer of all Christianity. The *Lord's Prayer* gives us the model prayer, so that we can know how to pray. Most importantly, however, he gives himself—in the Holy Spirit—to help us pray! As St. Paul wrote:

> **The Spirit helps us in our weakness; for we do not know how to pray as we ought, but the Spirit himself intercedes for us with sighs too deep for words. (Rom 8:26)**

We might think that prayer is our own doing or that everything depends on our own efforts. However, every effort we make to pray is simply our response to the working of the Holy Spirit. We cannot pray effectively without the help of the Holy Spirit. As we learn about prayer, we need to ask the Holy Spirit to help us to pray. He will be with us at every step, giving us the desire to pray, as well as the words we will say in prayer.

### THE POWER OF PRAYER

Whenever we feel in our hearts a desire to improve, a desire to respond more generously to Our Lord, and we look for something to guide us...the Holy Spirit will remind us of the words of the Gospel that we "ought to pray continually and never be discouraged". Prayer is the foundation of any supernatural endeavor. With prayer we are all powerful; without it, if we were to neglect it, we would accomplish nothing. (St. Josemaria Escriva, *Friends of God*, 238)

Prayer is the most powerful weapon a Christian has. Prayer makes us effective. Prayer makes us happy. Prayer gives us all the strength we need to fulfil God's commands. —Yes! Your whole life can and should be prayer. (St. Josemaria Escriva, *The Forge*, 439)

The spirit of prayer which fills the entire life of Jesus Christ among men teaches us that all our actions—great or small—ought to be preceded by prayer, accompanied by prayer and followed by prayer. (St. Josemaria Escriva, *The Forge*, 441)

# HOW TO PRAY

***We must set aside time for our prayer life.***

**Prayer is the life of the new heart. It ought to animate us at every moment...But we cannot pray "at all times" if we do not pray at specific times, consciously willing it. These are the special times of Christian prayer, both in intensity and duration. (CCC 2697)**

Like anything worthwhile, prayer takes hard work. Learning how to pray is like learning any other skill. If you want to learn to play the guitar, you will have to set aside time each day to practice, you will need an instructor, and you will need a plan for advancing in your knowledge of the guitar. Most importantly, you will need discipline and perseverance. All these things are necessary as well for learning to pray.

**Set aside a time and place.** One of the most important things to do in order to pray well is to set aside a time and place for prayer each day. If you don't set aside a specific time, there is a good chance you will forget to pray, or something else will come up. So set aside time to pray each day, perhaps when you first get up in the morning. Further, you need a specific place for your prayer time. It could be your bedroom, or somewhere quiet in your house. Having a statue, crucifix, or religious picture there will help you focus on God.

**No distractions.** It is very difficult to go even a few minutes without distractions—texts, TV, music, phone calls. But in order to hear God speak to you, you need to make sure you are listening. And how can you listen if you are distracted? So during the time set aside for prayer, be sure that your cell phone is turned off or in another room, and that there are no distractions.

**Make a plan.** When you have a time and place set aside, and have made sure you have no distractions, then what? You need a plan. Perhaps during your prayer time you will read a little of the Bible or pray a Rosary. Plan ahead and know what you want to do during the time you have set aside. If you are not sure, discuss it with one of your parents, your sponsor, or a priest at your parish.

**Start small and build up.** Once you realize how important it is to pray everyday, you might feel you

## THE LORD'S PRAYER (Our Father)

**The Lord's Prayer "is truly the summary of the whole gospel." (CCC 2761)**

The most important prayer to learn came to us directly from Christ. When the Apostles asked Christ to teach them to pray, their humble and honest petition opened the door for Christ to reveal the most perfect prayer: "Our Father, who art in heaven..." Since this comes from the mouth of Christ, it is called the *Lord's Prayer*. It is also simply called the Our Father.

The *Lord's Prayer* includes seven petitions. Here is what each of them means:

- **Hallowed be thy name.** We begin by addressing God's holiness; *hallowed* means "holy." By calling him Father, we wish to draw nearer to his holiness.
- **Thy kingdom come.** We acknowledge our desire for the Kingdom of God. This refers to the perfection of the Church on earth. It also refers to our anticipation of his eternal kingdom in heaven and Christ's second coming.
- **Thy will be done.** We want to submit to God's will ahead of our own wants and desires.
- **Give us this day our daily bread.** We ask God to provide for our earthly needs. We also express our eagerness for the Body and Blood of Christ in the Eucharist.
- **Forgive us our trespasses, as we forgive those who trespass against us.** We ask God's pardon for our own sins, and the grace to forgive our enemies.
- **Lead us not into temptation.** We ask for God's help so that we can be strong enough to avoid sin and grow in holiness.
- **Deliver us from evil.** We beg God to protect us from evil. We also ask God to allow us to share in Christ's victory over sin and death.

should pray for a long time everyday. But it is best to start small and then work your way up. If you don't spend any set time praying now, just start with 5-10 minutes. After you have done that for at least a month, then you could add 5-10 more minutes. You may continue to do that until you are praying an hour a day.

St. Paul said, "pray constantly" (1 Thes 5:17), so does this mean that every moment should be set aside for prayer? No. What St. Paul meant was that every moment should be lived for God, and offered up as a prayer to God. Although certain times should be set aside exclusively for prayer, every moment can be made a prayer. Always recognize that God is with you at all times and that you can always converse with him no matter where you are or what you are doing.

> **Prayer is both a gift of grace and a determined response on our part. It always presupposes effort. (CCC 2725)**

> **Our praying can and should arise above all from our heart, from our needs, our hopes, our joys, our sufferings, from our shame over sin, and from our gratitude for the good. It can and should be a wholly personal prayer. But we also constantly need to make use of those prayers that express in words the encounter with God experienced both by the Church as a whole and by individual members of the Church. For without these aids to prayer, our own praying and our image of God become subjective and end up reflecting ourselves more than the living God. (Pope Benedict XVI, *Jesus of Nazareth*, p. 130)**

> **The great men and women of prayer throughout the centuries were privileged to receive an interior union with the Lord that enabled them to descend into the depths beyond the word. They are therefore able to unlock for us the hidden treasures of prayer. And we may be sure that each of us, along with our totally personal relationship with God, is received into, and sheltered within, this prayer. (Pope Benedict XVI, *Jesus of Nazareth*, p. 133)**

## IDEAS FOR DAILY PRAYER TIME

There are many things you can do during your prayer time to make it fruitful. Here are some ideas to get you started:

- Pray a Rosary
- Read the Gospel passage for the day's Mass (the passages for each day can be found online at *www.usccb.org*).
- Read through a Gospel, a few verses each day
- Pray a Chaplet of Divine Mercy
- Read a good spiritual book, such as *Imitation of Christ*
- Engage in mental prayer
- Visit the Blessed Sacrament or attend Eucharistic adoration
- Pray before or hold a crucifix
- Pray before a statue of Our Lord, the Blessed Mother, or any of the saints
- Pray before an image of Our Lord, the Blessed Mother, or any of the saints
- Clasp a medal you are wearing
- Find a quiet place of solitude to contemplate a spiritual concern
- Pray for the Poor Souls in purgatory, especially loved ones

Although certain times should be set aside exclusively for prayer, every moment can be made a prayer.

"where two or three are gathered in my name, there am I in the midst of them." (Mt 18:20)

## PRAYING WITH THE CHURCH

***When we are praying with the Church, we are praying with the Communion of Saints.***

God desires that his people pray together. Christ proclaimed, "where two or three are gathered in my name, there am I in the midst of them" (Mt 18:20). Christ is present in a particular way whenever even a couple of people meet to pray or discuss their faith. We can pray with our fellow Catholics in many ways, such as a group Rosary, a Bible study, or family prayer before meals. In each case, Christ is present.

The liturgical celebrations of the Church, such as Mass, are particularly special times when the faithful gather to pray. Every liturgical celebration is an action of the whole Church. When you and your family join other people for Mass at your local parish, it is not just this small group that is praying together. You are praying in communion with the whole Church.

But praying with the "whole Church" is even more powerful than you might think. When two or more disciples gather to celebrate the liturgy and Sacraments of the Church, it is not only Christ but the entire Body of Christ who are present there.

## APOLOGETICS 101:

### DRYNESS IN PRAYER

(Adapted from the *Didache Bible*)

***How can we overcome dryness in prayer?***

**Rejoice in your hope, be patient in tribulation, be constant in prayer. (Rom 12:12)**

**Continue steadfastly in prayer, being watchful in it with thanksgiving. (Col 4:2)**

**Pray at all times in the Spirit, with all prayer and supplication. To that end keep alert with all perseverance. (Eph 6:18)**

Dryness in prayer is a common affliction among even the most devoted Christians. It means that one "feels" nothing when praying, or doesn't know what to say during prayer, or loses interest in prayer. Persistence and vigilance are necessary to overcome this.

Dryness in prayer occurs from time to time within almost everyone who prays regularly. Even some of the holiest men and women have spoken of dryness in their own prayer lives. St. John of the Cross wrote of his "dark night of the soul." St. Teresa of Calcutta (Mother Teresa), the twentieth-century nun known for her selfless work for the impoverished and dying in India, explained that she had long periods of feeling distant from God even in her prayer. It is a phenomenon we often associate with prayer of petition: God may hear our praise and thanksgiving, but when our requests go unanswered, we sometimes feel he is not listening to us.

Dryness characterizes the distance we feel from God when we do not feel his presence or interest in us or when we feel we are not generating enough passion or confidence in our prayers. At times we do not believe that we are praying effectively because we lack the right words, as if God would answer us if only we were eloquent enough. What is more at issue is whether we are praying "as we ought": if we are asking for the right things, if we are coming to God seeking to fulfill our passions rather than submit to his will in all humility.

The key to fruitful prayer is always perseverance and vigilance, based in true faith and humility. Our dispositions in prayer affect its effectiveness; only complete abandonment to the will of God will ultimately satisfy us. We must seek constant conversion of heart, forever conforming our hearts and wills to the will of God. We trust that like a loving Father he will always give us what we truly need.

### PRAYING TO MARY AND THE SAINTS

Many people do not understand why Catholics pray to anyone other than God. After all, if you can pray to God Almighty directly, why bother to pray to others, such as the Blessed Virgin Mary, the saints, or the angels?

The first thing to remember is that when Catholics say that we "pray" to the Blessed Virgin Mary, the saints, or the angels, what we really mean is that we are asking for their intercession. We are asking them to pray for us. Asking others to pray for us is something that all Christians do. When was the last time that someone asked you to pray for him or her? When was the last time that you asked a friend, a relative, or your parish priest to pray for you?

When we ask people to pray for us, we are asking them to intercede for us. When we do this, we are inclined to ask someone who prays regularly and has a strong, personal relationship with God. And the strongest relationships of all are between God and the saints and angels in heaven!

This is one of the great benefits to being part of the Communion of Saints. We can ask those who have gone before us and are now completely united to God to pray for us. We can explain to them things about our life, our feelings, and our worries, so they know what our needs are. Their prayers can help us to join them one day in heaven.

Praying *with the whole Church*, then, includes not just everyone in your parish, nor just every Catholic in the world. It includes all the faithful in Christ who have ever lived. This is the Communion of Saints: all of the members of the Church on earth, in heaven, and in purgatory. Many churches have statues, paintings, stained glass, and other representations of saints to remind us that we are not alone, that "we are surrounded by so great a cloud of witnesses" (Heb 12:1). In the liturgy we are united with the angels and saints in our prayer.

So if someone close to you has died in the friendship of God, you can be sure that he or she prays with you at every Mass and will be present at your Confirmation. Even your Catholic friends and relatives who cannot attend your Confirmation will be there "in spirit" as part of the same communion of faith!

## EXPRESSIONS OF PRAYER

***There are a variety of ways and methods of praying, and each is an encounter with God.***

**The Christian tradition comprises three major expressions of the life of prayer: vocal prayer, meditation, and contemplative prayer. They have in common the recollection of the heart. (CCC 2721)**

In Christian tradition there are three "expressions" of prayer. Christ himself taught *vocal prayer* to his disciples and also practiced *meditative prayer* and *contemplative prayer*. All three types of prayer are helpful in the Christian life.

### MARY, THE MODEL OF PRAYER

**Mary…represents the model of the Church at prayer…[F]or the People of God Mary represents the model of every expression of their prayer life. In particular, she teaches Christians how to turn to God to ask for his help and support in the various circumstances of life. (St. John Paul II, September 17, 1997)**

*The Blessed Virgin Mary at Prayer* by Sassoferrato.
Give yourself plenty of time in silence to listen for God's voice.

**Vocal prayer** is spoken prayer. It is well suited to prayer in common such as a liturgical celebration or a blessing before a family meal. It fits with our human need to integrate the activities of body and soul. It allows us to express through our physical senses what we feel and believe internally, in the depths of our hearts. This is how we pray with our whole being. Liturgical prayer, which is primarily based on Sacred Scripture, also forms us as a Christian community in the Word of God.

**Meditative prayer** involves concentrating on some spiritual topic. This can often be initiated by spiritual reading. For example, one could read a Gospel passage, such as the parable of the Prodigal Son, or the feeding of the 5,000. Instead of just reading it as you would any other book, you take time to think deeply about the passage and what it means, both for the people who first experienced it, and also for you. You can place yourself in the scene, pretending to be one of the persons present in the account. Think about what it would have been like to be there. What would your feelings about Jesus have been? What would you have said to him if he had walked right up to you through the crowd? Your new insights can help you live more fully as Christ's disciple today.

> **Meditation is above all a quest. The mind seeks to understand the why and how of the Christian life, in order to adhere and respond to what the Lord is asking. (CCC 2705)**

**Contemplative prayer** is the highest form of prayer. It is the "listening" part of the conversation we have with God in prayer. Instead of simply telling God what we want or how we feel, as we might do in vocal prayer or in meditative prayer, we listen to what God has to say to us. In this type of prayer, we allow God to speak to us and even to change how we think about things. Contemplative prayer is not something we "do." It is instead something we receive from God. Contemplative prayer usually follows meditative prayer. After you spend time in meditation, give yourself plenty of time in silence to listen for God's voice. You most likely won't hear it with your ears, but you will hear him in your heart.

> **Call to me and I will answer you, and will tell you great and hidden things which you have not known. (Jer 33:3)**

## ANOTHER WAY TO PRAY

Prayer is communicating with God, and communicating is more than just words. Think about how you communicate with the people around you. Sometimes you talk to them, sometimes you give them a hug, sometimes you might do something for them. In every case you are communicating something to them.

One way that we can communicate our love for God is through self-denial. Another word for this is "mortification," which we'll learn more about in the next chapter. Self-denial means giving up things that are good for us for something better. For example, we might give up eating chocolate during Lent. Or we might not eat meat on Fridays. Or we might do an extra chore around the house without being asked. In each case, we can lift these acts of self-denial to God, to show how much we love him. These acts then become a true form of prayer.

## FORMS OF PRAYER

***Praying can have many purposes, from worshiping God to asking forgiveness for sins.***

In Christian tradition there are multiple forms of prayer: blessing and adoration, petition, intercession, thanksgiving, and praise.

Prayers of ***blessing*** are our response to God's gifts to us: because God blesses us, we can in return bless him. Prayers of ***adoration*** acknowledge the greatness and power of God as we stand in his presence as his humble creatures.

Prayers of ***petition*** cry out to God with our needs, particularly our need for forgiveness. We know God is the source of everything we have, and so we go to him for help.

Prayers of ***intercession*** request things from God for other people, for example, our families, our friends, the Church, our community, our nation, the world, and even our enemies. When we intercede for others, we act as members of the common priesthood and as members of the Communion of Saints.

### FORMS OF PRAYER IN THE MASS

All five forms of prayer can be found in the Mass. Examples include:

- The *Gloria* ("Glory to God in the highest...") is a prayer of blessing and adoration.
- The Confiteor, when we ask God to forgive our sins, is a prayer of petition.
- The Universal Prayer, or Prayer of the Faithful, is a prayer of intercession.
- The entire Eucharistic Prayer is one of thanksgiving. In fact, the word "Eucharist" is from a Greek word that means "thanksgiving."
- The *Sanctus* ("Holy, Holy, Holy Lord God of hosts...") is a prayer of praise.

Prayers of ***thanksgiving*** can be offered in all circumstances: joy and suffering, abundance and want. There is literally nothing we have in this life that we did not receive from God. We thank him for all he has done for us. Most especially, we thank God for his great gift of salvation.

Prayers of ***praise*** are mindful of God for his own sake, for the very fact that he is God. We praise God because he is God, apart from what he has done for us.

The sacramental of holy water reminds us of our baptismal graces and our commitment as an adopted child of God.

## SACRAMENTALS AND DEVOTIONS

***Devotional signs and symbols can help you be open to receive grace.***

We use many sacred objects, blessings, gestures, and other signs in our prayers and devotions. They have been handed down to us from previous generations of Catholics. These signs are part of our "family history" that help us draw closer to Christ in prayer. They help us have a good disposition to receive or use the graces of the Sacraments. For this reason, we call these signs *sacramentals*.

> **Sacramentals do not confer the grace of the Holy Spirit in the way that the sacraments do, but by the Church's prayer, they prepare us to receive grace and dispose us to cooperate with it. (CCC 1670)**

Sacramentals invite us into a deeper union with Christ. The Church uses sacramentals in the liturgy, and churches themselves are often filled with sacramentals. These are some common sacramentals:

***Holy water*** reminds us of our Baptism. At Mass the priest might sprinkle the congregation with holy water. When we enter a church, we use holy water from a font or the baptistry to make the Sign of the Cross. This sacramental reminds us of our baptismal graces and our commitment as an adopted child of God.

The ***Sign of the Cross*** traces the symbol of Christ's Passion and Death on our bodies. The prayer that accompanies the gesture ("In the name of the Father, and of the Son, and of the Holy Spirit") calls on the three Persons of the Blessed Trinity. It reminds us of the redemption that Christ won for us through his Sacrifice on the Cross.

***Ashes*** remind us of our mortality. Just as God created human beings from the dust of the earth, so will our bodies return to the earth to await resurrection. This sacramental also reminds us of our need to repent from sin. We recognize that we are mere creatures in need of forgiveness. We receive ashes on our foreheads on Ash Wednesday.

A ***blessing*** marks something for a particular use. We are reminded of God's presence and goodness when we ask God's blessing before a meal, receive a blessing from a priest, or have our home blessed.

A ***sacred object*** such as a crucifix, religious painting, or rosary helps us focus our senses on God in prayer. These sacramentals can help us avoid distractions.

Sacramentals can become part of the fabric of our daily lives. This way we are continuously directed to Christ and reminded of God's presence.

The Miraculous Medal

The Brown Scapular

## THE HOLY ROSARY

One of the most popular Catholic devotions is the Holy Rosary. The rosary is a string of beads which one uses when saying certain prayers including the Our Father, the Hail Mary, and the Glory Be. Usually the person praying the Rosary focuses on five mysteries as he or she prays. These mysteries are events that occurred in the life of Jesus or Mary, which we meditate upon while praying the prayers. Nearly all of the mysteries of the Holy Rosary are revealed in Scripture. There are four different sets of mysteries that are commonly used:

- **Joyful Mysteries:** the Annunciation, the Visitation, the Nativity (Birth of Christ), the Presentation (of Christ in the Temple), and the Finding of Jesus in the Temple.
- **Sorrowful Mysteries:** the Agony in the Garden, the Scourging at the Pillar, the Crowning with Thorns, the Carrying of the Cross, and the Crucifixion.
- **Luminous Mysteries:** the Baptism of Christ in the Jordan, the Manifestation of Christ at the Wedding of Cana, the Proclamation of the Kingdom of God with His Call to Conversion, the Transfiguration, and the Institution of the Eucharist.
- **Glorious Mysteries:** the Resurrection, the Ascension, the Descent of the Holy Spirit, the Assumption (of the Blessed Virgin Mary), and the Coronation of the Blessed Virgin Mary.

For many people the Rosary is a daily devotion, and it is common for a family to pray it together. It is a good idea to have a Rosary for your own devotional use.

## APOLOGETICS 101:

### THE SIGN OF THE CROSS

(Adapted from the *Didache Bible*)

#### *What is the Sign of the Cross?*

> **Christ did not send me to baptize but to preach the gospel, and not with eloquent wisdom, lest the cross of Christ be emptied of its power. For the word of the cross is folly to those who are perishing, but to us who are being saved it is the power of God. (1 Cor 1:17-18)**

The Sign of the Cross is a gesture used at any time, especially at the beginning and end of prayer. It serves as a reminder of the Cross of Christ and of the Blessed Trinity, and it strengthens us during times of trial.

The Sign of the Cross dates back to the earliest days of Christianity. St. John may have been referring to this Christian practice in the Book of Revelation (Rev 7:4, 9:4, 14:1) when he spoke of the faithful having the seal on their foreheads. In the Old Testament we find a foreshadowing, or type, of the Sign of the Cross when Ezekiel writes of the faithful who mark on their foreheads the Hebrew letter *tav* (in Greek, *tau*), meaning a mark, a sign, or a cross (Ez 9:4).

As a sacramental the Sign of the Cross is used by Christians (Catholics, Orthodox, and some Protestants) to bless themselves when beginning and ending prayers and at other times throughout the day to strengthen them in faithfulness and virtue. It is not only a symbol of faith but also a manifestation of belief in the Blessed Trinity and in the Sacrifice of Christ on Calvary as the origin of all grace and salvation. Through this sign our prayers are offered to God in the name of each Person of the Blessed Trinity.

In the Western Church the Sign of the Cross is made with the right hand, fingers extended together, touching first the forehead and then the chest (forming the vertical beam of the cross) and next the left shoulder and then the right (forming the horizontal beam). In the Eastern Churches the thumb and first two fingers are joined together to represent the Blessed Trinity, and the last two fingers are tucked into the palm to represent the two natures of Christ; the "horizontal beam" is traced from the right shoulder to the left.

The Sign of the Cross is usually made while saying a short prayer such as the following:

- "In the name of the Father, and of the Son, and of the Holy Spirit. Amen."
- "By the Sign of the Cross, deliver us from our enemies, you who are our God."

A parish might hold a May Crowning, in which a crown and flowers are presented to a statue of the Blessed Virgin Mary.

## CATHOLIC CUSTOMS

***The customs of Catholic spirituality can help strengthen our interior life.***

Some of the great aids for our Christian lives are the numerous Catholic customs and traditions that mark the liturgical year. Every family has its own traditions and customs that it celebrates throughout the year. The Church family also has celebrations that highlight special feasts and seasons. These customs can help draw our focus to God and away from the many distractions that afflict our daily lives.

Some of these customs are almost universal in the Catholic world, and many vary from culture to culture. People of different cultures bring their own Catholic customs when they emigrate to a new land, enriching the Church in their adopted homeland with their expressions of diversity in faith.

During Advent a family might have an ***Advent wreath***. The family members light the four candles week by week as they get ready for Christmas. This custom reminds us that we are all waiting for Christ. Perhaps your family follows this practice.

During the Christmas season a family might set up a ***Nativity scene*** depicting the surroundings of Christ's Birth. Some families wait for Christmas day to place

A family might celebrate the Solemnity of the Most Holy Body and Blood of Christ (Corpus Christi) by attending a Eucharistic procession. The Eucharist will be placed in a monstrance, which is then carried either through the Church, around the Church, or through the streets of the town or city. In some places, the faithful line the streets to wait for the passing of the Eucharist, and some may follow the Eucharist in solemn procession.

the baby Jesus in the manger, which reminds us of the true meaning of Christmas. We give each other gifts usually on Christmas Eve, Christmas Day, or Epiphany.

During Lent a family might pray the ***Stations of the Cross*** together, whether at home or in a church. This custom includes prayer and meditation on each of fourteen events in the Passion and Death of Christ. On Palm Sunday many parishes hold a procession, and the faithful carry blessed palms to commemorate Christ's entry into Jerusalem.

A parish might hold a ***May Crowning***, in which a crown and flowers are presented to a statue of the Blessed Virgin Mary. This custom reminds us of her unique role in salvation history.

A family might celebrate the Solemnity of the Most Holy ***Body and Blood of Christ*** (Corpus Christi) by attending a procession. The Blessed Sacrament is displayed in a monstrance and carried through the streets to the church as the faithful follow behind, singing hymns.

We should try to incorporate Catholic customs into our family life and personal devotions. These outward expressions help our interior life of faith by focusing our minds and hearts on the actions of God in the world.

*Jesus Goes Up Alone onto a Mountain to Pray* by Tissot. The Holy Spirit helps us in our prayer, where we encounter and talk with God.

# CONCLUSION

***The faithful disciple is a praying disciple, following Christ's example of prayer and trust.***

Prayer is an essential ingredient for the disciple of Christ. The Holy Spirit helps us in our prayer, where we encounter and talk with God. We pray both individually and with other members of the Body of Christ. We can use prayers from our Catholic Tradition, or we may just speak to God in our own words. We can also ask others to pray for us, including the Blessed Virgin Mary, the saints, and the angels.

As we prepare for Confirmation, we are called to a life in the Holy Spirit. The foundation of this life is prayer. But we must ask the Holy Spirit to help us pray as we ought. He will guide us to have a continual conversation with God, recognizing his presence in our daily lives.

# POINTS TO REMEMBER

1. Prayer is essential to being a disciple of Christ. The Holy Spirit will help us to have a strong and active prayer life.
2. We must set aside time each and every day to pray.
3. The three expressions of prayer are vocal prayer, meditative prayer, and contemplative prayer.
4. The forms of prayer include: blessing and adoration, petition, intercession, thanksgiving, and praise.
5. The Lord's Prayer is important to Christians because it is what Jesus gave to his disciples as a form of prayer when they asked him to teach them how to pray. It is considered the perfect prayer as it includes all the different types of prayer, and Jesus himself was the one who taught it.
6. The Mass is the highest form of prayer that can be offered up to GOD. It is the source, the center, and the summit of the Catholic Church.

# Witness of Christ

## St. Kateri Tekakwitha

St. Kateri Tekakwitha was born in 1656 in present-day New York State. She was part Mohawk and part Algonquin. Her parents and brother died from a smallpox epidemic when she was four years old. She survived, but the disease made her eyes weak and scarred her face. After her eyesight deteriorated, she received the name "Tekakwitha," which means "she who bumps into things."

After the death of her parents and brother, Kateri lived with her uncle. He chose a young boy from the tribe to be her husband when they both became older, but Kateri wanted to dedicate her life to God. Her uncle eventually permitted her, at age eighteen, to begin instruction in the Catholic faith. On Easter Sunday 1676, Kateri was baptized. However, as a result of her conversion and Baptism, she was treated harshly by other members of her tribe. That same year she fled to a Jesuit mission in Canada.

At the mission Kateri grew profoundly in her faith and her devotion to God. She received First Communion in 1677, and in 1679 she made a vow of perpetual virginity. This meant that she promised never to marry and to remain chaste her entire life. She wished to give herself totally to Christ.

Kateri dedicated her life to teaching children to pray as well as working with the elderly and the sick. She was especially known for her kindness. Kateri's joy and works of charity received their strength and vigor from her prayer life, including her devotion to the Mass, the Blessed Sacrament, and the Cross.

Shortly before her 24th birthday, Kateri became sick and died. Her final words were "Jesus—Mary—I love you." The people who saw her die say that within minutes, her face was healed of its scars and became radiant with beauty.

After her death many miracles were attributed to her, and many people implored her intercession.

In 2006 a five-year-old boy named Jake Finkbonner, who is half Native American, contracted flesh-eating bacteria through a cut on his lip. Jake's parents took him to the hospital when his face swelled the morning after the injury. Doctors identified Jake's condition as Strep A. During the next few weeks, the doctors could not contain the rapid growth of the flesh-eating bacteria, and they told his parents that Jake would die.

Jake's parents turned to God with trust and hoped for a miracle. The family's parish priest advised them to ask for the intercession of St. Kateri (who was then Bl. Kateri) because of the disease that had left her face scarred. They began praying for her intercession. They were joined in prayer by their parish and Jake's school. A representative from the Society of Blessed Kateri even came to visit the boy. He put a pendant with an image of Kateri on the boy's pillow.

The day after the pendant was placed on the pillow, the infection that was killing Jake suddenly and inexplicably stopped. He began to recover. His doctors could not explain why the disease that had not responded to their efforts had suddenly reversed course. After a thorough investigation, Jake's recovery was deemed a miracle.

In 2012 Kateri Tekakwitha was canonized by Pope Benedict XVI. She is the first Native American to be named a saint. In the United States, her feast day is July 14 (April 17 elsewhere).

## VOCABULARY

### INTERIOR LIFE

The interior life is a life of prayer and the practice of living in the presence of God at all times. One with a strong interior life seeks God in all things.

## STUDY QUESTIONS

1. What is the interior life?
2. How does the Holy Spirit help us to pray?
3. What are the seven petitions of the Lord's Prayer?
4. What are the four most important things to remember when beginning to pray every day?
5. What does it mean to say that in the Mass we pray with the whole Church?
6. Why should we pray to the Blessed Virgin Mary, saints, and angels?
7. What are the three different expressions of prayer?
8. What are the five forms of prayer?
9. What is a sacramental?
10. What are the names of the four sets of mysteries of the Rosary?

## PRACTICAL EXERCISES

1. The importance of the Blessed Virgin Mary and the honor that we give her is misunderstood by many non-Catholics. Some people even believe that Catholics worship Mary as if she were a goddess! Imagine that an acquaintance sees you with a Rosary and makes a comment that you "worship" Mary. Explain to her the importance of Mary for our salvation, but be clear that worship is reserved for God alone.

2. Some Catholic customs can be confusing to non-Catholics. Imagine that it is Ash Wednesday and you have received ashes. Later you see a friend at the store. He says, "You have some dirt on your forehead." Explain to him why you have ashes on your forehead and what this sacramental means.

# Sealed in the Spirit

***Make a plan a part of your daily schedule, including mental prayer, to help you develop a happy spiritual life.***

You are reaching near the end of this book. You have read and learned many things about the Catholic faith and your call to be a disciple of Christ. You might be thinking, "This is a lot of information to understand all at once!" That is certainly true about the faith. Because there is so much depth and mystery to the Blessed Trinity, the Church, and our path to eternal life, we can learn our whole lives and still only scratch the surface.

Your vocation, your discipleship, your growth in holiness, and your journey to the everlasting happiness of heaven is the purpose of your life. The Church, the moral law, the Sacraments, Scripture, prayer, worship, discernment, and your conscience are all gifts that God gives you to help guide you toward greater happiness and holiness.

To respond to God's grace and his free gift of salvation, you need to act. *Decalogue for a Happy Spiritual Life* (on the following page) is a plan that you can follow. It asks 10 challenging questions, explains the implication of each question, and then suggests a goal or habit that you can develop. You might want to review this once a week so that you can be prepared to use the gifts of the Holy Spirit which you will receive in Confirmation.

Your vocation, your discipleship, your growth in holiness, and your journey to the everlasting happiness of heaven is the purpose of your life.

# Sealed in the Spirit

## How to Develop a Happy Spiritual Life

**1. Do I want to follow myself or God?**

If I want to follow God, then I need to seek his guidance every day about everything in my life, knowing that he is my loving Father.

***Suggestion:*** *Set aside some time every day to pray in conversation with God.*

**2. Do I want to be honest and do what is right, following my conscience?**

If I want to be honest, then I need to understand what is good and what is bad for me and for others. I need to form my conscience so that it can help me choose what is good.

***Suggestions:*** *Become familiar with the moral teachings of the Church. Do a short examination of conscience (three minutes) at the end of each day.*

**3. Do I want to be my true self? Do I want to have integrity?**

If I want to be myself, then I cannot pretend to be something or someone that I am not just to fit in and be accepted by others. I need to be sincere and truthful and live with integrity, which means living honestly and being trustworthy. I must do this even if it means making big sacrifices.

***Suggestion:*** *Make two or three personal resolutions that will help you to have the courage to live as your true self.*

**4. Do I want to discover God's plan for me?**

If I want to discover God's plan, then I need the help of the Holy Spirit to discover what God is calling me to do and what his mission is for me.

***Suggestion:*** *Meet with a spiritual director, such as your parish priest, every month for guidance.*

**5. Do I want to make use of the gifts and talents that God has given me in order to serve him and give him glory?**

If I want to use my gifts and talents, then I need to organize my time and efforts.

***Suggestions:*** *Set specific goals for the next day, week, and year. Develop a lifestyle—good habits—to help achieve those goals.*

**6. Do I want to make my life the best that I can out of love for God and others, imitating the life of Christ?**

If I want to live as God intended me to live, then I need to learn about the life of Christ. Only then can I work to imitate him in my own life.

***Suggestion:*** *Read and reflect on the Gospels for five to ten minutes every day.*

**7. Do I want to persevere in all the things that I want to achieve for God?**

If I want to persevere, then I need to be able to accept my own limitations and be patient with myself when I seem to fail. I need to be determined to begin again cheerfully, offering to God the efforts that I have made.

***Suggestion:*** *Go to Confession every month to receive the graces to be humble and to make changes in your life.*

**8. Do I want to make others happy and help them enjoy a good spiritual life?**

If I want to make others happy, then I need to love and serve them and bring them closer to God by my example, the Sacrament of Confession, and the Works of Mercy.

***Suggestion:*** *Ask for God's help at the beginning of every day, and decide to serve others, making a point to do at least one of the Corporal or Spiritual Works of Mercy every day.*

**9. Do I want to make priorities in my life so that I can use my freedom to make decisions and avoid laziness?**

If I want to make priorities, I need to live a simple life and give each activity its proper place, always keeping God first.

***Suggestion:*** *Make and keep a plan of life for every day of the week.*

**10. Do I want to receive and cooperate with God's grace to keep my spiritual life in good shape?**

If I want to receive and cooperate with grace, I need to pray to the Holy Spirit every day, accept challenges with a positive outlook, care for others, and go to Mass.

***Suggestion:*** *Offer the day to God through the Blessed Virgin Mary as soon as you wake up, and finish the day with three Hail Marys.*

# YOU AND YOUR PARENTS

***Praying as a family is a powerful way to support one another on the path to holiness.***

The family home is "the domestic church" and "a community of grace and prayer" (CCC 1666). It is within the family that most Christian children first learn to pray: bedtime prayers, grace before meals, and devotions such as the Rosary.

However, even in many good Christian families, life gets busy and the habit of family prayer can be lost or neglected. Even if your family has kept this tradition, it is always good to ask, "Do we pray enough as a family?"

Fr. Patrick Peyton, who was known as the "Rosary Priest," is being considered for canonization. The well-known saying, "The family that prays together stays together" is attributed to him. Prayer unites a family in faith and love.

Talk about these ideas with your parents:

1. Prayer is essential for our lives. It helps draw us closer to God and makes our relationships with each other stronger. Pray together with your parents for ten minutes every day for one week. Write down some of your thoughts and feelings about praying with your parents before the beginning of the week—do not share it with anyone yet—and have your parents do the same. After the week write down some of your thoughts and feelings, and have your parents do the same. How did your thoughts and feelings change this week? How did those of your parents?

2. Ask your parents what prayers and devotions they remember from their childhood. (You can ask some aunts, uncles, and grandparents the same question.) What did they like about these devotions? Do they still use any of these prayers and devotions today? If your parents stopped, why did they? Suggest that you pray one of these prayers or devotions together.

3. Ask your parents if they have a favorite image or story about the Blessed Virgin Mary. Why is this their favorite depiction or story of Mary? Did they grow up hearing this story or venerating this statue or painting? Did they have a specific prayer answered after praying in front of this image? What is your favorite story or portrayal of the Virgin Mary, and why?

4. Prayer can be a struggle. It requires that we set aside time for it. Discuss with your family how you all can make prayer a more significant part of your lives. Come up with a time that your family can pray together every week—if not every day—in addition to going to Mass together. Ask every member of your family to contribute his or her thoughts and suggestions.

Ask your parents what prayers and devotions they remember from their childhood. Ask your parents if they have a favorite image or story about the Blessed Virgin Mary.

# YOU AND YOUR SPONSOR

***Your Confirmation sponsor should become your partner in prayer and support for life.***

Whether or not you were close to your Confirmation sponsor when you began this Confirmation preparation course, by now you have probably formed a faith-based friendship.

Your sponsor's role will continue even after the day of your Confirmation. He or she should carry on as your guide and mentor for years to come. In particular, your sponsor should continue to pray for you as you grow in happiness and holiness. You can do the same for your sponsor.

As your Confirmation day gets closer, keep talking with your sponsor about prayer and the interior life. Here are some topics that you might want to cover:

1. Plan a day to participate in a weekday Mass with your sponsor. Before the Mass, either that morning or a day or two ahead, each of you should read the Mass readings on your own. (The readings can be found in a missal or online at *www.usccb.org*.) Each of you should write down some of your thoughts about the readings. After Mass, spend some time together, perhaps over a meal. Share with each other your thoughts about the readings before Mass and how they changed after Mass.
2. Ask your sponsor about his or her favorite Catholic devotions. Share your favorite devotion. Set up a day and time every week, even if you cannot meet together in the same room, when you will pray one of these devotions together. From time to time talk about what praying together and this devotion mean to you both.
3. Pray one of the "hours" of the Liturgy of the Hours, especially Morning Prayer or Evening Prayer, together with your sponsor. (The hours can even be found online.) Try this on a few occasions. Talk about what praying together and this liturgy mean to you both.
4. Write a prayer for your sponsor. You might want to include these elements:
   a. Recognition of some of the gifts of the Holy Spirit, especially those that your sponsor uses well in his or her life.
   b. Thanks to God for the example that your sponsor has given you in living the faith.
   c. Specific intentions for your sponsor.

*Station of the Cross, No. 8: Jesus Meets the Women of Jerusalem.*
Ask your sponsor about his or her favorite Catholic devotions.

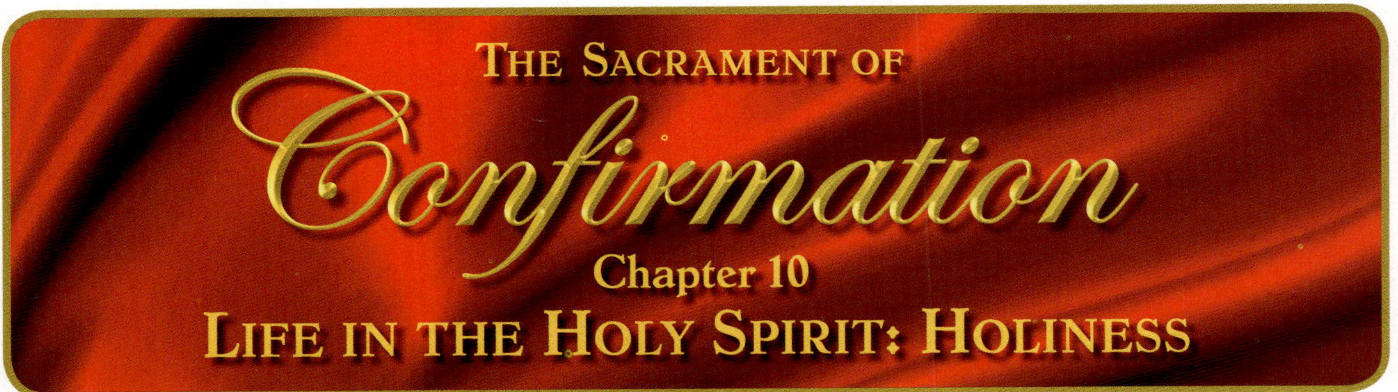


## INTRODUCTION

***To live as a disciple of Christ means to take seriously your vocation to holiness.***

In the last chapter you read about the foundation of life in the Holy Spirit: prayer. In this chapter you will read about how life in the Holy Spirit—life as a disciple of Christ—impacts the choices you make every day. In everything you do, conform yourself to Christ. This is called the life of *holiness*.

Perfect communion with God is the ultimate happiness. God is perfect, holy, and good. The closer we draw to God, the more we can share in his life of perfection, holiness, and goodness. We are created for happiness "by God and for God."

The Holy Spirit helps us in this life of holiness. He gives us strength to live the way God wants us to, and he always draws us closer to him.

> **At every time and in every place, God draws close to man. He calls man to seek him, to know him, to love him with all his strength....In his Son and through him, he invites men to become, in the Holy Spirit, his adopted children and thus heirs of his blessed life. (CCC 1)**

To be a Christian means to be grafted onto Christ like a branch is joined to the vine. This draws us into the divine life of Christ and the inner life of God.

Doing good things and staying away from evil are great. But living the Christian life is much more than imitating Jesus; having the life of Christ in you makes you a member of his Mystical Body. You can share in his relationship with the Father: This is the basis of the Christian life.

*Sermon on the Mount* by Bloch.
We are created for happiness "by God and for God."

After reading this chapter, you will be able to answer these questions:

- What is the universal call to holiness?
- How do we judge if an action is good or evil?
- How should we form our conscience?
- What is the importance of the Ten Commandments and the Beatitudes for living holiness?
- What is the Sacrament of Penance, and how does it heal us?
- What are virtues, and how can we foster them?
- What are the different vocations God might call us to?

# THE CALL TO HOLINESS

***Holiness is a lifelong journey that requires commitment to prayer and right living.***

What do we mean when we say disciples of Christ should strive to be "holy"? Many people believe that being holy means simply being good. In other words, following the rules, being polite, and never getting in trouble.

This is a misunderstanding of what it means to be holy. If you look at the holiest people who ever lived—the saints—they were not simply people who followed rules and never got in trouble. They lived very exciting lives! Being holy means being like Christ, who as God is all-holiness. Being holy means that all of your actions, thoughts, and words are directed towards God, no matter what everyone else around you is doing.

## ESSENTIAL ELEMENTS OF HOLINESS

Being holy is a way of life. What are some of the essential elements of this way of life? Here are a few:

***We are called to worship and love God as Christ did.*** Christ is the perfect model for our lives, and what Christ did above all else is worship and love God. If we are to be holy, we too must worship and love God as Christ did.

***We are called to model ourselves after Christ and his teachings.*** Christ gave us an example of holiness through his humility, life of prayer, detachment from worldly things, and acceptance of persecution. He always did the will of the Father and lived in perfect communion with him. If we want to be perfect, we must seek to imitate the love, virtues, and holiness of Christ.

***We are called to conversion.*** To become Christ's disciples, we respond to the gift of faith and become part of the Church through her liturgy and Sacraments. To live as a disciple requires continued repentance and conversion; it requires a conscious effort as part of our struggle against temptation and sin. Conversion happens in the heart through the grace of God, but it is fostered by spiritual practices and acts of love that open us up to grace.

*St. Teresa of Calcutta.*
Christ gave us an example of holiness through his humility, life of prayer, detachment from worldly things, and acceptance of persecution.

Holiness is not easy. Many of the saints have spoken of the path to holiness as a *struggle*, and indeed it is. Just as Christ faced temptation from Satan in the wilderness, so we face temptation in our daily lives. Keeping the work of grace strong through the Sacraments and prayer makes us more resistant to temptation and sin.

Sometimes people think that holiness is something that can be achieved by only a select few, meaning the saints. But holiness is for everyone. The Church proclaims a **universal call to holiness**, because Christ wants everyone to be holy. If you are a disciple of Christ, then it is your calling to be holy.

God wants to give you all the tools that you need to become holy. He offers you his grace in every moment of your life. You do not have to do anything *extraordinary* to grow in holiness; you only have to live your *ordinary* life well. Make sure your vocation to holiness is always the first priority in your life.

## THE PRECEPTS OF THE CHURCH

To help Catholics grow in holiness, the Church has established a set of minimum commitments for the practice of the faith. These requirements are called the Precepts of the Church.

> The precepts of the Church are set in the context of a moral life bound to and nourished by liturgical life. [They are] meant to guarantee to the faithful the very necessary minimum in the spirit of prayer and moral effort, in the growth in love of God and neighbor. (CCC 2041)

The Precepts of the Church remind us of what it means to be a member of the Church. Regular participation in the Mass and reception of the Sacraments are essential. We must also give attention to the interior life and to the faith community. We should do much more than what the Precepts require, of course. However, if we do not maintain this minimum level of participation, then we really cannot think of ourselves as being in full communion with the Catholic Church.

There are five precepts:

- ***Attend Mass every Sunday and on Holy Days of Obligation.*** The vigil Mass on Saturday or the evening before a Holy Day satisfies this obligation.
- ***Receive the Sacrament of Penance at least once per year.*** We must go to Confession once a year. However, it is a good and recommended practice to confess your sins more frequently, for example, monthly.
- ***Receive the Eucharist at least once during the Easter season.*** Again, it is best to receive the Eucharist weekly or even more frequently, as long as you are free from mortal sin.
- ***Observe the required days of fasting and abstinence.*** The days of fast and abstinence during Lent are a minimum exercise in self-discipline. Additional sacrifices should be part of our regular spiritual life.
- ***Provide for the needs of the Church.*** Give a portion of your income or wealth to your parish, to special collections, and to other Catholic charities. The mission of the Church requires some financial support to maintain her good works, schools, parishes, and dioceses, and to care for the poor and vulnerable.

## FREEDOM AND CONSCIENCE

***God gives each person the freedom to choose to do good.***

To live a life of holiness, we freely choose to follow the will of God, both in our daily activities and in our vocational call.

Love requires freedom. God does not force us to love him. If he did, we could not accurately call that love. Rather, God loves us so much that he gave us the power to accept or reject him. But he also gave us the ability to know right from wrong, and to understand the path to follow to live the way he calls us to live. This ability is called our "conscience."

Many people do not understand what conscience is. The most popular idea is that conscience results in feelings of guilt about a bad decision or freedom from guilt about a good decision. If this were true then any act that "feels" okay would be good. Any act that "feels" wrong would be bad. People who think this way might say something like this: "People say it's wrong to lie to my parents, but I don't feel bad because their rules aren't fair. My conscience is clear."

*Allegory of Free Will and Sin*, miniature, *City of God*. God loves us so much that he gave us the power to accept or reject him.

In reality, conscience is not a feeling, emotion, or hunch. It is not even a theoretical judgment about whether an act is good or evil. **Conscience** "is a judgment of reason whereby the human person recognizes the moral quality of a concrete act" (CCC 1778). It is a practical judgment about the good or evil of a particular act. This judgment is made in light of the moral law. Here is an example of a well-formed conscience: "I know everyone else at work takes change out of the register to use in the soda machine. Right now, I want to because I'm really thirsty and no one will know. But stealing is wrong, so I won't do it."

> **His conscience is man's most secret core, and his sanctuary. There he is alone with God, whose voice echoes in his depths. By conscience, in a wonderful way, that law is made known which is fulfilled in the love of God and of one's neighbor. (*Gaudium et Spes* 16)**

## DISCERNING RIGHT FROM WRONG

Whenever we act, there are three parts of our act—the object (which is the act itself), the intention behind our action, and the circumstances surrounding the action. The morality of an act depends on all three things:

- If the ***object*** of an act is evil, then doing the act would be morally wrong. Some objects are always evil. Some examples of these acts are killing innocent human life, torturing a person, and the marital act outside marriage. Good intentions or special circumstances, no matter how extreme, can never make an evil act "good."
- The ***intention*** can change how good or evil an act is. Giving your lunch to a person who is hungry has a good *object*, but if your *intention* is to impress your friends with your generosity, then that intention makes your good act less good. Likewise, good intentions can never make an evil act "good."
- The ***circumstances*** are all the things that affect an act. The circumstances can change how good or evil an act is. Talking behind a friend's back is morally wrong, but saying something to just one person is not as evil as saying it to dozens of people. Additionally, good circumstances cannot make an evil act "good."

The gifts of the Holy Spirit, which you received at your Baptism and which will be deepened at your Confirmation, increase the power of your conscience to make moral judgments; this is why you are studying (and should continue to learn throughout your life) the teachings of Christ, the teachings of the Magisterium, and the Commandments. As the *Catechism* teaches:

> **"When he listens to his conscience, the prudent man can hear God speaking." (CCC 1777)**

## FORMATION OF CONSCIENCE

***You have a duty to follow your conscience, and you have a responsibility to form it well.***

If one proper way to think of conscience is God speaking to us about right and wrong, can our conscience ever be in error? Yes. Sometimes you can mistake your own desires for your conscience. You might desire so strongly to make a particular choice that you do not want to think about what is truly right or wrong. Sometimes you might choose evil because you have convinced yourself that you have a good excuse. Sometimes you want to do good, but you choose bad things because you do not understand the moral issues properly.

*Pilate Washing His Hands* by Preti.
Sometimes you might choose evil because you have convinced yourself that you have a good excuse.

We rely on conscience to judge actions. Therefore we have the duty to form our conscience so that its judgments reflect the teachings of Christ and his Church.

God makes his law known in our hearts. Inside we understand that certain things are right and certain things are wrong. But there is more to learn about the moral law. We must also be taught how to evaluate moral situations. We must be able to apply what we know to the decisions we face each day. This training begins with learning the basics such as the Ten Commandments, the Beatitudes, and the virtues, which we will review next. This training continues throughout our lives.

The more truly our consciences are formed, the more effective and trustworthy they will be in guiding us to good moral choices. Because we encounter many different situations, forming the conscience is a lifelong duty.

Here are some ways to form your conscience:

- **Learn the moral teachings of the Catholic Church.** These teachings come from Christ, who entrusted them to his Church. The Magisterium of the Church is guided by the Holy Spirit. We can rely on what the Church teaches about what is right and wrong.
- **Be humble when you make a moral decision.** Have an attitude of faith and obedience when you learn about the Church's teachings. This is especially vital when you do not fully understand or agree with them. Trust the Church since she teaches with the authority of Christ.
- **Keep up your prayer life.** Prayer is conversation with God. God communicates his will through prayer. Prayer, therefore, is needed to form your conscience.
- **Ask someone.** When you are unsure about a moral decision, ask a priest or another practicing Catholic adult.
- **Make a daily examination of conscience.** Keep your conscience well-trained by thinking through your day, considering when you have sinned and where you could have acted more virtuously or served as a better example of Christ's love.
- **Go to Confession regularly.** When your soul is in communion with God, you are filled with sanctifying grace and free of serious sin. You are better able to discern God's voice. Actual grace will also help you in the moment of decision. Do not be afraid to ask questions of the priest in Confession if you need to understand a Church teaching better.

The more truly our consciences are formed, the more effective and trustworthy they will be in guiding us to good moral choices.

## ENDS AND MEANS

You've probably heard the expression, "The ends justify the means." This is used to excuse morally wrong acts if a bigger, final goal seems morally good.

This expression is simply not true. No matter how noble the good intention is, or how extraordinary the circumstances are, an evil act can not be "made" good.

Imagine that your high-school-age friend wants to be a doctor who serves in areas of the world without access to medical care. This is a good end, or goal. Of course, one requirement to become a doctor is to go to college. To get into college, she has to have good grades in her high school classes. This friend copies homework and cheats on tests to get good grades. She justifies these actions with her worthy goal of becoming a doctor. Cheating is morally wrong, but she does it anyway in order to achieve something good. But her actions are not justified. Her good intentions do not make her cheating "good."

# THE TEN COMMANDMENTS

***The law seems simple, but Christ's focus on love demands more than meets the eye.***

A compass is a tool that aligns with the earth's magnetic field to show which direction is north. If you are navigating a journey a compass can help you reach your destination. Christ and his Church have given you a "moral compass" to help you know how to make good moral decisions. This compass, the moral law, will help you on your journey to heaven. And one of the fundamental elements of the moral law is the Ten Commandments.

God gave Moses the Ten Commandments on Mt. Sinai during Israel's Exodus from Egypt. They were the model for how the people were to live in relationship with God and neighbor. Christ emphasized that his followers need to live according to the Commandments. He said that he had not come to abolish the Law but to fulfill it. In fact, his teachings provided a new depth and life to the Law.

Christ's teachings emphasized that we are to go beyond the letter of the Law. We should allow the spirit of the Law to penetrate our hearts. For example, Christ reiterated the Fifth Commandment, thou shall not kill. However, he added:

> **"I say to you that every one who is angry with his brother shall be liable to judgment; whoever insults his brother shall be liable to the council, and whoever says, 'You fool!' shall be liable to the hell of fire." (Mt 5:22)**

Christ taught that the Fifth Commandment forbids not just murder but also sins such as anger, holding grudges, and casting insults. Likewise, Christ discussed the Sixth Commandment against adultery. He taught, "Every one who looks at a woman lustfully has already committed adultery with her in his heart" (Mt 5:28). His teaching emphasized the need for purity not only in our actions but also in our hearts and minds. The Commandments cannot remain external practices but must fill our hearts with the love of God and neighbor.

The heart of the Ten Commandments is love. Christ taught us "the greatest Commandment" (Mt 22:37): We should love God with our whole heart, with our whole soul, and with our whole mind. He added that the second greatest Commandment was to love our neighbor as ourselves. The entirety of the Law can be summed up in the love of God and the love of neighbor.

*Moses Descends from Mount Sinai* by Bol.
If we truly love God and neighbor, then keeping the Commandments will come naturally.

This does not mean that we can ignore the Ten Commandments or the Church's moral law. Love does not eliminate the moral law. It is the *reason* for the moral law, and it should be our motivation to keep the moral law. If we truly love God and neighbor, then keeping the Commandments will come naturally.

> **The Law of the Gospel fulfills and surpasses the Old Law and brings it to perfection: its promises, through the Beatitudes of the Kingdom of heaven; its commandments, by reforming the heart, the root of human acts. (CCC 1984)**

This love, which is commanded by Christ, is much more than simply nice feelings or politeness. It is to love as Christ loved—a love so great that he gave his life for us. When we love God above all else, we are able to love and serve our neighbor with self-sacrificial love.

## The Ten Commandments

1. I am the Lord your God: you shall not have strange gods before me.
2. You shall not take the name of the Lord your God in vain.
3. Remember to keep holy the Lord's Day.
4. Honor your father and your mother.
5. You shall not kill.
6. You shall not commit adultery.
7. You shall not steal.
8. You shall not bear false witness against your neighbor.
9. You shall not covet your neighbor's wife.
10. You shall not covet your neighbor's goods.

*Sermon on the Mount* by Olrik.
Christ's teachings provided a new depth and life to the Law given to Moses by God in the Ten Commandments.

## The Beatitudes

The Beatitudes were revealed by Christ in his Sermon on the Mount. They illustrate his New Commandment of Love. They describe some of the virtues and dispositions that lead us to grow in happiness and holiness. Like the Ten Commandments, the Beatitudes are part of the Church's moral compass. They can help form your conscience.

The Beatitudes express a hope that goes beyond this world, which is often filled with suffering and persecution. This hope is for our eternal reward in the Kingdom of Heaven. The Beatitudes acknowledge the suffering and longing of people who seek the will of God. Though we suffer in this life, our hope will be satisfied with the happiness, glory, and peace of heaven.

Blessed are the poor in spirit, for theirs is the kingdom of heaven.

Blessed are those who mourn, for they shall be comforted.

Blessed are the meek, for they shall inherit the earth.

Blessed are those who hunger and thirst for righteousness, for they shall be satisfied.

Blessed are the merciful, for they shall obtain mercy.

Blessed are the pure in heart, for they shall see God.

Blessed are the peacemakers, for they shall be called sons of God.

Blessed are those who are persecuted for righteousness' sake, for theirs is the kingdom of heaven.

Blessed are you when men revile you and persecute you and utter all kinds of evil against you falsely on my account. Rejoice and be glad, for your reward is great in heaven.

(Mt 5:3-12)

## SIN AND REPENTANCE

***Conscience reveals our offenses so we can repent and restore friendship with God.***

Although we might desire to follow God always in our words, thoughts, and actions, we often fail to do so. This is called sin.

> **Sin is an offense against reason, truth, and right conscience; it is failure in genuine love for God and neighbor caused by a perverse attachment to certain goods. (CCC 1849)**

Sin can be categorized in many ways. We often think about a sin as a violation of a particular Commandment, Precept of the Church, Beatitude, or "rule" in the moral law. For example, hitting someone out of anger is against the Fifth Commandment, and sneaking into a movie theater without paying is against the Seventh Commandment. But there are other ways of classifying sins that are helpful to know.

*Christ and the Adulteress* by Turchi.
No matter how we sin, Christ is always ready to offer us his mercy and forgiveness.

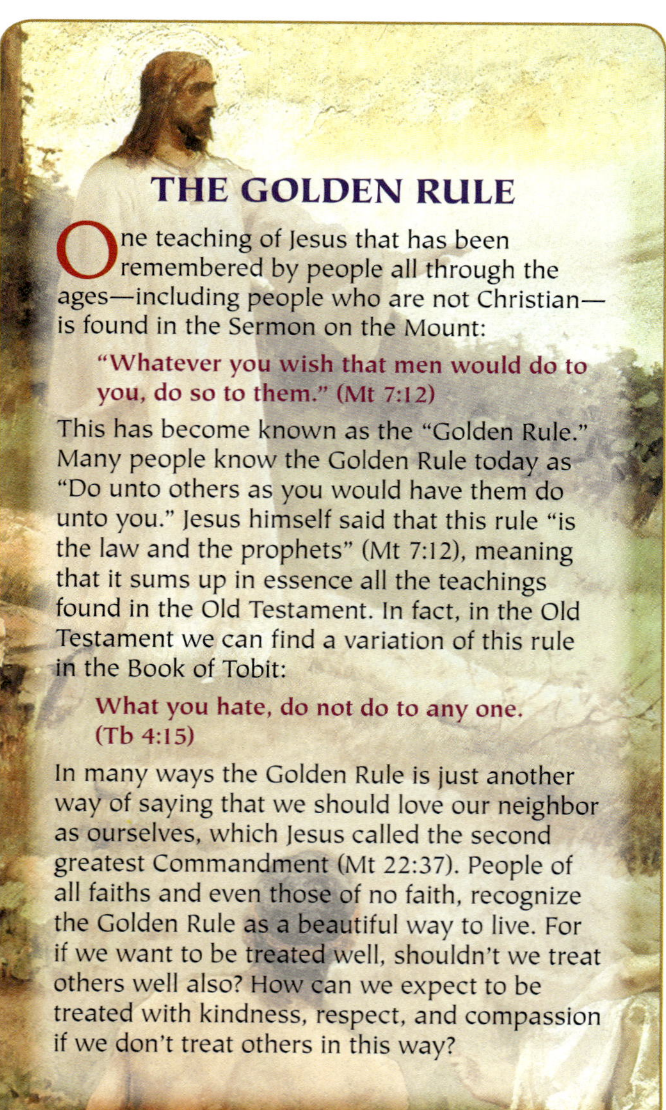

### THE GOLDEN RULE

One teaching of Jesus that has been remembered by people all through the ages—including people who are not Christian—is found in the Sermon on the Mount:

> **"Whatever you wish that men would do to you, do so to them." (Mt 7:12)**

This has become known as the "Golden Rule." Many people know the Golden Rule today as "Do unto others as you would have them do unto you." Jesus himself said that this rule "is the law and the prophets" (Mt 7:12), meaning that it sums up in essence all the teachings found in the Old Testament. In fact, in the Old Testament we can find a variation of this rule in the Book of Tobit:

> **What you hate, do not do to any one. (Tb 4:15)**

In many ways the Golden Rule is just another way of saying that we should love our neighbor as ourselves, which Jesus called the second greatest Commandment (Mt 22:37). People of all faiths and even those of no faith, recognize the Golden Rule as a beautiful way to live. For if we want to be treated well, shouldn't we treat others well also? How can we expect to be treated with kindness, respect, and compassion if we don't treat others in this way?

***Original Sin and actual sin.*** Original Sin is inherited as part of the human condition, passed down from our first parents. It is washed away in Baptism. Actual sin, also called *personal sin*, refers to the sins that a person commits.

***Sins of commission and sins of omission.*** Although sin is always an act of the will, it is not always actually doing something. A sin of *commission* is an evil act. It is choosing to do something that is wrong such as lying, stealing, or showing disrespect. A sin of *omission*, however, is different. The word "omission" means failing to do something. So a sin of omission is a sin we commit by failing to do a good act we should do, or choosing not to do something that is right. Failing to do your chores, missing Mass on Sunday, and wasting time are all sins of omission.

***Venial sin and mortal sin.*** Venial sins are less serious sins that wound our relationship with God but do not break our communion with him. We should avoid venial sins and stay close to the Sacrament of Penance so that these little sins do not lead to bigger sins. Mortal sins are serious sins that break our communion with God. These require urgent attention in the Sacrament of Penance to restore grace to our souls and friendship with God.

No matter how we sin, Christ is always ready to offer us his mercy and forgiveness. He offers his mercy to all those who seek it so that we can be reconciled to God. By the power of the Holy Spirit, he continually calls us to repentance so that we can walk the path to holiness and eternal life.

The gifts of the Holy Spirit help us form our consciences and keep the moral law. They also help us remain aware of our sins as we examine our consciences in preparation for the Sacrament of Penance.

### WHEN IS SIN MORTAL?

**For a sin to be considered mortal, three conditions are required:**

- The evil act must be ***serious***, what the Church calls "grave matter."

  *Grave matter* is specified by the Ten Commandments...The gravity of sins is more or less great: murder is graver than theft. One must also take into account who is wronged: violence against parents is in itself graver than violence against a stranger. (CCC 1858)

- You must commit the evil act with ***full knowledge***. You must be aware that the act is wrong and serious, either because you know the Church's teaching on the matter, or your conscience is telling you so. Of course, pretending or telling yourself that the act is "not all that bad" would not mean you do not have full knowledge.

- You must commit the evil act with ***full consent***. You must want to do the evil act. At times a person is forced to do an evil act, or isn't in a condition where he or she can think straight. For example, the person is being threatened or taking prescribed medication that clouds his or her thinking. That person cannot give full consent. The evil act would still be wrong, but the coerced or confused person did not fully consent to it.

If any of these conditions is not met, then the sin is not mortal; it is venial.

## THE SACRAMENT OF PENANCE

***Through his priest and with your sincere Confession, Christ forgives your sins.***

On the night of Christ's Resurrection, his Apostles were hiding behind locked doors when he appeared to them. He breathed on them and said:

> **"Receive the Holy Spirit. If you forgive the sins of any, they are forgiven; if you retain the sins of any, they are retained." (Jn 20:19-23)**

With that, Christ established the Sacrament of Penance, giving his Apostles the power to forgive sins just as he did during his earthly ministry.

Christ bestowed this power on his Apostles, and they then handed it on to their successors, the bishops. Our bishops, who share this same power with their priests, participate in Christ's healing ministry through the celebration of the Sacrament of Penance.

The Sacrament of Penance is essential for being a disciple and growing in happiness and holiness. Through this Sacrament your sins are forgiven and you are restored to full communion with Christ. You are strengthened for your journey to heaven through the grace of the Holy Spirit.

*Christ Appears Behind Locked Doors* by Duccio. Christ established the Sacrament of Penance by giving his Apostles the power to forgive sins.

Recall when you might have fallen short of your duty to love God and neighbor.

Like all the Sacraments, Penance has a matter, form, and minister:

The ***matter*** of the Sacrament of Penance consists of the actions of the person who confesses (the *penitent*). These are the actions of the penitent:

- ***Be contrite.*** Contrition is true sorrow and hatred for sin along with the resolution not to sin again. Sorrow may be *perfect contrition*, which is felt because of a pure love for God. Or it can be *imperfect contrition*, which is felt because of the fear of hell or punishment. Your contrition will lead you to make a "purpose of amendment," which is a commitment not to sin again by improving both your interior life and your actions.
- ***Confess your sins.*** Confession is a full and honest accounting for sins that you committed that have not yet been forgiven in the Sacrament of Penance.
- ***Give satisfaction.*** Satisfaction is doing the penance that the priest assigns.

The words of absolution, which are prayed by the priest, constitute the ***form*** of the Sacrament of Penance:

> **God, the Father of mercies,**
> **through the death and resurrection of his Son**
> **has reconciled the world to himself**
> **and sent the Holy Spirit among us**
> **for the forgiveness of sins;**
> **through the ministry of the Church**
> **may God give you pardon and peace,**
> **and I absolve you from your sins**
> **in the name of the Father, and of the Son,**
> **and of the Holy Spirit.**
> **(*Rite of Penance*, Rite for Reconciliation of Individual Penitents, no. 46)**

The ***minister*** of the Sacrament of Penance is a bishop or priest.

Because of the graces that we can receive in the Sacrament of Penance, it has many other positive effects in our lives:

- It restores us to God's grace, repairing the damage done to us by sin.
- It gives us a peaceful conscience, for we know our sins are forgiven.
- It gives us spiritual consolation, for we know we are in communion with God.
- If mortal sins were forgiven, it restores us to full communion with Christ and his Church.
- It helps us prepare for the judgment at the end of this life; with a pure soul, we are prepared to meet God.

For help learning how to prepare for and go to Confession, see *Sealed in the Spirit* at the end of this chapter.

To help us confess our sins, and to avoid committing them, the Church encourages every person to examine his or her conscience on a regular basis. When you examine your conscience, you look back on your day (or however long it has been since you last examined it). Recall when you might have fallen short of your duty to love God and neighbor. Make this practice a habit in your life. It will help you greatly on your path to holiness.

## THE ACT OF CONTRITION

Even if we are not in a state of mortal sin, we should strive to be sorrowful for our sins. A powerful prayer that you might incorporate into your prayer life is the Act of Contrition. By praying an Act of Contrition, you acknowledge that you are a sinner and need the grace of our all-loving and merciful God.

There are several forms for an Act of Contrition. This is one of the more popular ones:

> **O my God, I am heartily sorry for having offended you. I detest all my sins, because I dread the loss of heaven and the pains of hell; but most of all because they offend you, my God, who are all good and deserving of all my love. I firmly resolve, with the help of your grace, to confess my sins, to do penance, and to amend my life. Amen.**

This is a very short prayer that you can say throughout the day:

> **Jesus Christ, son of God, have mercy on me, a sinner!**

# THE VIRTUES

***To seek holiness, practice these good habits and dispositions.***

A *virtue* is "a habitual and firm disposition to do good" (CCC 1833). To be virtuous people, we need to develop interior dispositions that make choosing what is good a habit.

Virtues form the foundation of a life of holiness. Practicing the virtues conforms us to Christ. It also makes it easier to practice them in the future. Just as one must repeatedly perform any activity—sports, music, art, etc.—in order to improve at it, so too must we repeatedly perform the virtues to improve in a life of holiness.

There are many virtues, but the primary virtues fall into two groups: the *theological virtues* and the *cardinal virtues*.

## The Theological Virtues

You received the theological virtues first in the Sacrament of Baptism, and they were strengthened in the other Sacraments. They help us to live in God's grace. They also help us to be in communion with the Blessed Trinity.

- ***Faith*** means believing in God and all that the Catholic Church teaches. True faith is living—it is made visible in the way you live.
- ***Hope*** means trusting in God above anything else and making eternal life with God the focus of your happiness.
- ***Charity***, or ***love***, is the "virtue by which we love God above all things for his own sake, and our neighbor as ourselves for the love of God" (CCC 1822).

The theological virtues will be strengthened and increased in you in the Sacrament of Confirmation.

## The Cardinal Virtues

Four human virtues are central to the Christian life: prudence, justice, fortitude, and temperance. Many other virtues stem from these four. These virtues are called "cardinal" because of their importance.

- ***Prudence*** helps us recognize the good in every situation and the correct way to do what is right. It leads our conscience to discern the best action in a particular situation. People who do not practice prudence let their impulses, emotions, and temptations lead them to do what is wrong.
- ***Justice*** helps us recognize the love and devotion that is due to God. It also helps us give every person the dignity and respect that he or she is due. People who do not practice justice devalue others, treat them unfairly, and fail to respect their rights.
- ***Fortitude*** strengthens us to choose good and resist evil in every situation. It helps us overcome fear, especially in times of trials or persecution. People who do not practice fortitude let fear lead them away from the faith and into sin.
- ***Temperance*** helps us enjoy everything in a balanced and responsible way. It helps us control our desire for worldly pleasure so that our desires do not control us. The temperate person does not let himself be controlled by greed, lust, gluttony, and laziness.

*Return of the Prodigal Son* by Tissot.
Four human virtues are central to the Christian life: prudence, justice, fortitude, and temperance.

## MORTIFICATION

Mortification is an important part of the Christian life of holiness. What is mortification? The simplest definition of mortification comes from Jesus himself:

> **"If any man would come after me, let him deny himself and take up his cross and follow me." (Mt 16:24)**

In other words, mortification is self-denial: giving up good things for something better. People exercise self-denial all the time. For example, someone on a diet might not eat certain food in order to lose weight. Or an athlete will endure demanding training in order to become better at his sport. In each case, that person gives up something good (certain food, comfort) for something better (a healthier body, success at an athletic event). Our life is full of self-denial, even if we don't realize it.

Mortification is specifically Christian self-denial. We deny ourselves certain pleasures, or we endure certain pains, in order to draw closer to God. We might decide to get up each morning a half hour earlier than usual in order to pray. We refrain from complaining when given a chore by our parents. We complete all our homework assignments before going out to play with our friends. We offer these things to God and ask that they help us become more like his Son Jesus Christ, who gave up his life for us.

If we want to be saints—and we should all want to be saints!—then we need to practice mortification. And when we do so, we should be sure to offer our mortification for the glory of God and in prayer for those around us.

God gives everyone a vocation to love, serve, and seek holiness in a particular **state of life**.

## WHAT IS GOD ASKING OF YOU?

***God is calling you to holiness; he also calls you to use your virtues and talents to serve him.***

Living a life of holiness is not confined to avoiding evil and doing good. It includes the call we first receive at Baptism to love and serve God. It also consists in following the specific call God has for *your* life. Does he want you to be a priest or religious sister? A husband and father, or a wife and mother? The path we choose will be the path that draws us closer to God and deepens our life of holiness.

> **He calls his own sheep by name and leads them out. When he has brought out all his own, he goes before them, and the sheep follow him, for they know his voice. (Jn 10:3-4)**

The specific way in which you will serve God is called your *vocation*. A vocation is a calling from God. In Baptism he calls everyone to love, serve, and seek holiness. Further, he can also call people to a specific vocation in a particular **state of life**. The Church recognizes particular vocations to three states of life: marriage, Holy Orders, and the consecrated life. Further, some people live out a life of holiness outside one of these three recognized states, such as in the single life. Each of these is oriented toward love and service.

People often use the word *vocation* to refer to a job or professional career. A person may indeed feel "called" by God to become, for example, a doctor or a teacher. Such options may be a matter of discerning the best use of the gifts God has given you. But for this discussion "vocation" does not refer to a career choice. Your vocation means much more than that.

How do we know our vocation? Finding out is called **discernment**. Discernment is the process of prayerfully coming to understand what God is asking of you. It is a process that must be undertaken in conversation with God, in other words, with *prayer*. It is a process that uses our reason, too. When discerning God's will, we must look at ourselves honestly and recognize the gifts that God has given us—our talents, practical skills, personal skills, and interests. We should also consider what gifts we need to develop. Using and developing our gifts and talents can help us come to find where God is directing us.

Each vocation consists of a unique call by God for you to serve him in the way best suited for you. Through your vocation, you can live the life of true happiness and holiness to which God has called you. As you read about the different vocations in the Church, prayerfully reflect about your own call to serve God. He might not reveal your exact vocation to you yet, but if you keep an open heart, he will as you get older.

## THE VOCATION TO MARRIAGE

Marriage is the vocation that is written in the nature of man and woman. (This does not mean that everyone who does not marry is going against his or her nature.) The majority of Christians are called to marriage. God gives fewer people the vocations of Holy Orders and the consecrated life.

The Church teaches that the family unit of a husband, a wife, and their children is an essential building block of a healthy society. The Christian family is regarded as a ***domestic church***. The family is where children are introduced to the faith, taught how to pray, and raised to live their lives loving God and their neighbors.

Catholics who have a vocation to the married state of life are encouraged to marry other Catholics. Their shared faith and values should make for a more harmonious home and give them common goals in raising their children. Marriages between Catholics and Christians who are not Catholic—or between Catholics and people who are not Christian—present particular challenges that need to be considered.

## THE VOCATION TO HOLY ORDERS

The Sacrament of Holy Orders is a special vocation for men who carry out the mission entrusted to the Apostles in the life of the Church. There are three degrees of the Sacrament of Holy Orders: bishops, priests, and deacons.

The Sacrament of Holy Orders was instituted by Christ at the Last Supper. He established his Apostles as his first priests and bishops. He gave them the power to celebrate the Eucharist, forgive sins, and teach in his name. They handed on this power to their successors, the bishops. As the Church grew, bishops primarily watched over large areas of the Church, and priests primarily celebrated the liturgy in local communities. The Apostles established a third order, deacons, as a ministry of service.

It is the constant Tradition and teaching of the Church, in keeping with the practice of Christ, that only men can receive Holy Orders.

## THE VOCATION TO THE CONSECRATED LIFE

God calls some men and women to dedicate themselves completely to him. We call this *the consecrated life*. There are various forms of consecrated life, such as religious sisters (nuns), religious brothers, monks, and consecrated virgins. Although their lifestyles might vary greatly, they share one commonality. All profess to live what are called the ***evangelical counsels*** of poverty, chastity, and obedience.

While a person in the married state is a sign of God's presence in the world, a person in the consecrated life is a sign of the world to come. In the world to come, God's children will not have or need possessions. And as Jesus said, "They neither marry nor are given in marriage" (Mk 12:25). By taking vows professing the evangelical counsels, consecrated men and women are anticipating this heavenly arrangement here and now.

## THE EVANGELICAL COUNSELS

Commitment to living the evangelical counsels of poverty, chastity, and obedience is central to the consecrated life. They are called *evangelical* because they come from the Gospel. They are a living witness of Christian discipleship. They are called *counsels* because Christ counseled his disciples to choose these virtues as a means of growing in holiness.

***Poverty*** means detachment from worldly things. The practice of poverty is manifested in a simple lifestyle sharing in the plight and sufferings of the poor.

***Chastity*** means the appropriate disposition toward sexuality within a person's state of life. For the unmarried, this means complete abstention from sexual expression.

***Obedience*** means submission to proper authority. For those in the consecrated life, it means obedience to their religious superiors.

## THE COMMITTED SINGLE LIFE

The committed single life is not one of the vocational states of life recognized by the Church, but it is a way that some people live out their universal call to holiness. They make a firm, permanent decision to remain single permanently but without entering Holy Orders or the consecrated life. (This does not include people who happen to be single but are still discerning a vocation to one of the other three states of life.) Like those with vocations to Holy Orders and the consecrated life, they devote themselves wholeheartedly to the service of God and others. Unlike marriage, Holy Orders, or the consecrated life, there is no public vow, promise, or Sacrament attached to the single life. It is not overseen by a bishop or any Church authority.

A person in the committed single life enjoys the ability to allot time, resources, and attention to the Church and to good causes. He or she can bring the Good News into all areas of life. Those with vocations to particular states of life may not be able to do so. The family obligations of people in the married state, for example, might take up much of their time. The pastoral obligations of priests might not let them get away from parish work very often. People in the single life, on the other hand, do not have these obligations. This allows them to serve the needs of others, in many different forms and circumstances.

*The Forerunners of Christ with Saints and Martyrs* by Fra Angelico.
Every person is called to holiness, which means becoming more and more like Christ and conforming yourself to him by the help of the Holy Spirit.

## CONCLUSION

***Every person is called to a life of holiness.***

A disciple of Christ is called to a life of holiness. The essence of holiness is completely conforming your life to Christ's. By following the Commandments, forming your conscience, and practicing the virtues you will become more like him. Such a life isn't easy. This is why Christ gave us the Sacrament of Penance. There we receive healing when we fail to live up to the call of holiness.

God has a specific call for your life's work, a vocation through which you will grow in holiness. He may call you to marriage, Holy Orders, the consecrated life, or the committed single life. Each state of life is a means toward love, service, holiness, and eternal communion with God.

Discernment is the prayerful process of seeking and knowing God's plan for your life. By understanding the gifts and talents that God has given you, you can come to know the path to which he calls you. It is a process that requires humility, patience, honesty, and openness to the will of God. By following God's will for your life you will find the indescribable happiness that God desires for you.

## POINTS TO REMEMBER

1. Every person is called to holiness, which means becoming more and more like Christ and conforming yourself to him by the help of the Holy Spirit.
2. Conscience "is the judgment of reason whereby the human person recognizes the moral quality of a concrete act" (CCC 1778). We are all obliged to form our conscience through prayer, learning the moral teachings of the Church, and going to Confession.
3. The Sacrament of Penance restores us to Christ after we have fallen through sin.
4. God calls each person to a specific vocation. The three vocational states of life recognized by the Church are marriage, Holy Orders, and the consecrated life.
5. God gives the necessary graces for every person's state of life and personal vocation, whether that person is in the state of marriage, Holy Orders, or the consecrated life.

# WITNESS OF CHRIST

## ST. JOSEMARIA ESCRIVA

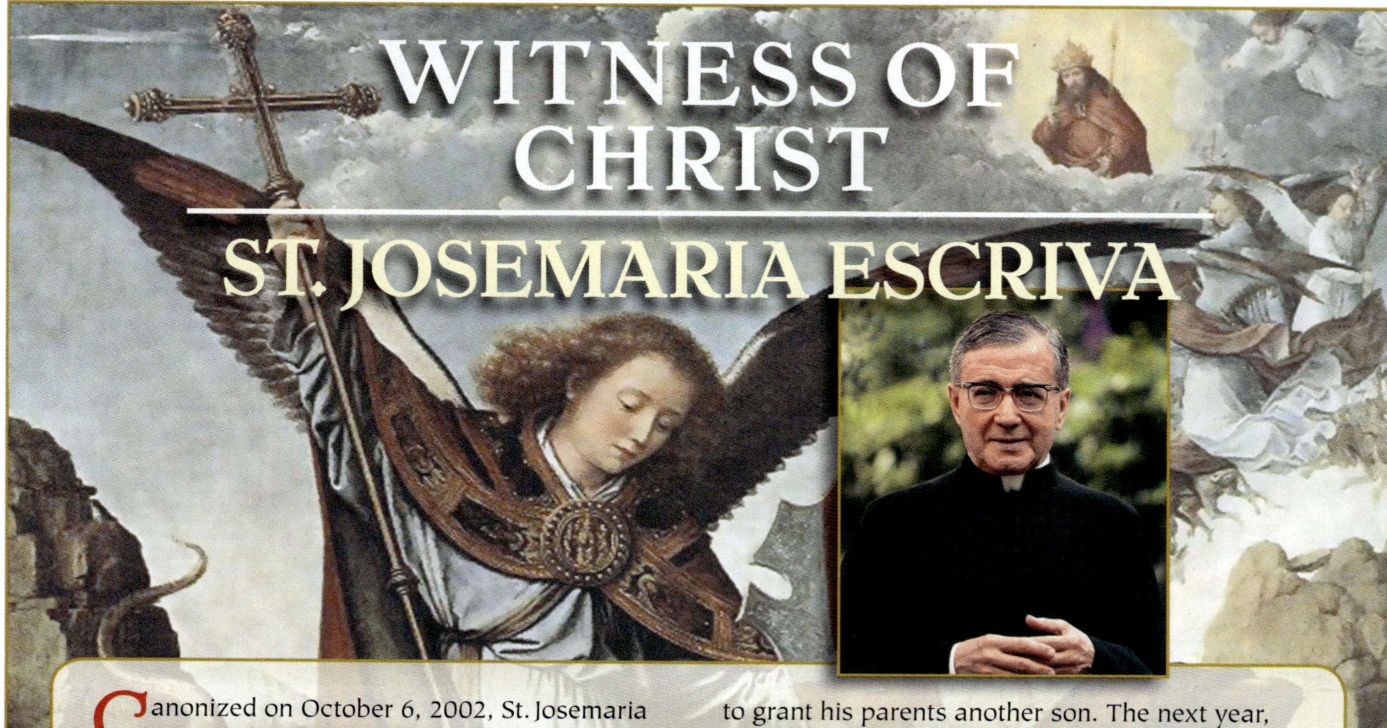

Canonized on October 6, 2002, St. Josemaria Escriva helped point the way to holiness for lay men and women. Born in 1902 in the town of Barbastro, Spain, he was the second child and first son of Jose and Dolores Escriva. Four girls also were born to the Escrivas, but only Josemaria and Carmen, their oldest daughter, lived to adulthood. When he was young, nothing set him apart from any other boy in town. He played "roll-the-hoops" and "cops-and-robbers" with his friends in the streets and backyards where he grew up.

His parents were devout, cheerful Catholics who taught their children the importance of serving God. When he was six, Josemaria made his First Confession, which was followed by First Communion at ten.

During the Christmas season of 1917, he noticed the footprints of a discalced Carmelite priest in the snow. He had a sudden sense that it was Christ himself who had walked in the snow. It was a moment of great grace. From that time forward, he attended daily Mass and made frequent confessions. He soon decided to enter the seminary and become a priest.

His father had wished his son to be a lawyer, but he supported Josemaria's choice to become a priest instead. Josemaria's vocation to the priesthood, however, meant there would be no one to carry on the family name, so he asked God to grant his parents another son. The next year, 1919, his brother Santiago was born.

Josemaria was ordained a priest in 1925 and soon moved to Madrid, where he spent the first part of his priesthood in a poor community where he was noted for his loving care of all. When his father died, he became the sole support of the family. To care for his mother, sister, and little brother and pay for his studies, he gave Latin lessons, lectured, and taught civic and Canon law. He spent his little spare time with the poorest of the poor and the incurably ill. In return for his care, he asked those to whom he ministered to pray for the success of his priesthood.

From these poor beginnings was born his life's endeavor, Opus Dei, which means the "Work of God." In 1928 God graced him to see that his priesthood would be devoted to helping lay men and women understand that ordinary persons could become saints. His mission was to lead all to sanctify their lives and their work for the good of the Church through a personal apostolate with others. He taught them to approach their ordinary daily lives with cheerfulness and happiness and to sanctify themselves, their work, and others for the glory of God. In this way, the faithful can transform their very lives into continuous prayer.

His life showed, above all, the gift of fortitude and the theological virtue of hope.

## VOCABULARY

### CONSCIENCE

A practical judgment about the good or evil of a particular act that a person makes using reason in light of the moral law.

### DISCERNMENT

The process of prayerfully coming to understand what God is asking of you.

### DOMESTIC CHURCH

The Christian family, where children are introduced to the faith, taught how to pray, and raised in the moral virtues.

### EVANGELICAL COUNSELS

Poverty, chastity, and obedience.

### STATE OF LIFE

One of three vocations recognized by the Church that is oriented toward love and service; marriage, Holy Orders, and the consecrated life. Some people choose to live out the universal call to holiness, for example, in the single life, which is not one of the Church's officially recognized vocational states of life.

### UNIVERSAL CALL TO HOLINESS

Refers to the fact that every baptized person is called to seek holiness regardless of his or her state in life. This call was reaffirmed by the Second Vatican Council.

## STUDY QUESTIONS

1. What is the universal call to holiness?
2. What is conscience?
3. Name and describe the three elements of a moral action.
4. How do the Commandments and Beatitudes serve as a "moral compass"?
5. Name and describe the three elements of a mortal sin.
6. What are the two types of contrition? Explain each one.
7. When did Christ institute the Sacrament of Penance, and how did he do it?
8. What are the theological virtues?
9. What are the Cardinal Virtues?
10. What are the three states of life God might call a person to?

## PRACTICAL EXERCISES

1. What virtues did your Confirmation saint practice best? List at least three. What virtue was the biggest challenge for your saint to practice?

2. Write an Act of Contrition in your own words. Make sure it expresses love for God, sorrow for sin, and a resolution to avoid sin in the future.

# Sealed in the Spirit

***Living the Sacraments—and going to Confession on a regular basis—requires prayer, preparation, and interior conversion.***

The Sacrament of Penance should be received often, but it must not be taken lightly. Sin is a serious matter, and your desire to be absolved of sin and reconciled with God must be sincere. It should reflect a true conversion of your heart. This is a guide to help you prepare for this wonderful Sacrament and for the sacramental rite itself.

***Examine your conscience.*** Examine your conscience regularly, ideally in your daily prayer. Ask the Holy Spirit to reveal your sins to you. Recall times you have failed to practice virtue. Do this especially before receiving the Sacrament of Penance so that you can make a "good Confession," one that is complete and heartfelt.

In your examination, you might consider the Ten Commandments, the Beatitudes, and the Precepts of the Church. Think about events in your life and how you may or may not have lived up to the Christian ideal.

***Experience sorrow for your sins and resolve to avoid all sin.*** Sin separates us from God, and every time you sin, you should regret it and determine never to sin again. Your sins are not like computer files that you need to delete in Confession just so you can have room for more. God is always ready to forgive, but you must cooperate with his grace. Make a firm commitment to avoid sin and remain faithful to Christ.

***Confess your sins in the Sacrament of Penance.*** Almost every church has a confessional or reconciliation room set aside. Go at the scheduled times, or make an appointment with a priest. The Rite of Penance usually proceeds as follows:

- Make the Sign of the Cross, and tell the priest how long it has been since your last Confession.
- Tell the priest how you have sinned. Do not go into great detail, but say enough so that the priest can understand the seriousness of each sin. If a sin happened more than once, then state how many times. Do not make excuses for your sins.
- Feel free to ask questions of the priest. He may ask questions of you, too, to clarify the nature of your sins. He may offer some advice on handling these sins or on spiritual practices to help strengthen you against sin.
- The priest will ask you to say an Act of Contrition. You can use your own words or one of the forms that you have memorized.
- The priest may then assign you a penance to perform, usually involving prayer, Scripture reading, meditation, or an act of kindness or charity.
- The priest will give you absolution for your sins in these words:

  **God, the Father of mercies,<br>through the death and resurrection of his Son<br>has reconciled the world to himself<br>and sent the Holy Spirit among us<br>for the forgiveness of sins;<br>through the ministry of the Church<br>may God give you pardon and peace,<br>and I absolve you from your sins<br>in the name of the Father, and of the Son,<br>and of the Holy Spirit.**

  **(*Rite of Penance, Rite for Reconciliation of Individual Penitents*, no. 46)**

- The priest will then dismiss you with the words, "Go in peace." Thank the priest, leave the confessional or reconciliation room, and perform your penance as soon as possible.
- Before you leave the church, say a very simple thanks to God in your own words for all his kindness to you.

# You and Your Parents

***Every family is a domestic church whose members grow in holiness and love.***

Our first experience of community is the family. But the family is much more than that as well. God designed the family to be an image of the communion of the Holy Trinity. When family life is lived according to the will of God, the members of the family see one another as his children. They see their connection and responsibility to others in the world.

Those sound like high ideals, but they are true. Think about these questions. How well does your family live up to its calling as a domestic church? Do prayers and discussions about your Catholic faith play an important role in your family life?

These questions are not meant to embarrass you or your family. No family is perfect. All families can do a better job of being a domestic church. Individuals can get distracted from the life of prayer. In the same way, entire families can become so caught up in day-to-day life that there seems to be little or no time for shared prayer, reflection, and discussion.

Here are some questions to help you and your parents reflect on your life as a domestic church:

1. Read the Parable of the Talents (Mt 25:13-40) with your parents. Explain to them what you read in this chapter about holiness and virtue. How can we live better as a domestic church?
2. Some families read a few verses from the Bible together, perhaps after they get back from Mass on Sunday or after dinner on weeknights. Others make use of a good video or audio series on the *Catechism*. How can we deepen our knowledge of the Catholic faith?
3. Many Catholics have relatives and friends who are priests or living the consecrated life. Do you know anyone living out these vocations? What most impresses you about him or her? Did you ever think about a vocation to the priesthood or consecrated life?
4. Parents have a good perspective on their children's gifts and talents. What gifts and talents do you see in me? Which of my gifts do you think would be helpful if my vocation is to the married state? Which of my gifts do you think would be helpful if my vocation is to the consecrated life?

How well does your family live up to its calling as a domestic church?

# YOU AND YOUR SPONSOR

***Talking about the signs of holiness that you see in your family can help you on your own path to Christ.***

You read in earlier chapters about the responsibilities of your sponsor, including accompanying you as a spiritual partner as you prepare for the Sacrament of Confirmation. You also read that his or her role does not end at the Confirmation Mass. Instead, your sponsor can help form you throughout your life as a faithful disciple of Christ. With the help of the Holy Spirit he or she can help you fulfill your calling as a disciple of Christ.

Talk with your sponsor about holiness. Share some of the things you read in this chapter. Listen to what your sponsor has to say about his or her own successes and struggles with holiness and what advice he or she has for you. Ask your sponsor to pray for you to be a true disciple of Christ. Offer to do the same for him or her.

If you find that talking about holiness with your sponsor is hard, here are some questions that might help:

1. What is the best advice that you can give when it comes to being a disciple of Christ? How do you live a life of holiness in your family life?
2. What is your vocation, or if you are still discerning it, what vocations are you considering? What advice do you have for me as I continue to discern my vocation?
3. What is one of your favorite parables of Christ from the Gospels? (Read it together.) What do you think it reveals about becoming holy?
4. What person in your life best demonstrates holiness, and why?

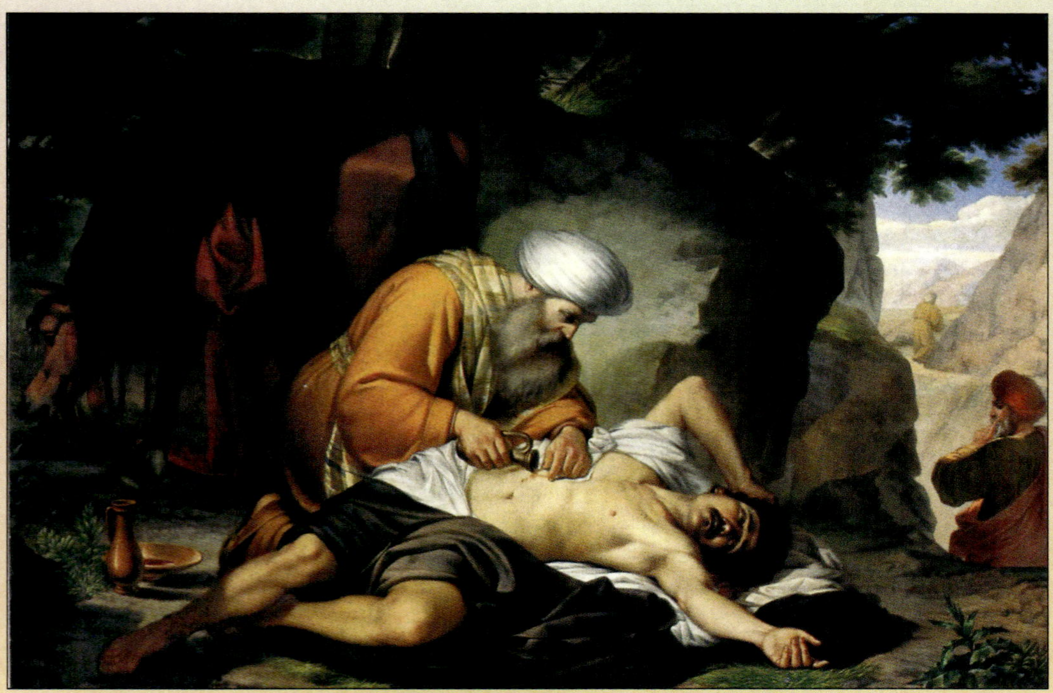

*Parable of the Good Samaritan* by Conti.
What is one of your favorite parables of Christ from the Gospels?
Read it with your sponsor.

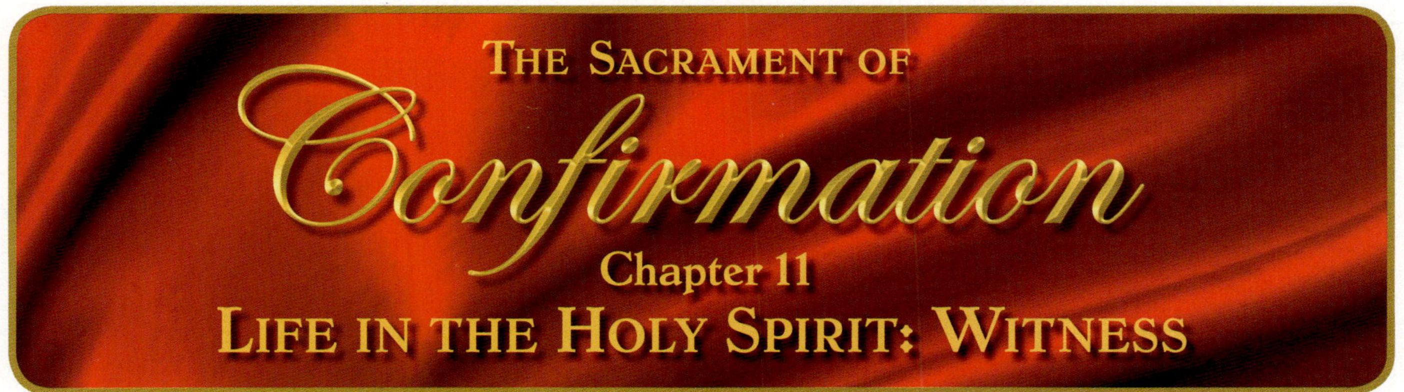


# INTRODUCTION

***Disciples of Christ share the Good News of salvation with others.***

**The ultimate purpose of mission is none other than to make men share in the communion between the Father and the Son in their Spirit of love. (CCC 850)**

So far, in understanding life in the Holy Spirit, we have focused on making your life more like Christ's. You do this through prayer, following the Commandments and Beatitudes, living the virtues, and following God's vocational call for your life. But your discipleship in Christ should not be solely focused on yourself. It is also about helping others, both spiritually and physically. As a Catholic about to be confirmed, you will be given a great gift: life in the Holy Spirit. Wouldn't it be great if everyone received this gift? They can, but someone has to give it to them.

Think about your own life as a Catholic. You received the faith from someone else, most likely your parents. They brought you to baptism, taught you your first prayers, took you to Mass, and helped you understand the Church's teachings. Without others showing you the way to Christ, it is unlikely that you would be his follower today.

Since you have been given this wonderful gift, you should now be inspired to give it to others by sharing your faith with them. As we will see in this chapter, Jesus calls all his followers to be witnesses for him to the world. This is an essential duty of those who bear the name "Christian."

*Ministry of the Apostles*, Russian icon.
This complex icon illustrates scenes of the Apostle's lives, their ministries, and martyrdoms.

After reading this chapter, you will be able to answer these questions:

- What is the Great Commission and what does it mean for me?
- How will the anointing at Confirmation link me to Christ and the Church's mission?
- What is evangelization, and how can I be part of the New Evangelization?
- How can I become a solid witness for Christ?

*Appearance While the Apostles Are at Table* by Duccio.
"Thus it is written...that repentance and forgiveness of sins should be preached in his name to all nations, beginning from Jerusalem. You are witnesses of these things. And behold, I send the promise of my Father upon you...." (Lk 24:46-49)

# THE GREAT COMMISSION

***Christ's final instructions to his Apostles to live as his witnesses extend to all the baptized.***

Before Christ's Ascension into heaven, he gave his Apostles what is called the **Great Commission**:

> **"All authority in heaven and on earth has been given to me. Go therefore and make disciples of all nations, baptizing them in the name of the Father and of the Son and of the Holy Spirit, teaching them to observe all that I have commanded you." (Mt 28:18-20)**

The Apostles were not to remain in and around Jerusalem. They were to go to all peoples and tell them about Jesus and his Good News. The work that Christ sent them to do in the world is also called **evangelization**, a word which is rooted in the word *gospel* (which in Greek is *euangelion*). These words mean "good news," and so evangelization is the work of spreading the Good News of salvation that was won for us by Christ.

> **The Church, in obedience to the command of her founder and because it is demanded by her own essential universality, strives to preach the Gospel to all men. (CCC 849)**

How would the Apostles accomplish such a mission? They would have the power of the Holy Spirit, which Christ promised to send after his Ascension. Following Christ's instructions, his Apostles waited for this gift in the Upper Room, spending their time in prayer. The Holy Spirit descended upon them on the day of Pentecost. They immediately went out to preach the Gospel, carrying out the Great Commission.

> **In [the apostles], Christ continues his own mission: "As the Father has sent me, even so I send you." The apostles' ministry is the continuation of his mission; Jesus said to the Twelve: "he who receives you receives me." (CCC 858)**

While baptizing converts is usually the work of priests, the Great Commission more broadly includes the work of all Christians: telling people the Good News about Jesus. The Church teaches that lay people "carry out for their own part the mission of the whole Christian people in the Church and in the world" (LG 31).

As a disciple of Christ you have a role in Christ's continuing mission on earth. The graces of the Holy Spirit that come to you in the Sacraments give you the help you need for this mission.

## THE CHURCH GROWS THROUGH EVANGELIZATION

***The Church exists to evangelize.***

Evangelization is not a secondary aspect of the Catholic faith. It is essential to it. In fact, you could say that the history of the Church is the history of Catholic evangelization. For how did the Church go from being a small group of uneducated men and women in an obscure part of the Roman Empire to the largest religion in the world today? Evangelization.

Picture the first Christians at Pentecost. They were a frightened group whom the governing authorities viewed with suspicion. Anyone observing them from the outside would be convinced that they wouldn't last more than a few months as a religious movement. But from the very beginning we see that they shared their faith with others. They worked hard to spread Christianity to all corners of the Roman Empire and even beyond. The Acts of the Apostles tells the story of that early growth. It begins in Jerusalem, and by the end of the book, Christianity has reached Rome, considered the center of the world at that time.

The work of evangelization did not end with the Apostles. It continued to happen wherever Christians lived. By various means—preaching to large crowds, teaching small groups, passing on the faith to family members, sharing the Good News in the marketplace—Christianity continued to grow. By the fourth century it was such a powerful movement that the Emperor himself, Constantine, became a Christian. After his conversion, most of the Roman Empire became Christian. And the growth of Christianity continued. After the Empire was largely Christian, missionaries were sent to all known lands to convert others to the faith. St. Augustine of Canterbury went to England, St. Patrick went to Ireland, and St. Boniface went to Germany, all in an effort to bring souls to Christ. Eventually the lands that were largely inhabited by Christians reached from England to Russia.

As the Church learned of new lands, such as parts of Asia or the "new world" (America), it continued to send out missionaries. The mission was always the same: to witness to the faith given by Jesus Christ and help souls find salvation in him through the Church.

That mission continues today and will continue until the end of time. For Christ's Great Commission is still in effect. We are to make disciples of "all nations." And this Great Commission is not the responsibility of just a few of Christ's disciples. It is the duty of each and every one of us.

> **It is from God's love for all men that the Church in every age receives both the obligation and the vigor of her missionary dynamism, "for the love of Christ urges us on." Indeed, God "desires all men to be saved and to come to the knowledge of the truth"; that is, God wills the salvation of everyone through the knowledge of the truth. (CCC 851)**

*A missionary priest of the Institute of the Incarnate Word (IVE) in Papua, New Guinea.*
IVE places a high priority on sending missionaries to places that have a greater need, either because of a lack of missionaries or because the faithful are in urgent need of them.

# THE TRAVELS OF ST. PAUL

St. Paul became one of Christianity's greatest evangelizers, traveling and spreading the Gospel throughout the Roman world, far beyond the borders of Palestine, founding some of the earliest and most prominent early Christian communities along the way. By some estimates, St. Paul's travels totaled well over 10,000 miles and brought him to every corner of Asia Minor, into Arabia, across Macedonia and Greece, and finally to Rome. Some scholars believe he may have traveled even as far west as Spain. For his troubles, however, this "Apostle to the Gentiles"—once a fervent persecutor of Christians—was severely persecuted for the faith.

St. Paul also spent a good deal of time in prison. He was arrested in Philippi, and again later in Jerusalem, after which he spent two years in prison in Caesarea, and two more years under house arrest in Rome. He eventually was martyred by beheading in Rome around AD 64.

## St. Paul's First Journey, ca. AD 46-48

*St. Paul Healing a Lame Man in Lystra* by Dujardin.
"And when the crowds saw what Paul had done, they lifted up their voices, saying... "The gods have come down to us in the likeness of men!" (Acts 14:11)

## St. Paul's Second Journey, ca. AD 49-52

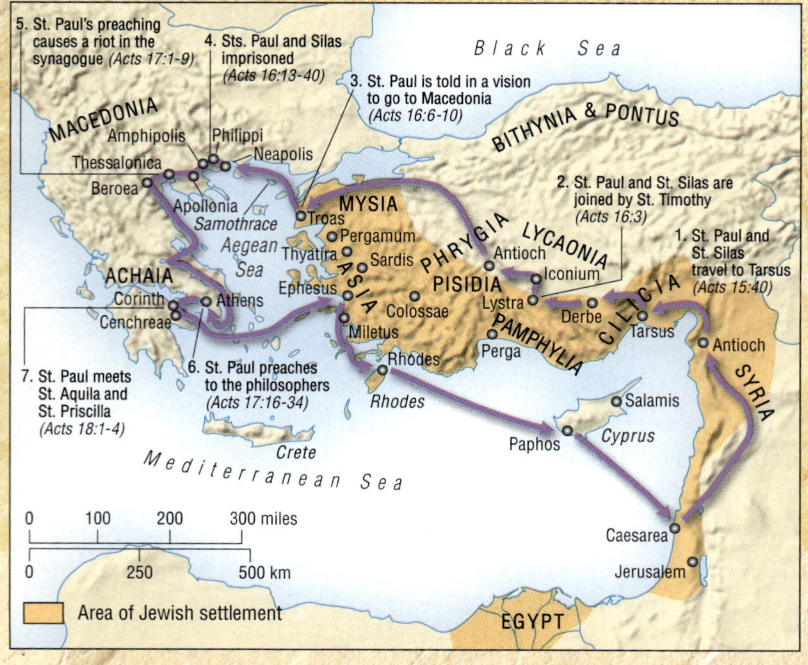

## THE TRAVELS OF ST. PAUL *Continued*

### St. Paul's Third Journey, ca. AD 53-57

### St. Paul's Voyage to Rome, ca. AD 61-62

## PLACE OF DEATH OF EACH APOSTLE

All of the Apostles other than St. John died a martyr's death. By looking at the location of their death, we can see how they spread out to their known world in their missionary travels. They were driven by their desire to fulfill Christ's Great Commission.

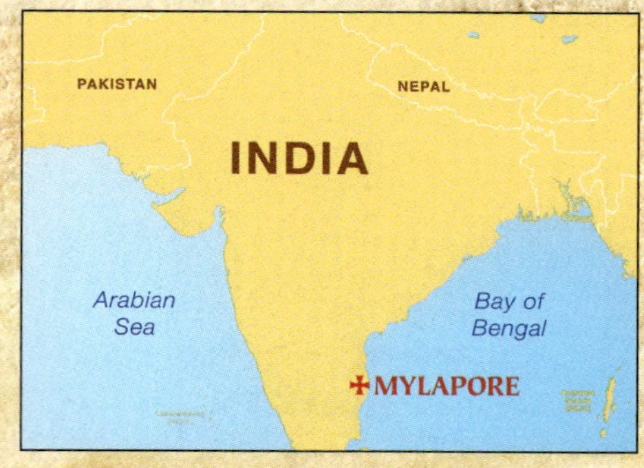


**ST. PETER:** Rome

**ST. ANDREW:** Patrae, Greece

**ST. JOHN:** Island of Patmos

**ST. JAMES THE GREATER:** Jerusalem

**ST. PHILIP:** Hierapolis, Phyrgia (Turkey in antiquity)

**ST. BARTHOLOMEW:** Albanopolis, Eastern Armenia (Azerbaijan)

**ST. JAMES THE LESS:** Jerusalem

**ST. JUDAS THADDAEUS:** Persia (Iran)

**ST. SIMON THE ZEALOT:** Persia (Iran)

**ST. THOMAS:** India (possibly Mylapore)

**ST. MATTHEW:** Ethiopia (or Persia, or Pontus)

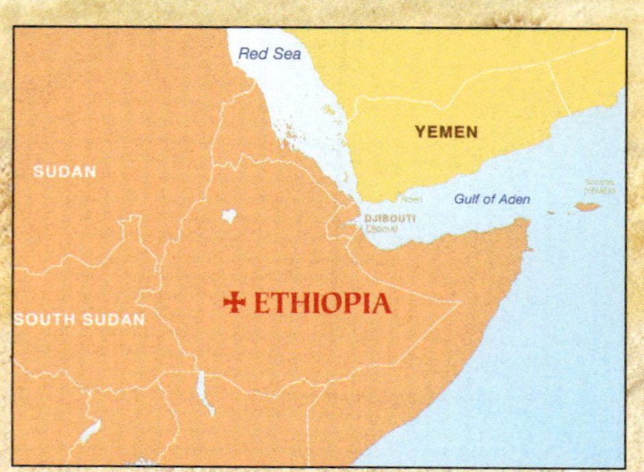


*Maps show modern-day national borders.*

## CONFIRMATION LINKS US TO CHRIST'S MISSION

***The anointing and gifts of Confirmation fill us with the Holy Spirit and make us disciples.***

The mission of Christ is to save the world. He did this by his life, Death, and Resurrection. But his mission continues on in his followers. He gave his disciples the Great Commission, and then sent the Holy Spirit at Pentecost to give them the strength to fulfill that Great Commission. Confirmation, which is in a sense our own individual Pentecost, gives us the strength to continue this mission. It is the Holy Spirit, in whom we are sealed at our Confirmation, that powers the missionary impulse of the Church.

> **The Holy Spirit is..."the principal agent of the whole of the Church's mission." It is he who leads the Church on her missionary paths. (CCC 852)**

The Sacrament of Confirmation will give you the strength to bear witness to Christ. Often when we think of being a witness to the world, we think of missionaries to faraway places. However, sharing the Gospel is not something we do just for strangers who are "out there" somewhere and have never heard of Christ and his Church. Your mission begins with those closest to you.

As a faithful Catholic in the world, your witness originates with the example you give in your everyday life: in your home, in your family, in your school, among your friends, and in your community. Sometimes witnessing to those around you is more difficult than doing so in a faraway land. But remember that you will have the benefit of the gifts of the Holy Spirit no matter where you go.

## BIBLICAL EVANGELIZATION

One of the great examples of evangelization is found in the book of Acts, chapter 8. It recounts the story of the deacon Philip. He encounters an Ethiopian man who was interested in God but did not know anything about Jesus. The Ethiopian is curious to know more, so he asks Philip to help him understand God's plan of salvation. Philip patiently answers the man's questions, and leads him to understand why Jesus came to earth. Once Philip sees that the Ethiopian is ready to convert, he offers to baptize the man. The Ethiopian accepts Philip's offer and becomes a Catholic.

Read the account below and think about how you can model your own evangelization efforts on Philip's.

> **An angel of the Lord said to Philip, "Rise and go toward the south to the road that goes down from Jerusalem to Gaza." This is a desert road. And he rose and went. And behold, an Ethiopian, a eunuch, a minister of Candace the queen of the Ethiopians, in charge of all her treasure, had come to Jerusalem to worship and was returning; seated in his chariot, he was reading the prophet Isaiah. And the Spirit said to Philip, "Go up and join this chariot." So Philip ran to him, and heard him reading Isaiah the prophet, and asked, "Do you understand what you are reading?" And he said, "How can I, unless some one guides me?" And he invited Philip to come up and sit with him. Now the passage of the scripture which he was reading was this:**
>
> **"As a sheep led to the slaughter**
> **or a lamb before its shearer is silent,**
> **so he opens not his mouth.**
> **In his humiliation justice was denied him.**
> **Who can describe his generation?**
> **For his life is taken up from the earth."**
>
> **And the eunuch said to Philip, "Please, about whom does the prophet say this, about himself or about some one else?" Then Philip opened his mouth, and beginning with this scripture he told him the good news of Jesus. And as they went along the road they came to some water, and the eunuch said, "See, here is water! What is to prevent my being baptized?" And he commanded the chariot to stop, and they both went down into the water, Philip and the eunuch, and he baptized him. And when they came up out of the water, the Spirit of the Lord caught up Philip; and the eunuch saw him no more, and went on his way rejoicing. But Philip was found at Azotus, and passing on he preached the gospel to all the towns till he came to Caesarea. (Acts 8:26-40)**

## YOUR ROLE IN EVANGELIZATION

***Confirmation, like Pentecost, sends you forth to spread the Good News.***

All of the graces and gifts that you will receive in Confirmation will prepare you to practice what is known as the apostolate. This word is rooted in apostle, which means "one who is sent."

> **In our day Jesus' command to "go and make disciples" echoes in the changing scenarios and ever new challenges to the Church's mission of evangelization, and all of us are called to take part in this new missionary "going forth." (Pope Francis, *Evangelium Gaudium*, 20)**

All of the baptized share in the Church's mission of evangelization. Those who were touched and healed by Christ during his earthly ministry told others about him and what he had done for them. You, too, are called to proclaim what he has done for you! Your baptismal commitment will be strengthened soon by the graces and gifts that you will be given in Confirmation. This is a commitment to evangelize through your discipleship in the midst of the world.

In recent years the Church has promoted a **"New Evangelization."** This is a title that describes newer, fresher efforts to teach or renew the Gospel message. It is directed towards those regions of the world where the faith was once strong but where people "have lost a living sense of the faith, or even no longer consider themselves members of the Church, and live a life far removed from Christ and his Gospel" (St. John Paul II, *Redemptoris Missio*, 33). This effort sometimes requires proposing the faith in new and innovative ways in order to draw people back into the mystery of the faith.

Chances are you live in an area of the world with many Catholics who have fallen away or become apathetic to the faith. You do not need to go off to a foreign country to get involved in the New Evangelization. You can start right in your own back yard!

### WITNESS AND SALVATION

**The disciple of Christ must not only keep the faith and live on it, but also profess it, confidently bear witness to it, and spread it... Service of and witness to the faith are necessary for salvation: "So every one who acknowledges me before men, I also will acknowledge before my Father who is in heaven; but whoever denies me before men, I also will deny before my Father who is in heaven" (Mt 10:32-33). (CCC 1816)**

Every day gives us opportunities to evangelize; we just have to be open to them. Here is one example of "real-life" evangelization:

**Your friend Robert:** I can't believe it.

**You:** What?

**Robert:** I just found out my grandmother's in the hospital. She's really sick and they don't know if she's going to make it.

**You:** I'm really sorry. Is there anything I can do?

**Robert:** I don't think so, but thanks for asking.

**You:** Well, I'll pray for your grandmother and your whole family.

**Robert:** Thanks, but we don't really believe in God.

**You:** I know, but when something bad happens to me I always talk to God about it and it always helps. Even if the situation is still bad, I feel better. I know that he understands what I'm going through and I don't have to be fake with him. I can just tell him what I really think. I'll pray that your whole family feels comfort even though I know it's difficult for you all.

**Robert:** Thanks, I appreciate that.

**You:** And if you need anything, just let me know!

## MORTIFICATION IS NECESSARY FOR EVANGELIZATION

**Unless a grain of wheat falls into the earth and dies, it remains alone; but if it dies, it bears much fruit. (Jn 12:24)**

Mortification (self-denial) is necessary to achieve any goal. If you want to win a race, or do well on an exam, or learn a musical instrument, you have to work hard and sacrifice certain things in order to succeed. The same is true for evangelization. After Pentecost, the Apostles went to the ends of the earth to proclaim the Gospel. Doing so was hard work, and it involved great self-denial. Ultimately, all the Apostles except John were killed for their faith. But God blessed their efforts and brought about many, many conversions to the Catholic faith.

A famous saying from the early Church was "The blood of the martyrs is the seed of the Church." This meant that the example of the Christians who denied themselves everything—even their lives—for Christ led many people to become Catholic. We might not be asked to give up our lives literally, but God is calling each of us to practice mortification for the sake of the Gospel. If we want to be witnesses to the world, we must deny ourselves for love of God and neighbor.

# A TRUE WITNESS FOR CHRIST

***Make disciples by knowing, living, talking about, and defending your faith.***

To "make disciples" may sound like a gigantic task. And it truly is a great responsibility. Yet when Christ gives you a mission, he also gives you the help you need to fulfill that mission. With the gifts of the Holy Spirit which you will receive in Confirmation, you can go forth in confidence that you have all the graces to be an effective witness for Christ.

To understand how you should go about this mission, you only have to look at the example of the Apostles. Evangelization comes down to four things: knowing your faith, living your faith, sharing your faith, and defending your faith when you are called on to do so. We will look at each of these aspects of evangelization in turn.

## TELLING YOUR STORY

You might be intimidated by the idea of "sharing your faith." After all, you probably feel you don't know everything there is to know about Catholicism. Also, what if you say something wrong, and the person decides not to become Catholic? It is natural to be nervous—it's a big subject!

The best way to start evangelizing is to simply tell your story. In other words, why are you Catholic? You might not have thought about this before, and you might not have an answer at the tip of your tongue. But it is good to know why you are Catholic. Once you can answer that question to yourself, you can help others see why being Catholic is God's desire for everyone. When others see how much joy being Catholic brings you, they might be interested in becoming Catholic too.

## KNOW YOUR FAITH

***You can only share your faith if you know it well.***

You read in this book that your religious formation is a lifelong journey. Confirmation is surely an important milestone. But it is not your "graduation" from learning about the faith. It is one step along a journey of living your faith in a deeper way.

There is a popular saying, "You can't share what you don't have." You cannot talk about your faith with others if you do not know it yourself. It is true that even saints, bishops, and theologians do not always have ready answers to some of the most difficult questions, but you do not want to have that problem when you are asked about the basic beliefs of the Church. So take your study of the Catholic faith seriously, and continue to learn by reading Scripture, the *Catechism*, and other Catholic literature. Attend some classes when they are available at your parish, and listen to the homilies at Mass. Perhaps there is a Catholic radio or television station available in your area with shows that explain the faith.

When asked questions about the faith that you can't answer, don't be afraid to say, "I don't know." No one will expect you to have all the answers. But always be willing to find out. The best place to start is the *Catechism*, which contains the answers to all the most common questions about Catholicism.

### KNOWING THE SCRIPTURES

The Bible is the inspired story of God's work in this world. It tells of how God created us, and then saved us after we fell away from him. Knowing this story well will help you to witness your faith to others.

Many people think that Catholics don't know the Bible. They think that only Protestant Christians really know what that Bible says. But this doesn't have to be true. By reading the Bible every day, and using Catholic study guides to help you to understand it, you will become familiar with Scripture and know how to share its story with others. This will also help you when people challenge your faith and claim that the Bible contradicts what the Church teaches.

### THE MESSAGE OF SALVATION

Sometimes it can be overwhelming to talk about God's message of salvation to someone. Where do I begin? What is most important to say? We must remember the end goal: salvation, or reaching heaven after death. There are many things we can say when we share our faith, but they should revolve around four principal points:

- **God is one and Triune.** The Revelation of the Trinity is the essential component of the Revelation given to the world by God. It reveals *who God is* and, thus, informs our worship and proclamation of him.
- **Jesus Christ is the Son of God and the Second Person of the Trinity become man.** The entire Christian message centers on the historical fact that God became man in Jesus of Nazareth. The Church has always proclaimed —and defended—the truth that Jesus Christ is fully God and fully man.
- **Salvation is a gift of God by grace through Jesus Christ.** Due to the Fall of man at the beginning of time, the human race is incapable of attaining our complete fulfillment with God in heaven. But God in his mercy has made salvation available to us through the life, Death, and Resurrection of his Son, Jesus Christ.
- **Each person is called to holiness by participation in God's love now and eternally.** The Church boldly proclaims that man's true calling is not only to be with God forever in heaven, but to also become more and more like him. Through Baptism, we are sanctified and are called to become, by God's grace, images of Christ.

## LIVE YOUR FAITH

***No one will listen to you if you don't witness your faith with your life.***

The Catholic faith is not just something to be talked about. It is a way of life. In fact, in the early days of the Church the faith was called "the Way" (Acts 9:2). This showed it is more than just a set of beliefs. As you read in the previous two chapters, living as a disciple of Christ requires a strong prayer life and a commitment to strive for holiness each day.

Living your faith is just as important as talking about your faith. If your life does not reflect the Gospel message, then your words may not impress anyone. You will be called a hypocrite. But if you live as an authentic disciple of Christ, people will be inspired by your example. They will want to know who gives you such joy, peace, and a loving and virtuous disposition in all that you do. This will then allow you to speak of the source of your good example: Jesus Christ.

The Acts of the Apostles and the letters of St. Paul and others describe how the Apostles and the early Christians lived their lives as a witness to their faith. They prayed frequently and met every week to celebrate the "breaking of the bread." Many converts were won to the Gospel by the way Christians loved one another with the love of Christ. Their strength in the face of persecution and even martyrdom revealed the depth of their convictions.

### WHAT TO DO WHEN YOU DON'T LIVE YOUR FAITH

Nobody's perfect. There will be times that you make decisions and do things that aren't in line with what Jesus wants of us. When that happens, you might be worried that you gave a bad witness of Catholicism to others. Remember though that the Church is here for sinners, not for perfect people. So after you fall, be sure to go to Confession, and if others saw you do something wrong, admit your mistake to them. Doing so is actually a great example of living your faith.

## TALK ABOUT YOUR FAITH

***Words are necessary to let others know about Christ.***

You do not have to be a street-corner preacher, proclaiming the Gospel to people who pass by. You do not have to go door-to-door offering to explain the Catholic faith to people in their living rooms. You can do these things, of course, but evangelization is usually much simpler than that. When there is a chance to share your faith or offer someone counsel, ask the Holy Spirit to give you the words you need. You may be surprised at how easy it is to speak the truth with love when you have the Spirit guiding you.

Some opportunities come up because of your lived witness. If you are at a restaurant with an acquaintance, you can make the Sign of the Cross and invite him or her to join you in saying grace. Even a little gesture like that can prompt someone to ask about what you believe. If someone is going through a difficult time, a word of spiritual encouragement or sharing an experience in which your faith helped you through a rough spot might be appropriate. God will put people in your path who need to hear the Good News.

### WHAT IF I'M NOT GOOD AT TALKING TO OTHERS?

When people think of an evangelist, they usually think of someone who is naturally outgoing and good in front of crowds. But what if you aren't like that? What if you prefer small groups and get really nervous when talking to groups? That's okay—that's how God made you. But he still wants you to witness your faith.

Talking to others about your faith doesn't have to be done in front of large groups, or on a street corner to strangers. It can happen at the lunch table, on the ball field, or at the movies. You can just naturally talk to your friends about what you believe and why you believe it. We all feel comfortable talking about the things we love to the people we care about, and this is no different!

## HOW TO EVANGELIZE

What are some practical steps for sharing your faith with others? Everybody will do it differently, but here are seven suggestions.

**Step 1: Pray, Pray, Pray.** Prayer is the foundation of any spiritual activity, and sharing your faith is no different. You need to form a habit of prayer in your life—praying every day for at least some amount of time—and you need to pray for those around you.

**Step 2: Live Your Faith.** As mentioned earlier, the best witness to the Catholic faith is living it. Further, no one will listen to you talk about your faith if you don't live it yourself: why should they follow something you don't?

**Step 3: Tell Your Story.** If you are trying to be a disciple of Jesus Christ, you have a story to tell. Why do you want to be confirmed? What is the most important part of being a Christian to you? What is hardest about being a Christian?

**Step 4: Don't Argue—Invite.** Sharing your faith isn't the same thing as being in a debate. People will disagree with you—that's all right. Always be willing to share your faith with others, but don't start arguments. Instead, invite others to consider your beliefs respectfully and with an open mind.

**Step 5: Be Natural.** When sharing your faith, you should be as natural as you are when talking about your favorite hobby or sports team. Don't feel like you have to follow a script. Talk about what appeals to you about being Catholic.

**Step 6: Be a Friend.** No matter what your friends may believe, always be a friend to them. In other words, support and encourage them when they are down, and rejoice with them when they have success in life. Being a friend has always been the best way to share the love of Jesus Christ with others.

**Step 7: Trust God.** In the end, you are not going to "make" someone Catholic. They are going to become Catholic because of their own decision and—most importantly—because of the work of the Holy Spirit. Always trust that God will work in the lives of your friends to bring them closer to him.

The New Testament is full of accounts of the Apostles and early Christians speaking openly about their faith. It is interesting to note that the Apostles, most of them simple men with little education, became eloquent preachers of the Gospel after they received the gifts of the Holy Spirit!

## DEFEND YOUR FAITH

***Sometimes you will have to explain and defend your faith to others.***

One of the surest things about being a disciple of Christ is that your faith will be attacked. Christ himself endured much ridicule, abuse, and opposition. Ultimately, he was crucified for preaching the Good News. You probably will not suffer in such an extreme way, but your acquaintances, friends, and even family members might make fun of you for living your faith or because they know that you are Catholic. Modern culture tends to be anti-Catholic and anti-Christian. Therefore much of what you believe as a Catholic may go against what much of modern society tells you is true.

You will need strength to endure this persecution. You will also need to be able to answer honest

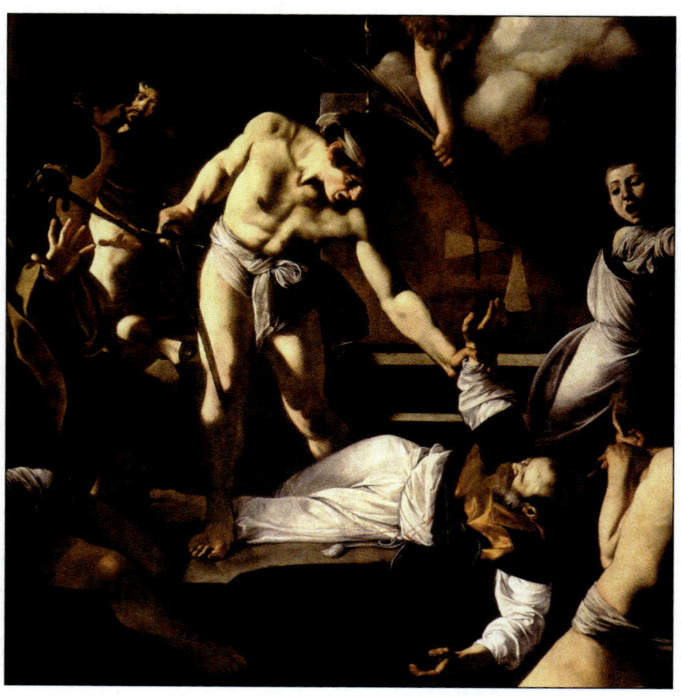

*Martyrdom of St. Matthew* by Caravaggio.
Modern culture tends to be anti-Catholic and anti-Christian. You will need strength to endure this persecution.

questions about your Catholic faith. Knowledge of the faith is important, and you must also know how to explain the faith to others. You must be able to present it in a reasonable way that is filled with love and compassion for the questioner. St. Peter, who suffered much for the faith and in the end was even crucified, writes:

> **Always be prepared to make a defense to any one who calls you to account for the hope that is in you, yet do it with gentleness and reverence. (1 Pt 3:15)**

Evangelization must be anchored in the ability to explain and defend the Catholic faith. Presenting reasoned arguments that explain the faith is called **apologetics**. People who are searching for God often have many questions. You should be able to direct them to the answers that will lead them closer to Christ and his Church. Of course, there will be times when you find yourself without an answer or too tongue-tied to give a good answer. This happens to everyone. Then, it is best to simply say something like, "I'm sorry, but I don't know the answer to that. But I'll try to find the answer and let you know." If you continue to pray for guidance from the Holy Spirit, you will find that such situations will happen less and less often.

*Martyrdom of St. Peter* by Gandolfi.
Evangelization must be anchored in the ability to explain and defend the Catholic faith.

## PRACTICAL APOLOGETICS

Although Catholicism is the largest religion in the world, many people don't understand what the Church teaches—even Catholics sometimes! You will often be called upon to explain to those around you the teachings of the Church. This work of apologetics can be vital in helping others to follow Christ. Here is an example of real-world apologetics:

**Your friend Sarah:** Is that a rosary? Why do you pray to Mary when you can just pray directly to God?

**You:** Let me ask you something first: do you ask others to pray for you?

**Sarah:** Sure, all the time.

**You:** Who do you usually ask?

**Sarah:** Well, I guess I ask my parents sometimes. And my friends from youth group. And there is this nice woman at church who is always praying, so sometimes I ask her.

**You:** So you ask people you think are already close to God?

**Sarah:** Yeah, I guess you could say that.

**You:** Now, let me ask you another question. What do you think happens to Christians when they die?

**Sarah:** They go to heaven, of course.

**You:** So they are close to God, right?

**Sarah:** Absolutely. Are you ever going to answer my question?

**You:** Yes! When Catholics pray to Mary, what we are really doing is asking her to pray for us, just like you ask your parents or your friends or that lady at your church. Since Mary is in heaven, she is closer to God than you or I, which makes her prayers extra powerful.

**Sarah:** Well, I guess that makes sense. I don't think I'll be praying the Rosary anytime soon though.

**You:** I understand, but I'll ask Mary to pray for you!

*Miracles of St. Francis Xavier* by Rubens.
The Holy Spirit will help inspire your courage and your words through the gifts that you will be given in Confirmation.

## CONCLUSION

Confirmation is not the end of a journey but a new beginning in the Christian life. At your Confirmation you will be given the graces that you need to live the Catholic faith as a fully initiated member of Christ's Church.

The Sacrament of Confirmation and the gifts of the Holy Spirit will help you live as a true witness for Christ. In Confirmation you will take on a greater share of the Great Commission to spread your faith. You will fulfill this by the example of your life and by being ready and willing to share your faith with others. The Holy Spirit will guide you and lead you in discipleship.

You must know your faith first in order to share it. You must live your faith, be willing to talk about your faith, and be prepared to defend your faith.

Learning to articulate your faith through apologetics will teach you how to give the reasons behind the teachings of the faith. As always, the Holy Spirit will help inspire your courage and your words through the gifts that you will be given in Confirmation.

## POINTS TO REMEMBER

1. Christ commanded his followers to make disciples of all nations, which we call "the Great Commission."
2. Evangelization is an essential part of the Catholic faith, and by our Confirmation we are called to share the Good News of salvation with others.
3. In order to be a good witness for Christ, you should know your Catholic faith, live it, talk about it, and defend it when questioned.

# WITNESS OF CHRIST

## ST. FRANCIS XAVIER

In 1506, a boy named Francis was born in the Castle of Xavier in the Kingdom of Navarre, which is now part of Spain. Francis was a member of a noble family. His father was an advisor to the king. By all accounts, Francis could have lived a life of comfort and ease like his peers, but God chose a different path for the young man.

At the age of nineteen Francis left for Paris to study at the university. There he met the man who would change his life: Ignatius of Loyola. Ignatius had a profound effect on Francis. When Ignatius began his own religious order, Francis was one of its first members. The order was called the Society of Jesus, more commonly known as the Jesuits. In 1536 Francis was ordained a priest, and a few years later he was sent to Asia as one of the first Jesuit missionaries.

Being a missionary in a far-off land isn't easy in any age, but it was particularly difficult during the sixteenth century. Travel by sea was dangerous, and often included many hardships. For a young man born to nobility, such hardships might seem impossible to endure, but instead of complaining Francis offered them up for the success of his mission. His desire to preach the Gospel far outweighed any difficulties he encountered.

Francis traveled throughout the Far East, including India, many Asian islands, and particularly Japan. Wherever he traveled, he would learn the language, care for the sick, catechize the young, and preach the Gospel to anyone who would listen. During his missionary travels, his powerful preaching and faithful witness led many thousands of people to convert to Catholicism.

After spending 2-1/2 years in Japan, Francis set his sights on China. He had heard many things about it, and greatly desired to spread the message of Jesus throughout the pagan land. However, on his way to China he fell ill and died on an island off the coast of the mainland. The year was 1552. By the time of his death he had traveled thousands upon thousands of miles, driven by the desire to bring people to Jesus Christ and the Catholic Church. For all this he lived, above all, on the gift of knowledge.

Seventy years after his death, Francis, along with Ignatius of Loyola, was canonized a saint of the Catholic Church. St. Francis Xavier is the patron saint of Catholic missions.

## VOCABULARY

### APOLOGETICS
The practice of articulating a defense of the Catholic faith.

### EVANGELIZATION
The work of spreading the Good News of salvation that was won for us by Christ, which the graces and gifts of Confirmation prepares a Christian to practice.

### GREAT COMMISSION
Christ's departing instruction to his Apostles: "Go therefore and make disciples of all nations, baptizing them in the name of the Father and of the Son and of the Holy Spirit, teaching them to observe all that I have commanded you" (Mt 28:19-20).

### NEW EVANGELIZATION
Efforts to teach or renew the Gospel message in the regions of the world where the faith was once strong but where the people have ceased practicing it.

### SELF-DENIAL
Giving up a good thing for something better.

### WITNESS (TO CHRIST)
A person who knows, gives testimony, or offers evidence or proof of Christ and his power.

*St. Peter Preaching in the Presence of St. Mark* by Fra Angelico.
"Go therefore and make disciples of all nations."

## STUDY QUESTIONS

1. What is the Great Commission?
2. Who helped the Apostles bring more and more people to Christ?
3. Who is responsible to fulfill the Great Commission?
4. What are some of the towns in which St. Paul preached the Gospel?
5. How is the Sacrament of Confirmation linked to the mission of the Church?
6. What is the apostolate?
7. What is the New Evangelization?
8. What are the four things we can do to be witnesses for Christ?
9. Why is it important that we know our faith well?
10. What is apologetics?

## PRACTICAL EXERCISES

1. Pick one of the Twelve Apostles and do a study on his life after Pentecost. Find out where he travelled, who he preached to, and how he died. Write a short biography of the Apostle.

2. In your class, divide into groups of two. Choose one of the following topics to debate, with one person taking the Catholic position, and another taking the non-Catholic position. (Note that not all of these topics have been covered this year, so ask your teacher for resources to inform your debate.)

   a. The infallibility of the Pope.
   b. The existence of God.
   c. The immorality of abortion.
   d. The existence of purgatory.
   e. The Real Presence of Christ in the Eucharist.

3. Make an effort this week to talk to someone about your faith. For example, you might tell someone about your upcoming Confirmation and what it means to you. Or, perhaps you could invite someone to attend Youth Group or other Catholic event with you.

Make an effort to talk to someone about your faith. You could invite someone to attend a Youth Group or other Catholic event with you.

# SEALED IN THE SPIRIT

***The Holy Spirt gives you the ability to witness your faith to others.***

All of us have some fear about sharing our faith with others. We know if we do, we could be ridiculed or rejected. It's not always easy being a Catholic, and it's definitely not always easy to talk about our Catholic faith with others. In many ways, we are like the Apostles who were hiding in the Upper Room before Pentecost. When you receive Confirmation, a little "Pentecost" occurs in your life. In Confirmation, we receive the same Holy Spirit that the Apostles received. And it can give us the same strength to witness to others as the Apostles received on Pentecost.

How exactly does the Holy Spirit help us to witness our faith?

**The Holy Spirit gives us courage.** It is often said that courage is not the absence of fear, but the ability to do the right thing in spite of our fear. Even if sharing our faith with others might be frightening at times (What if I'm made fun of? What if I lose my friends?), the Holy Spirit allows us to overcome those fears to help others draw closer to Jesus Christ.

**The Holy Spirit gives us the words to say.** Sometimes we don't know what to say when someone challenges our faith. Sometimes we fumble over our words trying to explain what we believe. Through the power of the Holy Spirt that we receive at our Confirmation, we are given the words to say when they are needed. As Jesus said,

> **Do not be anxious beforehand what you are to say; but say whatever is given you in that hour, for it is not you who speak, but the Holy Spirit. (Mk 13:11)**

**The Holy Spirt gives us opportunities.** We may know non-Catholics whom we would like to invite to learn more about the faith, but we don't ever find the "right time" to do it. However, if we are praying to the Holy Spirt and asking his help, he will give us the opportunities we need to share our faith. In fact, rather than having to seek opportunities, often our friends and family will approach us if we ask for the Holy Spirit's help!

The most important thing to remember when witnessing the faith is that we are unable to convert anyone. Only the Holy Spirit can bring about a person's conversion. So we must simply follow the Holy Spirit's lead and trust that he will open hearts so that our witness can help others to embrace the Catholic faith.

The most important thing to remember when witnessing the faith is that *we* are unable to convert anyone. Only the Holy Spirit can bring about a person's conversion.

# You and Your Parents

***Your parents have had to witness and defend their faith.***

Every Catholic has to be a witness to his or her faith. Whether it is going to a far-off land to preach the Gospel, or living faithfully in your own neighborhood, we are all witnesses. Your parents, too, have been witnesses for Christ in their lives. By having you baptized, helping you to receive your First Communion and Confession, taking you to Mass, and helping you prepare for Confirmation, your parents have witnessed the importance of the Catholic faith to you.

But your parents have been witnesses to other people in other ways, perhaps even in ways they don't realize. Sit down with them and talk about how they have witnessed to the faith in the past. Here are a few questions you could ask to get started:

**1. Can you think of a time when you shared your faith with someone else?** It might have been a simple comment or a long discussion, with a friend or a stranger. When did you tell someone else about Catholicism? What was the reaction?

**2. Have you ever had to defend your faith?** When? How was it being challenged? How did you respond?

**3. Have you ever looked back and realized you missed a good opportunity to witness your faith?** We all make mistakes. Can you recall a time when you could have said something but didn't? What was the situation? What should you have said? What would you do differently?

By helping you prepare for Confirmation, your parents have witnessed the importance of the Catholic faith to you. Talk to your parents about how they have witnessed to the faith in the past.

# You and Your Sponsor

***You can witness to your faith with your friends and relatives.***

In "You and Your Parents" you talked to your parents about times in the past they may have witnessed their faith. Now talk to your sponsor about ways that both you and he (or she) can witness your faith in your lives.

Every person has a "circle of influence." These are people we interact with regularly whom we impact through our words and actions. Talk to your sponsor about how you can each witness your faith to your circles of influence. Here are some questions to get you started:

**1. With whom do you interact most during a typical week?** Think about the people you encounter most frequently: family members, fellow workers or students, even the grocery bagger! Some will be Catholic, some non-Catholic Christians, and some might be of a completely different religion or no religion at all.

**2. How can you help these people to understand Catholicism better?** Unfortunately, most people don't understand the Catholic faith very well. They have misperceptions and errors in their understanding of the teachings of the Church. Further, they may know very little about the Sacraments, prayer, or the saints. Think of ways that you can help them to understand Catholicism in a more complete way.

**3. How can I witness my Catholic faith to them?** Our faith calls us to serve those in need (see Chapter 12). We have a particular obligation to help those who are closest to us. So if you know that one of your friends or family members has a need, try to help them as best you can. This witnesses the love that Christ has for each one of us.

Also, always remember to pray each day for all those you will encounter during that day. Ask the Holy Spirit to bless them, and to give you the wisdom and courage to witness your faith to them.

*Miraculous Draught of Fishes* by Raphael.
"And Jesus said to Simon, 'Do not be afraid; henceforth you will be catching men.' And when they had brought their boats to land, they left everything and followed him." (Lk 5:10-11)

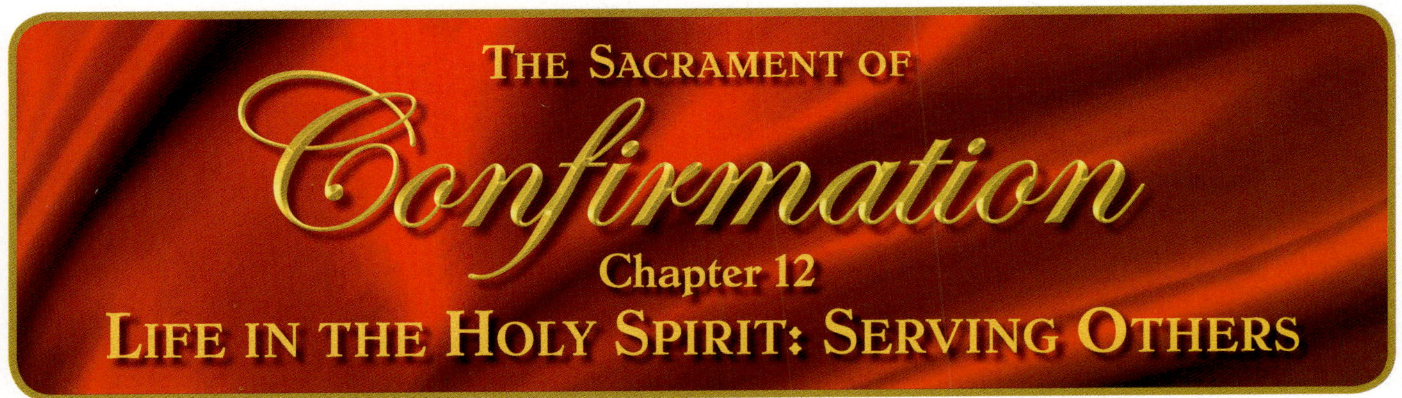


# Chapter 12
# Life in the Holy Spirit: Serving Others

## INTRODUCTION

***Loving service to others is an essential part of being a true disciple of Christ.***

Most dioceses ask young people who are preparing to receive the Sacrament of Confirmation to perform some kind of service for their parish or community. The purpose of this stipulation is to strengthen the connection between being a disciple of Jesus Christ and serving others.

You understand that the Sacrament of Confirmation gives you divine strength to witness to the Gospel. In this chapter we will learn more about the great importance of serving our neighbor. Christ cared for the "least" in the world, and he calls us to imitate him in all that we do.

Christian service is much more than a box to check off in order to meet the requirements of our Confirmation preparation course. It's not just something "nice" that Christians should do. Christian service is a mandate of Christ. It is part of what it means to be his disciple.

After reading this chapter, you will be able to answer these questions:

- Who is the source of human dignity?
- Why is the right to life essential to preserve human dignity?
- What is the difference between charity and justice?
- What is meant by "Catholic social teaching"?

## THE DIGNITY OF THE HUMAN PERSON

***Our worth or value is based on our status as God's special creation.***

A fundamental principle of Catholic teaching is the **dignity of the human person**—a dignity that comes from God.

Every person possesses dignity regardless of race, beliefs, physical condition, class, or age. A person's dignity does not depend upon his job, possessions, accomplishments, physical strength, or even virtues or holiness. It derives from the fact that each of us is made in the image and likeness of God. This imprint

*Christ Healing the Sick at Bethesda* by Bloch. Christ cared for the "least" in the world, and he calls us to imitate him in all that we do.

of God that human persons bear makes each one worthy of respect and honor. The divine image can be obscured by sin, but it can never be taken away. Everyone—even the most sinful person—deserves to be treated with dignity.

Every person is equal in dignity in the eyes of God. All people have the same nature and the same origin. All are called to enjoy the same destiny: to be sons and daughters of God, in communion with him forever in heaven. Jesus Christ shed his Blood and died on the Cross for all, and God desires the salvation of everyone.

What is our guiding principle for respecting human dignity? We must see every person as someone with rights and dignity equal to our own, for all are created in the image of God. This principle is another expression of what Christ taught when he commanded us, "Love one another as I have loved you" (Jn 15:12) and "Love your neighbor as yourself" (Mt 19:29).

*Christ and the Good Thief* by Titian.
Everyone—even the most sinful person—deserves to be treated with dignity.
"And he said, 'Jesus, remember me when you come into your kingdom.' And he said to him, 'Truly, I say to you, today you will be with me in Paradise.'" (Lk 23:42-43)

## WE ARE CALLED TO SERVE

***All followers of Christ are called to serve those in need.***

The truth that every human person has dignity has important consequences. First and foremost, it should impact how we treat others. Do we treat others with kindness? Do we help those in need? Do we treat every person with respect?

Being a disciple of Christ means that we are always ready to help those in need and to defend the dignity of others when it is threatened. This is a command of Christ. The way that we treat our neighbors and the charity that we show them is part of our path to salvation.

Our love and worship of God cannot remain on the spiritual or mental level. It must be expressed in concrete, visible acts of love. As Christ taught in the Parable of the Sheep and the Goats, we will be judged on how we treated and cared for the least of our brothers and sisters:

> **"When the Son of man comes in his glory...the King will say to those at his right hand, 'Come, O blessed of my Father, inherit the kingdom prepared for you from the beginning of the world; for I was hungry and you gave me food, I was thirsty and you gave me drink, I was a stranger and you welcomed me, I was naked and you clothed me, I was sick and you visited me, I was in prison and you came to me. Truly, I say to you, as you did it to one of the least of these my brethren, you did it for me.'" (Mt 25:31, 34-36, 40)**

Christ even showed us by example that serving others is necessary to following him:

> **"If I then, your Lord and Teacher, have washed your feet, you also ought to wash one another's feet. For I have given you an example, that you also should do as I have done to you...If you know these things, blessed are you if you do them. (Jn 13:14-16, 17)**

In this chapter, we will see that serving others is something we do both individually and as a society. Let's first explore how we can each help serve others.

*Cain Kills Abel* by Novelli.
God, and God alone, decides when a human life will begin or end.

## DEFENDING HUMAN LIFE

***Every human being deserves lifelong protection and support—from conception to natural death.***

The most fundamental attack on the dignity of the human person is the denial of the right to live. Because God is the author of life, every human person has a special connection and relationship to his or her Creator. As a result, God, and God alone, decides when a human life will begin or end. As Catholics we are called to defend human life from dangers that threaten it.

You know the Fifth Commandment—"You shall not kill" (Ex 20:13). Obviously murder is a serious offense against human life. These specific violations of the Fifth Commandment are important to understand:

**Abortion**, which is the killing of a human being before he or she is born, is the paramount right-to-life issue. There is never moral justification for directly or intentionally ending the life of an unborn baby, the most vulnerable and innocent of human beings. Using drugs in order to end a pregnancy early is the taking of human life just as surely as is a surgical abortion. Harming or destroying a human embryo for the sake of helping others (for example, to create new medicines) likewise kills a human life and offends human dignity. In cases where the mother's physical life is in immediate danger and treatment cannot be postponed, every effort must be made to avoid harming the child while treating her.

> **Since the first century the Church has affirmed the moral evil of every procured abortion. This teaching has not changed and remains unchangeable. Direct abortion, that is to say, abortion willed either as an end or a means, is gravely contrary to the moral law. (CCC 2271)**

**Euthanasia, suicide, and assisted suicide** are sins against the Fifth Commandment at the other end of life. Euthanasia is an action or omission that directly causes the death of a handicapped, sick, or dying person. Some people try to justify such acts by calling them "mercy killing" because they aim to end suffering. However, euthanasia arises from a devaluing of human life—a belief that certain lives are not worth living because they involve conditions that are difficult, painful, or embarrassing.

> **Intentional euthanasia, whatever its forms or motives, is murder. It is gravely contrary to the dignity of the human person and to the respect due to the living God, his Creator. (CCC 2324)**

Suffering has profound meaning in Christian life. The Cross of Christ, with all its pain and humiliation, is the symbol of our redemption. Everyone is called to "take up his cross" (Mt 16:24), in order to share the life of the Son of God. As St. Paul wrote:

> **We are children of God, and if children, then heirs, heirs of God and fellow heirs with Christ, provided we suffer with him in order that we may also be glorified with him. (Rom 8:16-17)**

The Fifth Commandment extends also to respect for our own lives and bodies. **Suicide**, the willful taking of one's own life, violates this Commandment. God alone is the master of life, and we are forbidden to take human life, even our own. Suicide is a denial of God's sovereignty, his plan, and his ability to bring good out of suffering. It also brings lasting harm to those left behind.

**The Church does recognize, however, that there may be circumstances that reduce the culpability of suicide. For example, a person who had psychological problems might not have much responsibility for his or her suicide. "The Church prays for persons who have taken their own lives." (CCC 2283)**

It is a grave offense to help another person commit suicide. Thus, *assisted suicide*, whether or not it is committed by a healthcare professional, is also forbidden by the Fifth Commandment.

The **death penalty** can be used as a means to protect society. However, the Church holds that the death penalty is rarely if ever necessary in modern societies.

**Assuming that the guilty party's identity and responsibility have been fully determined, the traditional teaching of the Church does not exclude recourse to the death penalty, if this is the only possible way of effectively defending human lives against the unjust aggressor...**

**Today, in fact, as a consequence of the possibilities which the state has for effectively preventing crime, by rendering one who has committed an offense incapable of doing harm —without definitely taking away from him the possibility of redeeming himself—the cases in which the execution of the offender is an absolute necessity "are very rare, if not practically non-existent." (CCC 2267)**

## SERVICE FOR THE RIGHT TO LIFE

There are many ways you can use the gifts of the Holy Spirit in support of the right to life. Here are a few examples:

- Volunteer or help raise funds for a pregnancy-counseling center that does not refer clients for abortions.
- Visit the sick and elderly in their homes, hospitals, or retirement centers, especially those who have few loved ones to visit them. Your love and friendship can help people who are suffering and aging avoid loneliness and despair.

*St. Thomas Aquinas* by Crivelli.
The first theologians of the "just war doctrine" were St. Augustine and St. Thomas Aquinas. The spirit behind the Church's teachings on "just war" is that the objective is self-defense and not simply to destroy or punish the enemy.

**War and self-defense** are areas where the direct killing of another person, although regrettable, may be justifiable. War should be a last resort to resolve conflicts. When it is necessary, acts of war should be limited. They should be the least violent means possible of ending the conflict. They must never intentionally target noncombatants.

To kill in self-defense requires the existence of a serious and immediate threat to life. In such a situation, one may use only the minimum level of force necessary—non-lethal, if at all possible—to repel the attacker.

## SERVING THE NEEDIEST

***Following the example of Christ, we offer special love and care for the neediest among us.***

There can be no doubt that Christ showed a special love for people who were poor, oppressed, and outcast. He touched those who were considered "unclean" and marginalized by society. He taught his disciples to favor the disadvantaged:

**"When you give a feast, invite the poor, the maimed, the lame, the blind." (Lk 14:13)**

In fact, he defined his earthly life as a mission to the poor:

> **"The Spirit of the Lord is upon me, because he has anointed me to preach good news to the poor. He has sent me to proclaim release to the captives and recovering of sight to the blind, to set at liberty those who are oppressed." (Lk 4:18)**

Christ addressed the poor directly and called them "blessed":

> **"Blessed are you poor, for yours is the kingdom of God. Blessed are you that hunger now, for you shall be satisfied." (Lk 6:20-21)**

The other side of this blessing, moreover, is a warning for the rich and those whose bellies are full (Lk 6:24-25). Christ told one wealthy man:

> **"If you would be perfect, go, sell what you possess and give to the poor, and you will have treasure in heaven; and come, follow me." (Mt 19:21)**

The Lord did not condemn wealth in itself. He condemned hoarding wealth to the neglect of the poor. He had some friends who were wealthy and generous, and he showed them great love:

- Zacchaeus was a tax collector who gave half of his possessions to the poor (Lk 19:8).
- Joanna and Susanna helped fund Christ's earthly ministry (Lk 8:3).
- Nicodemus, a disciple of Christ, was a ruler and a man of means (Jn 3:1, 19:39).

When Christ came into the world, he was born into poverty. Even though he was God, he humbled himself, identifying with the poor and lowly. Throughout his earthly ministry he showed a special love and care for the poor.

In his Parable of the Sheep and the Goats, which is about the Final Judgment, Christ admonished his followers to see the poor and needy of the world as himself:

> **"'Lord, when did we see you hungry and feed you, or thirsty and give you drink? And when did we see you a stranger and welcome you, or naked and clothe you? And when did we see you sick or in prison and visit you?'**
>
> **"And the King will answer them, 'Truly, I say to you, as you did it to one of the least of these my brethren, you did it to me.'" (Mt 25:37-40)**

The "goats" who did not help the poor were banished to everlasting fire. By denying such help to the needy, they denied Christ himself.

We are called to follow the example of Christ. This is not an option for a select few but a requirement of all disciples.

Christ's Parable of the Rich Man and Lazarus (Lk 16:19-31) demonstrates the proper attitude towards the poor. The rich man wore nice clothes and ate good food. Meanwhile Lazarus was outside the rich man's gate. He would have been satisfied with the rich man's scraps. When both men died, the angels brought Lazarus to the company of Abraham. The rich man was sent to a place of torment and suffering. The rich man was able to see Lazarus and begged him for some comfort. Abraham answered the rich man, saying:

> **"Son, remember that you in your lifetime received your good things, and Lazarus in like manner evil things; but now he is comforted here, and you are in anguish." (Lk 16:25)**

*Parable of the Rich Man and Lazarus*, codex illumination. Top panel: Lazarus at the rich man's door. Middle panel: Lazarus's soul is carried to Paradise by two angels, and Lazarus is in Abraham's bosom. Bottom panel: The rich man's soul is carried off by two devils to hell, and he cries out to Abraham.

We all have a Lazarus at our doorstep.

## THE WORKS OF MERCY

The Church has traditionally identified some forms of service to be of particular importance. They are called the "Works of Mercy." There are seven Corporal Works of Mercy and seven Spiritual Works of Mercy that the Church recommends to the faithful.

> The *works of mercy* are charitable actions by which we come to the aid of our neighbor in his spiritual and bodily necessities...Among all these, giving alms to the poor is one of the chief witnesses to fraternal charity: it is also a work of justice pleasing to God. (CCC 2447)

**The Corporal Works of Mercy** are acts of loving service by which we help our neighbors with their material and physical needs.

- ***Feed the hungry.*** Share part of your lunch with someone who does not have one or help with an organized meal service for the poor.
- ***Shelter the homeless.*** Some organizations use volunteer labor to build simple homes for people with little money. Even people who are not handy can help by fetching supplies and tools for the other volunteers.
- ***Clothe the naked.*** Help sort and hang clothing at a thrift store.
- ***Comfort the sick.*** Visit an elderly relative in a retirement home. Many people there are lonely as well as infirm.
- ***Visit the imprisoned.*** Write a letter to someone who is in prison.
- ***Bury the dead.*** Attend funeral Masses and burial services of family, friends, and acquaintances to pray for the soul of the deceased.
- ***Give alms to the poor.*** Contribute to your parish collection and to other worthy charities.

**The Spiritual Works of Mercy** help our neighbors with their emotional and spiritual needs.

- ***Instruct the ignorant.*** Study your Catholic faith and help others understand it better.
- ***Admonish the sinner.*** Encourage your friends to turn away from sin and to live in virtue. Correct their bad behavior with gentleness and love.
- ***Counsel the doubtful.*** Help others when they face challenges to their Catholic faith.
- ***Comfort the sorrowful.*** Talk with family, friends, and neighbors who are grieving or going through some hardship.
- ***Forgive all injuries.*** Do not hold grudges. Be kind to and pray for people who have hurt you.
- ***Bear wrongs patiently.*** Work to be less critical and more understanding of people who do not treat you well or seem inconsiderate.
- ***Pray for the living and the dead.*** Offer your prayers for the benefit of people on earth as well as the Holy Souls in purgatory.

Christ made clear the danger of being indifferent to the difficulties of the plight of the poor. We all have an obligation to look after the needs of our brothers and sisters. We all have a Lazarus at our doorstep.

## SERVICE FOR THE POOR AND NEEDY

There are many ways you can use the gifts of the Holy Spirit in support of the poor and needy. Here are a few examples:

- Encourage your parish youth group to take on some charitable projects, and help organize them. Perhaps your group can help an outreach to the homeless, work at a local soup kitchen, or help families with yard work.
- Work through your library or youth center to help a child or young adult with homework skills.
- Contribute part of your income to charity. When you earn money or receive it as a gift, consider giving ten percent of it away. You can research charities that help the needy or give your donation in your parish offering or poor box.
- Look for opportunities to help people in need. There may be someone in your neighborhood who could use some help. Sometimes it is hard to see the poor and needy right in front of us! Think and pray about what you can do for others.

We are called to take care of the earth and use its resources for the good of society.

## STEWARDSHIP OF GOD'S CREATION

***God gave us the world and its resources, but we must care for it so that everyone benefits.***

> **The climate is a common good, belonging to all and meant for all. At the global level, it is a complex system linked to many of the essential conditions for human life.** (Pope Francis, *Laudato Si'*)

When God gave Adam dominion over the earth, he delegated responsibility not simply for the use of creation but for its care and custody as well. Adam was called to exercise stewardship over all earthly goods. God made them to serve him and all future generations.

Thus, to abuse the earth's resources—to overuse them, mishandle them, or deplete them without need—is really to steal them from other people.

> **God created man in his own image, in the image of God he created him; male and female he created them. And God blessed them, and God said to them, "Be fruitful and multiply, and fill the earth and subdue it; and have dominion over the fish of the sea and over the birds of the air and over every living thing that moves upon the earth." (Gn 1:27-28)**

The Church bases her teaching on God's instruction to Adam in Genesis. He received authority to plan for the wise use of all the resources that he was given.

Creation is a gift from the Father. When God created the heavens and the earth, he said that it was good. Animals, plants, and natural resources are gifts that "speak" of the glory of God. The high point of creation, however, is the human being. The Father placed us as stewards over the created world. We are called to take care of the earth and use its resources for the good of society.

We are called to care for the earth, subdue it, and use it for the benefit of others. This means that the fruits of creation are to be used for good. The plants, animals and various resources should be cherished and protected from undue harm. We are free to make use of them, but we must also take care of them.

> **The earth is the LORD's and the fulness thereof,**
> **the world and those who dwell therein;**

**for he has founded it upon the seas,
and established it upon the rivers. (Ps 24:1-2)**

The things of the earth should not be treated in a way that robs future generations of their use. Rather, we must respect creation and make efficient use of it, always remembering that creation is a gift given to us by the Creator.

> **Our insistence that each human being is an image of God should not make us overlook the fact that each creature has its own purpose. None is superfluous. The entire material universe speaks of God's love, his boundless affection for us. Soil, water, mountains: everything is, as it were, a caress of God. (Pope Francis, *Laudato Si'*)**

## SERVICE FOR GOOD STEWARDSHIP OF THE EARTH

There are many ways you can use the gifts of the Holy Spirit in support of good stewardship. Here are a few examples:

- Use, but do not waste, material goods. If there are "leftovers" from last night's dinner, do not turn your nose up at them. Think of the many people who have little or nothing to eat. If you have too many clothes in your closet, offer some to people who can use them or donate them to a charitable organization.
- Use, but do not waste, resources. Limit the time you spend in the shower, turn off lights and appliances when they are not in use, and make sure your doors and refrigerator are closed. Wasted energy adds up across a household, neighborhood, city, state, and nation.
- Reuse, or perhaps recycle, material goods. Send whatever has outlived its usefulness to a recycling program. Learn what services are available in your area, and encourage your family, friends, neighbors, and local businesses to do the same.
- Avoid littering. Volunteer to clean up city parks and highway roadsides. When you go camping or hiking, make sure you do nothing to harm the environment you are enjoying.

## USING CREATED THINGS WISELY WITH THE GIFT OF KNOWLEDGE

> **God saw everything that he had made, and behold, it was very good. (Gn 1:31)**

Knowledge enables us to discover the divine plan contained in God's creation, in order to accomplish our mission on earth, and following the path that we should follow in our journey—to give glory to God and to reach heaven.

> **There is something holy, something divine, hidden in the most ordinary situations and it is up to each of you to discover it. (St. Josemaria Escriva, *Passionately Loving the World*)**

The knowledge that comes from the Holy Spirit, however, is not limited to human knowledge; it is a special gift, which leads us to grasp, through creation, the greatness and love of God and his profound relationship with every creature.

We discover how everything speaks to us about God and His love. We manage to accept man and woman as the summit of creation, as the fulfillment of a plan of love that is impressed in each one of us and that allows us to recognize one another as brothers and sisters.

God gives us this gift of knowledge in order to understand better that creation is a most beautiful gift of God. He has done many good things for the thing that is most good: the human person.

All this is a source of serenity and peace and makes the Christian a joyful witness of God. It brings a profound sense of gratitude! It is the sensation we experience when we admire a work of art or any marvel whatsoever that is borne of the genius and creativity of man.

Pope Francis taught,

> **Custody of creation is precisely custody of God's gift and it is saying to God: "Thank you, I am the guardian of creation so as to make it progress, never to destroy your gift." God forgives always, we men forgive sometimes, but creation never forgives and if you don't care for it, it will destroy you. (Pope Francis, *General Audience*, May 21, 2014)**

This gift allows us to live a life of detachment: understanding the role of created things and using them as God intended. Then we will be able to love with the love of God.

Creation is a gift, it is the marvelous gift that God has given us, so that we will take care of it and harness it for the benefit of all, always with great respect and gratitude.

# CHARITY AND JUSTICE

***You should work not only in direct service but also for social and structural change.***

We have so far discussed the importance of each one of us serving those in need. We call this service to others "charity." Charity involves direct service to persons in need. It seeks to help meet their short-term requirements for living in human dignity. Giving shelter to a person who is homeless, giving companionship to a person who is in prison, giving groceries to a person who is hungry, giving clothing to a person who is cold, and giving health care to a person who is ill are examples of acts of charity.

It is no coincidence that the word *charity* is associated with *love*; in Scripture they are synonymous. Acts of charity are acts that show love of neighbor.

Justice, on the other hand, involves work or advocacy for changing the culture, institutions, and laws that make and continue social problems. Justice focuses on long-term solutions by trying to remove the root causes of poverty, violence, and other social problems. Organizing campaigns to improve public policy, changing practices in an organization or workplace to align with human dignity, and petitioning political leaders to take action to correct unjust laws are examples of work for justice.

*Youth for a United World*, the youth sector of the Focolare Movement, provide aid locally and on a global level to the homeless, the elderly, prisoners and immigrants, victims of war and natural disasters. Often, it is only when people band together to advocate for positive change that social progress is made.

> **Justice is the moral virtue that consists in the constant and firm will to give one's due to God and neighbor. (CCC 1807)**

Charitable service is a private, individual act, sometimes carried out within a larger group. The charitable work of parish youth groups and organizations like the St. Vincent de Paul Society or the Knights of Columbus are examples of this. Efforts for social change, however, usually require the support of a large number of people. Often, it is only when people band together to advocate for positive change that social progress is made.

*Here are some examples of charity and justice:*

## RIGHT TO LIFE

**Charity:** Making baby blankets and donating them to the local crisis pregnancy center.

**Justice:** Going to your state capital and lobbying your representatives to pass a law that protects the unborn from abortion.

## SERVING THE NEEDIEST

**Charity:** Volunteering at your local soup kitchen.

**Justice:** Encourage local restaurants to donate their leftover food to homeless shelters, food pantries, and soup kitchens.

## STEWARDSHIP OF GOD'S CREATION

**Charity:** Organizing some friends to pick up litter in your neighborhood.

**Justice:** Proposing to your local city council the construction of a new park, and working to gain support for the project in your community.

*The virtue of justice must always be at the service of charity*, which helps to keep all of the virtues centered on the love and mercy of God. For centuries the Catholic Church has thought through carefully the principles behind a just society. The teachings that flow out of that careful reflection are usually called "Catholic social teaching," which we will explore in the next section.

## CATHOLIC SOCIAL TEACHING

***You were made to live in society, and you have a part to play in serving the common good.***

**The human person needs to live in society. Society is not for him an extraneous addition but a requirement of his nature. (CCC 1879)**

Because human beings are social by nature, we need to find ways of living together: tolerating differences, ensuring justice and fairness, and keeping order. We need moral principles to guide our societies. God revealed his moral law and established his Church to guide us in knowing and keeping this law. The principles of the law that governs human society are referred to as **Catholic social teaching**.

**The Church's social teaching comprises a body of doctrine, which is articulated as the Church interprets events in the course of history, with the assistance of the Holy Spirit, in the light of the whole of what has been revealed by Jesus Christ. (CCC 2422)**

Catholic social teaching, if observed by everyone, would bring the world much closer to resembling the Kingdom of God. It takes time to change the world, however. It is up to individuals like you—faith-filled disciples of Christ committed to living their faith—to make it happen.

**"Whoever would be great among you must be your servant, and whoever would be first among you must be your slave; even as the Son of man came not to be served but to serve." (Mt 20:26-28)**

The foundation of Catholic social teaching is Christ's New Commandment of Love:

**"A new commandment I give to you, that you love one another; even as I have loved you." (Jn 13:34)**

The Apostles and early Christians understood this command as the foundation of the Good News. In their New Testament letters, Sts. John, Peter, and Paul emphasized that loving one's neighbor is the mark of a disciple of Christ.

**Concerning love of the brethren you have no need to have any one write to you, for you yourselves have been taught by God to love one another. (1 Thes 4:9)**

*Christ and the Rich Young Ruler* by Hofmann. When we show God's love by working for Catholic social principles, we become the "light of the world" and attract others to Christ.

Everything in Catholic social doctrine is an application of the principle of neighborly love. This love is not simple affection or "getting along." It is the self-sacrificing love that Christ demonstrated for all people, especially by dying on the Cross. Charity requires the gift of our very selves.

The Blessed Trinity is our model for love. The Father, Son, and Holy Spirit exist in perfect communion with one another. We as humans are incapable of perfect communion, but we are created to grow in communion and friendship with God and with the other members of the Body of Christ. In this way we share in the joys and sufferings of others.

**God has so composed the body, giving the greater honor to the inferior part, that there may be no discord in the body, but that the members may have the same care for one another. If one member suffers, all suffer together; if one member is honored, all rejoice together. Now you are the body of Christ and individually members of it. (1 Cor 12:24-27)**

The Holy Spirit unites the members of the Church in love. The Church is made up of people of diverse ethnicities, languages, occupations, educational backgrounds, and professions, and yet we are all intimately united in faith through the Holy Spirit.

We have already discussed some of the principles of Catholic social teaching, including the dignity of all human persons, the right to life, the importance of caring for the poor, and stewardship of God's creation. Here are some other important principles of Catholic social teaching:

***Family, community, and participation.*** Family is the fundamental unit of society. When families break down, the larger community suffers. In the family we normally have our first experience of community and our first instruction in the social virtues, which contribute to the improvement of society. The family is based on marriage, and therefore good, strong, faithful marriages are important to the stability of both family and society.

***The dignity of human work.*** Work is essential for making a living. More importantly it is a way of participating in God's creation and contributing to the good of society. The basic rights of workers must always be respected.

***Solidarity among all people.*** The right to human dignity knows no borders. We have a responsibility to serve our brothers and sisters of all races, nations, languages, faiths, and cultures (Gn 4:9). We must work for human rights, justice, and peace throughout the world.

***Human Freedom.*** As images of God, human persons have the freedom to use their intellects and choose the actions they believe are best for themselves and others. Although the Catholic Church lays out principles for a just society, people have the freedom to determine the best practical ways to implement those principles in their various cultures and societies.

***Universal destination of goods.*** God created the earth and its goods to benefit every human person. They should be distributed in such a way that meets the basic needs of all, including sufficient food, water, shelter, clothing, security, and opportunity.

In Confirmation the Holy Spirit will strengthen us to be disciples who draw others into the Body of Christ. When we share God's love through acts of charity, we are living images of God in the world. When we show God's love by working for Catholic social principles, we become the "light of the world" and attract others to Christ. Working for justice is an important part of our mission of evangelization.

## LIVING OUR LIVES AS TRUE CHRISTIANS

Let love be genuine; hate what is evil, hold fast to what is good. Love one another with brotherly affection; outdo one another in showing honor. Never flag in zeal, be aglow with the Spirit, and serve the Lord. Rejoice in your hope, be patient in tribulation, be constant in prayer. Contribute to the needs of the saints, practice hospitality.

Bless those who persecute you; bless and do not curse them. Rejoice with those who rejoice, weep with those who weep. Live in harmony with one another; do not be haughty, but associate with the lowly; never be conceited. Repay no one evil for evil, but take thought for what is noble in the sight of all. If possible, so far as it depends upon you, live peaceably with all. Beloved, never avenge yourselves, but leave it to the wrath of God; for it is written, "Vengeance is mine, I will repay, says the Lord." No, "if your enemy is hungry, feed him; if he is thirsty, give him drink; for by so doing you will heap burning coals upon his head." Do not be overcome by evil, but overcome evil with good.

Let every person be subject to the governing authorities. For there is no authority except from God, and those that exist have been instituted by God. Therefore he who resists the authorities resists what God has appointed, and those who resist will incur judgment. For rulers are not terrors to good conduct, but to bad. Would you have no fear of him who is in authority? Then do what is good, and you will receive his approval, for he is God's servant for your good. But if you do wrong, be afraid, for he does not bear the sword in vain; he is the servant of God to execute his wrath on the wrongdoer. Therefore one must be subject, not only to avoid God's wrath but also for the sake of conscience. For the same reason you also pay taxes, for the authorities are ministers of God, attending to this very thing. Pay all of them their dues, taxes to whom taxes are due, revenue to whom revenue is due, respect to whom respect is due, honor to whom honor is due. (Rom 12:9-13:7)

## WHAT CAN YOU DO?

### *Can one person, especially a newly confirmed person, really make a difference?*

> **Let him ask his own heart; if he loves his brother, the Spirit of God abides in him. (St. Augustine, *Treatise on the Epistle of St. John*, VI, 10)**

It does not take a lot of thought to realize that building up the Kingdom of God on earth is hard work. The Catholic Church has been doing it ever since Christ ascended into heaven. Sometimes it seems that the world is no closer to living Christ's teachings now than it was then. It might even appear that it has all gotten worse.

The problems of the world are so vast. Poverty is widespread in some parts of the world, and even exists in developed nations. There are always wars, violence, abuse, natural disasters, a lack of education, political and religious oppression, and so many other troubles. Where can we begin? And with problems so large, how much can it matter if you—one person—attempt to do anything about it?

In a modern parable, a man walks along a beach as the tide brings in thousands of starfish. When the tide begins to go out again, many of the starfish are left on the shore to dry up and die. As this man continues to walk, every time he comes across a starfish, he picks it up and throws it back into the ocean so that it can survive.

A woman walking the other way crosses his path. Noticing what he is doing, she asks him, "Why do you bother? There are thousands of starfish here. You cannot possibly save them all. What difference does it make?"

The man smiles, picks up another starfish, and just before throwing it back in the water replies, "It matters to this one."

You will not likely be able to solve all the world's problems. You certainly cannot solve them by yourself. But you can make a difference by using the gifts of the Holy Spirit that you will receive in Confirmation. You can cooperate with God's grace to do acts of charity and work for justice.

Christ taught his disciples, "The poor you always have with you" (Jn 12:8). He did not mean to say that since the problem of poverty would never go away, we should not try to help people. He had something else in mind, something God had commanded his people for a long time:

> **You shall give to [the poor man] freely, and your heart shall not be grudging when you give to him; because for this the LORD your God will bless you in all your work and in all that you undertake. For the poor will never cease out of the land. (Dt 15:10-11)**

People who are poor give us opportunities to love and serve, to be generous, and to sacrifice. Christ assures us that we will be richly blessed for everything we do "to one of the least of these" (Mt 25:40).

### FIND YOUR OWN CALCUTTA

In 1950, St. Teresa of Calcutta, known affectionately as Mother Teresa, founded the Missionaries of Charity and devoted herself to serving the poorest of the poor on the streets of Calcutta, India. She and her sisters took in and cared for the sick and elderly who had been abandoned.

A woman once wrote to Mother Teresa saying that she wished she could join in her work in India. The humble servant of the poor sent this reply:

> **Stay where you are. Find your own Calcutta. Find the sick, the suffering, and the lonely right there where you are—in your own homes and in your own families, in your workplaces and in your schools. You can find Calcutta all over the world, if you have the eyes to see. Everywhere, wherever you go, you find people who are unwanted, unloved, uncared for, just rejected by society—completely forgotten, completely left alone.**

There is missionary territory right where you are, wherever you are. The mission is all around you. All you have to do is love and serve wherever you are.

## CONCLUSION

***The gifts that you will be given in Confirmation will help you love charity and justice.***

God created every person in his own image and likeness. In so doing he bestowed on each of us an inherent dignity that can never be taken away. Because this dignity resides in our fellow human beings, we are called to serve others when they are in need. We do this by defending the right to life, caring for the poor, being good stewards of God's creation, and other acts of charity.

The greatest threat to justice in our time is the attack on the dignity of human life, especially of the unborn and the elderly. As a confirmed Catholic, you will need to stand against these attacks. This can be done by helping women in crisis pregnancies, volunteering at a home for the elderly, working to pass laws that protect life, and a whole host of other activities.

As Catholics, we are also called to serve all the poor, especially through acts of mercy. We can help those who are materially poor by helping at a soup kitchen, or organizing a clothing drive at our school. We can help those who are spiritually poor by sharing with them our faith in Jesus and comforting those who have experienced suffering or loss.

We are also responsible for the world God has given us. This entails being good stewards of the earth, which means we take care of it and all those who inhabit it. We can help to plant trees in our yard or at a local park, or we could make sure we don't waste food, either when we are at home or out to eat. As stewards, we can use creation for the good of humankind, but always while respecting the fact that everything created is from God.

And, our help for those around us is not limited to individual acts of charity. We are also called to make our world a more just place to live. This is done by applying Catholic social teaching to our societies, working to conform our human laws to the just laws of God.

Each one of us can make a difference toward solving the world's social problems and building God's kingdom on earth. You can do your part to love and serve as Christ did in your home, school, and community.

*St. Lawrence Distributing Alms* by Fra Angelico.
Each one of us can make a difference toward solving the world's social problems and building God's kingdom on earth.

## POINTS TO REMEMBER

1. Every person has an inherent dignity that comes from being made in the image and likeness of God.
2. As disciples of Christ, we are called to serve those around us, both in charity and justice.
3. The principles of the law that properly govern human society are called "Catholic social teaching."
4. Our goal is to live as true Christians in our minds and in our actions.

# WITNESS OF CHRIST

## ST. GIANNA BERETTA MOLLA

All Christians are called to holiness and to living out the Gospel in our daily lives. Ultimately, discipleship brings sacrifice, and in hard times we put our own desires aside for the good of others. St. Gianna Beretta Molla was a modern-day saint who exemplified this in her life.

Gianna was born in Italy in 1922 as the tenth child of thirteen siblings. From a young age Gianna was devoted to the Catholic faith and trusted in the power of prayer. This trust in God guided and helped her throughout her life. When Gianna reached adulthood, she devoted time to serving young people and was an active member of groups that assisted the poor. Gianna even wanted to go to Brazil to help serve the poor with her brother, who was a missionary. However, because of ill health, she was unable to go.

Gianna earned degrees in medicine and surgery and eventually opened her own medical clinic, specializing in caring for children. In her clinic she served and took care of the needs of mothers, babies, the elderly, and the poor. She made sure that she cared for those who were "least" in the eyes of the world. Even with all of her work, she still loved to spend time outdoors, especially skiing and mountain climbing.

Eventually, Gianna discerned a call to the vocation of marriage, and God put a good man in her life named Pietro. They married, and within a few years Gianna gave birth to three children.

Gianna's next pregnancy would be different. Toward the end of her second month, she started to feel pain. The source of the pain was a fibroma on her uterus. Gianna needed to have the tumor removed for her health, and her doctors gave her three choices: have an abortion, have a hysterectomy, or risk complications by removing only the fibroma. The abortion or hysterectomy would have killed her child. The only way for the child to live was for the fibroma to be removed, but Gianna was told she might suffer serious complications from the surgery.

Gianna told the surgeon to save the life of the child that she was carrying. If only one of them was to live, Gianna wanted it to be her child. She commanded that the child's life be saved at all costs. She said, "If you must choose between me and the baby, no hesitation; choose—and I demand it—the baby. Save her!" This is one example of her living the gift of piety and trusting in God completely. The child's life was saved; a little girl was born on April 21. After enduring terrible pain, Gianna died seven days later of the complications. As she suffered she kept repeating, "Jesus, I love you. Jesus, I love you." She was 39 years old when she gave up her own life for her daughter.

In a culture that disregards human life and mocks self-sacrifice, we can look to Gianna Beretta Molla as a model and a powerful intercessor in heaven. She gave up her life so that her child could live. Gianna's trust in God shines brightly in a world darkened by sin and disbelief.

## VOCABULARY

### ABORTION
The killing of a human being before he or she is born.

### ASSISTED SUICIDE
Any action or omission of action that assists another person in bringing about his or her own death. Responsibility may be aggravated by the scandal given because every human being must be absolutely respected and protected in his or her integrity. It is forbidden by the Fifth Commandment.

### CATHOLIC SOCIAL TEACHING
The principles of the law that govern human society that God has revealed and the Church teaches.

### DIGNITY OF THE HUMAN PERSON
The quality of being worthy or honorable; worthiness, nobleness, excellence. Every human person, by reason of his or her creation in the image and likeness of God, has intrinsic dignity. Certain characteristics that are distinctive in human beings—such as work and freedom—are endowed by God with a special dignity.

### EUTHANASIA
An action or omission that causes the death of a handicapped, sick, or dying person.

### SUICIDE
The act of taking one's own life; self-murder. This is forbidden by the Fifth Commandment.

## STUDY QUESTIONS

1. Why do Catholic youth groups and Confirmation preparation courses emphasize service?
2. Why does every human person have innate dignity?
3. Why is the right to life fundamental to human dignity?
4. What are some of the offenses against the right to life?
5. What does the Parable of the Sheep and the Goats reveal about our relationship with people who are in need?
6. Why do we have a responsibility to be good stewards of creation?
7. What are *charity* and *justice*?
8. What is the foundation of all Catholic social teaching?
9. Who unites the members of the Church in love?
10. What is the "universal destination of goods"?

## PRACTICAL EXERCISES

1. Choose a saint, preferably the saint you chose to honor in your Confirmation name. How did this saint serve the needs of the poor or other disadvantaged persons? Where are people in need in your everyday life (family, school, work, and so on)? How can this saint inspire you to serve them?

2. As a class, choose a local charity to support through your sacrificial actions. Perhaps there is a soup kitchen nearby at which you can volunteer. Or perhaps you could organize a food drive for a local food pantry.

# Sealed in the Spirit

***As a disciple endowed with the gifts of the Spirit, be mindful of the poor and needy.***

> **If you pour yourself out for the hungry
> and satisfy the desire of the afflicted,
> then shall your light rise in the darkness
> and your gloom be as the noonday. (Is 58:10)**

When Christ traveled through the city of Jericho, a tax collector named Zacchaeus desperately wanted to meet him. Zacchaeus was short, so he ran ahead of the crowds and climbed a tree to get a better view of Jesus. As Christ was passing by, he saw the man in the tree and said to him, "Zacchaeus, make haste and come down; for I must stay at your house today" (Lk 19:5). The people were shocked at Christ's words. Why was he seeking this person?

When Jesus arrived at the house, Zacchaeus repented of his sins and vowed to make restitution to anyone that he had cheated. And Christ said to him:

> **"Today salvation has come to this house, since he also is a son of Abraham. For the Son of man came to seek and to save the lost." (Lk 19:9-10)**

There are many people like Zacchaeus in the world—outcasts who are despised by everyone around them. Some of these people, through their sins, have removed themselves from the mainstream of society. Their actions pushed others away. They may have made themselves lonely outsiders, yet they need our love.

Other people may be considered outcasts through no fault of their own. They might be a part of an ethnic minority or speak a different language. They might have a disability or be shy. They might be socially awkward or poor. They need our love, too.

Christ sought out people who were considered outcasts during his earthly ministry. He reached out to sinners and touched the lepers and the sick. He found people who needed love and healing and offered it to them. We who call ourselves his disciples should perform these same actions. We must bring the Good News to the outcast.

Make it a point to reach out to the lonely and rejected around you. Befriend them. Show them Christian love. Other people might tease or reject you for trying to be a friend to the outcast. Remember that there were many who criticized Christ for the same reasons. Try to live and love like Christ anyway.

*Zacchaeus in the Sycamore Awaiting the Passage of Jesus* by Tissot.
We must bring the Good News to the outcast.

# You and Your Parents

***Your mother and father have experience with the spirit of service.***

Most parents have personal experience with some of the issues in this chapter: crisis pregnancies, helping the poor, charitable giving, and serving others. Talk with your parents about what they have learned about charitable service and social justice in their personal experience.

Here are some questions to start your discussion:

1. What kinds of acts of charity have you done? How have your experiences drawn you closer to Christ?
2. How would you explain the *right to life* to someone who is "pro-choice"? What have you done to help women who face crisis pregnancies or young mothers who need help with their children? What were your experiences, and how have they drawn you closer to Christ?
3. What is your experience with work? Do you see your work as a share in doing God's work? Have you ever had to campaign or advocate for better wages or working conditions, either for yourself or for others? Have you ever had an impact on the faith of a coworker?
4. How have you been involved in social justice in your community? Have you ever signed petitions, worked with an advocacy group, or contacted a corporation for a change in policy as a matter of justice? How do social issues affect your vote for government officials?

*Washing of the Feet* by Agostino.
Talk with your parents about what they have learned about charitable service and social justice in their personal experience.

# You and Your Sponsor

***We are all consumers, but consumerism and materialism inspire greed and selfishness.***

Consumerism is a culture or mentality that supports the excessive consumption of goods. It is a pressing spiritual problem in developed nations. Consumerism values wealth, material possessions, and earthly pleasures as the goal of all human effort.

The virtue of *temperance* helps us overcome consumerism. Temperance is the moderate use of goods. It takes our focus off the accumulation of excessive goods for our own enjoyment. It helps us place more importance on sharing them or making them available to people who can not meet their basic needs.

Most entertainment media and commercial advertising tends to promote or glorify consumerism. It is easy for people who grow up in the developed world to be attracted to this. Pope Francis issued this challenge to young Catholics:

> **Confront the daily vanity, that poison of emptiness which creeps into our society based on profit and possession and on consumerism which deceives young people (Pope Francis, *Angelus*, August 5, 2013).**

Talk with your sponsor about consumerism. Does he or she have any insights on this?

These questions might help you begin your discussion:

1. How have you practiced the ideals that are in this teaching of the *Catechism*?

   **Goods of production—material or immaterial—such as land, factories, practical or artistic skills, oblige their possessors to employ them in ways that will benefit the greatest number. Those who hold goods for use and consumption should use them with moderation, reserving the better part for guests, for the sick and the poor. (CCC 2405)**

2. What do you think Pope Francis meant when he called modern society a "culture of waste"? How does a "culture of waste" relate to consumerism?

   **It is no longer man who commands, but money, cash commands. And God our Father gave us the task of protecting the earth—not for money, but for ourselves: for men and women. We have this task! Nevertheless men and women are sacrificed to the idols of profit and consumption: it is the "culture of waste." If a computer breaks it is a tragedy, but poverty, the needs and dramas of so many people end up being considered normal. (Pope Francis, *General Audience*, June 5, 2013)**

3. In what ways are you a responsible consumer, and how can you grow in the virtue of temperance?

*Parable of the Man Who Hoards* by Tissot.
Talk with your sponsor about consumerism.

## INTRODUCTION

***You are part of God's great plan.***

When you began this book, you read about the work of God in this world. You learned how he reveals himself to mankind. You read about the marvelous ways he has worked to save us. You met amazing people like Noah, Abraham, Moses, and David. God used them to bring his message of salvation to the world. Then of course you read about God's Son, Jesus Christ, through whom God brought about reconciliation between all of mankind and himself. You also learned about the Church, that institution which over the centuries has counted billions of people as its members, including the greatest saints the world has ever known: St. Augustine, St. Francis of Assisi, St. Joan of Arc, St. Therese of Lisieux and a multitude of others.

You might have asked yourself, *What does this have to do with me? What do I have to do with God's plan of salvation? Who am I compared to all these great men and women whom God has used to do his work?*

The answer lies in the Sacrament of Confirmation. By being confirmed, you are uniting with this great work of salvation and being counted among the many men and women who have lived their lives for the cause of Christ and his Church. You are part of the Church—*you are part of Salvation History.* And no matter where your life takes you, never doubt that God has a plan for you that is integral to his plan for the whole world. We have seen that God always works through people—ordinary, regular people—to change the world. Look at the Apostles. Before Pentecost, they were ill-educated working-class men with no theological background. By the power of the Holy Spirit, these same men became the instruments God used to convert one of history's largest pagan Empires to Christianity. Amazing! That is the power of the Holy Spirit—power that you, too, receive at Confirmation.

*St. Joan of Arc* by Ingres.

*Who am I compared to all these great men and women?* The answer lies in the Sacrament of Confirmation. God has a plan for you that is integral to his plan for the whole world.

## ENTERING A BATTLE

***Through Confirmation God provides you with a powerful secret weapon.***

Perhaps you still wonder how your life can be like that of the Apostles or the other saints. After all, you are just a student, living with your family, and living a life much like your friends'.

What you might not realize is that you, by being confirmed, are entering into a battle—a cosmic battle with eternal consequences. Imagine the battle scenes in popular movies. Aliens or super villains attack, and heroes come to the defense of the world and all who live in it. These scenes pale in comparison to the battle you are joining. "For," as St. Paul wrote, "we are not contending against flesh and blood, but against the principalities, against the powers, against the world rulers of this present darkness, against the spiritual hosts of wickedness in the heavenly places" (Eph 6:12).

At Confirmation young people traditionally are told that they are now "soldiers of Christ." This reflects the nature of life here on earth. It is a constant and lifelong battle between good and evil. By being confirmed, you choose a side in this cosmic battle—one that has eternal consequences for both you and those around you.

If we are honest with ourselves, we realize that we don't have the strength, or the courage, or the abilities for such a fight. Like St. Peter, we are often more likely to run in times of crisis than to stand with Christ. Eventually, however, St. Peter himself died for his faith. How was St. Peter transformed from one who would betray Christ to one who would die for him? It happened by the power of the Holy Spirit—the same power you receive at Confirmation.

The great secret weapon of the battle we are engaged in is the Holy Spirit. He gives us the strength, the courage, and the abilities to fight in God's army against those who oppose it. And it is through the Sacrament of Confirmation that we receive the fullness of the Holy Spirit in our lives. Confirmation transforms the soul so that it is no longer ordinary—it literally becomes *extraordinary*.

Paradoxically, the soul is called to extraordinary things in the ordinary things of life. Although the battle we are in is far greater than any that Hollywood can conceive, it is largely unseen and quiet.

*Christ Denying Satan* by Bloch.
The Holy Spirit gives us the strength, the courage, and the abilities to fight in God's army against those who oppose it.

What are some of the places in our lives where we wage this battle? Let's find out.

## BATTLES OF DAILY LIFE

***You will overcome temptation and persecution through the power of the Holy Spirit.***

The greatest struggle many young people face today is the struggle for purity. Purity is the continual choice to not allow one's heart to become entangled by sights of the human body or impure thoughts. It is not the absence of temptation but the strength to turn away from temptation. It's the will's reaction to the senses. Purity does not mean the absence of temptations of the flesh, but the choice (over and over again) to keep your heart from getting tangled up in them. Unfortunately, we live in a culture where modesty has been devalued, and so the battle for purity can be incredibly difficult. However, this battle is of the utmost importance, and the graces received in the Sacrament of Confirmation give each person the strength to win it.

Do I look at each person around me as an image of God, a brother or sister whom I want to lead to heaven? Or do I look at them as instruments for my own pleasure? We need the Holy Spirit to transform our entire way of looking at others. Then we can see others as God sees them: beloved children he wants to be united with him forever in heaven.

One practical way to fight this battle for purity is to say a prayer to the Blessed Mother when tempted against purity. Ask her to intercede for you in remaining pure. Another important practical help is to do all we can to avoid what is called "the near occasion of sin." This just means: don't put yourself in bad situations! If we are committed to avoiding sin and remaining pure, we should be committed to avoid any situation that could lead us to lose our purity.

Another battle is self-centeredness. This is something all those impacted by Original Sin must face, but it can be particularly acute today. Movies, TV shows, and even many people we know emphasize the importance of making yourself happy, even if what you're doing harms others. Christ calls each of us to put him first, others next, and then ourselves last. The two great commandments, "Love the Lord your God with all your heart, all your soul, and all your mind," and "Love your neighbor as yourself" direct our thoughts and actions away from our own passions and desires. They turn us toward serving God and those around us.

A young person spends a good deal of energy thinking about the future, and this is understandable. Whatever the future holds for you, keep in mind that true fulfillment is found not in striving to be happy, but in striving to make others happy. Practically speaking, find some service project that you can engage in on a regular basis—helping at a soup kitchen, volunteering at a pregnancy center, working at a nursing home. Keep those you help foremost in your thoughts, even when confronted with the desire to put yourself first.

*Pope Francis Prays at the Vatican Lourdes Grotto.*
One practical way to fight the battle for purity is to say a prayer to the Blessed Mother to intercede for you in remaining pure.

Still another battle is faithfulness to God and his commands. For almost 1,700 years Western culture, of which you are part, has been fundamentally Christian in nature. Now, however, many are calling our age a "post-Christian" era—one in which Christian values and beliefs should no longer impact our society. In this arena, the Sacrament of Confirmation is vital for living a truly Christian life. Although many of the commandments of God may now be mocked, we as Christians know that following them is the path to a happy, fulfilled life. It may seem that everyone around you urges you to break these commands, falsely promising happiness and contentment. You need the power of the Holy Spirit to recognize that lie and resist those temptations.

One way to remain faithful to God's commands is to read the lives of the saints regularly. This allows you to see how others were able to remain faithful to God even in the midst of great struggle.

*St. Francis Embracing Christ on the Cross* by Murillo. As Jesus sacrificed himself for the salvation of others, so we too should make sacrifices for the good of others.

## MAKING DISCIPLES

### *Your words and actions will witness to the Good News.*

As we learned in Chapter 11, Jesus said to his disciples, "Go therefore and make disciples of all nations, baptizing them in the name of the Father and of the Son and of the Holy Spirit, teaching them to observe all that I have commanded you" (Mt 28:19-20). Christ's first disciples took this command literally. They went out to all the known world seeking converts to the Christian way of life, facing rejection and even death all along the way. Yet they never wavered.

We, too, are called to make converts. We may not be called to a far-away land to convert pagans to Christ. But in everyday life we will witness to the love and life we receive from him. This witnessing can take many forms—inviting a friend to Mass, practicing the virtues, telling others how much Christ has impacted your life, or opposing evil in your community such as abortion.

We are also called to serve those most in need in this world. By being confirmed, you are given the charge to serve others. How are those around you suffering and in need? What can you do to help them? By serving the poor, the defenseless and the needy, you serve Christ himself. Putting the needs of others before your own needs is an essential aspect of the Christian life. As Jesus sacrificed himself for the salvation of others, so we, too, should make sacrifices for the good of others.

## STRIVING FOR HOLINESS

### *God gives us the grace we need to become more like him each day.*

Ultimately, the battle being described here can be summed up in one phrase: the quest for holiness.

Holiness, as we read in Chapter 10, means being *conformed to Christ*, who is all-holy. One who is holy wants what he wants, loves what he loves, and even hates what he hates (sin). As we learned in Chapter 2, through Original Sin we have fallen from the life God originally intended for us. We are incapable under our own power of achieving that perfect life. We see our own incapability every day, for example, when we say nasty things to others without even thinking about it, when we lazily refuse to do our chores, or when we think of ourselves instead of others.

Jesus said, "You, therefore, must be perfect, as your heavenly Father is perfect" (Mt 5:48). Read that command of Christ again—be perfect! And just in case it was not clear, Jesus reveals the heights of the standard he is setting—"as your heavenly Father is perfect"! Impossible! Yet as Christ says elsewhere, "With men this is impossible, but with God all things are possible" (Mt 19:26). One of the primary means that God uses to make the impossible possible is the Sacrament of Confirmation. Holiness is not unattainable—it is not something that only people whose images will end up as statues in churches can achieve.

Also, holiness is not something practiced only in extraordinary circumstances, as was done by Christians during the Roman persecutions or in Nazi Germany. In fact, holiness is usually practiced in the ordinary circumstances of life, at home, at school, and in everyday life. For example, when your mom asks you to put away the dishes, this is an opportunity to grow in holiness. Do you do it without complaint, and a cheerful heart? Or do you resist at first, and then only grudgingly perform the task? Another example would be when a number of students are picking on someone. Do you join them, or simply ignore their actions? Or are you willing to stand up for someone else, even if it means that you will be made fun of or shunned? These situations, which occur so often in daily life, are the crucible in which holiness is forged. It is in these situations that we must depend on the grace we receive in the Sacraments to be faithful to the teachings of Christ. For if we do not practice holiness in the ordinary events of everyday, how could we ever stand strong for Christ in times of persecution or even martyrdom?

All the Sacraments work together, so by receiving Confession and Communion regularly, the graces of Confirmation become more activated in our lives.

## COOPERATING WITH GRACE

***These three steps will help you activate the graces God will give you in Confirmation.***

Remember, however, that the grace of the Sacraments is not magic. In other words, being confirmed does not mean that you immediately become like Christ in all things. You probably know people who have been confirmed yet do not live as God wants them to live. Does that mean that Confirmation doesn't "work"? Not at all—it shows that when we receive grace we must *cooperate* with that grace to make it effective. Think of the person born with incredible athletic talent. From an early age he can run, throw, and jump better than all his peers. But if he does not cooperate with this God-given talent—by exercising, practicing, and working hard—he will never become a world-class athlete who can win championships. It takes both the talent he was gifted with and the development of this talent to make it happen. Likewise, when we receive Confirmation, God gives us incredibly powerful gifts, but these gifts can lie dormant and unused if we don't cooperate with them—like the gifts of a supremely talented athlete who spends his days eating junk food in front of the TV.

In this book we compared the spiritual life to the physical life. Just as we need to breath, eat, and exercise to live and stay healthy, so we must **pray**, **receive the Sacraments**, and **practice the virtues** in order to spiritually live and stay spiritually healthy.

**Pray:** Imagine having a best friend that you never talk to. Is that even possible? If you are truly close friends, you will have a desire to communicate with that person on a regular basis. In fact, going any long period of time without talking together will be difficult. Likewise, our relationship with God should be such that we desire to communicate with him frequently. This is prayer. Spend time every day in prayer—10 minutes, 30 minutes, or an hour if possible. Talk to God and listen to him. We usually don't hear God's voice with our ears, but by spending time in prayer we come to know more clearly his will for us.

**Receive the Sacraments:** The Sacrament of Confirmation is of course received only once, and its

Now you have chosen to mark yourself with the Sign of Christ and to be his disciple, his witness, and his soldier. Your life will never be the same.

graces last a lifetime. On the other hand, there are certain Sacraments—particularly Confession and Communion—that we should receive over and over. All the Sacraments work together, so by receiving Confession and Communion regularly, the graces of Confirmation become more activated in our lives. Practically speaking, we should of course go to Mass every Sunday and on Holy Days. We should also make an effort to go more often. We should go to Confession at least monthly, so that we can combat sin in our lives.

**Practice the Virtues:** The Christian life is not simply a life of prayer and going to church, however. It also entails modeling our lives after the life of Christ, who followed his Father's will perfectly. We must strive each day to practice the virtues: to be just with others, to have self-control, to be courageous in resisting sin, and to choose the right path in all our decisions. Practicing the virtues is only truly possible if a person is praying and receiving the Sacraments regularly. All these things go together. They form the armor of God we need for our spiritual battles in this life.

## CONCLUSION

### *Live for Christ!*

The Sacrament of Confirmation marks a dramatic turning point in your life. No longer are you simply following the desire of your parents for you to be Catholic. Now you have chosen to mark yourself with the Sign of Christ and to be his disciple, his witness, and his soldier. Your life will never be the same. It might appear to others that nothing dramatic has happened, but you know that your life is transformed. If you embrace this Sacrament and live the gifts of the Holy Spirit, you will live the most exciting life that can be lived: a life for Jesus Christ!

# ART AND PHOTO CREDITS

## Cover

*Students receive the Sacrament of Confirmation, administered by Cardinal Francis E. George at St. Clement Church in Chicago.* (Karen Callaway/Catholic New World); ©New World Publications

## Front Pages

iii *See* Cover Credit
iv *The Holy Trinity*, Francesco Cairo; Museo del Prado, Madrid, Spain
ix *Suffer the little children to come unto me, and forbid them not*, Rev. James Wills; The Foundling Museum, London, UK
xii *The Good Shepherd*, Bernhard Plockhorst; Zion Lutheran Church, Baltimore, Maryland

## Introduction

1 *Pentecost*, Max Bentele; ©Free Christ Images
2 Adobe Stock (retouched); ©gracel21
3 Adobe Stock; ©BillionPhotos.com
4 *Sacrament of Confirmation at St. Francis de Sales Oratory*; ©Institute of Christ the King Sovereign Priest, Archdiocese of St. Louis, Missouri; ©Jerry Naunheim Jr.
7 *Sacred Heart of Jesus*, Charles Bosseron Chambers; restoredtraditions.com
9 background: *Altarpiece of St. Michael*, Gerard David; Kunsthistorisches Museum, Vienna
inset: *St. Dominic Savio*, Public Domain, MTF Archives
10 *St. Philip Baptizing the Ethiopian*, alternate title *The Baptism of the Eunuch*, Rembrandt; Private Collection
11 Adobe Stock; ©4Max
13 Adobe Stock; ©Monkey Business
14 left: Design Pics, Stock Image
right: *Prayer*; Willows Academy, Des Plaines, Illinois; Julie Koenig, Photographer; MTF Archives
16 *Sacrament of Confirmation*; St. Paul the Apostle Catholic Church; MTF Archives

## Chapter 1

17 Adobe Stock; ©4Max
18 *The Conversion of St. Augustine* (detail), Fra Angelico; Musee d'Art Thomas Henry, Cherbourg, France
19 *God, the Eternal Father*, Giovanni Francesco Barbieri Guercino; Pinacoteca Sabauda, Torino, Italy
20 *St. Thomas Aquinas*, Jose Risueno; restoredtraditions.com
22 *Transfiguration of Christ*, Giovanni Bellini; Museo Nazionale di Capodimonte, Naples, Italy
23 *Holy Trinity*, Hendrik van Balen; Sint-Jacobskerk, Antwerp, Belgium
24 *The Supper at Emmaus*, Velazquez; Metropolitan Museum of Art, New York
25 left: *St. Paul Preaching in Athens*, Raphael; Victoria and Albert Museum, London, UK
right: *The Qumran Isaiah Scroll* from Qumran Cave 1 (The Great Isaiah Scroll); Shrine of the Book, Israel Museum, Jerusalem
26 *St. Matthew and the Angel*, Guido Reni; Pinacoteca, Vatican
27 *The Magnificat*, James Tissot; Brooklyn Museum, New York
29 Inset: *St. Pedro Calungsod*, Rafael del Casal; Archdiocesan Shrine of Saint Pedro Calungsod, Cebu City, Philippines
31 *Pentecost*, Jean Restout II; Musee du Louvre, Paris, France
32 *Celebration of Confirmation in Mostar*, Luiggi Pezzuto, Apostolic Nuncio to Bosnia and Herzegovina; Zvonimir Coric, The Catholic News Agency of the Bishops' Conference of Bosnia and Herzegovi
33 Adobe Stock; ©flairimages
34 *Confirmation* (retouched); St. Paul the Apostle Catholic Church; MTF Archives

## Chapter 2

35 *Christ Carrying the Cross*, Lorenzo Lotto; Musee du Louvre, Paris, France
36 *The Lord's Prayer* (detail), James Tissot; Brooklyn Museum, New York
37 *The Garden of Eden* (retouched), Erastus Salisbury Field; Shelburne Museum, Vermont
38 *The Rebuke of Adam and Eve* (retouched), Domenichino; National Gallery of Art, Washington, D.C.
40 *Eve, the Serpent, and Death* (detail), Hans Baldung Grien; National Gallery of Canada, Ottawa, Canada
41 *Noah releases the Dove from Stories of Noah Mosaic*; San Marco Basilica, Venice, Italy
43 *The Transfiguration*, Lodovico Carracci; Pinacoteca Nazionale, Bologna, Italy

# ART AND PHOTO CREDITS

44 *Entry into Jerusalem*, Unknown Master; National Museum in Warsaw, Poland
45 *The Resurrected Christ*, Salvator Rosa; Musee Conde, Chantilly, France
46 The Last Supper, Stained Glass (retouched); ©Free Christ Images
47 *Last Judgment Triptych* (detail), Hans Memling; Muzeum Narodowe, Gdansk, Poland
49 inset: *Bl. Chiara Badano*; MTF Archives
50 *The Incarnation of Jesus*, Piero di Cosimo; Galleria degli Uffizi, Florence
51 *Northridge Preparatory School*, Niles, Illinois; Julie Koenig, Photographer
53 *Nicene Creed Papyrus Fragment*; John Rylands University Library of Manchester, UK
54 left: *St. Catherine of Alexandria, The Olera Polyptych*, Cima da Conegliano; Parish Church of St. Bartolomeo, Olera (Bergamo), Italy
right: *St. Christopher with the Infant Christ and St. Peter* (detail), Cima da Conegliano; Private Collection

## Chapter 3

55 *The Trinity in Glory*, Titian; Museo del Prado, Madrid, Spain
56 *The Holy Trinity*, El Greco; Museo del Prado, Madrid, Spain; Archivo Oronoz
57 Adobe Stock; ©Konstantin Sutyagin
58 *Anointing of David* (detail), Felix-Joseph Barrias; Musee du Petit-Palais, Paris, France
59 *The Holy Trinity*, Andrea Previtali; Accademia Carrara, Bergamo, Italy
60 *Madonna in the Forest*, Fra Filippo Lippi; Staatliche Museen, Berlin, Germany
61 *Baptism of Christ* (detail), Pietro Perugino; Sistine Chapel, Vatican
62 *Pentecost*, Fray Juan Bautist Maino; Museo Nacional del Prado, Madrid, Spain; Archivo Oronoz
63 *St. Peter Preaching* (flipped), Masolino; Cappella Brancacci, Santa Maria del Carmine, Florence
67 *The Israelites Passing Through the Wilderness*, William West; Bristol City Museum and Art gallery, Bristol, England
68 inset: *St. Peter Holding the Key of the Paradise* (detail), Pierre Puget; Parish Church, Grandcamp,France
70 left: Adobe Stock; ©robyelo357
right: Adobe Stock; ©PathomP
71 Adobe Stock; ©luckat
72 top: *Pope Francis during the Sacred Chrism Mass*; ©L'Osservatore Romano
bottom: *Pentecost* (detail), Alvise Vivarini; Gemaldegalerie, Berlin, Germany

## Chapter 4

73 *Christ Handing the Keys to St. Peter* (detail), Pietro Perugino; Sistine Chapel, Vatican
74 *The Last Supper* (detail), Simon Vouet; Palazzo Apostolico, Loreto, Italy
75 *Christ Healing the Blind* (detail), El Greco; Metropolitan Museum of Art, New York
76 *Sacrament of Baptism;* Photo from *The Catholic Priest Today*, (Midwest Theological Forum, 2007)
77 *St. Mary of the Angels Church*, Chicago, Illinois; Julie Koenig, Photographer
78 *Tridentine Mass*; ©Joachim Specht
79 *His Excellence Bishop Jan Babjak SJ Celebrating Mass*; St. John the Baptist Cathedral, Presov, Slovakia; AG Archives
80 *Sacrament of Confirmation*; ©W P Wittman Photography
81 *Catholic High School Students Volunteering at a Nutrition Center*; Julie Koenig, Photographer
82 *St. Peter's Square, Canonization of St. Josemaria Escriva*; Wojciech Dubis, Photographer; MTF Archives
84 *The Last Supper* (detail), Carl H. Bloch; Frederiksborg Palace Chapel, Denmark
85 left: *Pope Benedict XVI Ordains Twenty-two Men to the Priesthood*, St. Peter's Basilica, April 29, 2007; ©L'Osservatore Romano
right: *Pope Francis and the College of Cardinals in the Sistine Chapel*; ©L'Osservatore Romano
86 *St. Peter's Basilica*, "Good Shepherd" Sunday Mass, May 7, 2006; ©L'Osservatore Romano
87 Inset: *St. John Paul II*; MTF Archives
89 *World Youth Day*, Palm Sunday, April 5, 2009, St. Peter's Square; ©L'Osservatore Romano
90 *Auxiliary Bishop George Rassas administers the Sacrament of Confirmation at St. Stephen Deacon & Martyr, Tinley Park.* (Karen Callaway/Catholic New World); ©New World Publications
91 left: *Cross of Ashes, Ash Wednesday*; ©W P Wittman Photography
right: *"Bless our Food"*; ©W P Wittman Photography
92 *Easter Mass 2007*; Puebla, Mexico, Church East of the Cathedral; Wojciech Dubis, Photographer; MTF Archives

# ART AND PHOTO CREDITS

## Chapter 5

93 *Pope Benedict XVI Baptized Fourteen Babies*, 2010, Sistine Chapel, Vatican; ©L'Osservatore Romano
94 *St. Peter Baptizes the Neophytes*, Masaccio; Cappella Brancacci, Santa Maria del Carmine, Florence, Italy
95 *Immaculate Conception*, Bartolome Esteban Murillo; Museo del Prado, Madrid, Spain
96 *The Crucifixion*, Giovanni Battista Tiepolo; St. Louis Art Museum, St. Louis, Missouri
97 *The Baptism of Christ* (detail), Jean Baptiste Camille Corot; Church of St. Nicolas-du-Chardonnet, Paris, France
98 *The Resurrection* (detail), Carl H. Bloch; Frederiksborg Palace Chapel, Denmark
99 *Disciples of Jesus Baptizing* (detail), Giulio Procaccini; Palacio Real, Segovia, Spain; Archivo Oronoz
101 *Baptism*, St. Thomas the Apostle Church, Naperville, Illinois; Photo Courtesy of Debbie Snyder
102 *Jesus with the Children*, Stained Glass; Unknown Master; MTF Archives
103 left: *Already He Knew God as His Father*, Frederick Goodall; Private Collection
top right: *Angels Worshiping* (detail), Benozzo Gozzoli; Chapel, Palazzo Medici-Riccardi, Florence, Italy
104 *First Communion*; Wojciech Dubis, Photographer; MTF Archives
105 Inset: *Bl. Pier Giorgio Frassati*; Public Domain; MTF Archives
106 *The Fall of Man* (detail), Hendrick Goltzius; National Gallery of Art, Washington, D.C.
107 Adobe Stock; ©mylu
108 *Jesus Preaching on the Mount*, Gustave Dore; Private Collection
109 *Baptism*; Wojciech Dubis, Photographer; MTF Archives
110 *Holy Water*; Julie Koenig, Photographer; MTF Archives

## Chapter 6

111 *Northridge Preparatory School*, Niles, Illinois; Julie Koenig, Photographer; MTF Archives
112 *The Last Supper* (detail), Church Fresco, Vienna; Adobe Stock; ©Renata Sedmakova
113 *The Signs on the Door* (detail), James Tissot; Brooklyn Museum, New York
114 *Miracle of the Bread and Fish* (detail), Giovanni Lanfranco; National Gallery of Ireland
115 *The Gathering of the Manna* (detail), Master of the Gathering of the Manna; Musée de la Chartreuse, France
116 *Mass of St. Gregory*; National Museum of Archaeology, Madrid, Spain; Archivo Oronoz
117 *St. John Paul II*; MTF Archives
118 *Lamentation Over Christ* (detail). Fra Angelico; Museo di San Marco, Florence, Italy
119 *Roman Missal*; Published by Midwest Theological Forum
121 Adobe Stock; ©stefania57
123 Photo from *Remain with Us, Lord: Reflections on the Mass in the Christian Life*; (Midwest Theological Forum, 2013)
125 Inset: *Silver Ostensorium Containing the Miracle of Lanciano*; Church of St. Francis, Lanciano, Italy; ©Franco Colacioppo
126 *Perpetual Adoration Chapel*; St. Mary Help of Christians Catholic Church, Aiken, South Carolina
127 *Most Reverend John Bura Celebrates the Divine Liturgy*; Epiphany Ukrainian Catholic Church, St. Petersburg, Florida
128 *The Blessed Sacrament Chapel*; Cathedral of Chihuahua, Mexico; AG Archives
129 *Mass at St. Paul of the Cross Church*, Park Ridge, Illinois; Julie Koenig, Photographer; MTF Archives
130 *Communion*; Willows Academy, Des Plaines, Illinois; Julie Koenig, Photographer; MTF Archives

## Chapter 7

131 *Orlando Sanchez receives the Sacrament of Confirmation from Bishop Robert Guglielmone of the Diocese of Charleston, South Carolina, at St. Anthony of Padua, Greenville, South Carolina*; ©Octavio Duran, Photographer, CNS
132 left: *Pentecost*; Church Art; Adobe Stock; ©Renata Sedmakova
right: *Sts. Peter and John Laying Hands Upon the People*; Book of Hours Illustration, Flanders ca. 1484-1529; MS 7, f. 27r, Syracuse University Library, Department of Special Collections
133 *St. Paul Preaching in Athens*, Raphael; Victoria and Albert Museum, London, England
134 *Joyful Recipients of First Communion*; ©W P Wittman Photography
135 *Sacred Chrism Mass*; ©Diocese of Fort Wayne-South Bend, Indiana
136 *Sacrament of Confirmation*; ©Mazur/catholicfaith.org.uk
137 *Auxiliary Bishop George Rassas talks to Confirmandi shortly before they received the Sacrament of Confirmation at St. Stephen Deacon & Martyr, Tinley Park*. (Karen Callaway/Catholic New World); ©New World Publications
138 *Abby Sherlock receives the Sacrament of Confirmation from Bishop Robert Guglielmone of the Diocese of Charleston, South Carolina, at St. Anthony of Padua, Greenville, South Carolina*; ©Octavio Duran, Photographer, CNS
139 *Sprinkling Holy Water, The Rite of Blessing*; ©W P Wittman Photography
140 *Sacrament of Confirmation*; ©Today's Catholic, Diocese of Fort Wayne-South Bend, Indiana
141 *Sacrament of Confirmation at St. Francis de Sales Oratory*; ©Institute of Christ the King Sovereign Priest, Archdiocese of St. Louis, Missouri; ©Jerry Naunheim Jr.

# ART AND PHOTO CREDITS

142 *Sacrament of Initiation for Adults*; ©W P Wittman Photography
143 *Sacrament of Confirmation at St. Francis de Sales Oratory*; ©Institute of Christ the King Sovereign Priest, Archdiocese of St. Louis, Missouri; ©Jerry Naunheim Jr.
145 *Sacrament of Confirmation at St. Theresa Catholic Church, Sugar Land, Texas*; ©Brandon Vos; Studio Vos, Inc.
146 inset: *St. Josephine Bakhita*; Private Collection; Public Domain
147 *Sacred Chrism Mass*; ©Diocese of Fort Wayne-South Bend, Indiana
148 *Sacrament of Confirmation*; ©W P Wittman Photography
149 *Sacrament of Confirmation*; ©W P Wittman Photography
150 *Sacrament of Confirmation*; ©St. Mary Catholic Church, Muncie, Indiana, Diocese of Lafayette
151 *Boy Praying*; Adobe Stock; © *Vibe Images*
152 *Sacrament of Confirmation at St. Francis de Sales Oratory*; ©Institute of Christ the King Sovereign Priest, Archdiocese of St. Louis, Missouri; ©Jerry Naunheim Jr.
153 *Sacrament of Confirmation*; ©Chicago Catholic

## Chapter 8

155 *Battle of Lepanto*, Luca Cambiaso; Royal Monastery of St. Lawrence of Escorial, Madrid, Spain; Archivo Oronoz
156 *Scenes from the Life of Christ: 1. Nativity: Birth of Jesus* (detail), Giotto; Cappella Scrovegni (Arena Chapel), Padua, Italy
157 *The Disciples of Jesus Baptize*, James Tissot; Brooklyn Museum, New York
158 *Madonna with Angels Playing Music* (detail), Pere Serra; Museu Nacional d'Art de Catalunya, Barcelona, Spain
159 *The Emmaus Disciples*, Abraham Bloemaert; Musees Royaux des Beaux-Arts, Brussels, Belgium
160 *Joseph's Dream* (detail), Gaetano Gandolfi; Private Collection
161 *The Martyrdom of St. Stephen*, Jacques Stella; Fitzwilliam Museum, University of Cambridge, England
162 *St. Bernadette Soubirous*; Public Domain
163 *Apotheosis of St. Thomas Aquinas* (detail), Francisco de Zurbaran; Museum of Fine Arts of Seville, Spain
164 left: *St. Josemaria Escriva*; MTF Archives
right: *St. Therese of Lisieux*, MTF Archives
165 left: *The Vision of St. Teresa of Avila*, Domingo Chavarito; Museum of Fine Arts, Granada, Spain; Archivo Oronoz
right: *"I Am with You Always."* (detail); ©Free Christ Images
166 *Domine quo vadis?*, Annibale Carracci; National Gallery, London, England
167 *Sts. Teresa of Calcutta and John Paul II, India, February 1986*; AP File Photo
168 *The Holy Spirit* (detail); Unknown Master; Public Domain
169 Inset: *Mary and Child with Saints Felicity and Perpetua (Sacra Conversazione)*; National Museum in Warsaw, Poland
172 *Virgin and Child with Saints* (detail), Boccaccio Boccaccino; Gallerie dell'Accademia, Venice, Italy
173 *Parable of the Lost Sheep*, Alford Usher Soord; Standard Bible Story Readers, Book One by Lillie A. Faris, The Standard Publishing Company, 1925
174 *The Adoration of the Trinity*, Albrecht Durer; Kunsthistorisches Museum, Vienna, Austria

## Chapter 9

175 *St. Mary of the Angels Church*, Chicago, Illinois; Julie Koenig, Photographer; MTF Archives
176 *St. Francis*, Albert Chevallier Tayler; Private Collection
177 Inset: *St. Maria Goretti*; Public Domain
178 *Good Friday Morning: Jesus in Prison*, James Tissot; Brooklyn Museum, New York
179 *The Two Trinities* (detail), Bartolome Esteban Murillo; National Gallery, London, England
180 *Young Woman Reading Bible*; Adobe Stock; ©xxknightwolf
181 *St. Mary of the Angels Church*, Chicago, Illinois; Julie Koenig, photographer; MTF Archives
182 *St. Roch Asking the Virgin Mary to Heal Victims of the Plague* (detail), Jacques-Louis David; Musee des Beaux-Arts, Marseille, France
183 left: *Virgin at Prayer*, Il Sassoferrato; restoredtraditions.com
bottom right: *Agony in the Garden* (detail), Giovanni Bellini; National Gallery, London, UK
184 left: Photo from *The Catholic Priest Today*, (Midwest Theological Forum, 2007)
right: *Holy Water Font/Stoup*; Adobe Stock; ©gabe9000c
185 bottom left: *The Miraculous Medal*; Xhienne, photographer; AG Archives
bottom right: *Brown Scapular of Mount Carmel*; Sarah Sofia, photographer; AG Archives
top right: *Praying the Rosary*; Adobe Stock; ©nyul

# ART AND PHOTO CREDITS

186 *May Crowning*; Julie Koenig, Photographer; MTF Archives
187 *Eucharistic Procession*; 2005 Southeastern Eucharistic Congress, Charlotte, North Carolina
188 *Jesus Goes Up Alone onto a Mountain to Pray*, James Tissot; Brooklyn Museum, New York
189 Inset: *St. Kateri Tekakwitha*, Claude Chauchetiere, SJ; Diocese de Saint-Jean-Longueuil
191 *Sacrament of Confirmation*; St. Paul the Apostle Catholic Church; MTF Archives
193 *Father and Son Reading the Bible*; Adobe Stock; ©Gino Santa Maria
194 *Station of the Cross, No. 8*; Sts. Peter and Paul Church, Naperville, Illinois; Julie Koenig, photographer; MTF Archives

## Chapter 10

195 *Sermon on the Mount* (detail), Carl H. Bloch; Frederiksborg Palace Chapel, Denmark
196 *St. Teresa of Calcutta at San Gregorio in Rome*; ©Manfredo Ferrari
197 *Allegory of Free Will and Sin*, Francois Maitre; Illustration for *City of God* by St. Augustine (ca. 1475-80); Museum Meermanno Westreenianum, The Hague, Netherlands
198 *Pilate Washing His Hands*, Mattia Preti; Metropolitan Museum of Art, New York
199 Adobe Stock; ©*Mary Camomile*
200 *Moses Descends from Mount Sinai with the Ten Commandments* (detail), Ferdinand Bol; Royal Palace of Amsterdam, Netherlands
201 *Sermon on the Mount* (detail), Henrik Olrik; Altarpiece in Sankt Matthæus Kirke, Copenhagen, Denmark
202 left: *Sermon on the Mount* (detail), Jose Moreno Carbonero; St. Francis the Great Church, Madrid; Archivo Oronoz
top right: *Christ and the Woman Taken into Adultery*, Alessandro Turchi; Private Collection
203 *Appearence Behind Locked Doors* (detail), Duccio; Museo dell'Opera del Duomo, Siena, Italy
204 *Penance*; Willows Academy, Des Plaines, Illinois; Julie Koenig, Photographer
205 *Return of the Prodigal Son*, James Tissot; Brooklyn Museum, New York
206 left: *Christ Carrying the Cross*, Titian; Museo del Prado, Madrid, Spain
top right: *Dominican Friars, Province of St. Joseph with students from Our Lady of Grace School, Kisumu Kenya*; Br. Jacob Bertrand Janczyk, OP, Photographer; Used with permission
207 Adobe Stock; ©rio
Photo from *The Catholic Priest Today*, (Midwest Theological Forum, 2007)
208 *Communion of the Apostles*, Luca Signorelli; Museo Diocesano, Cortona, Italy
209 *The Forerunners of Christ with Saints and Martyrs* (detail), Fra Angelico; The National Gallery, London, England
210 *St. Josemaria Escriva*, MTF Archives
213 *Family Time*; Adobe Stock; ©biker3
214 *Parable of the Good Samaritan*, Giacomo Conti; Church of the Miraculous Medal, Messina, Italy

## Chapter 11

215 *Ministry of the Apostles*, Russian Icon, Fyodor Zubov; Yaroslavl Museum–Preserve, Yaroslavl, Russia
216 *Appearance While the Apostles Are at Table*, Duccio; Museo dell'Opera del Duomo, Siena, Italy
217 *IVE Missionary Priest in Papua, New Guinea*; CBEtheridge, Photographer, ©Institute of the Incarnate Word
218 *St. Paul Healing the Cripple at Lystra*, Karel Dujardin; Rijksmuseum, Amsterdam
223 left: *The Martyrdom of St. Ignatius of Antioch*, Unknown Master; MTF Archives
right: *Jesus Teaches the People by the Sea*, James Tissot; Brooklyn Museum, New York
224 *Northridge Preparatory School*, Niles, Illinois; Julie Koenig, Photographer; MTF Archives
226 *The Martyrdom of St. Matthew* (detail), Caravaggio; Contarelli Chapel, San Luigi dei Francesi, Rome, Italy
227 *The Martyrdom of St. Peter*, Gaetano Gandolfi; Church of St. Peter the Apostle, Carignano (Parma), Italy
228 *Miracles of St. Francis Xavier* (detail), Peter Paul Rubens; Kunsthistorisches Museum, Vienna, Austria
229 inset: *St. Francis Xavier* (flipped), Elias Salaverra; Javier Castillo Church, Navarra, Spain; Archivo Oronoz
230 *St. Peter Preaching in the Presence of St. Mark*, Fra Angelico; Museo di San Marco, Florence, Italy
231 *World Youth Day, 2005*; ©W P Wittman Photography
232 Adobe Stock; ©Vibe Images
233 Adobe Stock; ©Monkey Business
234 *Miraculous Draught of Fishes*, Raphael; Victoria and Albert Museum, London, UK

# ART AND PHOTO CREDITS

## Chapter 12

235 *Christ Healing the Sick at Bethesda* (detail), Carl H. Bloch; Frederiksborg Palace Chapel, Denmark
236 *Christ and the Good Thief*, Titian; Pinacoteca Nazionale, Bologna, Italy
237 *Cain and Abel*, Pietro Novelli; Galleria Nazionale d'Arte Antica, Rome, Italy
238 *St. Thomas Aquinas*, Carlo Crivelli; The Demidoff Altarpiece, The National Gallery, London, UK
239 *Parable of Lazarus and Dives*, Illumination from Codex Aureus of Echternach; German National Museum, Nuremberg, Germany
240 *Poverty in Mexico*; Luke Mata, Photographer; MTF Archives
241 *Children Celebrating the Beauty of Nature*; ©Crestock Stock Photos
243 *Youth for a United World*, Focolare Movement USA; Used with permission.
244 *Christ and the Rich Young Ruler*, Heinrich Hofmann; Riverside Church, New York
246 *St. Teresa of Calcutta in India*; AP File Photo
247 *St. Lawrence Distributing Alms* (detail), Fra Angelico; Cappella Niccolina, Palazzi Pontifici, Vatican
248 Inset: *St. Gianna Beretta Molla*; saintgianna.org
250 *Zacchaeus in the Sycamore Awaiting the Passage of Jesus*, James Tissot; Brooklyn Museum, New York
251 *Washing of the Feet*, Giovanni Agostino da Lodi; Gallerie dell'Accademia, Venice, Italy
252 *Parable of the Man Who Hoards*, James Tissot; Brooklyn Museum, New York

## Epilogue

253 *Joan of Arc at the Coronation of Charles VII*, Jean-Auguste-Dominique Ingres; Louvre, Paris, France; Archivo Oronoz
254 *Christ Denying Satan*, Carl H. Bloch; Frederiksborg Palace Chapel, Denmark
255 *Pope Francis Prays at the Vatican Lourdes Grotto*; ©L'Osservatore Romano
256 *St. Francis Embracing Christ on the Cross*, Bartolome Esteban Murillo; Museum of Fine Arts of Seville, Spain
257 Photo from *The Catholic Priest Today*, (Midwest Theological Forum, 2007)
258 *Pope Francis Celebrates the Sacrament of Confirmation*, ©L'Osservatore Romano

*Holy Family* by Claudio Coello.
Museum of Fine Arts, Budapest, Hungary

# INDEX

# INDEX

# INDEX

# INDEX

# INDEX